Other books by the same authors

THE BEAVER PAPERS

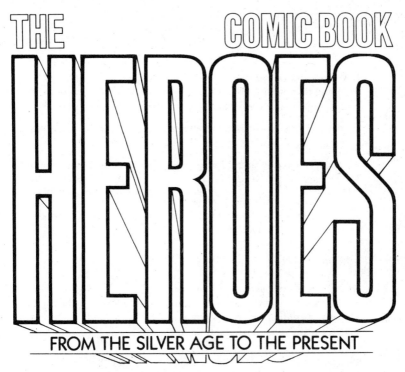

THE COMIC BOOK HEROES

FROM THE SILVER AGE TO THE PRESENT

WILL JACOBS
AND
GERARD JONES

CROWN PUBLISHERS, INC.
NEW YORK

Dedicated to
JOE FILICE, MIKE FORRESTER, AND MIKE JENSEN
who helped us think
and spotted our goofs

Copyright © 1985 by Will Jacobs and Gerard Jones

Published by Crown Publishers, Inc., One Park Avenue, New York, New York 10016 and simultaneously in Canada by General Publishing Company Limited

Manufactured in the United States of America

CROWN is a trademark of Crown Publishers, Inc.

Library of Congress Cataloging in Publication Data

Jacobs, Will.
    The comic book heroes.

    Includes index.
    1. Comic books, strips, etc.—United States—History and criticism. I. Jones, Gerard. II. Title.
PN6725.J3   1985   741.5'0973   85-7721
ISBN 0-517-55440-2

Design by Jake Victor Thomas

10 9 8 7 6 5 4 3 2 1

First Edition

Contents

Acknowledgments

The research for this book was greatly speeded by the attention and comments of a number of present and former professionals in the comic book business, most notably: Messrs. Murray Boltinoff, E. Nelson Bridwell, Dick Giordano, and, especially, the very generous Julius Schwartz of DC Comics Inc.; Archie Goodwin, Peter Sanderson, and Jim Shooter of Marvel Comics; Richard Bruning of Capital Comics; Dean Mullaney and Cat Yronwode of Eclipse Comics; Steve and Bill Schanes and David Scroggy of Pacific Comics; along with John Broome, Gardner F. Fox, Mike Grell, Jack and Roz Kirby, Joe Kubert, Doug Moench, and the extremely helpful Jack Schiff. Thanks also to Rich Morrissey (and others in Interlac) for information and encouragement; and many thanks to John Clemons and Scott MacAdam of The Comic Zone in Fremont, California, and Tom Kee and Theresa Marovich of Comics and Comix in Palo Alto for their great generosity. And a special tip of the cowl to Peter Cannon, a real thunderbolt of an editor.

List of Abbreviations

AA	Amazing Adventures	HH	Hero for Hire	PM	Power Man
Act	Action Comics	HOM	House of Mystery	PS	The Phantom
Adven	Adventure Comics	HS	House of Secrets		Stranger
Am. Fan.	Amazing Fantasy	Hulk	The Incredible Hulk		
An.	Anthro			R	Rima The Jungle
AT	Astonishing Tales	JA	Jungle Action		Girl
Atom	The Atom	JI	Justice Inc.		
Av.	The Avengers	JIM	Journey Into	SA	Strange Adventures
			Mystery	SavT	Savage Tales
Bat	Batman	JLA	Justice League of	SF	Sgt. Fury
BB	The Brave and The		America	Shad.	The Shadow
	Bold	JO	Jimmy Olsen	Show	Showcase
BH	Blackhawk		(Superman's Pal)	SM	The Amazing
BJB	Bomba The Jungle				Spider-Man
	Boy	K	Kamandi	SS	The Silver Surfer
		KD	Kull the Destroyer	SSWS	Star Spangled War
C	Conan the Barbarian				Stories
CA	Captain America	LL	Lois Lane	ST	Strange Tales
CC	The Claws of the		(Superman's	Sub.	The Sub-Mariner
	Cat		Girlfriend)	Sup	Superman
CL	Creatures on the			Supb	Superboy
	Loose	MF	Monster of		
CM	Captain Marvel		Frankenstein	T	Tarzan
CU	Challengers of the	MGA	My Greatest	TA	Tales to Astonish
	Unknown		Adventure	TD	Tomb of Dracula
		MIS	Mystery in Space	Thor	Thor
DD	Daredevil	MM	Metal Men	TS	Tales of Suspense
Def.	The Defenders	MOKF	Master of Kung Fu	TU	Tales of the
Det.	Detective Comics	MP	Marvel Premiere		Unexpected
DP	The Doom Patrol	MPr.	Marvel Presents		
DS	Dr. Strange	Mr. M	Mr. Miracle	U	The Unexpected
D.Sav.	Doc Savage	MS	Marvel Spotlight		
		MSH	Marvel Super Heroes	W	Warlock
F	The Flash			WBN	Werewolf By Night
FF	The Fantastic Four	NAS	The New	WF	World's Finest
FP	The Forever People		Adventures of		Comics
			Superboy	WL	Warlord
GL	Green Lantern	Nex.	Nexus	WW	Wonder Woman
GL/GA	Green	NG	New Gods	WWo	Weird Worlds
	Lantern/Green				
	Arrow	OAAW	Our Army At War	XM	The X-Men
		OFF	Our Fighting Forces		
H&D	The Hawk and The				
	Dove				

Overview

The comic book field is exploding. In just the last few years, a wave of new publishers, new creators, new ideas, and new philosophies have raised it to unprecedented heights, promising to make it, at last, the medium of boundless possibilities that its guiding lights have long hoped it would be. A great new breadth and sophistication within the comics themselves, accompanied by increasing attention from the world at large, might soon liberate the medium from its subculture status and make it, in America as it is in Japan and parts of Europe, a significant force in mainstream entertainment. And a growing number of strong individual creative visions may make it as rich and varied as any other medium.

Yet at the same time the field seems to hover at the brink of disaster. New, untested strategies of marketing and distributing may fail, confusion as to the true size and nature of the market may limit publishers, and old misunderstandings of the medium may impede general interest. At the same time an inbred, esoteric fan market may apply creative restraints, and conservative editorial decisions may dampen the current blaze of creativity. Within a few years, comic books may prove themselves an entertainment medium and art form to be reckoned with, or they may slide into creative oblivion as a mere curiosity for some hard-core hobbyists.

This book is the story of how comic books pulled themselves from the doldrums of the mid-1950s, when they were only an endangered subspecies of children's entertainment, to their current, unprecedented watershed. There are many periods to discuss along the way: the years when the comic book heroes regained their position as supremely delightful entertainers for kids; the years when ambitious writers and artists tracked down and captured an adolescent and collegiate readership; the grim years of the 1970s, when everything good seemed doomed to failure and everything mediocre flourished; and now the unexpected resurgence of quality, invention, and sincere dedication. It is an extremely varied, complex, and colorful story, and—with luck—one that is only now beginning its most fascinating chapter.

This book serves a number of purposes. In its search for causes and effects, trends and goals, it is a narrative of the hows and whys of comic books' long journey to their present state. As a critical history, it is a guide for those interested in reading comics to the many styles and approaches employed in the field; it should give many ideas as to which comics succeed as entertainment, which do not, and why. In its details and descriptions it is a record of the innumerable forms taken by costumed character and adventure comics over the last three decades. And for those who remember the old comics fondly, it should provide many moments of nostalgia.

Of necessity, our scope has been somewhat limited. Because the medium has been dominated since the late 1950s by costumed heroes and related sorts of fanciful adventure characters, these form the focus of the book. Other genres, such as war, horror, and western comics, are mentioned only insofar as they have made a real impact on the field as a whole. Since the two most productive and influential publishers of comics in these years have been DC and Marvel, they are almost the sole recipients of our attention; only when treating the 1980s do we deal with alternative publishers. Thus, such contributions to the comics of the 1960s as Carl Barks's superb funny animal stories, the Warren line of quality horror and war magazines, and the many heroes of Radio Comics, Charlton, Gold Key, and others have been mentioned only incidentally, if at all. It must be left to future historians to treat these other currents of comic book history.

The comics covered in this book represent the mainstream of the field. The broadest possible range of styles, concepts, and aims falls within our scope. That range, in fact, has made the job of criticism especially challenging. It would be foolish to judge by the same standards an adult, cynical comic about the misadventures of a police officer in a decadent, near-future world and a children's adventure story about a costumed crime-fighter who runs with the speed of light; one or the other would inevitably be judged either too ambitious or too juvenile, even though they might both be perfect realizations of their concepts and genres. Thus we have striven to criticize every comic by its own standards: by the creator's goals, by the demands of its particular type, and by the needs of its intended readership. The only standards we have applied to all comics are the basic qualities of good storytelling, both verbal and visual.

The book is divided into three parts: the first deals with the "Silver Age" of the late 1950s and 1960s, the second with the troubled years of the 1970s, and the third, a closing chapter, with the promise of the 1980s. The structure and approach of each part varies according to the material being covered. When discussing the 1960s we have attempted to take an adequate look at nearly every series, as these were the years when the foundations were being laid; in the 1970s, when comic book titles proliferated at a startling rate, and innumerable titles either fell quickly to cancellation or contributed nothing to the growth of the field, we have dealt only with those comics that time and hindsight have shown to be significant. The reader may also notice that the early portion of the book includes biographical material on the creators of the comics, which the later portion omits; these biographies have been used to explore aspects of the history of comics in the 1940s and 1950s that fall outside the scope of this book but have greatly influenced its subject matter. Lastly, in the final chapter, we have had to take a flexible, open-ended approach to discussion, as the decade, still in process, obviously cannot yet be analyzed from a historical perspective.

This book represents the first attempt to provide an overview of the history of comics from 1956 onward. With it we hope to give the regular followers of comics a keener perspective on the field they enjoy, to encourage former readers of comics to rediscover a past joy, and to alert the world at large to the boundless possibilities of the medium. Finally, it is hoped that this book will be but the first of its kind, and that discussions of comics will grow more thorough and more frequent in the years to come.

Presenting the Silver Age

A kid looking for good comic books in 1956 would have found it a rough year. He could always find a few, of course. Maybe he'd have put down a dime for a fairly good science fiction title or a decent western or something else mimicking the current Saturday matinee fashions. But something was missing. The heart had gone out of the comic book business. The heroes had vanished.

Slipping sales figures a few years before had put an end to those dozens of costumed crime-fighters of the so-called Golden Age of Comics, the late 1930s and 1940s. Flash, Green Lantern, the Human Torch, the Sub-Mariner, Captain Marvel, even the Justice Society of America, in which DC Comics' greatest heroes banded together to battle the most nefarious of menaces, had all been swept away by the early 1950s; without them, the comics were scarcely more than movies without movement, pulp novels with pictures. Sales and quality were both falling, and without those masked vigilantes and super-benefactors, without the one type of character truly indigenous to comic books, it was doubtful that the medium itself could survive.

Spinning the squeaky comics rack on a late summer afternoon that year, a kid would find only three heroes still surviving in their own titles. There was Superman in great quantity, but with very little quality. An unimaginative editorial policy pitted the first and greatest of heroes against an unending stream of petty crooks full of tiresome schemes and armed with kryptonite. A hero capable of moving worlds wasted his talents trying to outwit hoodlums with names like Bullets Barton and Mr. Wheels. His old friend Batman had not sunk quite so low, but anyone who remembered his atmospheric adventures as "the dark-night detective" in the 1940s would have been disappointed at the lackluster stories and coarse drawings of a decade later. The third survivor, Wonder Woman, also a DC property, had lost both the original writer and the original artist who had made her so idiosyncratic and so interesting in her first ten years; their successors were unable to make her either.

There was nothing to satisfy a kid's hunger for superhuman feats and high aventure, nothing to make thrilling those last days before school started again, nothing that drew his hand irresistibly to the rack. Every comic seemed to speak of a glorious past, a mediocre present, and a dismal future.

Except for one.

There was one that begged to be bought. Across its cover undulated a strip of movie film. From frame to frame in the film a red-garbed figure was running, running fast, running so fast that his speed hurled him out of the film and right at the reader. "Presenting the Flash!" read the copy. "Whirlwind Adventures of the Fastest Man Alive!"

Whirlwind they were. A flip through the pages showed this new hero, this Flash, outracing a bullet, zipping up and down the sides of skyscrapers, battling an ultra-slow villain called the Turtle, thwarting a scientific thief from the future, and then—as a coup de grâce—breaking the time barrier by his sheer velocity.

There was no question about this one. Any kid who had ever dreamed of running fast—and was there ever a kid who hadn't?—would have dashed for the cash register without a pause, dime in one hand and Flash in the other.

If the kid had looked up a couple of feet, he might have noticed someone else buying the very same comic; maybe a teenager who liked science fiction adventure, or a young English student who had loved comics too much as a child ever to turn his back on them completely, or even a grown-up science professor whose hobby was collecting Golden Age comics. These people might have seen the Flash in a different light: the art carried the action with dynamic clarity and fluidity; the plot was fast and complex but remarkably well developed. Not only had DC revived, in a new version, one of its best heroes of the 1940s, but it had done so with a tautness and refinement very rare in comics. It had brought the eight-year-old and the English student together under one cover.

In his origin story, the new Flash tipped his hat to his older readers. Barry Allen is a police scientist always ridiculed for his slowness, though

Herald of the Silver Age: Barry Allen opens his ring and becomes the Flash in an early adventure. Pencils by Carmine Infantino, inks by Joe Kubert, script by John Broome. From *Showcase* 4, October 1956.

he is fascinated by the fast-running Flash, comic book hero of his boy-hood. When lightning strikes a cabinet of chemicals beside which Barry is standing, at once dousing and electrocuting him, he is endowed with "supersonic speed, undreamed-of speed." He dedicates his life to fighting crime, taking the name of the Flash.

Here, then, was a hero who seemed to bespeak a return to the Golden Age, but who also, with a streamlined style and science-fictional milieu, was purely of the new decade. These were, after all, the years of monsters in the matinees and saucers in the skies, and the mounting science fiction fad was only one year shy of exploding into a craze. Whoever was behind this new hero's creation clearly both loved old comics and had his finger firmly on the pulse of contemporary childhood. A man combining such virtues could be the one, if anyone could, to launch a new phase in comic book history and give the medium a second chance at life.

The man in question was a good-natured perfectionist named Julius Schwartz, and because of his background he proved to be the perfect man for the task. As a boy he had known two consuming passions: the New York Yankees, particularly Babe Ruth, and the nascent field of sci-ence fiction. Along with a friend named Mort Weisinger he launched a magazine called *The Time Traveller*, the first fan magazine devoted en-tirely to science fiction. With it and its successor, *Science Fiction Digest*, the two boys helped lay the foundations of the zealous, noisy world of science fiction fandom.

After a while the two friends decided to earn a little spending money by acting as literary agents for the many writers they had met; but Weisinger ended the partnership when he took editing jobs, first with the Standard Magazines line of pulp science fiction titles in 1936, then with DC Comics in 1941. Schwartz continued the work alone, becoming, while still in his early twenties, the premier agent in his field. He gained a reputation for working with his clients, making demands of them, nursing them, until he felt they were doing their best work. Acting more like a big brother than an agent, he helped a young Ray Bradbury find his unmistakable voice; he taught Alfred Bester to play pinochle and bridge when he wasn't market-ing his stories. (An oft-repeated anecdote about Schwartz grew from a year he and Edmond Hamilton roomed together in California. While Hamilton typed up his *Captain Future* space operas, Schwartz would doze on a couch, jokingly tallying his ten-percent commission; whenever the typewriter bell would ring, indicating that Hamilton had typed another ten words, and thus another ten cents worth of fiction, Schwartz would cry out, "Another penny!") This science fiction background would pro-vide the foundation for his key contributions to comics in the late 1950s.

As the wartime paper shortage and the rapid growth of both the comic book and paperback book industries crippled the pulp magazines in which most science fiction stories were published, Schwartz found his in-come dropping. It was his friend and client Alfred Bester who told him about an editorial opening at All American Comics in 1944. Bester himself was a writer there under editor-in-chief Sheldon Mayer, one of the seminal comics editors of the Golden Age.

Mayer said of Schwartz, "Though I liked him at once, I remember feeling that background-wise, Julie didn't have too much going for him. . . . I don't think he had ever read a comic book before he had bought a few of ours and read them in the subway on the way to the interview." But Mayer saw in Schwartz and his background as an agent the sort of editor he wanted: "the kind of guy who would be sympathetic to the needs of writers and artists . . . and yet be able to cajole, coerce, and/or inspire them to do their best work."

The year after Schwartz got the job with All American, the company merged with its business partner, National Periodical Publications, who published the Superman-DC line of comics. Simultanously DC found itself the giant of the industry and Schwartz found himself working with his old partner in fandom, Mort Weisinger.

Schwartz taught himself the job of editing on *The Flash, Green Lantern,* the *Justice Society,* and other heroic series until the hero market ran dry. In the early 1950s he focused on westerns (with *All-Star Western* and *Western Comics*) and science fiction, which was steadily making its presence felt more and more strongly in comics, as DC scrambled for success in the marketplace. Schwartz proved to be as tough and patient an editor as he had been an agent, building around himself a stable of young artists and writers whom he could groom and train to create comics as he conceived them. The watchword in Schwartz's office was consistency—the same writer and artist on every episode of a series. Over the years he developed a faultless sense for matching just the right men to just the right material.

DC's search for a winning title gave birth to a new kind of comic book in 1956. Called *Showcase,* it auditioned new series concepts in one-issue appearances. Schwartz says that it was during an editorial session to air *Showcase* ideas that "someone, some unknown inspirational genius, suggested that we bring back the Flash. We decided not to revive the old Flash from the forties but to modernize him." So it was that the small miracle of *Showcase* 4, "Presenting the Flash," found its way to the stands, and a new age of comics was sparked (Show 4, cover-dated Oct. 1956, in the postdating custom of comics).

The Flash sold well enough to return next spring in *Showcase* 8 (dated June 1957), then again in issues 13 and 14 (dated Apr.-June 1958), until at last, taking up where his namesake had left off a decade before, he earned his own title (with *The Flash* 105, Mar. 1959). In doing so, he opened the door for a return of the heroes and showed that fantastic adventure stories, if told properly, could still appeal to a new generation of kids. For the next several years, under editor Schwartz, writer John Broome, and artist Carmine Infantino, the Fastest Man Alive would scarcely miss a step,

6

The dynamism of the mature Infantino: Flash and the Elongated Man tackle the Pied Piper. Inks by Joe Giella, script by Broome. From *The Flash* 138, August 1963.

setting the standards for what was promising to be a new Golden Age of comics.

That perfect union of talents came very close to having never occurred. Infantino was still in art school in 1947, when he and a friend went around to DC looking for work. He had a rough, angular style with a good sense of movement, but little polish. As he put it, "My work had a lukewarm reception by most of the editors and was disliked by one in particular." That one in particular was Julius Schwartz. But Sheldon Mayer saw Infantino's potential and hired him, eventually assigning him to Schwartz's Golden Age Flash. At first reluctantly, later happily, artist and editor began to educate each other.

Schwartz himself was quick to admit that he knew very little about art in his early editing days, but he stuck by one creed: "If it's not clean, it's worthless. So I look at the artwork from my point of view, an ordinary, average Mr. Joe."

This insistence upon clarity helped Infantino mature into one of the finest visual storytellers ever to work in his field. During the new Flash's first few years, he refined a style of sparse backgrounds, novel page layouts, and relaxed lines that gave his stories an open, fluid feeling never before seen in comics. A wealth of poised, energetic characters and visual speed-gimmicks propelled each story from panel to panel to its climax. To all this he added a subtle skill for characterization and a sophisticated eye for the settings and situations of American life.

He had the perfect partner in writer John Broome. Although Robert Kanigher wrote the lead stories in Flash's *Showcase* appearances, Broome's superior backup stories earned him the job of regular Flash scripter. A close friend and client of Schwartz's from the days of the pulps, he was a faultless plotter, who could weave a major conflict between Flash and a villain into fourteen pages, or a clever human-interest story into eight. His most complex plots never stinted any element of the story: character, setting, mystery, suspense, action, the inevitable showdown, or the happy resolution. Although he often wrote stock comic book fare (colorful villain commits gimmicky robberies, Flash hunts villain down, villain traps Flash in a diabolical device, Flash ingeniously escapes and hauls villain off to jail), Broome had a genius for finding the little twist that would make an old plot feel fresh. His expanding repertoire of speed tricks for Flash, for example—running on water, turning invisible, passing through walls, whipping up tornadoes—kept kids spellbound for years.

The later history of comics has shown how difficult it is to make characters seem real without soap-opera interludes that cause the plots to lag, but Broome had a sensitivity to the little strokes of characterization that quickly gave reality even to his most absurd creations. The villains he invented for Flash were a rogues' gallery of colorful eccentrics, the likes of Captain Boomerang, the Weather Wizard, Grodd the gorilla genius, and the magical Abra Kadabra. Yet when the fiendish Mirror Master sits in jail, fretting because the Trickster and Captain Cold have edged him out in the prison newspaper's "Most Successful Criminal Poll," we have no choice but to believe it (F 136, May 1963). And when Captain Cold himself falls in desperate love with every woman who catches his eye—from an Asian princess to a popular idol named Miss Twist to Barry Allen's own girl-friend—we find out hearts going out to him a little even as he makes us laugh.

Broome gave even more character to Flash's friends than to his enemies. In early 1960 (F 112, May 1960) Flash met Ralph Dibny, the Elongated Man, a stretchable sleuth with a love of attention; he became the only DC hero to announce his true identity to the world at large. The Elongated Man was an incorrigible seeker of mysteries, and it was not unusual for him to find himself shrunk by aliens while vacationing in the Yucatan (F 115, Sept. 1960), or hypnotized by undersea conquerors during his honey-moon in the Caribbean (F 119, Mar. 1961); but whatever transpired, he always came up smiling. Broome's affectionate handling of the camaraderie between Barry Allen and Ralph Dibny made their team-ups some of the most appealing episodes in the Flash's career.

It was in this human dimension that Broome most needed Infantino. Infantino drew everything—a hidden city of scientific gorillas, a harlequin committing crimes with toys, Flash strapped to a giant boomerang—as if he believed absolutely in its existence. His subtly witty drawings, full of character, and his grasp of the artistic tricks that cast an illusion of reality, pulled the reader magnetically into his world. Barry Allen, with his crew-cut and rumpled trench coat, became a real man. The tension and affec-tion were palpable whenever Barry's girlfriend, ambitious reporter Iris West, chided him for his incurable sloth.

Infantino even made Kid Flash believable. When Iris's nephew, Wally West, gained speed identical to Flash's through a convenient fluke of na-ture in late 1959 (F 110, dated Jan. 1960), many readers reacted with out-rage: After all, junior sidekicks are certifiable baby stuff. But Infantino's art can evoke so fully the quiet of a small-town afternoon or the coolness of a shaded lawn that we forgive the teen-oriented plots full of beatniks, schoolteachers, and singing idols. As children, we may have resented finding Kid Flash stories in the backs of so many *Flash* comics, but seen now, through adult eyes, they can be hypnotically nostalgic.

Scarcely anything about the Flash was altogether new, as experimenta-tion would never be Schwartz's great virtue. But heroes had never before been handled with such humor and humanity, art that was at once so dy-namic and pristine, stories so entertaining to children and so satisfying to adults. If the heroes were indeed to return, it could never be with the in-nocent abandon and crude vitality that had made the Golden Age seem so golden in retrospect; but the high standards of plotting and drawing set by the Schwartz stable would at the same time ensure that they would have to keep their quality higher than they ever had before. And in the first few years after the Flash's debut, Schwartz's own work in science fic-tion comics would raise those standards still higher, bringing such a dy-namic new perspective, such increased complexity, such abundant new themes, and such heightened craftsmanship into the field that the coming years would have to be, at the very least, a "Silver Age of Comics."

Strange Adventures in Space

The year after the new Flash appeared, the growing American interest in science, outer space, and the future exploded into an all-consuming craze. The launching of *Sputnik* in October 1957 broadcast a clear message to the makers of American popular culture, and of comic books in particular: science fiction was the only way to go.

Almost immediately, the center of DC's editorial conferences became the creation of two space-faring heroes, one to be set in the far future, in the Buck Rogers tradition, the other in the present, à la Flash Gordon. Each of DC's science fiction editors was asked to develop one. Jack Schiff, an editor with a more fanciful and juvenile slant, took the future hero. Julius Schwartz, with his instinct for blending the fantastic and the plausible, set about the creation of a space hero for our time. This would be the second step in the building of the Silver Age.

Schwartz had launched two science fiction comics, *Strange Adventures* and *Mystery in Space,* in 1951. Originally working with a large and fluctuating stable of free-lancers, he had gradually pared his regular staff down to two writers (John Broome and Gardner Fox) and five artists (Carmine Infantino, Murphy Anderson, Mike Sekowsky, Sid Greene, and Gil Kane) who could deliver the kind of complicated but clear, gimmick-filled stories that he wanted. The craftsmanship in these late-fifties tales was high but somewhat inconsistent, and the comics in general were short on character and pizzazz. Adam Strange, Schwartz's science fiction hero, was a shot in the arm to the whole stable.

The first problem presented by the notion of a present-day spaceman was transportation. No primitive rocket could carry a man far enough or fast enough to have any exciting adventures in space. The ingenious solution was a flash of light, the Zeta-Beam, a teleportation ray fired at Earth years before by the scientists of Rann, a planet orbiting Alpha Centauri; when it strikes archaeologist Adam Strange while he is on a dig in South America, it hurtles him instantaneously twenty-five trillion miles across the gulf of space. And, just as a flashlight cast on the pages of a hidden comic book under the covers at night can transport a child to a world of wonder, so did the Zeta-Beam hurl Adam Strange to the beautiful, perilous, scientifically advanced planet Rann.

Adam Strange is swept from Earth to the beautiful vistas of Rann . . .

. . . to meet his interplanetary sweetheart, Alanna. Pencils by Infantino, inks by Murphy Anderson, script by Gardner F. Fox. From *Mystery in Space* 91, May 1964.

But there was a catch: the rays of the Zeta-Beam would wear off at unpredictable times, throwing Adam back to Earth and the imprisonment of reality. To heighten the drama, Adam fell in love with Alanna, beautiful daughter of the chief scientist of Rann, and his enforced separation from her was an agony. His only solace lay in waiting for the next Zeta-Beam, for a long series of them had been fired toward Earth, and Adam was able to calculate when and where each would strike. And so he would wait, gazing at the indifferent stars, for his next fabulous adventure.

The first Adam Strange stories, featured in *Showcase* magazine, were fairly standard Flash Gordon fare, in which the swashbuckling off-worlder turned back would-be tyrants of his adopted planet. But shortly after beginning his regular appearances in *Mystery in Space* in 1959, Adam's life took a decided turn for the peculiar. No sooner would he materialize on Rann than he would find himself facing a man-eating vacuum cleaner, a giant sentient atom, a huge magnifying glass that floated in the sky and burned the cities below it with sunlight, or even a giant duplicate of himself. Soon even Adam was wondering wryly why some impossible menace always seemed to strike Rann when he arrived. He would not have had to wonder if he'd known his adventures were being written by Gardner F. Fox.

Fox was among the most prolific and wildly creative writers ever to work in comics, and a highly productive author of paperback fiction. He once described his usual output as "a comic book a week, four or five novels a year." Under at least six pseudonyms he produced science fiction novels, horror stories, mysteries, gothics, romances, and historical adventures. None of them was particularly artful, but most displayed a very free imagination.

Most of Fox's early comic book work had been for costumed heroes, but when reading tastes ran to science fiction in the 1950s, he was able to combine his imagination with a remarkably varied store of knowledge. Fox held a law degree and was fascinated with magic and science, and he filled thousands of index cards with odd facts of all descriptions. His Adam Strange stories always revolved around some peculiarity of chemistry or physics, often turning some commonplace item into a menace, and it was usually through a combination of Yankee know-how and scientific knowledge that Adam triumphed. How do you defeat a gang of intelligent, evil dust devils? Well, if you're able, as Adam was, to deduce that they are a sodium-based life-form—which would have to be animated by high internal temperatures—then you simply throw sand on them; by doing so, our hero tells us, "I added the silicate needed to transform the sodiums and calciums in their bodies . . . to glass!" (Mystery in Space 68, June 1961). An unspoken challenge to the reader was always to spot the nemesis' scientific Achilles' heel before Adam could. We rarely succeeded.

Only one artist could hope to render this parade of outlandish creations amazing and not laughable: Carmine Infantino. With the master of the magically plausible to make his ideas real, Fox was truly able to flex his creative muscles, and under the writer's pressure, Infantino produced some of the most inventive and beautiful art of his career. Though sacrificing some of the fluidity he brought to the Flash, Infantino concentrated on dizzying upshots of Adam soaring skyward with his rocket-pack, scenes of passion between him and the exotic Alanna, and breathtaking backgrounds of futuristic cityscapes full of sweeping curves, delicate spires, and swirling aerial pathways. And turning these exquisite designs into a lush and solid world was the work of the series' regular inker, Murphy Anderson.

Standard comic book production procedure resembles an assembly line. One artist turns in only a pencil drawing of each story, usually sparse in detail, which another artist then finishes in ink. Where Joe Giella inked Infantino airily but a little scratchily on *The Flash*, Murphy Anderson finished *Adam Strange* with pristine sleekness and polish.

Anderson and Infantino were the most unlikely of artistic partners. Where Infantino was inclined to distort reality a little to create effect, Anderson believed in strict naturalism and neatness. Anderson reportedly found the task of inking Infantino maddening and objected to the penciler's "impossible" character poses. Schwartz, however, proving that he had advanced far beyond his "average Mr. Joe's" understanding of art, saw past their superficial differences. "Carmine and Anderson," Schwartz said, "were both just at the point in their artistic development when they could balance each other and be a great team." The result of this union gave Adam Strange's adventures a solid, dynamic quality that is perhaps unparalleled in comics' history.

If the wild stories in the Schwartz science fiction comics challenged the skills of the artists, the artists were able to respond with a challenge of their own. In a system devised for the pulp magazines by his old friend Mort Weisinger, Schwartz would work out the cover design for each issue of his comics with an artist and have it drawn *before* the story was written. This ensured that every comic would have an eye-catching, child-thrilling cover. Often Schwartz would have a plot idea to go with the cover, but sometimes he and the writer would have to make up a story from scratch to go with some outlandish picture conceived solely for its visual appeal, such as a man with a miniature planet Saturn in place of his head, or a fisherman in a flying boat reeling in a green alien from a "fishing hole in the sky." The result was a stable of comics that united visual imagination and story more completely than any of their contemporaries; this was to be one of the greatest appeals of the stable's hero comics in coming years.

Schwartz's science fiction comics formed the matrix from which his hero revivals of the next few years would spring; *Strange Adventures*, although not featuring anything that could strictly be called a hero, revealed in its purest form the science fiction fad that dominated the first phase of the Silver Age, and helped set the style for the comic book renaissance of the early 1960s. In that title the tremendous ingenuity and freedom of the stable's imagination was shown best, for there the keynote was pure, unadulterated fun. Where most science fiction in comics to that time, when raised above the Saturday-matinee level, had tended toward the somber or cautionary, Schwartz saw that a lighter approach to that unique genre could be better suited to his medium. The scope of his science fiction would never exceed the accepted limits of comic books, but within those limits *Strange Adventures*, with an upswing beginning in 1959, would attain unprecedentedly high standards of quality—of which the foremost standard was sheer entertainment.

An important factor in the title's success was Schwartz's sensitivity to the taste of his young audience. From science fiction he drew primarily those elements that were most suitable to comics: wonder, mystery, and delight. The themes of the unrelated stories that comprised the bulk of the comic seemed to spring from the fantasies of ten-year-old children. Half the charm of those stories lay in the details around which they were woven, the stuff of childhood, the people and things that held magical significance for kids at the beginning of the 1960s—astronauts, aliens, pets, dinosaurs, cavemen, toys, ray guns, apes, contests, scientists, lost civilizations, and heroic fathers—details both fantastic and comfortingly familiar, skillfully blended together into a special enchantment. Schwartz's own boyhood love of athletics surfaced in many stories of sports in the future and on other worlds. (Such stories nearly received their own title when five issues of *The Brave and the Bold* [45–49, Jan.–Sept. 1963] were turned over to *Strange Sports Stories*, featuring imaginative Fox and Broome stories with Infantino art.) Many stories even featured children as protagonists, as in "Earth Boy Meets Spaceboy," a futuristic twist on *The Prince and the Pauper* (SA 123, Dec. 1960). But such themes did not give the stories the rambling, shapeless nature of children's fantasies, for the craftsmanship of Broome and Fox rendered them in such neat, sophisticated plots that they are delightful to the fathers of the children as well as to the children themselves.

As in *The Flash*, these stories were woven with great complexity, of which the classic example is "The Two-Way Time Traveller" (SA 143, Aug. 1962). Nuclear scientist Tod White goes to bed for a nap and awakens on a grassy plain. He finds out from a passing motorist that it's April 6, 1917, and that the United States has just declared war on Germany. But before the astonished Tod can mull over his sudden shift in time, he blacks out, only to reawaken in the year 2007. A patrolman decides to take him down to headquarters, but as they motor along a futuristic landscape, Tod suddenly vanishes again. His next stop is two hundred years backward from his own time, where Indians chase him until he disappears once again. Tod then finds himself in the year 2187 and realizes that his shifts are carrying him farther and farther away from his own time. He makes contact with a doctor and, just before he shifts again, instructs him to make a record of his visit so that future generations might be able to help him when he travels forward in time again. Tod is then flung hundreds of years into the past, where he witnesses the fall of a meteor, and again forward to the year 3087, where, as he had hoped, the world is expecting him. Doctors in this era have determined that Tod's time shifts are being caused by "omega radiation," a rare type of energy given off by certain meteors. The doctors can cure Tod, but they require a favor in return. Earth, it seems, has been contaminated by a gas cloud that can only be canceled by none other than omega radiation. The rub is that omega meteors have become so rare that they can only be found in the past. By reducing the amount of omega radiation in Tod's body, future science can send him back to precisely one year after the landing of the meteor that originally filled him with radiation. Tod obligingly travels to the past, brings back enough omega-radiated rock to save the future world, and in exchange is returned to his present.

All of this, without a sense of being crammed, was beautifully crafted into only seven pages.

In addition to such anthologized stories, Strange Adventures featured three regular series, alternating with one another, which reflected the growing interest in hero series and helped the stable broaden its range. The first, and best realized, was Space Museum, which debuted in issue 104 (May 1959). It was an unusual series in that the only recurring characters were the narrator, Howard Parker, and his son Tommy. Once a month the Parkers visit the Space Museum, one of the wonders of the twenty-fifth century, where, behind every fabulous object on display, ". . . there's a story of heroism, daring, and self-sacrifice." And these were the very stories that comprised the series as, on every visit to the museum, Tommy picks out an object and his father furnishes him, and us, with the heroic space-faring tale behind it.

The stories themselves always revolved around a spaceman who met and conquered a threat to star-flung humanity by an ingenious use of his or her wits. When Tommy Parker points to a silver medal on display, for example, we learn of astronaut Mike Dillon, cursed for his whole life to finish in second place in every contest and activity he undertook, who stumbled upon a secret alien invasion of our universe; deducing by oblique clues that only silver can power the one device that might stop the invasion, Dillon sacrificed his numerous second-place medals to become the champion of mankind (SA 136, Jan. 1962). Other intricate stories tell of a magpie (now stuffed in the museum) whose natural attraction for shiny objects saved the earth from conquest by a group of telepathic jewels, of a tin soldier that an ingenious old toymaker used to repel an invasion of the planet Jorga, and of a blonde hair that served as the cross hair on the scope of a weapon that tipped the balance in a mighty war against tyranny; the owner of that hair, to Tommy's delight, turns out to be his own mother, a war hero (SA 124, Jan. 1961).

All twenty of the stories were written by Gardner Fox and, with the exception of the first, drawn by Carmine Infantino. But this was not the same pristine Infantino of the Flash and Adam Strange; this Infantino was startlingly different. This great departure in look had nothing to do with Infantino's pencils, but rather with the inks. Instead of being shaded by the meticulous Anderson or the light Giela, Infantino was here inked by himself, and his inking style, raw and scratchy, lent his pencils a racy, bold line that whipped along in wild, exuberant action sequences. With plots of unfailing ingenuity, beautiful art, and never a false note, *Space Museum* may well have been the most consistent product of the Schwartz stable.

The next regular strip in *Strange Adventures* was *Star Hawkins*, concerning the ace private detective of the twenty-first century and his "amazing robot secretary," Ilda (SA 114, Mar. 1960). From Star and Ilda's association emerged the basis for the strip, the humorous interaction between the two; virtually every story revolved around one of the two protagonists getting him or herself into some wacky jam, from which he or she was eventually bailed out by the other in some mock-heroic feat of physical prowess or cleverness. *Star Hawkins* was a charming and boisterous entry in the Schwartz stable, even if plots were fairly predictable and the humor (as in most adventure comics) was usually cornball.

The artist on the series was Mike Sekowsky, a man of nearly the same age and Schwartz-tenure as Infantino and Kane. Often maligned for his strange interpretation of human anatomy and his messy lines, Sekowsky had an intelligent sense of storytelling that was fluid and dynamic. But a further assessment of his abilities must wait until his work on the *Justice League of America* is discussed in Chapter 5.

The Atomic Knights, the third strip featured in *Strange Adventures*, was the closest to being a hero series and began as the most distinct and promising of the three; but ultimately it proved the most frustrating. Although the individual stories were generally of a much higher quality than those in *Star Hawkins*, the reader could not help being painfully aware of the series failing again and again to live up to its great potential.

Atomic Knights, written by John Broome and penciled and inked by Murphy Anderson, is set in the wake of World War III, where plant life has been eradicated, the animal kingdom is nearly extinct, and man barely lingers on. The *Atomic Knights* themselves, so named because of the ancient suits of armor they wear—suits capable of shielding them from nuclear radiation—comprise a small "organization determined to represent law and order and the forces of justice and to help right wrong and prevent evil." The team includes an ex-schoolteacher, one of the last scientists left alive on earth, two ex-soldiers, a pretty girl, and Gardner Grayle, their levelheaded leader.

What made the series unique from its very inception was that it represented the only instance in the Schwartz science fiction universe in which science, rather than elevating and benefiting mankind, has wrought terrible destruction. The series got off with a bang in issue 117 (June 1960)

The Atomic Knights gaze out over a pristine Murphy Anderson landscape . . .

. . . then go into action through a ruined Earth. Script by Broome. From *Strange Adventures* 123, December 1960.

when the Atomic Knights were formed to battle and depose the Black Baron, an evil despot who was hoarding a badly needed food supply. The story suggested that rather than fight aliens or powerful villains, the *Atomic Knights* would examine a post-holocaust earth in realistic terms, yet another factor contributing to the strip's uniqueness. Indeed, this vein of realism continued very nicely when the Knights, in issue 120 (Sept.

1960), settled in Durvale, the first post-atomic-war pioneer village. Here the Knights manage to grow food, start a school, form a political structure to benevolently rule the town, and generally help start the long, hard climb back to civilization.

But with issue 129 (June 1961) the trouble began. In "World Out of Time," the Knights found themselves in Atlantis, of all places, a startling departure from the realism that until then had made the strip so captivating. Many other departures followed—Knights fight Atlanteans twice again (132, Sept. 1961, and 135, Dec. 1961), Knights domesticate giant dalmatians (138, Mar. 1962), Knights fight aliens (141, June 1962)—until these deviations from reality ceased to be deviations at all but instead became the series norm. The Atomic Knights hit rock bottom in "When the Earth Blacked Out" (144, Sept. 1962) when they tangled with a race of subterranean mole creatures who, we discovered, were the real perpetrators of World War III. In one stroke, the realism and daring on which the strip had been based was once and for all voided.

Yet despite the overall failings of the series, there were many delightful Atomic Knights stories, particularly those in which they visited the ruins of once-proud cities. Among these were "Cavemen of New York" (123, Dec. 1960), in which the Knights helped a band of humans who had devolved to savagery regain their humanity; "The King of New Orleans" (147, Dec. 1962), in which the Knights defeated a ruthless monarch with Dixieland jazz; and "Danger in Detroit" (153, June 1963), in which the Knights were made a present of the first postwar automobile for overthrowing a futuristic Gestapo. These stories—as well as the entire series—were heightened by the lovely pastoral scenes and stark ruins that poured from Murphy Anderson's pencil.

One other series ran in the Schwartz science fiction universe, although only for a few issues of *Mystery in Space* (from 66, Mar. 1961) and later for two of *Strange Adventures*. This was *The Star Rovers*, and the brevity of its career was just as well, for it was far and away the weakest of Schwartz's series. Demonstrating the greatest danger of that stable's style of gimmick-based stories, Gardner Fox built the entire series around one plot trick: Three space-faring adventurers experience three almost identical action-packed mysteries, retell them later to each other, and discover a single explanation for all. These mysteries were not only similar but rather dull, and to have to sit through each one three times taxed the reader's patience. The series was further weakened by the art of Sid Greene, who, although one of the finest inkers in the field, was not a penciler suited to the Schwartz approach. Greene had an attractive cartoonish style, but lacked the ability of Infantino and Anderson to make the fantastic palpable.

All the series continued without loss of consistency until 1964, when *Mystery in Space* and *Strange Adventures* were shifted to editor Jack Schiff to make way for the expanding Schwartz hero line. That marked the end of *Space Museum, Atomic Knights,* and *Star Rovers,* while *Adam Strange, Star Hawkins,* and the non-series stories continued under the hands of an entirely different staff and style. By then, however, new fashions were on the rise in comic book history, and Schwartz's science fiction titles had already completed their contributions to the quality and concerns of the Silver Age. Like westerns, romance, and the other old genres, science fiction was giving way to the new era. But it had one more contribution to make in the late 1950s—it was to spur the revitalization of the greatest hero of all.

3 The Superman Mythos

Mort Weisinger enjoyed telling this anecdote about his teenage days with Julius Schwartz and their science fiction club: "We were hiking in New Jersey's Palisades Park—Julie, Otto Binder, myself, and some of the other Scienceers—when suddenly we woke up in the hospital! A car had hit us and knocked us over like a row of clay pigeons. We could have all been wiped out but we were very fortunate. I often wonder, immodestly, what would have happened to science fiction and comics if we'd all been obliterated there."

What indeed? Schwartz's contribution has been suggested already. But comics would have been no less poor for the absence of Weisinger and Binder. Their lives crossed many times from 1935 to 1970, and each time something new was added to comics or science fiction. One of those crossings, in the late 1950s, made possible the second step in the history of the Silver Age—the revitalization of Superman.

Otto Binder had been among the most prolific pulp science fiction writers in the 1930s. For a while his agents had been Mort Weisinger and Julius Schwartz; later one of his biggest markets was *Thrilling Wonder Stories*, of which Weisinger was the young editor. But Binder feared the pulps would not last and sought something more secure. His brother Jack, a comic book artist, told him about the explosion in the comics market, especially among costumed-hero titles. Through Jack, Otto became a writer for Fawcett Comics, and from 1941 on, he made himself the principal writer for Fawcett's big star, Captain Marvel.

"Comics were like a drug, or a hypnotic spell, to me," Binder once said. "The moment I began writing them . . . I was a captive of this new and colorful way of writing stories." During his career, Binder would write more than two thousand stories for twenty publishers, including well over half of the Captain Marvel family lore, a contribution that made him, along with Gardner Fox, one of the two most important writers of the Golden Age.

Of all the heroes who had sprung up in the wake of Superman's success in the late 1930s, none copied the nature and powers of its inspiration more than Captain Marvel. DC shortly sued Fawcett for copyright infringement and a battle began—of lawyers, of sales figures, and of loyal young readers—that would rage through the 1940s and into the 1950s.

The same year that Binder took the helm of Captain Marvel, DC's Whitney Ellsworth hired Mort Weisinger to edit Superman and a number of other titles. A hard taskmaster and an editor with a clear vision of what he wanted, Weisinger (working with Ellsworth and co-editor Jack Schiff) would make as deep an imprint on the Man of Steel as Binder would on the World's Mightiest Mortal. For the next twelve years the two friends would be competitors and in the process would make their characters the two prominent heroes of the Golden Age, but with creative approaches that were nearly opposite.

Weisinger's Superman was almost a god. He had no private life, except as meek Clark kent, no personal quirks, no failings, only an awesome array of powers. He was aloof, mysterious, all business. Weisinger had his writers subordinate all else to the rigid, complex plots he demanded. Superman's world was rarely colorful or imaginative. The focus of his stories was the very concept of a costumed hero.

Binder's treatment of Captain Marvel, by contrast, was affectionate and humorous. The captain was a powerful but amiable, sometimes bumbling, fellow who often depended on the wits of his child alter ego, Billy Batson, to save his skin. Binder was never as careful with plot as were Weisinger's men, but his imagination poured forth an unending stream of wonders: a world-conquering worm, a gentlemanly talking tiger, a bickering family of mad scientists. If Weisinger fascinated his readers with his concepts and plots, then Binder charmed his with his characters and inventions.

Even the mightiest heroes, unfortunately, were not invulnerable to the hard times that beset costumed characters in the 1950s. Failing sales and the DC lawsuit forced Fawcett to abandon its comics in 1953.

Meanwhile, money had tightened up at DC, and Weisinger had lost some of his best writers. Superman's popularity continued largely because of the television show about him that had premiered in 1952. The show, sadly, only made the quality of the comics worse. Television, by its nature, permitted only a rather limited range of mundane problems for Superman to tackle, and the comics were forced to follow suit. Even more detrimental to the comics was the fact that editorial director Ellsworth left for Hollywood to produce the program, with Weisinger functioning as story editor; at the same time, co-editor Schiff's work load increased, and Superman languished for lack of attention.

In November 1957 the Superman show ceased production, and Weisinger brought his full attention back to the comics (the next year, an editorial reshuffling at DC made him the sole editor of nearly all the Superman titles, while relieving him of the burden of co-editing other DC comics). He couldn't fail to sense the lack of vitality in the Man of Steel, especially if he saw the care going into the new Flash, just down the hall. It was clear that something had to be done with DC's premier hero, and the new company policies made it clear that science fiction would have to be part of it. But the regular writers, after nearly twenty years with the character, seemed virtually drained of ideas. Weisinger himself, long known as an idea man, appeared to have little notion where to turn for Superman's new direction. He needed a new element on his staff, one that was not conditioned by sixteen years of Weisinger training. He found that element in Otto Binder.

Binder had been contributing stories for the Superman family of comics—*Action Comics, Adventure Comics, Superman, Superboy, Jimmy Olsen*, and, later, *Lois Lane*—since Captain Marvel's demise in 1953, but it was a few years before Weisinger began drawing on his talent and science fiction background to remake Superman's world. Their relationship would be a tense one personally, and ultimately unsatisfying for both men. Binder was not a careful enough plotter for Weisinger, and they would butt heads frequently over Weisinger's demand for story changes. But theirs was a productive union, and in 1958, 1959, and 1960 they introduced a constellation of changes that turned Superman from a concept into a character and gave him as delightful a universe as any that Captain Marvel had ever inhabited.

There is no point in trying to determine which ideas were Binder's and which were Weisinger's; most of them were born in conference, and the two men themselves later disagreed over who had contributed what. (Other writers, especially the just-returning originator of Superman, Jerry Siegel, also augmented many of the ideas.) But it is safe to guess that none of them could have existed without the marriage of Binder's imagination and Weisinger's sharp editorial eye. It was as if the spirit of Captain Marvel had entered the body of Superman.

Weisinger had long been fascinated with Superman's origin—his birth on a distant advanced scientific planet called Krypton, the planet's destruction, and baby Kal-El's Moses-like exodus to Earth. Now, with science fiction in the air, the space-travel theme seemed especially appealing. Somehow, though, he had never been able to wring a good story out of the Krypton idea until he and Binder, in 1958, pitted Superman against an alien villain called Brainiac. Brainiac, as Superman's first good outer-space foe, was interesting enough; but he paled beside what Superman discovered aboard his spaceship, for Brainiac's hobby was shrinking cities from many worlds and imprisoning them in bottles, and one of those cities was Kandor, from the planet Krypton (Act. 242, July 1958).

Kandor was like a child's most private fantasies made real. It was all of childhood's dollhouses, ant farms, secret hiding places, and imaginary playmates rolled into one. When Superman turned a shrinking ray on himself and entered the Bottle City, he plunged into a tiny world in which the ancient ways of Krypton had never died. There the people welcomed him as one of their own; some of them had even been friends of his mother and father. There, among brilliant-colored skyscrapers, wizened men in togas performed miracles of science. There, strange animals labored in farms beneath an artificial sun.

22

Superman shares his private retreats with a pal: the Fortress of Solitude and Kandor. Pencils by Curt Swan, inks by George Klein. From *Superman* 158, January 1963.

No one on Earth dreamed of Kandor's existence, for Superman hid it in his Arctic Fortress of Solitude. This Fortress, introduced a month before Brainiac in a story quietly celebrating *Action Comics'* twentieth anniversary, gave the Man of Steel his first opportunity to appear not merely as a hero but as a character—putting his feet up, playing a little high-speed chess with a robot, painting a Martian landscape with his telescopic vision, joking with his old pal Batman (Act. 241, June 1958). The Kandorians there were his secret friends, putting their wisdom and scientific wizardry always at his disposal. And when he tired of his lonely life as the Superman of Earth, he could always shrink into that sheltered world and walk among his own people as Kal-El of Krypton.

As thrilled as the kids were by Kandor, none of them could have been more excited than Mort Weisinger himself. He saw immediately that the focal point of Superman's new direction would have to be his Kryptonian background. For one thing, Kandor enabled Superman to shed his powers occasionally, for when he entered the Kryptonian conditions of the city he became a normal being once again; this opened up many plot avenues that had been closed by the hero's near-omnipotence. For another, Kandor and the Fortress ended Superman's days as an impersonal symbol of justice. Suddenly he was an individual, with a people and a past, with hobbies and friends, an object of interest in and of himself.

The logical encore to Kandor was Krypton itself. Through the device of time travel, Binder took us there, first with Jimmy Olsen (JO 36, Apr. 1959), and soon with Superman himself (Sup. 133; Nov. 1959). Though other writers would set stories on that planet, Binder was its protean geographer. He and his successors gave us a wonderland of robot factories, jewel mountains, sky palaces, fire-falls, scarlet jungles, interplanetary zoos, jet taxis, fire-breathing dogs, scientific tribunals, and even antigravity swimming pools.

This was the setting for one of Weisinger's finest stories, variously attributed both to Binder and Jerry Siegel, which marked the first of a type of epic, emotional adventure that would come to distinguish the Superman line: "Superman's Return to Krypton" (Sup. 141, Nov. 1960). This full-issue story—thus three times the length of the usual Weisinger tale—tells of Superman's struggle, bereft of his powers and acting as his father's laboratory assistant before his own birth, to prevent the approaching doom of Krypton. His desperation is further fueled when he falls in love with a mysterious beauty, Krypton's leading actress. But destiny cannot be changed; in the end Kal-El returns to the earth of the present, orphaned and homeless. This introduction of pathos to Superman, the realization that not even all his powers could give him back what he loved most in life, raised him from a mere costumed crime-fighter to something close to a tragic figure. Weisinger had discovered that Superman grew more heroic as he grew less powerful.

The last Weisinger-Binder contribution to this theme arose from the letters of inquisitive young fans. For most of his history, Superman's great prowess had been attributed to the lighter gravity of Earth in contrast to that of Krypton. That explanation had worked well at the character's inception in 1938, when his only real power had been unusual strength. But the argument grew less plausible as Weisinger added new powers to his hero. How, these new science-minded kids wondered, would lesser gravity create the ability to fly, or X-ray vision, or a super memory, or super-ventriloquism?

Weisinger answered that Krypton had orbited a red sun, and that somehow, under Earth's yellow sun, Kryptonians are granted remarkable powers. More than a convenient explanation, this provided the springboard for a number of adventures in which Superman found himself stranded on savage, inclement planets orbiting red suns. The first of these stories, by Binder, was little more than an exercise in cleverness, as Superman slipped out of danger after danger by his wits (Act. 262, Mar. 1960).

But during the 1960s, under other writers, they would become some of the most imaginative and suspenseful of Superman's adventures.

The genesis of the "red sun" stories shows clearly the Weisinger method of developing the Superman mythos. He encouraged his writers to try whatever they could imagine, and threw in many twists of his own. Then he listened to the fans. Whatever they liked he would give them again, but with a new wrinkle added. Gradually a whole body of lore grew around the figure of Superman.

Since his days with Schwartz in science fiction fandom in the early 1930s, Weisinger had respected the desires and opinions of even his youngest readers. As an editor of the pulps, he attended fan meetings and early science fiction conventions. As an editor of comics, he listened to kids.

In 1958, as the revitalization of his comics was just picking up steam, he opened a forum for kids' opinions and questions by introducing the first letter pages in hero comics. After twenty years of costumed heroes, someone was finally asking the people who bought the comics what they wanted to read.

Many of the letters he received were devoted to nitpicking ("How come, when Superman takes his Clark Kent clothes out of the secret pouch in his cape, the clothes are not wrinkled?") or the kinds of questions that only kids can conceive ("Will Superman ever give a signal-watch to Perry White?" or "Will Superman ever marry? Please answer or I'll go mad!"), but many told the editor what his readers wanted to see. The idea of Kandor captivated them, for example, but they were less curious about Krypton itself; they wanted Superman to show more of his human side; they wanted to go inside the Fortress of Solitude more often; and they were hungry for new characters.

When Weisinger, in 1958, issued a story that centered on a woman with extraordinary powers, hundreds of girls wrote in to demand a female counterpart for Superman. Supergirl, a teenage Kryptonian with powers nearly equal to her cousin Superman's, debuted in a Binder story in early 1959 and was promptly awarded a series of her own in the back of *Action Comics* (Act. 252, May 1959). Aside from Krypto the Super-Dog, Supergirl was the first Kryptonian to join Superman in his life on Earth. Although Binder's stories tended toward condescension and contrivance, Kal-El's cousin Kara did bring another element to his life—a sense of family—around which new types of stories could be woven.

One of the long-term benefits of the innovations of those years was the enormous increase in the variety of possible Superman stories. The writers would no longer be restricted to formula plots—Superman meets crook, crook stymies Superman, Superman overcomes crook—but would be free to give the Man of Steel adventures alone or with Supergirl, with his powers or without, on Earth or in Kandor. In seeking to broaden the range of possible plots still further, Weisinger and Binder introduced a pair of concepts that were like nothing the comics had ever seen.

The first was red kryptonite. This aberration of the notorious green kryptonite, the only substance in the universe capable of weakening Superman, had the ability to work weird transformations in Kryptonian minds and bodies for up to forty-eight hours. This gave Superman's writers an open field for bizarre story angles, turning him into a fire-breathing dragon, making him a giant or a midget, giving him a third eye in the back of his head, even splitting him into two beings, one good and one evil. Red K also induced nightmares, such as one in which Superman and Supergirl imagine they have destroyed the earth (Sup. 144, Apr. 1961).

The use of dreams to tell "impossible" stories intrigued both writer and editor. After all, why should a character as fanciful as Superman be bound by a single invented reality? Why not write stories—not dreams, but self-proclaimed "imaginary stories"—showing what might happen to Superman if something drastic were to occur in his life? Then anything could be done: Superman could give up his powers, could grow old and decrepit, could even die.

The Imaginary Stories started small, as a series of tales in Lois Lane comics in 1960, speculating on what Lois's life might be like if she were ever to realize her dream of marrying Superman. Binder wrote the earliest of them, but he left DC before Weisinger saw their full potential and spread them throughout the Superman line. As with so much of Binder's work for the Man of Steel, these stories would blossom only later, under other writers.

It often happens in the creation of a new kind of comic book that the most significant developments do not occur in the best-crafted stories. Binder was never able to plot with the facility of Weisinger's veterans, Jerry Siegel and Edmond Hamilton. And some time would pass before those men were fully able to assimilate the new ideas and begin weaving them into their intricate stories. The art, too, was getting a little stale, having been dominated by Wayne Boring since the 1940s. Boring had a good imagination for fantastic landscapes, which helped such stories as "Superman's Return to Krypton," but he used a very overt, dramatic approach to characterization and expression that clashed with the new, intimate treatment of Superman. Overall, the effect was of craft far below that of the Schwartz stable, in both writing and art; Superman's best years still lay ahead. But by the summer of 1960, Superman and his world were already infinitely more interesting than they had been a mere three years before.

The contributions of Otto Binder did not stop at these. He also helped give Jimmy Olsen a stretchable alter ego called Elastic Lad and invented such menaces as a giant gorilla with kryptonite eyes named Titano. With Siegel and Weisinger he introduced a breed of moronic pseudo-Supermen called Bizarros, who lived on a square planet and did everything backwards.

One of his then least-noticed creations proved to have perhaps the greatest potential of all. In a story from early 1958, a trio of teenage heroes from the distant future—one a telepath, one a master of magnetism, one a living conductor of lightning—journeyed to the twentieth century to meet Superboy (Adven. 247, Apr. 1958). It was an undistinguished story and lay forgotten for a year and a half. A few fans, however, thought the idea of a futuristic band of heroes showed potential, and they demanded a return appearance. Beginning in late 1959, this Legion of Super-Heroes would play an ever-greater role in Superboy's life, and would grow into the biggest and most complex hero team in comic history. But that, too, would be the work of Siegel and Hamilton and later writers, and must be saved for Chapter 11 of this book.

In 1960, Otto Binder left DC to pursue a career in science article writing. He complained that with Weisinger he had been required to rewrite so many stories that he was unable to complete enough assignments to make a living. But he had done his job. He had given Superman a new lease on life. With his imagination he had given him greater fictional freedom than any character before or since. Pulling on his experience in early science fiction, he had helped his editor lay the foundation of a charming, dazzling, and endearing new universe. As he once did for Captain Marvel, he had helped create a family to bring companionship and drama to his hero's life. He had helped give the comics' greatest hero, at last, a world worthy of him.

Now it would be up to Mort Weisinger and his staff to make Superman himself a figure as fascinating as any in his world. Already the seeds had been planted for a new Man of Steel, one who would be less steel and more man.

Bizarre Characters and Fantastic Weapons

Even as the science fiction rage was helping revitalize the work of Julius Schwartz and Mort Weisinger, it was producing more mixed results from the third prominent DC stable, that of Jack Schiff.

Schiff had begun as a pulp editor at Standard Magazines in the 1930s, and had, in fact, helped hire Mort Weisinger to his post there in 1938. When Weisinger entered the military during World War II, he completed the circle by having Schiff hired to take his place at DC. By the time of Weisinger's return, Schiff had made himself an indispensable part of the company; acting as DC's managing editor for over twenty years, he coordinated production schedules, issued writing and art assignments, and acted as liaison between the company's front office—mainly publisher Jack Liebowitz and dedicated editorial director Whitney Ellsworth—and its many creative free-lancers. He also worked as a contact between the company and such agencies as the Comics Code Authority (the industry's self-censorship body since 1954) and the U.S. government (for various educational and international projects). A man of deep social conscience who held a firm belief in the power of the comics medium to educate children, Schiff put his greatest energies into a series of "institutional pages," one-page messages about issues as diverse as racial tolerance, consideration for neighbors, and the joys of public libraries; all in effective comic strip format, they were coordinated with the National Social Welfare Assembly and appeared in every DC comic from 1950 to 1967.

In addition to these considerable chores, Schiff was also responsible for editing a wide range of comics, including the three titles featuring DC's second most popular hero: *Batman, Detective Comics,* and *World's Finest Comics.* During the 1950s he also launched the western *Tomahawk,* along with *House of Mystery, House of Secrets, My Greatest Adventure,* and *Tales of the Unexpected,* a quartet of titles featuring supernatural mystery and adventure in what Schiff describes as "the Ambrose Bierce tradition." Like his friend Weisinger, Schiff believed in being deeply involved in the creation of his comics, down to plotting most of the stories himself. He says, "I insisted on good, tight plots with characterization and gimmicks, but pictures with colorful locale and sweeping action," along with factual accuracy and good taste. Thus from his desk came what were perhaps the best crafted and most colorful tales of DC's Golden Age.

Because of the size of his work load, Schiff's comics were usually handled by a team composed of the editor himself (who gained the nickname "Schiff on skates" for his never-ending scramble to enforce deadlines), veteran art director Murray Boltinoff, and copy editor George Kashdan, with frequent assistance by Weisinger. When Weisinger and Whitney Ellsworth left New York to work on the "Superman" TV program, still more responsibilities fell onto Schiff's shoulders; perhaps for that reason, and perhaps because of the general malaise afflicting comics at the time, the mid-1950s saw a dip in the quality and pizzazz of his stable's work. The stories—scripted mainly by Dave Wood, Jack Miller, France E. Herron, and DC veteran Bill Finger—grew less inspired. The art began to look rushed, and even artists who had made great names for themselves in years past—Mort Meskin, Alex Toth, Howard Sherman—were mere shadows of their former selves. A certain sameness set in that took away even from the more attractive art of Ruben Moreira, Lee Elias, and Nick Cardy. (Much of the problem was a shortage of inkers: Charlie Paris, the stable's best, was unable to handle a sizable portion of the work load; the smooth Stan Kaye was busy with a great deal of work for Weisinger; while the mainstay, George Roussos, was kept too busy to produce good work.)

After 1957, the solution for all such difficulties imposed by DC management was the same: turn everything into science fiction. But in the case of the Schiff titles, the loosest possible definition of "science fiction" was imposed, as his stories were forced to toss up a ceaseless parade of dinosaurs, monsters, and aliens both bizarre and comical. Schiff claims he hotly opposed this "monster craze," but to no avail. Because his comics were inherently more down-to-earth than most of Schwartz and Weisinger's (and perhaps also because he resented the new craze), Schiff was unable to integrate the new elements into his stories as effectively as his fellow editors. In the four mystery titles, rather than juxtaposing the fantastic with the commonplace in the Fox-Broome manner, he and his writers tended to stick to the completely fantastic, with stories hurtling from one explosive event to another—from battle to chase scene to battle again—without the complexity he had always prized. The mindlessness of the featured monsters also precluded the characterization and interesting motivation Schiff valued; thus the pages were soaked in such dialogue as, "The Shrawthca is senselessly destroying everything in its path!" (TU 54, Oct. 1960). Such stories could often thrill the little kids of the late fifties—for Schiff's artists produced the most toothsome and colorful monsters ever in comics—but with time they became sadly repetitive.

These elements were much more successful when incorporated into a series from its inception than when slapped on reluctantly afterward. *Space Ranger,* born of the same editorial conference that created Adam Strange in 1957, epitomized the colorful, exotic, childlike slant of Schiff's science fiction as charmingly as Adam epitomized Schwartz's more complex approach. With the ingenious, fantastic imagination of new writer

Arnold Drake setting the tone, the series told of the adventures of future policeman Rick Starr as he patrolled our Solar System, a constellation of planets, moons, and asteroids populated by colorful alien creatures. Operating out of his asteroid headquarters, Space Ranger was aided by his girlfriend Myra and a pink, scrappy little alien shape-changer named Cryll. Neatly and attractively drawn by Bob Brown, these light, pleasant stories ran in *Tales of the Unexpected* from 1959 to 1964 (TU 40–82), after his trial in *Showcase* issues 15 and 16 (Aug.–Oct. 1958).

Less colorful, and less successful, was *Tommy Tomorrow*, created by Schiff and Weisinger in 1947 (for their educational *Real Fact Comics*) as a forum for real scientific speculation, but transformed during the 1950s into a minor backup strip about an interstellar police force called the Planeteers. The stories (mostly by Jack Miller) avoided bug-eyed monsters in favor of little mysteries, but uninspired scripting and muddy Jim Mooney art kept Tommy trudging along in the back of *Action* and *World's Finest;* some tryouts in *Showcase* (41, 42, 44, 46, 47; 1962 and 1963) with Lee Elias art were fun, but came to naught.

The greatest problem of the stable in those years, however, was not at all with the science fiction comics themselves, but with the effect the craze had on other titles. For under an indiscriminate DC editorial policy, Batman was made to suffer through the strangest days of his career.

When created by Bill Finger and Bob Kane in 1939, Batman was a dark-night avenger of crime in the pulp-magazine tradition of the Shadow and the Spider. Soon he picked up the comics' original kid sidekick, Robin the Boy Wonder, along with a utility belt full of remarkable gadgets, and a subterranean Batcave housing scientific criminological devices and such sleek vehicles as the Batmobile and the Batplane; yet through it all Schiff and his associates kept him to the eerie shadows of the city, hunting down murderers and thieves. During the early 1950s, Batman and Robin spent more and more time traveling the world and donning exotic disguises, yet still their adventures remained squarely in the realm of what was plausible for a costumed master-sleuth without special powers. But beginning in 1957 (and accelerating after Ellsworth's retirement the next year, when Schiff lost an ally of great integrity and consistency), science fiction came to Gotham City, and during the next few years the Dynamic Duo went haywire.

No longer would Batman match wits with such colorful psychotics of urban gangland as the Joker, the Catwoman, and the Penguin. First it was a thug armed with an "energy radiator" from the planet Skar (Det. 250, Dec. 1957), then the winged bat-people from another dimension (Bat. 116, June 1958), next Garr of Planetoid X (Bat. 117, Aug. 1958). Within three years Batman found himself embroiled with so many aliens and weird creatures that on one cover he was driven to remark, "Great Scott! Another bizarre creature with a fantastic weapon!" (Det. 287, Jan. 1961). Some new villains were created for him, but they were nearly all in the

Batman undergoes a bizarre transformation (*left*), with pencils by Bob Kane. A member of the cartoonish Bat-Family: Batgirl joins Robin and Commissioner Gordon (*right*). From *Detective Comics* 322, December 1963.

pattern of the Fox, the Shark, and the Vulture, a trio of renegade inventors who used wild devices and animallike getups in place of the personal lunacies that had made the old villains so intriguing (Det. 253, Mar. 1958).

Suddenly Batman and Robin were wrenched from their world of dark alleys and rooftops and hurled to other dimensions and distant solar systems. As the distortions of his mythos accelerated, Batman found that he himself was subject to weird transformations. Beginning with "The Merman Batman" (Bat. 118, Sept. 1958), in rapid order he became an invisible man, a Zebra Batman, a robot, a Negative Batman, an alien, a baby, a "colossus," a mummy, and the "bizarre Batman Genie."

To add to the confusion, Schiff began populating the comics with a burgeoning "Batman family," evidently in emulation of the growing supporting cast of Superman. The first, from 1955, was Ace the Bat-Hound, inspired by Superboy's dog, Krypto. He was a generic-looking dog who battled criminals wearing a black mask over his eyes, presumably to prevent thugs from recognizing him and striking at him through his loved ones. A year later followed Batwoman, a more original creation, as Supergirl's debut still lay three years ahead. Bat-Girl arose in 1961, with the primary role of kissing Robin on the cheek and making him blush, and briefly in 1958 there was even a Bat-Ape, testament to DC's all-pervasive love of simians (on any given month we were bound to find either Flash's enemy Grodd, Superman's foe Titano, Superboy's pet Super-Monkey, the backup feature *Congorilla*, or one of the dozens of gorillas who swung through the science fiction comics). The most extravagant new cast member was Bat-Mite, an interdimensional imp modeled on Superman's pesky Mr. Mxyzptlk, who, beginning in 1959, took to dressing like a sloppy midget Batman and kicking off wacky adventures under the guise of trying to help his crime-fighting idol. Instead of keeping company only with the night, Batman and Robin thus found themselves besieged by a Bat-family whose gay demeanor and colorful attire destroyed the atmosphere of the shadows.

In 1962 and 1963 Schiff brought back the Penguin, Mirror Man, and some of his other old villains; he also pointed to the booming sales of his *Eighty-Page Giant Batman Annuals*, composed of reprints from the 1950s, as proof that kids didn't demand an exclusive diet of monsters, despite what the B-movies suggested. "I believe that there is such a thing as developing tastes in children," he says, "instead of just succumbing to them." Eventually his superiors would see his side, and another editor would be allowed to do what he was not permitted to do (to great effect, for Schiff's idea of reviving the old villains would lead to Batman becoming a popular mania in the mid-1960s); but for now they kept serving up stories of creatures and weird transformations until the children themselves began turning their backs.

While the stories grew more harebrained, the art became steadily more crude and childlike, reduced to page after page of simple figures pressed into small, repetitive panels. The great bulk of the stories were drawn by Bob Kane, Batman's principal creator and original artist (he was sometimes aided by "ghosts," such as Phil Kelsey, although many fan/historians—perhaps perplexed by the fact that all the Batman stories were signed "Bob Kane," regardless of the actual artist—have greatly exaggerated their role). Kane's figures had always been stiff and his faces rather crude, but over twenty years of drawing the same series he had gradually reduced his characters to mere ciphers of human beings. Nonetheless, his work often showed a rough, juvenile vitality, and his aliens could be genuinely amusing. Now and then, when Schiff, the writers, and Kane put no fetters on their flights of imagination, they created tales so inventive and exotic that even their rough execution was made charming.

These virtues shone brightest in the title Schiff called his "pet baby," *World's Finest Comics*, which held three advantages over *Batman* and *Detective*. First, it was there that Schiff thought of teaming Batman regu-

The Hero of Heroes comes to the aid of his pals Batman and Robin in ancient Egypt, through the charm and excitement of Dick Sprang. From *World's Finest Comics* 107, February 1960.

larly with Superman, whose fantastic nature made their outlandish adventures believable. Second, it enjoyed several scripts by a master of space adventure, Edmond Hamilton. Third, and most importantly, it was drawn from 1955 to 1961 by Dick Sprang. Although working in the same small-figured, childlike style as Bob Kane, Sprang brought into his panels a unique wit and dynamism capable of breathing life into the most farfetched story. To this he added a caricaturist's ability to give all his miniature figures a sense of character and personal charm, while his backgrounds exceeded all others' in detail.

In one intricate, colorful gem of a tale, a beast of living fire terrorizes the picturesque Mediterranean. The quest of Batman, Robin, and Superman to find the key to defeating it leads from a distant planet of odd geometric forms, through the bustling streets of ancient Greece, to exquisite miniature landscapes in the Egypt of the Pharaohs (WF 107, Feb. 1960). Another story finds a charming little alien movie producer unleashing three of the most peculiar creatures ever conceived by a comic book artist—one looks like a giant smirking golf tee, issuing from its head a floating roadway along which scurry an army of tiny robots—and filming our heroes' battle with them for his next extravaganza (WF 108, Mar. 1960). Sadly, when Sprang left DC in 1961, his successor, Jim Mooney, was unable to sustain the same charm, and the title grew gradually stale.

While Batman struggled along, three other old costumed crime-fighters in the Schiff stable were afflicted with problems not quite so outrageous but also, unfortunately, not as interesting. Green Arrow and Aquaman were the first comic creations of Mort Weisinger; the Martian Manhunter was a product of 1950s science fiction; but all three, until 1962, were only backup series in other hero comics.

33

Green Arrow began in 1941 as a modern-day Robin Hood, foiling thugs with his masterful archery, but quickly became a Batman imitation. In his secret identity as Oliver Queen, he was, like Bruce "Batman" Wayne, a wealthy socialite, and was joined in his adventures by his ward, Roy Harper, who was secretly his boy sidekick, Speedy. There was an Arrow-Cave, an Arrow-Plane, and an Arrow-Car, and Green Arrow sported a quiver of trick arrows with as many surprises as Batman's utility belt. Although an occasional Lee Elias or Jack Kirby guest shot perked the art up a little, the strip was usually blandly drawn by George Papp, a stiff, undistinguished penciler. It ran for years in *Adventure* and *World's Finest*, but, not surprisingly, never graduated to its own title.

Aquaman, also from 1941, was a "Sea King" who communicated telepathically with fish, a variant of the old Timely Comics' popular Sub-Mariner; it was a limited premise but was handled with a little more imagination than Green Arrow. Aquaman, also assisted by a boy sidekick, in this case Aqualad, solved many short mysteries involving smugglers, modern-day pirates, and occasional mad scientists. His adventures were drawn by Ramona Fradon, a competent penciler whose attractive, distinctive inking lifted the look of the series above the usual run of backup features. Aquaman was apparently more popular than Green Arrow, because in 1962 (after runs in *Adventure* and *Detective*) he began in his own title, where the stories grew longer but were now plagued by more monsters.

The youngest and best of the three was the Martian Manhunter, developed by Schiff and writer Joe Samachson for *Detective Comics* in 1955. Accidentally brought to Earth by a scientist, J'onn J'onzz was a big, green, beetle-browed humanoid with the ability to shift shape. In his early adventures he fought crime by adopting different appearances, but soon he was limited to one secret identity, that of police detective John Jones, and to battling thugs with an array of Superman-like powers: Martian Strength, Martian Breath, Martian Vision, and others in the same vein, plus the ability to elongate his body.

J'onn J'onzz, unlike other heroes of his time, had no boy sidekick, but after seven years he was joined by a semi-intelligent interdimensional pet named Zook (Det. 311, Jan. 1963). With his cartoonish face, super-pliable orange body, "highly sensitive antennae," and baby-talk, Zook brought a lighter and more fanciful element into the Manhunter's adventures. This element became dominant when the pair traded their backup spot in *Detective Comics* for a short-lived starring role in *House of Mystery* (HOM 143, June 1964 and after). The secret identity of John Jones was abandoned as the two spent their time battling the creations of the magical Idol Head of Diabolu, including such odd, dreamlike images as an orchestra of living musical instruments and a hole cut out of the sky as if out of a wooden dome, leading to a world above the stars. The regular creative team on the strip were writer Jack Miller and artist Joe Certa. Although not exhibiting any great artistic flair, they imbued J'onn J'onzz with a colorful charm that made the stories a delight to peruse.

In addition to his mystery-turned-science fiction titles and pre–Silver Age heroes, Schiff edited two comics not created by regular DC staffers. The first of the two was *Blackhawk*, about a team of World War II aviators, which DC bought from the Quality Comics Company in 1956. Superficially, the Blackhawks retained some of their Golden Age look, primarily through artists Chuck Cuidera and Dick Dillin, who had drawn them since the 1940s and came to DC with the title's sale. But at heart they were completely changed. Named after their intrepid leader, Blackhawk, they were originally formed as a band of aerial gladiators, a potpourri of allied nations—including a Frenchman, a Swede, a Dutchman, a Texan, a Chinese, and a Pole—who spearheaded the battle against the Nazi menace with no more than small planes, automatic pistols, and valor. At the end of the war, the team lost its basic purpose and languished for a decade, mopping up diehard Nazis and tangling with communists.

When DC took charge, their basic purpose faded completely from sight as the Blackhawks found themselves beleaguered by the usual store of monsters and aliens. Where the once-proud defenders of freedom had let sound their battle cry, "Hawk-a-a-a!" now they could only paraphrase their fellow unfortunate, Batman: "Great Scott! The eight-limbed Octi-Ape has escaped from the spaceship and has grabbed Chop-Chop!" (BH 152, Sept. 1960). Meanwhile, Dillin and Cuidera's art slipped far below the standard it had maintained into the 1950s, as they were forced to spend their talents on a menagerie of cartoonish beasts.

Unique among the DC comics of the time was the second title, *Challengers of the Unknown,* as it was created, drawn, and often written by a single man, free-lancer Jack Kirby. It fit the basic mold of monster-filled science fiction demanded then, but Kirby's pugnacious drawings, rapid storytelling, and grand imagination raised it a notch above the usual and made it thoroughly his own.

Jack Kirby stands as one of the great independent spirits of comic book history. Since the beginning of the Golden Age he had been perhaps the most seminal and productive action-artist in the field. He and his partner Joe Simon had created Captain America for Timely Comics in 1941, started a number of wartime features for DC, and then formed their own firm for the production of comics to be sold to a variety of publishers. They created the first romance comics and pioneered the genre of "boy gang" adventures. Kirby, himself a product of the tough streets of New York's Lower East Side, built a reputation as the premier artist of two-fisted action, heroic musculature, and fisticuffs that fairly flew off the page. He was also an artist who rebelled against working on someone else's assignments, and so he and Simon rarely stayed long with any publisher. In the mid-1950s they dissolved their partnership to go out and peddle their own creations separately.

35

Away from Simon, Kirby's imagination took a turn for the science-fictional and grandiose, a turn that brought him favorable reactions from the powers at DC. From the days of his boy-gang titles he carried a love of the manly camaraderie, team spirit, and rough-and-tumble action of street fights and school football. From his varied fascinations grew the Challengers, a team of four rugged adventurers who devote their lives over to battling dangers from "Out there— Places we cannot see! Things we fear to touch! Sounds that do not belong to this world! Riddles of the ages lurking beyond the bridge without a name!"

Wrestler Rocky Davis, skin diver Prof Haley, circus daredevil Red Ryan, and crewcut jet pilot Ace Morgan are flying through a storm when the controls jam and their plane plummets to the earth. By some miracle, all four crawl away from the crash alive. "We should be dead," says Red, "but we're not!" "We're living on borrowed time," says Ace, and the four of them throw in together to tackle exploits riskier than any they have dared before (Show. 6, Feb. 1957).

From Kirby's imagination poured such offbeat dangers as a sorcerous descendant of Merlin the Magician and an outer-space child who wants to keep the Challengers as pets. Even when relying on the device of an alien invasion of Earth, he gave us not the usual monster but a vast army of trained technological conquerors with a complex plan of attack (Show. 11, Dec. 1957). His art, very tight and forceful in action sequences, highly inventive with alien landscapes and machinery, gave punch to his suspenseful plots. Much of the art was further aided by inker Wally Wood who, as both a penciler and an inker for the deceased EC comics line, had been a highly influential science fiction artist in the early 1950s. Kirby's faults—a lack of character in his scripting and a rough-hewn quality to much of his drawing—were overshadowed by his vitality. He also took a liberty nearly unknown in those days of two-, three-, and four-story comic books, in allowing some of his stories to fill the full twenty-four pages of the magazine. It was a liberty he would carry over to his next publisher, to great effect.

True to form, Kirby soon seemed to grow dissatisfied with producing the Challengers for DC. After issue 8 of their own title (May 1959) he departed for other pastures. Schiff and his writers, with Bob Brown as penciler, maintained the series at a fun level, but Kirby's verve and vision could not be replaced.

That the Challengers were a commercial success is evidenced both by the fact that they went from *Showcase* to their own title in early 1958 and by the appearance of two similar adventure-team comics in 1959 and 1960. Rip Hunter, Time Master, blessed with superb art by the likes of Joe Kubert, Mike Sekowsky, and Nick Cardy in his early appearances, was the leader of a gang of time-travelers who had fast-paced and historically accurate adventures in different eras; Schiff reports that he and writer Jack Miller had "lots of fun" on the series, and it shows in the brisk storytelling.

Rip graduated his tryouts (Show. 20-21 and 25-26, June-Aug. 1959 and Apr.-June 1960) to his own title (Apr. 1961), but it lost much of its early beauty when Bill Ely became the regular artist. Less successful was *Cave Carson: Adventures Beneath the Earth*, about a squad of star-crossed speleologists, which, although also boasting some Kubert artwork, never got beyond *The Brave and the Bold* (beginning BB 31, Sept. 1960) and *Showcase*.

Clearly, by the beginning of the 1960s, the editorial styles of Weisinger, Schwartz, and Schiff had gone in such different directions that DC functioned essentially as three companies instead of one. Not only did each editor have his own titles and approach, but a stable of writers and artists who worked almost exclusively for him. Of the three, Schiff was the only one whose main character, Batman, had suffered from the changing times. No doubt, here was a case of a craze gone too far, for the science fiction that had worked for Flash and Superman had brought about Batman's downfall, and the stable that had possibly been DC's best was beaten silly by a thoughtless company policy.

The elements forced on Schiff in those years clearly did not suit the conventional hero. But new trends were coming, accompanied by redistributed editorial chores that would allow Schiff and his associates to develop new creations well suited to their talents and make a unique contribution to the progress of comic books.

5 The Return of the Heroes

When the Flash won his own magazine in 1959, Julius Schwartz began to get his first inkling that the world might be ready for costumed heroes again. But was this really the reopening of a field that most comic book professionals had dismissed as gone forever, or was the Scarlet Speedster's success only a fluke? Five times in the next two years, Schwartz would try to answer that question, each time with a modernization of a comic from the Golden Age.

First it was Green Lantern, in a version departing much further from his inspiration than had Flash. He shared with the Golden Age Green Lantern the concept of a normal man armed with a ring capable of performing miracles; in both the old and new versions, the ring was driven by the wearer's own willpower and energized by a sort of green railroad lantern. But the old Green Lantern was a semimystical character with an ancient magic lantern. The GL of 1959 drew his powers from a lantern-shaped "power battery" entrusted to him by a dying crime-fighter from another world (Show. 22, Oct. 1959).

This cosmic Green Lantern, with his nearly omnipotent "power ring," would become Schwartz's mighty hero, his answer to Superman. The very nature of his power would draw him to far planets, the future, and parallel dimensions, leaving the world of Flash and his Rogues far behind.

John Broome was able to draw from a new realm of his imagination in inventing stories for Green Lantern. Forgoing his lighthearted *Flash* style, he dipped into the mysteries of science, space, and time to create menaces that would stretch and challenge the powers of his hero. In GL's second appearance in *Showcase*, for example, the repressed, destructive side of a scientist's imagination springs to independent life as a faceless man, wreaking destruction with atomic weapons, until Green Lantern can exorcise and destroy it (Show. 23, Dec. 1959).

When Green Lantern began in his own magazine in the late spring of 1960, he—and the readers along with him—knew little of his origin and purpose, or the true scope of his powers. Answering the questions surrounding his unique hero in the first nine issues of *Green Lantern* comics, Broome plotted what remains one of the most impressive multiple-issue sequences in the history of comics.

It begins in issue 1, when Green Lantern's psyche is swept, bodiless, to the distant planet Oa. There we learn that he is only one of a corps of

Green Lantern performs tricks with his power-ring, displaying Gil Kane's budding action art. Inks by Giella, script by Broome. From *Green Lantern* 22, July 1963.

The romantic side of Schwartz: A quiet moment between the hero and his sweetheart/boss.

Green Lanterns, each from a different planet, commanded by a race of telepaths called the Guardians of the Universe (GL 1, Aug. 1960). (This was an idea Broome drew directly from his earlier science fiction experience, specifically a story in the *Captain Comet* series he did for Schwartz in the early 1950s, in which Comet is sworn into the service of the cosmic "Guardians.")

In issues 2, 3, and 4 (Oct. 1960–Feb. 1961) the emerald gladiator tangles with the "weaponers" of the dimension of Qward, where crime is the social norm and those who are "unlawfully honest" are punished. In issue 6 (June 1961) GL is summoned by a fellow Green Lantern, a fin-headed, bird-beaked gentleman named Tomar-Re, to a planet of living phantoms. Issue 7 introduces another Green Lantern, the renegade Sinestro, who would become the arch-foe of the Green Lantern of Earth (Aug. 1961).

Issue 9 brings it all to a climax that could put a lump in the throat of a devoted reader: Sinestro teams up with the weaponers of Qward to invade our dimension, and only the combined power of the Guardians and the Green Lantern Corps—replete with intelligent insects, plant-beings, living crystals, and bipedal fish—can defeat them. The battle won, the entire Corps charges its rings together on the mammoth power battery of Oa, in one stunning full-page drawing (Dec. 1961).

These cosmic spectacles were brought to life by the art of another Schwartz veteran, Gil Kane. Kane had come to the Schwartz stable in the early 1950s as a neat but undistinguished penciler, but during the next several years he had begun to work out a style of his own. His early Green Lantern drawings were notable for their compelling storytelling and muscular action, though his work generally looked rushed and undeveloped.

Kane's covers, however, showed his potential. His broad, bold layouts always started from the point of view that would give each scene its most dramatic angle. His characters seemed to fly, leap, and stagger right off the covers into the reader's lap. Though not yet the artist Infantino was, Kane's steady improvement promised a bright future. When that future was realized in the mid-1960s, he would change the look of comic art fundamentally.

Just as novel as Green Lantern's cosmic dimension was the nature of his alter ego, Hal Jordan. Jordan was no mild-mannered reporter, languid playboy, or infuriatingly slow police scientist in the classic DC mold. He was a dashing, handsome test pilot whose fearlessness had earned him his career as a costumed hero.

Paramount in Hal's life were his efforts to woo his curvaceous boss, Carol Ferris of the Ferris Aircraft Company. Carol was a typical Schwartz heroine, emotional but hardheaded, wanting both an ideal man and a successful career. She reached her most intriguing point in 1962, when a group of interdimensional amazons transformed her into the costumed villainess Star Sapphire, committed to humiliating Green Lantern and then forcing him to marry her. As she put it, "I seem to be two people. The dominant part of me wants to defeat Green Lantern! The other part wants him to defeat me!" Only Broome would have slipped such an insight into the mouth of a villainess (GL 16, Oct. 1962).

Another unusual supporting character was Hal's loyal "Eskimo grease-monkey" Pieface Kalmaku, the only human to share his secret identity. Many plots were built around Hal retelling his adventures for Pieface's Green Lantern Scrapbook, and the presence of a confident without special powers added an extra dimension to the hero.

But Broome's biggest twist on Green Lantern's alter ego was giving him a second one. When a group of scientists far in the future needed a hero, they yanked Green Lantern across the centuries to help them. In transit to A.D. 5700, however, he lost all memory of his own life. The scientists of the future gave him a false memory, an invented identity as asteroid explorer Pol Manning (secretly Green Lantern of the fifty-eighth century), and a lover named Iona Vane (GL 8, Oct. 1961). Many times GL would be pulled to the future, each time to pick up the threads of his second life and continue living where he had left off, before returning to Carol and Pieface and his Hal Jordan identity in the twentieth century.

Such innovations made Green Lantern an instant hit. A straw poll of readers, published in *Green Lantern* 3, showed him to be, for the moment, DC's most popular hero, with 888 votes to Superman's 600; Flash followed with 521, Batman with 512. Schwartz had scored twice now with his new, improved heroes. It was time to revive what many considered the greatest Golden Age comic of all.

"Just imagine!" read the ads. "The mightiest heroes of our time have banded together as the Justice League of America to stamp out the forces of evil wherever and whenever they appear! America resounds to the trumpetlike blast of their names . . . Superman! Batman! Flash! Green Lantern! Wonder Woman! Aquaman! Manhunter from Mars!"

This successor to the old Justice Society of America was Schwartz's most ambitious project yet. In this team he was entrusted not only with his own two heroes but with five from the stables of other editors: Weisinger's Superman, Robert Kanigher's Wonder Woman, and Schiff's Batman, Aquaman, and Martian Manhunter, to be joined in issue 4 (May 1961) by a fourth Schiff hero, Green Arrow. Only one writer could have been assigned to such a comic: Gardner F. Fox.

From Fox's imagination in 1939 had sprung the original Flash, Hawkman, the Sandman, Dr. Fate, and Starman, the core of Sheldon Mayer's stable of heroes. Through the 1940s he poured out story after story about these colorful crime-fighters, earning him a solid place in Golden Age history. More than anything else, however, his work was distinguished by his fifty-eight-page tales of his heroes' combined adventures in the Justice Society. Fox invented the idea of a hero team, and although the JSA was often copied during the 1940s, it was never equaled.

When Schwartz picked Fox to write the new Justice League, he affirmed the continuity of hero comics. It was a thrilling moment for DC's older fans. And there were signs—letters from grateful adults scattered throughout the country—that the number of those fans was steadily

"Hip" Snapper Carr exults in the greatness of his Justice League idols: Green Arrow, Green Lantern, Wonder Woman, the Atom, Aquaman, Superman, Batman, the Martian Manhunter, and Flash. Pencils by Mike Sekowsky, inks by Bernard Sachs, script by Fox. From *The Justice League of America* 16, December 1962.

growing. With his intelligent sense of fun, Schwartz was beginning to reach an audience who would normally have put comic books behind them. Taste and discrimination had usually been strangers to the world of costumed heroes, but now some readers were beginning to apply them to that strange genre of popular entertainment. Gardner Fox made sure that the Justice League would not disappoint them.

Fox had to refine his plotting style for the modern team. Economics had shrunk comic stories from fifty-eight pages to twenty-five, for one thing, and editorial standards were higher. In the early days of comics that mere idea of odd hero battling odd villain had been enough for most kids, so that a typical story just ran from conflict to conflict on artless enthusiasm. But Schwartz would no longer accept such simplicity. He took to calling himself "B.O. Schwartz" in the 1960s—"B.O." for "Be Original." Originality was the one criterion he demanded of every story by each of his writers.

Fox fell short in the JLA's first ten adventures (beginning BB 28, March 1960), which followed a rigid formula carried over from the 1940s: a menace creates disaters in three exotic corners of the world; the JLA splits up into three teams, each of which overcomes its particular challenge; at the end the heroes rejoin to defeat the villain himself. But by the end of 1961, Fox had broken his self-imposed bonds and turned his great imagination to charting unique and devious plots that played endless variations on a single theme, that the heroes must triumph by brain, not brawn. In the typical plot, a baffling mystery confronts our heroes in the opening pages; in unraveling it they fall prey to some highly scientific or magical schemer; and by the last few pages they are caught in a seemingly inescapable plight. Then, just when all seems lost, one hero unveils a brilliant plan—and the villain is undone.

In a classic example of this device, a trio of evil sorcerers has developed a set of spells, each perfectly attuned to paralyze a particular Justice League member. There seems to be no way to escape these spells until Aquaman has an inspiration: "Suppose each of us looked like some other member? For instance, I could look like Superman—and Superman could look like me! Then the sorcerers' spells—since they're always directed against individuals—couldn't hurt us!" Green Lantern's power-ring performs the camouflage. Ingeniously, the heroes simulate each other's powers—Aquaman, masquerading as Superman, has hidden whales and octopi destroy a ship while he pretends to destroy it with Kryptonian-strength—and the deception is maintained until the sorcerers are vanquished (JLA 11, May 1962).

Fox's plots always walked a strange line between predictability on the one hand and incoherent anarchy on the other. Perhaps no comic has ever posed as many difficulties to its writer as the JLA, especially in those days, when editorial policy did not allow stories to continue from one issue to the next. Fox had to sacrifice characterization almost completely to fit his complex plots into one comic, to the point that the liveliest personality on the team was their stereotypical teen hipster mascot, Snapper Carr. Sometimes the convolutions of the plot seemed arbitrary and the extraordinarily wordy storytelling became cumbersome. But in his best moments, and they were many, Fox made the Justice League the exemplar of how well a comic book can be plotted.

It was also an irresistible title to kids. Not only did it have all our favorite heroes under one cover, but Fox gave his stories so many ingeniously ludicrous quirks that we would gasp and laugh simultaneously. In his mind, a carnival fun house could be the gateway to another world, its concave and convex mirrors actually transforming our heroes into the ridiculous shapes they reflected (JLA 7, Nov. 1961). In his mind, an ordinary automobile from our science-based universe could be an unstoppable weapon in a universe that ran on the principles of magic, just as a magic spell would be in ours (JLA 2, Jan. 1961).

This last story contains a scene that shows artist Mike Sekowsky's eye for humor: A group of interdimensional thieves are shown loading the goose that lays the golden eggs, the fairy gold that vanishes each dawn, and the sword Excalibur into the trunk of a big yellow Pontiac. Sekowsky's peculiar figures, comical touch, and ability to master difficult problems of layout served him well in the strange world of the JLA. It became a cliché among fans who defended "Big Mike" to praise his skill at cramming a horde of heroes and villains into a single panel. But it was true, and making such busy layouts dynamic was no easy task. More than that, he could take whatever plot intricacies Fox threw at him and give them graphic sense. Sekowsky may never have been pretty, especially with the stiff inking of Bernard Sachs, but he always told one hell of a story.

With the Justice League, the Schwartz revival campaign was fully launched. In the next year and a half, Gardner Fox would take on three

Hawkman and Hawkgirl, in the rich, subtle rendering of Joe Kubert. Script by Fox. From *The Brave and the Bold* 34, March 1961.

more assignments that, though none were as successful as the first three revivals, would prove beyond a doubt that a good hero could not be kept down.

A Fox creation from 1939, Hawkman was a flying hero who wore a massive hawk mask, talked with birds, and fought modern crime with weapons of the past, including maces, crossbows, and whatever else Fox's research could turn up. The Hawkman of 1961 was a further extension of the theme, a highly scientific humanoid policeman from the planet Thanagar, visiting Earth in order to study our law-enforcement methods. He masqueraded as museum curator Carter Hall, a human identity that often led him into cases involving ancient artifacts and lost civilizations. This dual role enabled him to battle crime with the weapons of the past, the detective procedures of the present, and the science of the future. His role as an earthling was made easier by a unique Fox invention, a device called the Absorbascon, which transmitted all earthly knowledge on any given subject telepathically to its user.

Hawkman's most interesting feature, however, was Hawkgirl. His wife, fellow police officer, and associate curator, she was his equal partner in the battle with crime. Fox never even seemed to consider keeping her in the background, as she fought beside her husband with wits and wings and fists; and sometimes, when Hawkman was incapacitated, the final victory was hers alone. Hawkgirl, also known as Shiera Hall, joined level-headed Iris West and willful Carol Ferris in the ranks of Schwartz's gutsy professional women. Together, she and Hawkman marked the first married costumed heroes in comics.

For many fans they also marked the true return of the Golden Age. The letter page of Hawkman's first appearance—in *The Brave and the Bold,* a former adventure comic converted into a second *Showcase* (BB 34, Mar. 1961)—featured a reminiscence of the old Hawkman by Gardner Fox and a trio of letters from old-time fans ecstatic over rumors of the Winged Wonder's return. All of them were from adults, one of whom was Roy Thomas, soon to be one of the key figures in the birth of organized comic fandom.

Although he sparked great enthusiasm among the older set, Hawkman apparently failed to enthrall the children who comprised the bulk of DC's readership. After a three-issue run in *The Brave and the Bold,* his sales were not quite adequate to justify his own comic. Schwartz, out of fondness for the character, gave him another three-issue tryout a year later (BB 42–44, July–Nov. 1962), but again sales fell short.

Perhaps the concept of a birdman wasn't exciting enough in an increasingly technological age, as the strip's second artist, Murphy Anderson, would suggest. Or perhaps his slow start came because he was both blessed and cursed by the art of Joe Kubert. Kubert was a natural choice, having drawn Hawkman in the late 1940s, but in the intervening decade he had turned his art away from costumed heroes to become DC's principal artist of war and adventure stories. He was not regularly a member of the Schwartz stable, and so did not share the dynamic simplicity of Infantino and Kane. His unique, almost impressionistic use of line and shading baffled many of Schwartz's fans; the question of whether Kubert was right for Hawkman was the first serious issue to rise in DC's letter pages. Most of the older readers answered yes, many younger ones said no, while a few made a finer distinction: Kubert was a superb artist whose style simply wasn't right for the kinds of stories Gardner Fox was telling.

Whatever Schwartz's opinions, when Hawkman and Hawkgirl came back for their third tryout, this time backing up Adam Strange in *Mystery in Space* (from MIS 87, Nov. 1963), they were drawn by the radically different Anderson, and this time the series took.

Six months after Hawkman's debut, DC's older fans were given a treat served up especially for them, when Jay Garrick, the original Flash of the 1940s, returned. When Schwartz conceived this comeback, he wasn't sure how to make that ten-years-gone hero—about whom Barry Allen had been reading in a comic book in his origin story back in 1956—a real character in his new universe. Fox conquered the problem by imagining a second earth, existing in the same space as our own but "vibrating at a

Murphy Anderson's inks enhance Gil Kane's pencils in the Atom's battle with Dr. Light. Script by Fox. From *The Atom* 8, September 1963.

different speed," with a history closely paralleling ours except for the year in which costumed heroes first appeared. There the year was 1938, and the heroes were those of the Golden Age, not 1956 as in our world. When Barry Allen accidentally "vibrated" to this Earth-2, he found his boyhood comic book hero still living—older, gray at the temples, a little short on stamina, but still living—and still running fast (F 123, SEpt. 1961).

For the older readers, this story, "Flash of Two Worlds," brought the delightful surprise that their old favorites had not been abandoned. But for the younger ones it brought perhaps an even bigger thrill. True, they might not have known that there ever was an earlier Flash, but here was a new world, a world potentially chock-full of new heroes. And by now it was growing clear that that was what they wanted.

Schwartz and Fox's last revival of that period was a departure, owing less to its Golden Age namesake than any of its predecessors. "big— biG—BIG NEWS," read the ads, "about a SMALL—Small—small super-hero . . . The ATOM." In the 1940s, the Atom had been a minor hero with no extranormal powers, just a tough scrapper of small stature who seemed to stand for Everyman in the DC pantheon. In the science-minded atmosphere of 1961, however, the name suggested a completely different type of hero, one who could actually reduce himself in size from six feet to six inches and all the way down to the subatomic level.

Research scientist Ray Palmer discovers that he can control his size and mass by bathing himself in the emanations of a white dwarf star. With his "size and weight controls" he finds he can keep his weight at its full 180 pounds even at six inches high, or reduce himself to the weight of a feather. By shrinking himself to the size of an electron he can travel as part of an electronic impulse through telephone wires to any place in the world. He knows immediately that he will use his powers to fight crime, and thanks to the fact that his girlfriend is a lawyer, he find himself contacting a wide spectrum of thieves, hoodlums, and spies from the very beginning (Show. 34, Oct. 1961).

The concept of the Atom set him immediately apart from the rest of the costumed hero crowd. Where everyone else was bigger, stronger, faster than life, the Atom was smaller, forcing both him and Gardner Fox to rely heavily on their wits. To bring down a thug, for example, the Atom might waft into the air at feather weight, increase his weight suddenly, bounce off a convenient rubber eraser, and then drive his tiny fist into the crook's jaw with his full 180 pounds behind it (Atom 4, Jan. 1963). Such scenes gave artist Gil Kane an opportunity to show off his growing facility for action, while Murphy Anderson's inking gave the strip a tidy, everyday flavor that accented the charm of the Tiny Titan.

Although never as surprising as the *Justice League,* as grandiose as *Green Lantern,* or as wildly imaginative as *The Flash,* the early issues of *The Atom* set a standard for ceaseless invention and variation on the theme of smallness that made them gems of children's entertainment. Fox came up with a rogues' gallery of his own for the series, including such gimmick-foes as Dr. Light and Chronos, the Time-Wise Guy. But his best stories often came with little mysteries, neat as clockwork and surprising as a jack-in-the-box, about offbeat court cases (for which Fox's law degree came in very handy) or "impossible" burglaries. He also gave us another tough, charming Schwartz heroine in the person of lady lawyer Jean Loring, and a twist on the usual comic book romance: in this case it is Ray Palmer who proposes marriage every issue, and Jean who puts him off for the sake of her career.

The *Showcase* issues featuring the Atom in 1961 sold well enough to earn him his own title, and the question raised by Flash had been answered. All across America, in drugstores, supermarkets, candy stores, and newsstands, kids were casting their votes with the dimes they dug up from their pockets. They voted yes on costumed heroes. Now there could be no doubt that the best of them would live again. Meanwhile, just around the corner, as yet unknown to these veterans and followers of the Golden Age, a whole new breed of hero was getting ready to emerge.

The Fantastic Four

It is ironic that the most significant revolution in comics since the inception of costumed crime-fighters began as an act of overt imitation. The legend has it that Jack Liebowitz, publisher of DC Comics, once played a round of golf with an acquaintance named Martin Goodman. Goodman was the publisher of a number of slick-paper magazines, along with a minor, floundering line of comic books. Goodman's comic line was so minor, in fact, that it no longer even had a house name or trademark. At that time, early 1961, it was known simply as the Canam Publishers Sales Corporation.

During the course of the game, Liebowitz happened to mention his latest commercial success, *The Justice League of America*. That made an impression on Goodman. He had abandoned costumed heroes years before as a dead market, giving his comics over to westerns, romances, and monster stories. Now he wondered if he was missing something. When he returned to his office, he called in his comic book editor, art director, and head writer—who, at Canam Publishers Sales Corporation, were all one person, his cousin-in-law Stan Lee—and ordered him to whip up an imitation of the Justice League.

As it turned out, however, Stan Lee had recently been joined by the powerfully creative writer/artist Jack Kirby, and, soon after, he himself made the biggest creative decision of his career; what Goodman got back was not what he expected. It was indeed a comic book about a team of costumed heroes, and it did have a cover vaguely resembling that of the JLA. But this new group, this Fantastic Four, was like no set of heroes anyone had ever seen. They had the powers of heroes, true, but they didn't act like heroes. They acted, in fact, almost like real people.

The Fantastic Four were created when scientist Reed Richards, determined to beat the Reds to the moon, took his fiancée Sue Storm, her little brother Johnny, and an argumentative pilot named Ben Grimm on an ill-fated flight in a homemade rocket; bombarded by cosmic rays, the four crash-landed and then discovered that the mysterious rays had given them amazing powers: Reed's body stretches like rubber (a power borrowed from Schwartz's Elongated Man), Sue can turn invisible, Johnny bursts into flame and begins to fly (becoming, as with Schwartz's Flash, a modern version of a 1940s hero), while Ben becomes a monstrous mus-

Emotionalism, Marvel-style: Mr. Fantastic, the Thing, and the Human Torch confront the Invisible Girl and Sub-Mariner. Pencils by Jack Kirby, inks by Dick Ayers, script by Stan Lee. From *The Fantastic Four* 6, September 1962.

cleman with rocky orange flesh. They promptly pledge themselves to the defense of mankind, following old hero tradition (FF 1, Nov. 1961). But there the tradition ends. Heroes had always worn costumes and used secret identities, but the Fantastic Four fought monsters and aliens in their street clothes, and—although taking the dramatic titles Mr. Fantastic, the Invisible Girl, the Human Torch, and the Thing—they never considered concealing their true identities. Heroes never quarreled with one another, yet the Human Torch and the Thing were always at each other's throats. Except for bland junior sidekicks, heroes were adults. But the Torch was a car-crazy teenager with a healthy distrust of his elders.

Most of all, heroes were handsome and well-loved by the world, more content with their lives than most of us can ever expect to be. Until 1961, no comic writer would have suggested that acquiring strange powers might drive a wedge between a man and his society, bringing him more misery than contentment. But Ben Grimm, who would call himself only the Thing, had paid for his powers with an unalterably monstrous appearance; his enormous strength could not console him for the loss of his humanity. Resenting the world as strongly as he felt bound to protect it, he had to struggle as fiercely against his own bitterness and self-pity as against any villain. This was a turning point in comic book characterization.

That such a comic book could have come to exist at all is remarkable, but that it came from a company like Goodman's was especially shocking at the time. For years his small staff had been following the winds of fashion, churning out formula science fiction when science fiction was selling, formula westerns when westerns were selling. Following a cutback in 1957, their most noteworthy creations were a handful of Saturday-matinee-style monster titles. Yet suddenly they attempted the most radical change in adventure comics since the beginning of the Golden Age. And the motive for the change, surprisingly, was not so much commercial as personal, on the part of writer-editor Stan Lee and plotter/artist Jack Kirby.

Lee was unique among the men who shaped the Silver Age. He had begun his career as an office boy for Goodman at seventeen years of age in 1939. Soon he began filling in as a writer, than an editor, until eventually the whole show was his. Never a pulp writer or a science fiction editor, never a client of Julius Schwartz or an associate of Mort Weisinger, he was the only prominent writer or editor in the field who had been with comic books for his entire working life. (In that sense he was the prototype of the young people who dominate the field now, so many of whom have leaped directly from fan to professional status.) And it was this unique relationship with his field that made him the one man who could change the face of the medium completely.

In the Golden Age, when Goodman's company was usually called Timely Comics, three dominant heroes made deep impressions on young Stan's sensibilities. Bill Everett's Sub-Mariner, more antihero than hero, was the half-breed offspring of the queen of an undersea race and a human ship's captain, who often assaulted the cities of surface-people to avenge the despoilation of his beloved ocean. The android Human Torch started life as a misfit in society, whose ability to turn his body to flame at first threatened to be more of a danger than a blessing to mankind. These two not-quite-heroes fought a series of elemental battles against each other in the early 1940s, with neither clearly cast as good or evil. The third Timely hero, Captain America, created by Jack Kirby with his partner Joe Simon, was a living political symbol, wartime America's picture of itself, a colorful mouthpiece for patriotic sentiments.

The elements embodied in these characters—the antihero at odds with society, the extra-powerful being who is frail at heart, heroes who fight one another, and the hero as social or political symbol—were to remain in Lee's mind through the 1960s.

During the slump of the 1950s, when first costumed heroes were swept away by poor sales and then meaty horror stories were exterminated by public outcry against unsavory comics, Lee found himself grinding out reams of brainless stories in genres about which he cared nothing. His attention began drifting to other sources of income: advertising copy, news fillers, and magazine humor. But then, at the age of thirty-nine, a conversation with his wife changed the course of his career.

"Joan wanted me to bear down and make something of myself in the comic book field," he relates. "She wondered why I didn't put as much effort and creativity into the comics as I seemed to be putting into my other free-lance endeavors. The fact is, I had always thought of my comic book work as a temporary job—even after all those years—and her little dissertation made me suddenly realize that it was time to start concentrating on what I was doing—to carve a real career for myself in the nowhere world of comic books."

Joan's timing could not have been better. Kirby had recently joined the staff, determined to create something new and startling, "with a real human dimension," to reverse the company's fortunes. A short while later, Goodman asked Lee for the costumed hero team. Lee seized his opportunity; conditions were right for a revolution. After all, with a comics line like Goodman's there was very little to lose, giving Lee a freedom to experiment that his rivals at prosperous DC would never have. And so they refused to run off a mere conceptual copy of the Justice League. "No, this was to be something different—something special," Lee says, "something to stupefy my publisher, startle my public, and satisfy my wife's desire for me to 'prove myself' in my own little sphere." With *The Fantastic Four*, Lee did something that no one else in comics would have considered: he wrote for himself. Lacking the avenues of short stories and novels open to men like Fox and Binder, he kneew that if he was ever to say something of his own to the world, it would have to be through his costumed heroes.

Goodman had reservations about the new comic, but he let Lee have his way. In the late summer of 1961, *Fantastic Four* 1 hit the stands, laying the cornerstone of a remarkable publishing success story. After more than twenty years of Lee's powerful influence in the field, it is difficult to appreciate the impact that first issue must have had on the young hero fan spinning the rack in search of something new to read. Turning from the Justice League to Superman, for example, would have been an obvious shift to a different editorial style. But turning from them to the Fantastic Four was like stepping through the gateway to another dimension. Lee and Kirby did use a few of Schwartz's ideas, much as the Golden Age revival and the stretchable hero, but the emphasis of their stories was completely reversed. In their work, plot, pace, and mystery were shunted into the background while their brawling, bickering heroes took center stage, soaking the pages in pathos, anger, and romantic melodrama. Lee's writing was often rough, self-contradictory, and overdone. Perhaps his large work load prevented him from working carefully on any one project, and perhaps he was hampered by being both writer and editor, for there was no one to catch him in his failings or smooth his work out. But for him, neat craftsmanship was of far less consequence than innovation and raw enthusiasm. It was a risky alternative to put before the kids of America. But for a couple of reasons it worked.

One reason was Jack Kirby. After leaving *Challengers of the Unknown*, he had paused briefly his old partner Joe Simon kick off Archie Comics' attempt to get in on the hero business with a couple of minor costumed characters called the Fly and Private Lancelot Strong. Next he found his way back to Lee's offices (where he had worked in the early 1940s) in 1959, where his ability to plot and draw a lot of pages in a short time promptly made him the company's principal artist. Of the many types of stories he cranked out with Lee, those with the most distinctively fantastic, grandiose Kirby stamp were tales of monsters with names like Xom, Grottu, and the Creature from Krogarr. (Many of these monsters crept into the early issues of *The Fantastic Four* when, as often happened, Lee and Kirby were unable to think up any original foes for their heroes.)

Taking advantage of Kirby's background as a writer-artist, Lee utilized a method of story creation that would set his comics still further apart from the competition. In the most common comic book method, the writer submitted a detailed script to the artist, who then illustrated it faithfully. Lee, however, only discovered the story with Kirby; who then turned into a cohesive visual story as he saw fit. As a final step, Lee wrote in the dialogue and captions. (It is impossible, in fact, to say which man contributed which elements, although it seems safe to conclude that the essence and adventures of the Fantastic Four were mainly Kirby's, while the emotional nuances were Lee's). This freed Lee from the chore of plotting stories, which had grown onerous for him over the years, and let him give nearly all his attention to the characterization and human interaction he preferred. At first this new system took its toll, for Kirby would often stick to his straight-ahead action style of plotting, forcing Lee to cram his emotional angles into brief scenes overcrowded with verbiage (in FF 3, Mar. 1962, Lee wanted the Torch to leave the team in anger, but had no room for development or foreshadowing, and so had him suddenly and unconvincingly turn angry and buzz off in the last three panels). But as the two got the swing of collaboration, they came to use the system for a free-flowing interplay of ideas that made their comics, more than any others, visual creations as much as verbal ones.

Because Kirby drew so much for Lee, his art in the early 1960s suffered from muddiness and roughness (further impaired by a weak and overworked staff of inkers, including Dick Ayers, Chic Stone, Paul Reinman, and George Roussos), and his plots were often unevenly paced and repetitive. His plot contributions were largely ideas he carried over from *Challengers*, such as the use of full-issue stories and an origin story centering on four heroes crash-landing after a daring flight. The company's cheap production quality, with excessive use of gray in coloring and poor printing techniques, further contributed to the substandard look of the new comic. But none of it seemed to matter, for the star of the series was Stan Lee, with his ambitious human drama. And in that ambition lay the second reason for the Fantastic Four's success.

The number of older comic book readers had been growing since the Flash first appeared. Many of them were teenagers, still fascinated by the sheer fantasy of costumed heroes but becoming aware of the real emotional stresses of living. And, being teenagers, they were less comforted by familiarity than children and were hungry for change. To an adolescent eye, DC's comics often seemed simplistic and clichéd. Lee's conceptions came like a flash of lightning: heroes were human too, they could suffer and still be heroes; and comic books could experiment, could even aspire to be taken seriously. The FF gripped an audience smaller than DC's, but generally older, more vocal, and more conscious of what they read. Letters began arriving, unsolicited, at Lee's little office. He promptly instituted a Fantastic Four Fan Page, bearing such messages as "You are definitely starting a new trend in comics, characters who act like real people, not just lily-white do-gooders who would insult the average reader's intelligence." (Marvel staffer Dick Ayers has reported that many of those early fan letters were in fact written by Lee himself, but some, including one from DC fan Roy Thomas, were undoubtedly real.)

The fans forced Lee and Kirby into a couple of compromises with comic book hero tradition—they had to give their quartet skintight costumes and elaborate "scientific" headquarters—but most of the experiments were welcomed, and more demanded. They obliged them in issue 4 with the return of the original Sub-Mariner (shortly after Schwartz revived the Flash of Earth 2), the first entry of an antihero into the Silver Age. The Sub-Mariner declared war on all mankind, and therefore had to be fought as a villain. But his motivation—vengeance for the devastation of his people by an underwater atomic test—could not be dismissed as simple villainy. His tragic nobility also appealed to Sue Storm, the Invisible Girl, who grew infatuated with him—beginning three years of discord with her teammates and tension with her fiancée.

Here was a whole new complex of ideas: heroes who might be in the wrong, who are ambivalent about their enemy, who disagree with their plan of action, who are even caught in a romantic triangle with a villain. The fans were ecstatic.

The Sub-Mariner returned for "The End of the Fantastic Four," a story that, even after twenty years of innovation in comics, remains remarkably offbeat. In a few bad stock speculations, Reed Richards, a.k.a., Mr. Fantastic, loses all the team's money and gets them evicted from their skyscraper headquarters. Their only recourse is to hire themselves out as actors in a science fiction movie being promoted by a mysterious movie mogul. The mogul proves to be the Sub-Mariner, maneuvering them into position to attack them, not—as the traditional villain would do—to destroy them, but only to assuage his wounded pride for his earlier defeat at their hands. He battles them all to a standstill and goes his lonely way back into the sea (FF 9, Dec. 1962).

When the Fantastic Four's quick success prompted Lee and Kirby to bring out a second costumed hero title, it is not surprising that they produced a character still less like the traditional good guy. A blend of Dr. Jekyll and the Frankenstein monster, the new character was a respectable scientist named Bruce Banner who changed periodically into the Hulk, a powerful green-skinned brute whose twisted mind was capable only of thoughts of destruction. The Hulk was a step beyond the Thing as a product of Lee and Kirby's fascination with the idea of physical superiority as a wall between the hero and humanity. His only contact with mankind was a teenager named Rick Jones, whose sympathy was barely able to penetrate the Hulk's hate-clouded brain (Hulk 1, May 1962).

But they had perhaps launched the new character too quickly, for they seemed to have little idea just what to do with it. Soon ceasing to be an eloquent but evil Dr. Jekyll sort, the Hulk became an inarticulate brute on a perpetual rampage, then fell under Rick Jones's mental domination through a freak accident (Hulk 3, Sept. 1962). Next he was bombarded by a ray that gave him the mind of Bruce Banner along with the strength of the Hulk, but then the bestial side returned as the Hulk again thought of himself as a separate entity, scorning Banner and his entire weakling species (Hulk 5, Jan. 1963). His adventures also suffered because, although the character was cast as an antihero with no concern for human society, Lee insisted upon pitting him against evil communists; thus three of the Hulk's six issues involved ill-conceived battles with implausible Cold War stereotypes of Reds. Perhaps because of this poor planning—or perhaps because even Lee's followers were not yet ready for a protagonist so far from the heroic ideal—the Hulk did not enjoy the Fantastic Four's success.

There is no denying that the early products of what was to become the Marvel Comics Group left much to be desired in the realms of imagination, plot complexity, and polish. Even a mediocre Julius Schwartz comic showed far more craftsmanship than the best Lee and Kirby work of 1961 or 1962. But the raw vitality and enthusiasm of Lee's scripting and Kirby's art were infectious, and the kids took them to their hearts for their impish war on convention.

Lee himself was not the type to sit shyly in the corner waiting for someone to notice him. The cover of the third issue of the FF screamed, "The Greatest Comic Magazine in the World!!" Every issue from then on was mantled with a similar motto, and from there the self-advertisements only grew more emphatic. From a forgotten corner of the industry, after twenty years of creative stagnation, Lee would scream and joke and innovate his way to an unequaled position of influence in less than a decade. His work was filled with hype and pretension, crudity and excess. But it was equally full of sincerity, invention, humor, and love. In his comics, character was everything, and his best characters became more solid, beloved, and believable, more independent of their creator, than any before them in their medium. When he took us on an eleven-page "Visit with the Fantastic Four," in which nothing but conversation took place, he made it as interesting as any battle with a monster or mad scientist (FF 11, Feb. 1963). Stan Lee remains possibly the most controversial figure in the history of comics.

It would be with his third creation that Lee would truly discover not only his audience but his own greatest talents. He would soon find the key to unlock the deepest fantasies of his adolescent readers, launching his comics company on its long upward climb.

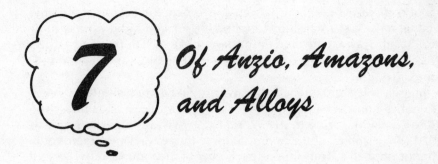

7 Of Anzio, Amazons, and Alloys

The writer-editor syndrome was not confined to the new Marvel Comics Group. At DC, in yet another small company-within-a-company, editor Robert Kanigher wrote nearly all of his own scripts, encountering the same problems that faced Stan Lee. Kanigher differed further from other DC editors in that he handled a very broad range of story types. In attempting to write and edit such diverse genres as costumed heroes, war, romance, and adventure, he seemed unable to arrive at a clear direction for his stable. Ideally, such a varied collection of titles, alone among the rigidly unified stables of DC, might have lent itself to great experimentation and liveliness. But Kanigher, perhaps because he lacked either an editor above him or writers below him off whom to bounce ideas, produced only one significant innovation in the hero realm.

Kanigher started writing for a number of comic book companies in 1940, quickly distinguishing himself for his speed and versatility; only three years later, in fact, he felt experienced enough to write a book entitled *How to Make Money Writing for Comic Magazines.* That same year, 1943, marked the beginning of his association with DC, for whom he would later estimate that he created, wrote, and edited at least twenty-three strips (he has said that he has written at least two scripts a week for forty years). He wrote for a time under Julius Schwartz, helping develop the new Flash in his *Showcase* appearances, but somehow, perhaps from lack of interest, he never developed a flair for conventional costumed-hero stories. This was never more painfully apparent than with *Wonder Woman,* which Kanigher wrote and edited consistently from 1947 to 1968.

The original conception of Wonder Woman could not have survived into the Silver Age. Created by William Marston, a psychologist with a keen interest in the female psyche, the Golden Age adventures of this battling Amazon were full of veiled sexual and fetishistic themes that drew fierce criticism during the anti-comic-book crusades of the early 1950s. In purging the strip of these subliminal contents, however, DC and Kanigher also bled it of the mythological and political themes that had made it unique. Wonder Woman now became just another invincible hero, whose gender was functionally irrelevant. Paradise Island, home of Aphrodite and her immortal women, degenerated into just another scientific hideaway. Instead of grappling with such issues as whether the way of women could bring peace to earth, Princess Diana spent dreary years fighting Angle Man, Mouse Man, and other hastily conjured bad guys, along with enough extraterrestrial creatures to make Batman's adventures seem provincial by comparison.

Among the costs of these quickly written, directionless stories was a collapse of Robert Kanigher's craft as a writer. He has described himself as a "spontaneous, instinctual writer": "I'm not a writer who sits down knowing what he is going to do in advance. That is not a writer but a *typist*. . . ." His approach often worked well with subtler human tales, but not with heroes. Plots hurtled from event to event with an illogic that even the most lax editor could not have approved had he himself not been the writer. One exemplary story opens with Wonder Woman as a teenager, called Wonder Girl, observing her future self in a "time and space screen" at her mother's behest; together they see Wonder Woman rush off to rescue her female fan club from kidnappers, then turn around and save the life of her boyfriend, who just happens to be crashing in an experimental jet at that very spot. Seeing these future triumphs, Wonder Girl is abruptly filled with a sense of inferiority, which sends her off to perform a series of random feats. In the course of these, she and a merboy who is infatuated with her blunder through a "crack in time" to the dinosaur age, where they battle a succession of mindless beasts, including one that gobbles up an island from beneath their feet, before rushing back to their own era. Just then, a messenger bursts into the chambers of our heroine's mother, Queen Hyppolyta, crying, "Satellite Lookout Station No. 3X22 reports hostile spacecraft heading directly toward our island!" So the queen flies up to fight a robot from Pluto, and at last the story rambles to the last page of the magazine. Kanigher titled this concatenation "The Island Eater," presumably because, of all the disjointed episodes in the story, that one allowed the biggest, ugliest monster for the cover (WW 121, Apr. 1961).

Although limping along with moderate sales from an audience who had no other extranormal females to buy, the more astute fans screamed their discontent, and Kanigher was courageous enough to print their letters and rebut them frankly. His most regular critic, Paul Gambaccini, once appeared in print saying, "It's too bad Mr. Kanigher cannot accept our criticism, and it's too bad we cannot accept his philosophies." In 1965 Kanigher tried to bend to his fans' demands for an older style of Wonder Woman, setting most of one year's worth of adventures in the 1940s and even instructing his artists, Ross Andru and Mike Esposito, to draw in the oddball manner of the strip's Golden Age artist (WW 156 and 159–164, Aug. 1965 and Jan.–Aug. 1966). The results were false and wooden, however, driving Kanigher back to two and a half years of increasingly campy and desperate retreads of tired themes.

Wonder Woman's artists, Andru and Esposito, were the most durable penciler-inker team in comics. They had been together before coming to DC in the early 1950s, and continued together steadily under Kanigher. Although occasionally falling prey to the same haste that afflicted his editor, Andru generally produced forceful and dramatic work, capable of telling a story with easy rapidity. Esposito inked him with a quick, scratchy line that was nevertheless good at revealing character and emotion.

Kanigher's talents were far better suited to war comics, and it was to them that he brought his most careful craftsmanship. In that field he edited *All American Men of War, G.I. Combat, Our Fighting Forces, Star Spangled War,* and *Our Army at War,* which featured the regular series *Sgt. Rock* and a superb, innovative new strip called *Enemy Ace.* These comics were distinguished mainly by their realism and deep emotion, in contrast to the wild fantasies abounding in *Wonder Woman,* and were further heightened by the superb art of Mort Drucker, Russ Heath, Ross Andru, and, primarily, Joe Kubert. Kubert, with his careful shading, rich use of blacks, and extraordinarily sharp eye for the nuances of characterization, was fast distinguishing himself as the subtlest and most sophisticated artist of the Silver Age. His strong storytelling technique gave form and substance to Kanigher's scripts, while the grittiness and pathos Kanigher saw in war were movingly captured by Kubert's evocative pencils. Kanigher, however, would reach his peak in 1968, when Kubert replaced him as editor of the war comics and Kanigher was able to devote full attention to his writing; discussion of that peak must wait until Chapter 26.

Kanigher had also been joined by Kubert in the late 1950s on *Viking Prince,* a strip featured in Kanigher's adventure title, *The Brave and the Bold.* The title contained a number of other series, including *Silent Knight* and *Robin Hood,* all rich in heroism and historical detail, but none were as well realized as *Viking Prince.* The strip is set in the tenth century and centers on an amnesiac young Viking named Jon. We learn that his father's throne has been usurped by the evil Torgunn the Claw, whose queen has tricked Jon into drinking a potion that has robbed him of his memory, rendering him unable to perform "Thor's twelve tasks" and thus claim the throne. The stories take us on Jon's quest to regain his memory through a colorful world of Vikings, dragon-ships, and bleak northern landscapes. As in his war stories, Kanigher's writing shines in these tales of action and adventure, masterfully rendered by the atmospheric art of Joe Kubert.

The Brave and the Bold next introduced *Suicide Squad,* a Kanigher adventure series set in the present, about a band of altruistic daredevils, with Ross Andru art (BB 25–27, Sept. 1959–Jan. 1960); they never graduated, however, beyond try-outs and backup strips. More fortunate were *Sea Devils* (Show. 27–29, Apr.–Aug. 1960), a squad of intrepid divers who found awesome dangers beneath the sea and gained their own title in 1961. Kanigher used the series to weave fantastic events around a framework of careful technical accuracy, but in the process gave it a disturbingly schizoid air, neither effectively realistic nor fanciful; it did, at least, display some fine art by Andru, Russ Heath, and others.

Ross Andru and Mike Esposito bring a light touch to the Metal Men. Script by Robert Kanigher. From *Showcase* 37, April 1962.

With respect to furthering comic history, Kanigher's one real contribution rested with the Metal Men. They began in the only way any truly offbeat series could have begun at DC in those years, for the concept was too strange to have passed an editorial conference: they were slapped together as a filler that everyone knew could have no future. The story goes that Irwin Donenfeld, a member of DC's publishing board, stopped by Kanigher's office one Friday afternoon in late 1961 with a problem: some scheduling mixup had left the next issue of *Showcase* without a feature, and less than two weeks remained before the deadline. Kanigher's reputation as the company's speed-demon won him the job of doing something about it, and he came through with a completely original feature, spun off the top of his head, by Monday morning. He handed the new script to Ross Andru, who raced through the twenty-four pages by the end of the week (despite the fact that, even under such pressure, Kanigher continued to scrutinize the art carefully and demand numerous revisions); by the time Mike Esposito finished the inking, only ten days had elasped since Donenfeld's request. The biggest surprise of the Metal Men, however, was not that Kanigher and his men had gotten the job done on time, but that the series caught on. DC kept them in *Showcase* for four issues, then in early 1963 awarded them their own title.

It was indeed a strange concept. The heroes were a sextet of robots, each composed of a single metal that determined its powers and name. Gold could be stretched and flattened to remarkable thinness. Iron was the muscleman. The slow-moving Lead could shield against radiation. When a liquid hero was needed, Mercury could melt. Platinum, a female robot nicknamed Tina, could spin herself into a fine, indestructible wire. The least useful member of the six was Tin, but his personality would soon make him a favorite of the fans. The leader of the group was Will Magnus, a brilliant scientist who created the Metal Men and developed a fatherly bond with them (Show. 37, Apr. 1962).

Robots and scientists, of course, were stock equipment in the Saturday-matinee style of science fiction that still held sway at DC, but this shape-shifting band of animated metals, drawn as extravagant caricatures of their various attributes by Andru, startled DC into a whole new perspective on heroes. For one thing, at the end of their first appearance—since Kanigher expected it to be a one-shot—all six of them died, only to be rebuilt in the next issue. Over the years they would be melted, smashed, repaired, and transmuted repeatedly. The only steady element, and the source of their charm, proved to be their personalities. Gold was noble and aloof; Iron strong and silent; Lead slow and complaisant; Mercury excitable, abrasive, and smart-mouthed. Tin, stuttering and self-effacing, won the group over with the purity of his heart, promising, "I'll do my best to be worthy of you all—if you give me a chance." Tina proved to be a very female robot, thanks to what Doc Magnus called a faulty "responsometer." She fell promptly in love with the Doc, making lighthearted soap opera a regular part of the strip.

This all fit in with Kanigher's basic credo, very unusual for DC in those years: "True plot is determined by characterization. . . . A character who acts and reacts makes a story." With the *Metal Men* this proved to be an especially effective belief, and as a consequence the series sported a number of highly unconventional but entertaining story lines. Among Kanigher's innovations were the multi-issue story and the running subplot, paralleling Stan Lee's experiments with the same devices.

Although the oddity of the Metal Men kept them from being a great commercial success, their emphasis on innovation, humor, and personality attracted a loyal body of the new breed of fan. Kanigher aimed the series very pointedly at those fans, eventually even going so far as to have his robots reading actual fan mail in the course of a story. It seems fans had been complaining that the Metal Men only fought such robotic and elemental foes as the Missile Men, Chemo, and the Gas Gang, and wanted to see more human opponents. To please them, the good robots rush off to capture villains of flesh and blood, only to find Flash, Batman, and Wonder Woman beating them to the punch every time. Tin, fearing the wrath of one of their most critical young correspondents, wonders, "What are we going to tell Irene Vartanoff?" Says Mercury, "My globules freeze up at the thought of it!" In the end they, and presumably Irene Vartanoff, must be content with a battle against Ethylene, Styrene, Silicone, and the other Plastic Perils (MM 21, Sept. 1966).

On three fronts, the spontaneous creation of the Metal Men helped spur DC to a new approach to comics. They eased the transition of emphasis from science fiction to characterization. They opened the gates to real innovation in quirky and experimental heroes. And they helped the company learn how to respond not only to the faceless buyers who added up to sales figures, but to the growing number of fans who every month sent in their personal views. Although Kanigher's strengths did not lie with costumed heroes, with the Metal Men he nevertheless made his mark on the development of the genre.

8 Spider-Man, the Hero Who Could Be You

If Stan Lee had astounded comic book fans with *The Fantastic Four*, it was his next creation, less than a year later, that electrified the growing body of critically astute readers. His new title was not only bolder but displayed a far greater craftsmanship than he had ever hinted at possessing before. With this superior workmanship, Lee was able to forge into effective drama the emotional themes that fascinated him, once and for all hooking the affection of the older kids who had been flirting with his comics.

The greatest part of Lee's improvement was his union with the exciting talent of Steve Ditko, an artistic collaborator far better suited to his interests than Jack Kirby. Ditko had emerged as a horror artist with a flamboyant, fantastical style at Charlton Comics during the 1950s. He had dabbled in science fiction, helping to launch Captain Atom, Charlton's closest equivalent to a costumed hero, in 1959. Once he joined Stan Lee's "bullpen" later that same year, science fiction became his stock-in-trade. Ditko's work combined a pervasive eeriness, a disconcerting sense of unreality in both figures and compositions, and a highly stylized brand of characterization that squeezed the perversities and weaknesses of his characters into every line. A disturbing undercurrent of madness seemed to flow through all his stories. His reputation as a loner—camera-shy and uncommunicative, creating these odd visions in the solitude of his studio—aded to the air of mystery about him. He still remains, though his reputation as an artist is universally high, one of the least known people in the field.

Soon after Ditko joined Lee's staff, Lee used the artist's peculiar talents to create a body of science fiction stories far more weighty and unsettling than the monster tales he cranked out with Kirby. The stories didn't catch on, however, and the title in which they were featured, *Amazing Adult Fantasy* (subtitled by Lee "The Magazine That Respects Your Intelligence," a clear bid for the atypical comic reader), quickly dropped off in sales. But Lee would make the most of his failure. When he learned that the last issue of that title would come with # 15, an idea began to play about in his mind. He saw an opportunity to create something even more daring than the Fantastic Four, a hero who would break every rule that they had left standing, since he now truly had nothing to lose. With Jack

62

Steve Ditko's blend of humanity, oddity, and adventure: Peter Parker in dejection, in turmoil, and in action. Script by Lee. From *The Amazing Spider-Man* 11, April 1964.

Kirby he began blocking out a set of powers and attributes—superficially, the hero would be based on the Spider of the old pulps, with a dose of Batman thrown in—and then set Kirby to work on the story. But the very first sketches showed one thing clearly: any hero Kirby drew would be manly, noble, bigger than life. Lee wanted to break away even from that tradition. So he gave the story to Ditko, and the Amazing Spider-Man was born.

The first page suggested that "we think you may find our Spider-Man just a bit . . . different!" The differences begin to show themselves quickly, as we meet high school student Peter Parker—skinny, bespectacled, and brilliant in science—who is doted on by the elderly aunt and uncle who raised him but ridiculed by the callow kids at school. "Someday I'll show them!" he sobs. "Someday they'll be sorry! Sorry that they laughed at me!" During a science experiment, Parker is bitten by a radioactive spider and, miraculously granted "the proportionate speed and strength" of that creature, he gets his chance. In any other comic book story, Parker would have immediately dedicated his life to fighting injustice, donned a costume, and turned his real life into a "secret identity." But not this bitter little egghead. He does make a strange costume, and invents a device to shoot sticky webs from his hands, but only to make himself a show-business sensation. He does conceal his identity, but only because he worries, "What if I fail? I don't want to be a laughingstock!"

Parker does not fail, however, and gets invited to show off his powers on "The Ed Sullivan Show." After his performance, while he gloats in the hall, he sees a thief run by, pursued by a guard. The guard hollers at Spider-Man to stop him, only to be answered, "Sorry, pal! That's your job! I'm through being pushed around—by anyone! From now on I just look out for Number One—that means . . . me!" But pride does come before a fall. Only days later, Peter's beloved Uncle Ben is murdered by a burglar. Insane with grief, Parker hunts down the killer, only to find that it is the very same thief he allowed to escape at the Sullivan show. And so, Lee tells us, Parker is devastated by guilt, "aware at last that in this world, with great power there must also come—great responsibility!" (Am. Fan. 15, Aug. 1962).

A solo hero—not a kid sidekick of a team-member—who was really a teenager . . . a meek alter ego that was the character's reality, not a coyly fabricated disguise . . . a costumed hero whose first thoughts were of money and glory, not of battling evil wherever it raised its head. It was a daring concept, but it was also tailor-made for the dreams and emotions of Lee's adolescent readers, who were eager for more innovation and who also, perhaps, saw a bit of themselves in the persecuted bookworm Peter Parker. Though conceived as a lark—like the Metal Men earlier that same year—letters and sales figures made it clear that the fans wanted more of this hero. Seven months later, Lee and Ditko launched him in his own title.

Two elements made Peter Parker utterly unique in comics. The first was that a need for growth had been programmed into his personality; unlike the stock personality traits to which all heroes, including the Fantastic Four, had been limited, Parker's character would have to grow to continue coping with the problems posed by his private life. Second, he came to heroics grudgingly. Rather than swearing an oath against evildoers everywhere upon receipt of his powers or the death of his uncle, Parker fell into the role as a logical outgrowth of his personal life; here was a believably ambivalent hero.

In the very first eight issues of his own title, Parker's new abilities put him through a tumultuous series of changes. In issue 1 we find him returning to his Spider-Man role reluctantly, again to make money performing, when his widowed Aunt May begins to run out of funds. Unfortunately, a crusading newspaper editor named J. Jonah Jameson has decided that Spider-Man is a potential menace to society and a bad influence on children, and soon his vicious editorials have destroyed Parker's hopes for a career. He tries to join the Fantastic Four, but backs out when he discovers that being a costumed hero isn't a paying job. A villain called the Chameleon tries to take advantage of Spider-Man's bad press by framing him for his own robberies, thus forcing him against his will into his first hero-style battle. Meanwhile, the money problems grow increasingly desperate. He laments, "Nothing turns out right . . . (sob) . . . I wish I had never gotten my super-powers!" (SM 1, Mar. 1963).

Parker's first good break comes when he hears that Jameson, his nemesis, is eager for pictures of a new villain, the Vulture. Spider-Man tracks the villain down—not at all planning to bring him to justice, but only to take pictures and sell them—causing the nervous Vulture to attack him first. Spider-Man beats this opponent while his automatic camera clicks, then, with secret smugness, sells the thrilling fight-pictures as Peter Parker to Jameson. For the first time he begins to enjoy his double life (SM 2, May 1963).

He also begins to crave action, however, and his new power goes to his head. "It's almost too easy!" he says, after rounding up a gang of thugs. "I almost wish for an opponent who'd give me a run for my money!" He gets one in Dr. Octopus (SM 3, July 1963), then another in the Sandman, and defeats them both, but in his cockiness he goes overboard, even beating up people on the street simply because they look suspicious. Soon his world comes crashing down in self-doubt: "Am I really some sort of crack-pot, wasting my time seeking fame and glory? Am I more interested in the adventure of being Spider-Man than I am in helping people?" (SM 4, Sept. 1963).

Next he is genuinely tempted by an offer to team up with the Fantastic Four's archvillain, Dr. Doom, but finds it in himself to refuse (SM 5, Oct. 1963). In the following issue, when he risks his life to come to the aid of a scientist who has unwittingly turned himself into the evil Lizard, Parker finally becomes a true hero: his narrow concerns broaden and his powers, formerly used only in his own interest, are finally used to help others (SM 6, Nov. 1963). The cost of this altruism is shown vividly when he sprains his arm in a return match with the Vulture, giving us the rare but moving sight of a hero struggling to overcome physical injury (SM 7, Dec. 1963). At last, making money as a photographer and at peace with his own motives, Parker even develops a little confidence in his private life, discarding his oversized glasses and making a successful play for Jonah Jameson's pretty secretary, Betty Brant (SM 8, Jan. 1964).

Peter Parker's growth from tormented egghead to confident, wise-cracking hero was a far cry from the jerky changes in editorial direction that afflicted the FF and Hulk in their early years. Lee had obviously found a perfect collaborator in Ditko. Whereas Kirby filled virtually every panel with action, forcing Lee to stick his emotional content in edgewise, Ditko not only wove emotional scenes into the stories but also infused the lay-out and rendering of every drawing with the dominant mood of each epi-sode. And Ditko's emotional portrayals were so effective—in levity, pathos, and rage—that Lee was no longer driven to overwrite in order to get his point across. Peter Parker could act out his anguish, unlike Ben Grimm and Bruce Banner, whose problems were allotted only enough space for occasional self-pitying soliloquies. Underlining all of this, Ditko melded a variety of symbolic images with his realism: when the specter of Spider-Man haunted Parker's life, he might be shown with a web-draped shadow, or overshadowed by a phantom Spider-Man, or with his face half-covered by his spider mask.

Ditko's most distinctive quality, however, was the unheroic "Everyman" mien of his characters, which Lee complemented in his scripting with a down-to-earth, confiding tone. We didn't *read* about Spider-Man; we gossiped about him with our good friends Stan and Steve. And it wasn't a bigger-than-life titan we gossiped about, but someone very much like us—perhaps, as Lee wrote, "the hero who could be you" (SM 9, Feb. 1964). It was this intimacy, more than anything, that opened the field of costumed heroes to an adolescent readership.

Further rounding out this intimate world was a supporting cast that both mirrored reality and lent the strip a complexity that was second to none. In addition to Aunt May, Jameson, and Betty Brant, the cast in-cluded a musclebound oaf named Flash Thompson who loved to perse-cute Peter Parker, his dizzy girlfriend Liz Allan—who was secretly intrigued by the bookworm Parker—and Ned Leeds, Parker's rival for Betty's affection. All of them remained in constant motion and growth, proving that although they had their roles to play, they would never freeze into stereotypes.

True to form, Lee and Ditko did not let their hero sit complacently in his new successes. With issue 9 (Feb. 1964) a whole new complex of problems began to appear. Aunt May falls ill, the first of a series of crises in her health that will keep Peter always on edge. Parker's new manner wins him the infatuation of the flightly Liz Allan, bringing jealousy and confusion into his budding romance with Betty Brant. Betty herself proves to have a brother with criminal connections, adding a note of ambivalence to her otherwise wholesome character. Spider-Man meets his biggest test in 1964, when Aunt May's desperate condition causes him to run away from a battle with his archfoe, the Green Goblin, branding him as a coward in the eyes of the world (SM 17, Oct. 1964). His problems overwhelming him, his own confidence shaken by the incident, he finds himself reduced to cowering in fear from his enemies. It is Aunt May's own plucky battle to survive that inspires him, however, and Parker finally affirms the course of his life: "Fate gave me some terrific super-powers, and I realize now that it's my duty to use them . . . without doubt . . . without hesitation! For I know at last that a man can't change his destiny . . . and I was born to be . . . Spider-Man!" (SM 18, Nov. 1964).

In this short run, Ditko's art improved further. Spider-Man took on a more powerful presence, action scenes grew more dynamic, and Parker, shedding his image as a social reject in favor of a more dignified alienation, came to look remarkably like James Dean. Through all the changes, however, Ditko's skill at emotional nuance did not diminish. Lee, improving apace, injected a breezy humor into his writing that complemented the inherent drama of the series. His fascination with irony and fate, themes with which he had struggled heavyhandedly before, now assumed a genuine strength with the star-crossed but intrepid Spider-Man.

Apart from the emotional angle, Lee and Ditko brought to their Spider-Man work many virtues that the other comics of the nascent Marvel Comics Group lacked. Ditko's plots were neater than Kirby's. The hero's nemeses were colorful hoodlums, not aliens, monsters, or commies. A number of interlocking mysteries ran through the entire series, particularly the hidden identities of the Green Goblin, a gangleader called the Big Man, and a stoolie named Patch.

Change would always swirl around Peter Parker as long as Lee and Ditko worked together, shaping not only his world but his heart. His life as Spider-Man would drive Betty Brant from him, and he would graduate from high school to pick up a new cast of characters in college. Sadly, despite the apparently seamless union of Lee and Ditko's talents, disagreements built up behind the scenes that prompted Ditko to leave the Marvel Group and return to Charlton in 1966 (after SM 38, July 1966). Spider-Man went on, but under artist John Romita a new approach was instituted. The old subplots were tied up all too neatly, characters were abruptly changed, and Parker was robbed of much of his complexity as he became a hip, motorcycle-riding Joe College sort. Spider-Man, it seemed, owed more to his artist than any character had before. But by the time Ditko left, Spider-Man's contribution to comics had already been made. Added to the kids who always comprised the bulk of comic buyers, to Julius Schwartz's nostalgic older readers, to the Metal Men's knot of loyal fans, were a bright pubescent bunch who would exult and suffer for years to come with the ever-changing Marvel heroes.

The Birth of Fandom

Although the idea of an active, influential body of fans was not altogether new to comic books, neither was it at all common. In the early 1950s, EC Comics—emphasizing sophisticated art and a grim, adult tone in its science fiction, horror, and adventure titles—inspired a voluble body of "fan-addicts" to send in letters and create their own mimeographed "fanzines." But the frightening, often violent material that resulted from EC's adult slant came under attack from parents, teachers, and lawmakers as public outcry drove comics back to a wholesome, innocuous, childlike level. For a few years it seemed that the only comic book readers with opinions worth considering had been driven from the field, and that editors would never show an interest in the remaining readers' thoughts. But when Mort Weisinger, drawing upon his experience in science fiction fandom, initiated his Superman letter pages in 1958, he showed that even though his readers might be very young, they had a lot to say about the comics they loved.

Almost all the letters sent to the Superman stable were indeed written by small children and, for the most part, expressed only their gut-level likes and dislikes. A great many kids also wrote in their suggestions for stories they'd like to see (for example, "How about a story where Superman gets a disease?"), and asked questions concerning details of Kryptonese lore. The most common missive received by Weisinger, however, was the "goof" or "boo-boo" type, in which readers gleefully pointed out what they felt to be mistakes made by the writer or artist ("In your story, 'When the World Forgot Superman' . . . the sun is out and everything is bright. But the calendar reads 'Dec. 11'!") and challenged the editor to squirm his way out of them. It was a modest start, but a start it was, toward reader participation in the development of comics.

The contacts between science fiction and comic book fandom did not cease with Weisinger. At a Pittsburgh science fiction convention in September 1960, two couples simultaneously conceived a pair of fanzines that devoted regular attention to comics: Dick and Pat Lupoff with *Xero* (a science fiction fanzine with a comic book column called *All in Color for a Dime*) and Don Thompson and Maggie Curtis with *Comic Art*. These enthusiasts were quite the opposite of Weisinger's young fans, all four being adults looking back on the Golden Age comics of their youth, with little interest in the comics of the present. Where Weisinger's followers had no sense of history or criticism, these nostalgic science fictioneers had little investment in the future of the medium. Before fandom could have any effect on the field, the gap between them would have to be bridged; and the engineer who began the bridge was Weisinger's old partner in fandom, Julius Schwartz.

When Schwartz started his letter pages in 1960, they were scarcely different from Weisinger's. But his high standards and Golden Age revivals were already attracting older readers—most notably neophyte English teacher Roy Thomas and a natural-science professor named Dr. Jerry Bails—and their lengthy, thoughtful letters began appearing frequently. This new intensity of interest in his work impressed Schwartz, and during 1961 he worked to encourage more serious correspondence, expanding his letter sections to two pages, printing longer missives in full, and even giving away original Infantino artwork as prizes for clever letters. The letter pages in *Mystery in Space* formed the first forum for real critical writing, as science fiction readers like Paul Seydor and Richard C. West subjected Schwartz's works to the same standards to which they subjected books and short stories. Soon controversy about Joe Kubert's art erupted in *Hawkman,* the question of whether human-interest stories or science fiction adventures were better suited to costumed heroes arose in *Green Lantern,* and juvenile readers were suddenly no longer just spotting goofs or suggesting stories; the kids had become the critics.

Schwartz built up a regular stable of letter-writers who stayed with him through the 1960s. Guy H. Lillian III appeared in 1962 (F 133, Dec. 1962) complaining about the "idiotic epistles" sent in by the "clods" among his fellow readers, and would go on to set the standards for fan letters as Schwartz's "favorite guy." Along with him came Buddy Saunders, Kenneth Gallagher, Gary Friedrich, Donald MacGregor, Bob Butts, and other fans; a slightly later generation would include Mike Friedrich, Irene Vartanoff, Marvin Wolfman, Peter Sanderson, Martin Pasko, and several others who would make their influence felt in years to come.

It was in the first issue of *The Brave and the Bold* featuring Hawkman that Schwartz had given full attention to his older readers; in the next issue of that same title (BB 35, May 1961) he made a slight adjustment in the letters, which might easily have been overlooked but had a dramatic effect on fandom. Until that time, all letter pages had published only the name, city, and state of the correspondent. Now Schwartz included street addresses, with the immediate effect that fans could contact directly the comrades they discovered through letter columns. Two of the correspondents in that first address-bearing issue were Roy Thomas and Jerry Bails, and only a few months later Thomas was helping Bails publish *Alter-Ego*—dedicated to studying "comic heroes of the past, present, and future"—the first fanzine to specialize in costumed heroes, and the first to deal with the dawning Silver Age. Fandom had begun its independent life, soon spreading through correspondence, fanzines, swap-meets, and clubs across the country.

But one element was still needed. These fans knew that they were a barely significant minority of comic buyers, a few odd aficionados standing on the outside looking in at a business still directed almost entirely at the faceless children who comprised DC's public. Although still loving their heroes, most of them found it hard to escape the teenager's contempt of "little kid stuff." They wanted some part of the field to respond directly to them and to their more complicated demands. *The Fantastic Four* was a hint that such a response might be coming: *Spider-Man* seemed tailored perfectly for them. And Stan Lee's approach to his readers during Marvel's first few years showed that those slightly older, mentally ambitious fans were in fact the prime targets of his creations.

Lee worked hard to maintain the feeling of intimacy with his readers that *Spider-Man* had sparked. By the end of 1962 he had switched the salutations of the letters he published from "Dear Editor" to "Dear Stan and Jack" (FF 9, Dec. 1962), and he and Kirby figured prominently as characters in one story (FF 10, Jan. 1963). To give the readers a sense of involvement in the company, he raised his pencilers and inkers from their usual anonymity to give them—and himself—credit at the beginning of every story. This wasn't a new practice; Schwartz had been giving Fox, Kane, and Anderson credit for *The Atom* for over a year. But Schwartz's credits seemed intended to acknowledge particularly careful work, while Lee gave everyone—soon even the men who lettered the captions and word-balloons—not only credit but cute nicknames and ostensible attributes, with the intention of creating a sense of family. Shortly he even began giving such nicknames to his heroes (Mr. Fantastic was called "Stretcho," the Hulk "Ol' Greenskin," and Spider-Man "Web-Head"), to be tossed around not only by editor and fans, but by characters in the stories as well.

Lee's letter-page style was one of easygoing, hip familiarity. He wanted to impress his readers with his honesty and self-effacement, admitting goofs openly and mixing unabashedly negative letters in with the praiseful ones, even when DC fan Paul Gambaccini let him know that he was not impressed with the "new realism": "I have tried to hold back for months but can't do it. My hatred of your mags has caused me to write. . . . Your heroes are lilly-lilly with obvious faking of emotions . . . [your] so-called heroes who act like 'real people' (if so, I pity the human race)" (FF 9, Dec. 1962).

This casual, humble attitude, however, stood in odd contrast to the growing hyperbole of Lee's self-advertisements. Ever since he had plastered "The Greatest Comic Magazine in the World!" on the cover of the FF's third issue, he had been screaming for the attention of fandom. With his May 1963 issues he finally gave his comics stable a name, the Marvel

Comics Group; only six months later his covers announced, "The Marvel Age of Comics Is Here!" and we soon saw issues that were "Bringing the Marvel Age of Comics to a Lofty New Pinnacle of Greatness!" (Apparently even this was too modest, for "The Brutal Betrayal of Ben Grimm" in FF 41, Aug. 1965, was proclaimed "Possibly the most daringly dramatic development in the field of contemporary literature!")

To give the young stable an image of identity, Lee added a Special Announcements Section, full of behind-the-scenes information and coming attractions (beginning with the Sept. 1963 issues), and a checklist of all Marvel titles (Dec. 1964) to his letter pages. In late 1964 he created a fan club called the Merry Marvel Marching Society, and began filling his writings with esoteric slogans ("Face front, True Believers!" "Excelsior!" " 'Nuff said!"), references to an invented company mascot named Irving Forbush, and florid promotions of the "Marvelous Marvel Manner." Most important, he addressed the fans directly with gratitude and praise, as in this blurb from the first page of a Spider-Man comic: "Dedicated to the new breed of comics magazine reader—to you, the modern Marvel fan, who will accept nothing less than the best in story and art!" (SM 23, Apr. 1965).

The pride and pretensions of his readers were so well fulfilled by these noble sentiments that a fierce feeling of loyalty to Marvel grew in the breast of much of fandom. Lee was always eager to publish letters attacking the unnamed competition, particularly when they came from converts like the former DC booster Gambaccini: "I don't know if their stuff has deteriorated or whether you have improved that much, but the competition now seems like ecch!" (SM 7, Dec. 1963). At first Lee modestly disagreed with DC's detractors, but by 1965 he found it impossible to keep himself off the bandwagon. "Chee!" he wrote. "Have you noticed the sorry mess of Marvel IMITATIONS making the scene lately? . . . We wanna make darn sure no dyed-in-the-wool Marvel madman gets stuck with one of those inferior 'Brand Ecch' versions of the real thing!" (Oct. 1965 issues). The battle between "Brand Ecch" and "Mighty Marvel" became such a rallying point for loyal Marvelites that letter pages soon abounded with credos from kids echoing Lee's own hyperbole. "When you're reading a Brand Ecch comic," wrote Matt Emmens and Jimmy Luzzi, "you're just reading a comic book, but when you're reading a Marvel mag, you stand a little taller, walk a little straighter, and talk a little prouder" (SM 33, Feb. 1966).

Whereas DC had quietly opened its doors to allow the fans in, Lee had gone out stumping to bring Marvel to fandom by whatever means he could find. In doing so, he succeeded not only in selling his own upstart company to comicdom at large, but in giving fans a sense of identity and giving them confidence that their opinions had clout in the hero business.

One event in 1965 made it clear that fandom would indeed be a force in comics' future. By then, fan conventions were popping up all over the country, the sale of old comics was becoming a business, and fanzines abounded. The most important of those was still *Alter-Ego*, now published and edited by Roy Thomas alone. The quality of his work attracted the notice of Charlton Comics, then planning to make their own plunge into the costumed-hero field, and Thomas sold them two scripts. A brief office job at DC followed (where he worked alongside E. Nelson Bridwell, a less prominent fan who had already broken through into professionalism), then an audience with Stan Lee. Lee was ready to break the Marvel monolith and hire a second writer, and Thomas—with virtually no credentials except those as a fan—got the job. Thomas's importance as both a writer and an editor would be great over the next several years, but just as important was the mere fact that he was hired, the fact that a widely known fan had broken into the inner offices of the comic book companies, and the implication that fans could now begin to shape the medium according to their own ideas.

Man and Superman

While Lee and Kanigher were experimenting with broader character relationships and deeper emotions, Mort Weisinger was quietly making his own brand of those qualities the very basis of his Superman mythos. Although the Man of Steel still fought crime and saved the world from natural cataclysms, the emphasis of his stories rested firmly on his relationships with friends and foes alike. Jimmy Olsen ceased to be merely a comic foil, eliciting now a warm, fatherly concern from Superman. Lois Lane and Lana Lang, no longer mere pests, entered unspoken but often turbulent affairs of the heart with the hero. The Kandorians were no longer just another exhibit in the Fortress of Solitude; Superman now toiled ceaselessly to restore his countrymen to their normal size. And Lex Luthor grew from his role of unqualified villainy to a broad humanity that lent his clashes with Superman an odd ambiguity. From these relationships poured, at a level clearly understandable to very young children, the gamut of human passion: grief, rage, love, and an all-pervasive irony.

Weisinger and his writers developed a storytelling technique designed to accentuate these passions almost to the exclusion of rock-'em-sock-'em action. The stories were presented in fairytale fashion, with the significant events presented simply and in isolation, at the expense of mood and a smooth narrative flow. A typical panel in nearly any given story would portray a climactic scene, omitting transitions and often the events that led to that climax. In the imaginary story "The Three Wives of Superman" (Lois Lane 51, Aug. 1964), for example, Superman marries Lois Lane only to bring about her death unknowingly with a serum intended to give her powers like his own. Afterward, just five sequential panels take us through a critical turn in the hero's life. In the first, Superman, who has given up his crime-fighting role, grieves on a "heartbreak asteroid." In the second, he returns inconsolable to his fortress on Earth. The next finds him reliving old times with Lois, and in the fourth he discovers that his serum killed her. The fifth panel finds him at her grave, where he makes peace with her memory by swearing to resume his Superman role. As in a child's storybook, such sequences were essentially static, but through the endearing qualities of his characters, set against the backdrop of the growing Superman lore, Weisinger, demonstrating an uncanny insight into the dreams of his young readers, imbued them with a vitality that made them a delight to read. In testimony to his success, Weisinger managed to break the immutable one-fight-per-story rule of hero comics and still make his the best-selling titles in the field.

His stable also forged a unique style of scripting, engineered to make every aspect of a story clear even to the youngest readers. Such statements as, "We're leaving the past! (Choke!) There's the explosion that destroyed our native planet Krypton! (Gulp!)" drew jeers from some older readers but vividly communicated both facts and emotions to Weisinger's chosen audience. (Perhaps the most extreme example of such scripting came in *Adventure* 301 (Oct. 1962) when, after a young man accidentally drinks a solution that subjects him to a bizarre transformation, a bystander cries, "Look . . . he's expanding—like a balloon!! He's lucky he's wearing clothing made of stretchable fiber!"—no doubt to keep kids from writing in to ask why his clothes didn't tear.)

A tireless worker as both an editor and a writer, Weisinger honed his commercial acumen through decades of work in many fields. He whipped out dozens of magazine articles all through his years as an editor, along with books as divergent as a diet plan, a novel about beauty pageants called *The Contest,* and the best-selling *1001 Valuable Things You Can Get Free.* Through it all, he not only edited his comics but fed his writers most of their plots himself. Some scripters rebelled against this monolithic control, but those who could live with it were given steady work for most of their careers.

More completely than any other editor, Weisinger shaped his comics to his personal vision. He was notorious in the business as a stern taskmaster, very demanding of both artists and writers. Artist Curt Swan described him as "very opinionated and difficult to deal with. And if anyone showed any weakness, he loved that, because then he would really lean on them. Sad thing to say." Perhaps so, but the result of this harshness was a collection of perfectly consistent and intricately interwoven titles.

Weisinger worked best with men he had known for many years. Otto Binder had been a friend in the 1930s; Edmond Hamilton had been one of his most reliable workhorses on *Thrilling Wonder Stories* and other pulps since the end of that decade. But the man whom Weisinger called "the most competent of all the Superman writers" had known not only the editor but the hero himself longer than any of them. Jerome Siegel first came to the attention of the science fiction world in 1933 as a fanzine editor eager to trade advertisements with Schwartz and Weisinger's *Time Traveller.* It was that same year that he dreamed of a hero from another planet, possessed of amazing powers, dedicated to righting the world's wrongs. With a fellow teenager, cartoonist Joe Shuster, he created Superman, and for five years struggled to sell it as a newspaper comic strip. When National Periodical Publications finally bought it in 1938, it proved to be the first great success of the young comic book field, making possible not only all the costumed heroes who would follow, but perhaps the field itself as a unique medium. Ten years later Siegel and Shuster began legal action to regain some ownership of the character from DC, as a result of which Siegel has said that the industry has blackballed and punished him ever since. Weisinger, however, rehired him to write Superman in 1959, and stood by him. "Siegel was the best emotional writer of them all," he said, "as in the unforgettable 'Death of Luthor' " (Act. 318, Nov. 1964). Siegel took delight in the burgeoning Superman mythos, handling innovations with great affection and a charming sense of humor.

One less venerable member of the stable was Leo Dorfman, a writer for Fawcett and Dell Comics in the 1950s whom Weisinger hired to fill Otto Binder's shoes in 1961. Dorfman was at his best in romantic, domestically oriented stories like "The Amazing Story of Superman-Red and Superman-Blue" (Sup. 162, July 1963), which explored nearly every possible wrinkle of Superman's future life after getting married and giving up crime-fighting, earned him the job of scripting *Supergirl* regularly.

A number of other writers worked for Weisinger in the 1960s, but none as regularly as Siegel, Hamilton, and Dorfman. Otto Binder returned in 1964, although he would never again be in a position to make significant contributions.

The art chores for Superman were handled primarily by Curt Swan, a penciler who never set out to be a comic book artist, and in fact had very little interest in storytelling art. His dream was to be a magazine cover artist, his youthful heroes such illustrators as Al Parker and John Whitcomb. But while drawing for *Stars and Stripes* in Paris during the war he met Eddie "France" Herron, former editor of *Captain Marvel*. When Herron joined DC after the war, he recommended that the jobless Swan show his portfolio to Weisinger, who promptly hired him.

After years of polishing his illustrating techniques on backup features, Swan got a crack at Superman in 1955. He carried his love of the sort of quiet scenes and human expression that dominate magazine illustration into his costumed-hero career, never warming to the increasingly fantastic approach to Superman in the late fifties. "To me the . . . supporting characters really had a personality. . . . Somehow they became a part of me. Then, when they started this business of flying around and Jimmy Olsen becoming some creature, Elastic Lad, . . . I'd want to take the script back and slam it down on Mort's desk and say, 'I want to get somebody else to do it. I don't want to do this.' " He never did take a script back, however, and when Wayne Boring left the stable in 1961, Swan became the Man of Steel's regular artist.

Rarely has an artist been matched with a strip so perfectly suited to his style. Ordinarily, an artist with so little interest in action and fantasy would have proved ill-suited to costumed heroes, but the new edge of soap opera in the Superman line demanded an artist of Swan's inclination. His skill with facial expressions and his penchant for realism gave him more in common with Norman Rockwell than with Carmine Infantino or Jack Kirby. Teamed with inker George Klein, whose neat, unassuming lines blended perfectly with Swan's pencils, Swan gave the Man of Steel his quintessential look, which continues to the presnt (Swan was unable to draw every Superman story, of which there were several per month, but Al Plastino, who had filled in for Wayne Boring in the fifties, ably pinch-hit for him on these occasions by assuming as similar a style as his abilities permitted).

The greatest developments in the Superman lore created by these men occurred in the titles *Superman, Action Comics,* and *World's Finest,* the last of which Weisinger had inherited from Jack Schiff in 1964. It was in the stories steeped in this mythos that the character of Superman and the nature of his unique world were rounded out. The elements that Weisinger and Binder had created in the late fifties were brought to full fruition as the 1960s progressed.

The central focus of Superman's development continued to be his Kryptonian origin. Most of the stories involving Krypton turned on Superman discovering new details of both his native planet's and his own personal histories. In "The Man Who Saved Kal-El's Life" (Act. 281, Oct. 1961) Superman discovers that a professor had invented a "matter radio" with which he had traveled to Krypton prior to its destruction. There, when baby Kal had been bitten by a "fish-snake," the professor had performed emergency surgery on him and thus saved the life of Earth's future benefactor. In "The Day Superman Became the Flash" (Act. 314, July 1964) it is revealed that Jor-El, Superman's father, had consulted a "computer forecaster," a machine capable of formulating a high-probability forecast of the future, in order to determine to what planet to send Kal-El. Before deciding on Earth, where Jor-El had seen that Kal would become a great hero, he had discarded five other planets on which Kal would have battled crime under such guises as a sea king, a tiny titan, a super archer, a speedster, and a dark-night detective—all modeled after his Justice League cohorts—but on which he would have been unhappy, alienated, or met an untimely end. In "Krypton Lives Again" (Sup. 189, Aug. 1966), Superman learns of a second Krypton that was created and populated with androids to act as a decoy against an alien armada. Unwittingly, Superman destroys the ersatz Krypton.

As Kryptoniana abounded, the Bottle City of Kandor became more prominent. The primary delight in these stories came from discovering new details about life in the Bottle City itself. In just a handful of stories, we learn of telepathic police hounds that can locate fugitives at any distance by reading their minds; of the scientist Van-Zee, who is Superman's exact double, and his wife, Sylvia, who is a double of Lois Lane; of duels fought with stun swords, of statues erected in honor of Kryptonian heroes; of bizarre native flora and fauna; and much, much more. Most notable among these tales were the ones in which Superman and Jimmy

Olsen, borrowing from Batman and Robin, assume the secret identities of Nightwing and Flamebird, Kandor's greatest crime-fighters.

One of the few bits of Superman lore introduced after Otto Binder's exit was the Phantom Zone, a "twilight dimension" where Krypton's worst criminals were banished as "disembodied wraiths"; it figured strongly in stories starting in late 1961. The Zone was like the dark flip side to Kandor, a nether-realm where the most horrible sides of the Kryptonian soul were preserved after the planet's destruction. No matter how much time passes, none of the Phantom Zone prisoners can age. A few of them gain wisdom through this purgatory and are freed by the Kandorian Phantom Zone Parole Board to become productive citizens of the Bottle City (Act. 310, Mar. 1964). But most, led by the incorrigible Jax-Ur, only allow their hatreds and frustrations to stew, while reliving with glee their evil deeds on Krypton; Jax-Ur takes special pride in having used a nuclear missile to destroy an inhabited moon. Although they can only speak to our dimension through the Zone-Ophone in Superman's Fortress of Solitude, they can see and hear everything that transpires here. Knowing that Superman's father was responsible for his conviction, Jax-Ur leads his cronies in schemes to avenge themselves on that scion of Krypton. The occasional escape of these criminals provided Superman with equal-powered foes to fight—another reversal of Kandor, where neither hero nor villain could possess great powers—and brought new revelations of Krypton's past into the stories.

"Red sun" stories also proliferated as Superman found himself, robbed of his special powers, on planets orbiting such suns more and more frequently throughout the sixties. Concerning these tales, Weisinger said: "To make him more of a likable character, the type of story I became fondest of was the one where ... Superman lost his powers and had to survive on his natural wits. ... You could identify with him then, an outstanding character deserving of your admiration, a real hero because of the clever things that he did when deprived of his super-powers." In "Superman Under the Red Sun" (Act. 300, May 1963), for example, Superman is tricked by the Superman Revenge-Squad into traveling thousands of years into the future, when earth's sun has turned red with age. Powerless, Superman's only hope to return to his own time is to find his way to his Fortress of Solitude. He succeeds, but only after journeying across a barren wasteland and warding off, with his quick wits alone, a number of odd, mutated beasts. In another story, Superman finds himself on a planetoid where the populace has reverted into a primitive, superstitious race. He is promptly captured by the natives and told that in order to free himself he must demonstrate "good magic powers" three times. How Superman, deprived of his powers, feigns such magic powers is another tribute to his resourcefulness and forms the backbone of this delightful yarn (Sup. 184, Feb. 1966).

Even Lex Luthor, long-time archenemy of Superman's, became more fully entrenched in the Superman mythos of the sixties. He not only figured prominently in the Imaginary Stories, under many different roles and guises, but Weisinger also built a body of lore around him that nearly equaled Superman's. During one battle we learn that Luthor, not to be outdone by Superman, has set up a "fortress of solitude" of his own, christened Luthor's Lair. Located in an abandoned museum in the heart of Metropolis, Luthor's Lair features telescreens with which to monitor the city outside, a Hall of Heroes including statues of Atila the Hun, Genghis Khan, Captain Kidd, and Al Capone, and a super-scientific workshop. Other elements paralleling Superman's life included Luthor's induction into a futuristic band of outlaws calling themselves The Legion of Super Villains, and the planet Lexor, on which Luthor is respected and admired as a great hero while Superman is feared and detested as a terrible villain (Act. 277, June 1961).

During this fertile period, Luthor also evolved from a common if ofttimes brilliant thug to a supreme evildoer against whom Superman fought his most epic battles. Although they scarcely ever threw a single punch, he and Superman became the mightiest rivals in comics. Their confrontations were often so monumental that Earth proved an inadequate arena; their clashes raged across all of time and throughout the entire universe. One of these confrontations produced a true Weisinger classic, an enormously complex full-length story, in which Luthor teams up with the evil android Brainiac and their struggle with Superman ranges for Lexor to Kandor (Sup. 167, Feb. 1964). With the very next issue (Sup. 168, Apr. 1964) Luthor returns for another three-part epic. With Luthor posing as both a costumed-hero and a newspaper editor, the battle again originates on Lexor, but this time is concluded in San Francisco in the year 1906, where, among other things, Superman must contend with the great San Francisco earthquake.

Lastly, the Imaginary Stories, in which events that *might* have happened were recounted, displayed more than any other tales in the Superman universe the storytelling techniques patented by Weisinger. Generally, many years were covered in these "what if" stories, which often followed characters along the full journey from birth to death. (Death ran rampant in these stories, but never as senseless annihilation; those who died usually did so in acts of heroic self-sacrifice.) They were extremely bittersweet in tone, and frequently modeled after the heroic epics of antiquity, in which defeat made the brave even braver and neatly rounded out their existence. Defeat, irony, and tragedy were preponderant, and the intense sorrow often endured by the characters was both touching and elevating. Classic examples are "The Three Wives of Superman," in which Superman marries Lois Lane, Lana Lang, and the mermaid Lori Lemaris in turn, only to have each die tragically; "Clark Kent's Brother" (Sup. 175, Feb. 1965), in which Lex Luthor is adopted by the Kents and eventually sacrifices his life to save his brother, in this case Superman, from death; and "The Death of

Superman and his pals: Perry White, Chief Parker of Smallville, the mermaid Lori Lemaris, Robin, Batman, Jimmy Olsen, an ersatz Clark Kent, Lois Lane, Pete Ross, Lana Lang . . . and John F. Kennedy. Art by Swan and Klein. From *Action Comics* 309, February 1964.

Superman" (Sup. 149, Nov. 1961), in which Luthor succeeds in slaying the Man of Steel, and Supergirl must carry on in his place. In the last panel, a classic ending in the Imaginary Story mold, Supergirl thinks, "Choke . . . All I feel is a great sorrow at the passing of the strongest, kindest, m-most powerful human being I've ever known! Sob—M-my cousin Super-man . . ."

As extensive as this lore came to be in the titles in which Superman starred, it was still so vast that it spilled over into the rest of Weisinger's stable. The participation of Superman's supporting cast in this mythos will be treated in the next chapter.

11 Superman's Pals

In addition to *Superman, Action Comics,* and *World's Finest,* Weisinger edited *Superman's Pal Jimmy Olsen, Superman's Girlfriend Lois Lane, Superboy,* and *Adventure Comics.* He also edited *Supergirl,* which was featured regularly in *Action Comics.* Although these titles weren't as successful, either commercially or artistically, as Weisinger's top three, they were all integral parts of the big picture.

Jimmy Olsen, Superman's pal and a cub reporter at the Daily Planet, was given his own comic in 1954. This was a risky move on Weisinger's part—Jimmy was, after all, a supporting character and not a hero—but frequent Superman appearances and a set of special Olsen gimmicks kept the title popular. At first, Olsen's specialty was disguise, leading him to play such diverse roles as a TV actor, a spy, a rock-'n'-roll star, and a mobster's moll in the cause of fighting crime. Very shortly, however, he fell prey to the same foolishness that afflicted Batman during the late 1950s, being transformed nearly every issue into such weird forms as a Giant Turtle Man, a Human Porcupine, Flame Boy, the Tom Thumb Jimmy, the Living Pinocchio, and, most frequently, a stretchable costumed-hero called Elastic Lad.

Olsen did, however, often intersect with Superman lore. Perhaps because of the quaintness and gimmickry of his adventures, he was at his best in stories revolving around Kandor, as in "Mystery of the Tiny Supermen," in which we meet the gnat-sized costumed-heroes from the Bottle City who call themselves the Superman Emergency Squad (JO 44, Oct. 1960). Later he battles four tiny desperadoes from Kandor who have been weirdly transformed by red kryptonite (JO 63, Sept. 1962) and soon after, as mentioned before, he enters the bottle with Superman to become the hero Flamebird (JO 69, June 1963).

Curt Swan did his first regular "Superman family" work on Olsen, and for over a decade he filled the strip with character and beauty. In 1965, unfortunately, he was replaced by Pete Constanza, a Golden Age cartoonist at the end of his career, while the stories grew increasingly goofier. The adventures of Superman's pal, by the mid-1960s, became the least appealing series of the Weisinger stable.

Olsen's early success prompted, in 1958, a comic called *Superman's*

Girlfriend Lois Lane. Lois was put through the same role changes and transformations as Jimmy—among them Lois the Super Brain, the Phantom Lois Lane, and Baby Lois—but the twin emphases of her stories were more trivial, one being Lois's never-ending scheme to discover Superman's secret identity, the other her dream of marrying him. She was esentially a one-dimensional character, and her adventures generally revolved around either threats to her feminine vanity or wacky schemes to trap Superman, reminiscent of Lucy Ricardo.

Because of this repetitiveness, Lois was usually at her best in imaginary stories. Those stories were originally created for her series, and from the beginning displayed a variety that lifted them above the strip's usual confines. In the first installment of the "Imaginary Series," Lois finds that being married to Superman is not the bed of roses she has always imagined. Because of his fear that his enemies will strike at him through his wife, Superman insists that Lois publicly marry Clark Kent, not the Man of Steel. While gossips whisper, "Poor thing! She's marrying Clark because she couldn't land Superman!" and other women boast about their successful husbands, Lois must bite her lip and hide all signs of her husband's special powers, even to burning a beautiful extraterrestrial gown he bought her. By the end she is shrieking in frustration (LL 19, Aug. 1960).

Lois's series was given some distinctiveness by the fact that it was the only one in Weisinger's stable not dominated by the art of Curt Swan. Artist Kurt Schaffenberger had developed his style drawing Captain Marvel for Fawcett, and so brought to the Superman family the same humor, charm, and vivaciousness with his art that Otto Binder had brought with his writing. He used an emotionally lively, caricature style that suited the light touch of most Lois Lane scripts, and a pristine simplicity that fit in well with Swan's more serious approach.

The Supergirl strip, which ran in *Action Comics* from 1959 to 1969 before moving over to *Adventure Comics,* was aimed strictly at young girls. The stories revolved largely around family problems, teen romance, and peer relations. Although much of the lore abundant in Superman stories was also present here, it usually provided only a backdrop to Supergirl's latest heartthrob. The strip's artist, Jim Mooney, although sketchy and unimaginative, was nevertheless suited to the strip as he imbued his facial expressions with all the sorrow, irateness, and wide-eyed delight that the strip's most regular writer, Leo Dorfman, made Supergirl undergo repeatedly. In "The Mutiny of Super-Horse" (Act. 294, Nov. 1962), for instance, Supergirl suffers great sadness when Super-Horse, in his secret identity as Comet, is sold to a Hollywood producer and consequently seems to prefer the company of Liz Gaynor, the actress with whom he co-stars in a movie, over that of Supergirl. In another story fraught with turbulent emotion, "Supergirl's Rival Parents" (Act. 310, Mar. 1964), Supergirl is first joyously reunited with her real parents—who had also managed to survive the destruction of Krypton—but must then choose which set of parents she would rather live with.

The one lesser series most closely tied in with the Superman mythos was Superboy—appearing in both *Adventure Comics* and *Superboy*—which made sense, as it told the adventures of Superman himself when he was a boy. Perhaps because he was more willing to experiment in titles less successful than *Superman* or *Action*, Weisinger introduced many of his principle innovations in Superboy stories, including the assorted new colors of kryptonite (red, blue, white, and gold), the Phantom Zone, the origins of Lex Luthor and that Fifth Dimensional imp, Mr. Mxyzptlk, and the Bizarros (who had their own would-be humorous series in the back of *Adventure* from issue 285 to 299, June 1961 to August 1962). This often created paradoxes in continuity, at least for older readers; it seemed peculiar, for example, that the Mr. Mxyzptlk whom Superman first met as an adult in 1944 suddenly proved to have been a pest to Superboy since high school. But to Weisinger's readers, the great bulk of whom were very young, every new issue was like the beginning of history, and these paradoxes went unnoticed.

Complementing the main body of the Superman mythos was a distinct Superboy lore, centering on his little hometown of Smallville. With a cast of characters including young Kal-El's kindly foster parents, Jonathan and Martha Kent, Superboy's devoted dog Krypto, a juvenile version of Lois Lane named Lana Lang, and Clark Kent's loyal pal Pete Ross (so loyal, in fact, that although he once accidentally discovered Clark's true identity, he never revealed the fact, even to Clark himself), this kid-centered lore added a new dimension to the Man of Steel's personality and broadened the stage upon which he acted. At their best, the Smallville tales exude an innocent, small-town charm that, though not quite as effective as Broome and Infantino's *Kid Flash* work, gave the series a distinctive flavor. Even when they fell short creatively, they gave Weisinger an opportunity to fill in the gaps in his hero's background which no other editor enjoyed. The art, regularly by George Papp, although also falling short of the likes of Infantino and Swan, was nonetheless competent and colorful, telling the stories in straightforward terms.

Among the many innovations of 1958 was an intermittent series called "Untold Tales," in which we discover episodes in Clark's life between his Superboy days and his full-blown Superman adventures. Weisinger took his revelations farther back in time with stories of Superbaby, cute tales of Clark's early experiments with his special powers. Occasionally we took a step back even farther, to see baby Kal-El on Krypton, giving us a toddler's view of that advanced planet. In "Life on Krypton," we meet Krypto as a puppy, feel Kal-El's parents' love for him, and discover amazing toys, such as a pipe that blows soap bubbles in complex geometric forms (*Superboy* 79, Mar. 1960).

The most significant development in the minor titles of the Superman family occurred in *Adventure* 300 (Sept. 1962), when the Legion of Super Heroes, until then limited to occasional guest appearances, inherited a comic of their own. To the original three members of that thirtieth-century team—Lightning Lad, Cosmic Boy, and Saturn Girl—had since been added several more powerful teenagers: Brainiac Five, whose twelfth-level brain makes him a human computer; Chameleon Boy, who can assume any shape he chooses; Triplicate Girl, who can split herself into three identical bodies; Sun Boy, who can generate heat and light; Shrinking Violet, who can reduce her size; Bouncing Boy, who can inflate his body and bounce like a ball; and others.

Around this band of futuristic crime-fighters Weisinger and his writers—first Jerry Siegel, then Edmond Hamilton—proceeded to weave a vast body of lore all their own. The team quickly came to feature a clubhouse, a vast array of advanced scientific gadgets, regular elections for team leader (later voted on by the fans), the Legion of Super Pets, the Legion of Substitute Heroes (composed of Legion applicants who had been turned away), a vast array of diabolical foes, and much more. Although none of the Legionnaires were provided with personalities, they each nevertheless possessed interesting origins and complex personal histories around which many enjoyable stories were produced. Superboy himself figured prominently as a member of the team, and several of the stories featured guest appearances by such members of the Superman family as Supergirl, Lana Lang, Jimmy Olsen, Krypto, Comet, and Streaky the Super Cat.

Regular Legion writer Edmond Hamilton had been, since 1928, one of science fiction's main inventors and popularizers of classic "space opera." His love of grandiose, cosmos-spanning adventures earned him the nickname "World-Wrecker" from his peers. With Weisinger he created the pulp series *Captain Future* (for which his agent was Julius Schwartz), then followed his editor to comics in the early 1940s. His old predilections surfaced during the 1960s in Legion stories that spanned space and threatened great cataclysms.

The regular artist through the first thirty-nine issues of *Adventure* that featured the Legion was John Forte. Forte was a stiff penciler, but his neat lines and quaint images, coupled with the varied and colorful costumes worn by the Legionnaires, made the final product attractive. In common with most of Weisinger's artists, additionally, Forte exhibited a penchant for very expressive facial emotions. Although he often ran to caricature, and one Legionnaire was indistinguishable from the next but for gender and costume, Forte nevertheless captured the rage and pathos that ran riot through the stories.

Classic early Legion fare is the "Death of Lightning Lad" sequence that ran in *Adventure* 304, 305, 308, and 312. Basically, Lightning Lad loses his life while battling Zaryan the Space Conquerer and is later resurrected through an act of self-sacrifice by another hero. The pathos is evident from this outline alone, but it is in the minor events strewn along the way that the strong emotional tone for the entire series was set. In "The Stolen Super Powers" (Adv. 304, Jan. 1963) Saturn Girl is warned by a friendly

Lightning Lad dies . . .

. . . and Legionnaires gather in mourning: Superboy, Sun Boy, Shrinking Violet, Cosmic Boy, Saturn Girl, Bouncing Boy, Chameleon Boy, and Supergirl. Art by John Forte, script by Jerry Siegel. From *Adventure Comics* 304, January 1963.

race on another planet that a Legionnaire will die using his powers against Zaryan. She schemes to rob her fellow Legionnaires of their special powers so that she will be the one to fulfill the prophecy, but Lightning Lad learns of her plan and sacrifices himself in her stead. In "The Return of Lightning Lad" (Adv. 308, May 1963) we learn of Lightning Lad's sister, who possesses her brother's power to generate lightning bolts. She removes his body to a "lightning world," takes his place in the crypt in the Legion clubhouse, and pretends to revive in order to carry on her brother's work in secrecy. In the end, however, her plot is unmasked, but she is inducted into the Legion as Lightning Lass. And in "The Super Sacrifice of the Legionnaires" (Adv. 312, Sept. 1963) Mon-El, another Legionnaire, discovers that Lightning Lad can be resurrected if someone uses his body as a conductor through which a lightning bolt can transfer that person's life force into the dead Legionnaire's body. Mon-El had meant to sacrifice himself, but the other Legionnaires decide to let fate, in the form of a stray lightning bolt, determine who the victim will be. The victim turns out to be Proty, Chameleon Boy's shape-shifting pet; he had impersonated Saturn Girl when he caught her in the act of tampering with her steel wand, with which that Legionnairess meant to attract a bolt of lightning, in order to ensure that she would be the one to die in Lightning Lad's place.

Although the first forty issues featuring the Legion of Super-Heroes were not nearly up to the level of Weisinger's three primary titles, they nevertheless established the strip's potential, which, in 1966, was brought to full fruition by the new creative team of writer Jim Shooter and artist Curt Swan. Swan took over the art chores with issue 340 (Jan. 1966), and although Hamilton stayed on as writer for another half a year, a change for the better became immediately apparent. In making the Legionnaires look older, the thirtieth century more sleekly futuristic, and the menaces more believable, Swan greatly broadened the series' appeal from its former childish orientation. But when thirteen-year-old Jim Shooter delivered his first story for issue 346 (July 1966), the writing itself took on a new sophistication, and the series firmly ensconced itself in the Weisinger front line.

At first glance it seems paradoxical that a thirteen-year-old should write more "adult" material than a veteran of sixty-two years, twenty-five of them writing for comics. From its earliest appearances, however, the Legion had established itself as a cult favorite and, although not yet one of DC's best-selliing titles, it elicited a far greater fan involvement than most comic books. Fans participated in the elections for team leader, sent in suggestions for new Legionnaires, flooded the mail room with requests for more background information on the lives of individual members, and demanded more romance between their favorite heroes and heroines. These concerns no doubt seem childish to an adult, but to teenagers they comprise the very core of their lives; and what teenager never took himself seriously? It is not surprising then that a thirteen-year-old, sharing both the concerns of his peers and the attitude toward those concerns, might be better equipped to write a comic strip that revolved around teenagers. What is surprising, however, is the superb craft that Jim Shooter utilized in his scripts.

"In the summer when I was thirteen," Shooter recalled, "I was reading *Adventure Comics* and it occurred to me that somebody got paid for writing this. . . . I thought, 'I can write better than this.' And so I did." He sent in a complete comic book, fully scripted and illustrated. Weisinger, at the time, knew that Hamilton was about to retire from comic book work and needed a replacement. He had already initiated the policy, new at DC, "of combing the slush pile to discover new talent"; shortly before, he had hired a grown-up fan named E. Nelson Bridwell as his assistant editor. Shooter's story was surprisingly good, plotted with the dexterity of a veteran, and the timing was right. He became the next fan to break into professional writing.

Furthermore, Shooter's unique perspective came from an appreciation of the Marvel style of characterization, to which Mort had paid no attention (for all the emotionality of his comics, his heroes had never displayed any flaws or been distinguishable from one another in personality). Shooter's stories were the first effective merger of the Marvel and DC styles.

Among Shooter's earliest contributions to the growing score of the series were four new Legionnaires: Princess Projecta, mistress of illusions; Ferro Lad, a mutant with the power to turn his body to iron; Shadow Lass, who could cast stygian shadows; and Karate Kid, a martial arts expert whose impetuous nature, additionally, marked the first appearance of a distinct personality in the Legion. Shooter also brought true tragedy into the strip when Ferro Lad, in "The Doomed Legionnaire" (Adv. 353, Feb. 1967), gave his life to save the galaxy from a huge cloud that devoured suns (unlike Lightning Lad, he has not been resurrected). And in creating the Fatal Five—a band of powerful villains consisting of the Persuader, whose atomic axe can slice through anything, including energy; Tharok, the half-human, half-robot leader of the group; the Emerald Empress, who commands the Emerald Eye of Ekron, an orb of nearly unlimited power; Mano, who, with one touch of the glowing disc in his right hand, can annihilate anything; and Validus, a mindless giant of incalculable strength who is controlled by Tharok—Shooter provided the Legion with truly evil opponents of such formidable power that their frequent clashes have provided some of the best Legion stories of the past seventeen years.

Despite these innovations, however, the strip did not live up to Weisinger's standards of success. Shortly after losing Swan in the late sixties, the Legion was reduced to a backup feature in *Action Comics*. Perhaps due to the shortened length of the stories, adventures featuring a good portion of the team were downplayed in favor of tales spotlighting individual members. Shooter, too, soon left, as he found the strain of leading a normal adolescence while trying to make a living as a writer too much, and the strip's popularity waned so severely that it was ousted even from its backup status. But the Legion was not dead. It would soon return, with the aid of a dedicated body of fans, to become one of the brightest lights of the next decade.

While upheaval rocked the comic book field during the 1960s, Mort Weisinger held steady, until his retirement in 1970, to the course he had plotted at the beginning of the Silver Age, keeping his comics solid and popular for over a decade. Rarely making a play for the adolescent fans who supported Spider-Man or the Metal Men, often accused by such fans of being stagnant and repetitive, he achieved success on his own terms by sparking the imaginations and touching the emotions of youngsters. His work remains unusual and unmistakable in the field of comics, and provides a yet-untapped well of invention, richness, and lore.

The Marvel Age
of Comics

With the success of the Fantastic Four, Stan Lee kicked his comics line into full gear in 1962. Launching eleven new series in the next two and a half years, he might at first have appeared to be cranking them out just to fill pages or capitalize on the growing market for costumed heroes; but Lee had a very clear idea of the type of innovative hero he wanted to create, and nearly all of his new strips fit the bill. It was only in the beginning that his work seemed aimless, for his radical ideas were as yet very general, and it took him some months to hit upon the specific elements that would make each series purposeful and consistent.

The Hulk had displayed many uncertainties from the beginning, with sudden changes in the character's psyche and his relationships with both Rick Jones and his own powers. Lee and Kirby's third title (released the same month as Spider-Man), would quickly fall victim to the same problem.

This was the Mighty Thor, and he was a strange combination of elements. When lame physician Don Blake finds a mysterious stone hammer, he is transformed bodily into the Norse god of thunder, complete with massive muscles, long golden locks, a winged Viking helmet, and a period costume. He discovers that he can fly by hurling the hammer with all his great might and letting it pull him through the air by the wrist-strap; soon it emerges that the hammer also lets him control the weather and gives him contact with Almighty Odin, father of the gods. With a tap of the hammer, Thor can transform himself back into puny Don Blake, the hammer itself becoming a humble cane; when Thor and his weapon are parted for more than a minute, the transformation occurs unwillingly.

The notion of a Norse god as a comic book hero was certainly an original one, but its creators seemed to have trouble deciding what to do with it. In his first adventure, Thor battled the Stone-Men from Saturn (*Journey Into Mystery* 83, Aug. 1962) in a rather standard Lee-Kirby plot, and in the second he thwarted a communist dictator in the republic of San Diablo (JIM 84, Sept. 1962). Next Thor met Loki, the legendary trickster among the gods, which promised a more appropriate mythological tone to the series and gave it its best story to date (JIM 85, Oct. 1962). But only two issues later we find a story called "Prisoner of the Reds," in which the elemental deity tumbles back into the humdrum routine of early Marvel plots (JIM 87, Dec. 1962). Although occasionally battling Loki and a futuristic thief called the Tomorrow Man (who hearkened back to Kirby's old *Challengers* work), Thor generally stumbled through highly inappropriate adventures for his first year and a half.

Lee himself appeared to lose interest in the project, throwing the writing chores to his brother and jack-of-all-trades, Larry Lieber; Lieber occasionally took on the penciling chores as well, for Kirby did not seem much more committed to the project than Lee did. The result was a haphazard and directionless comic, but with the good fortune falling on Marvel during those hero-hungry years, it sold well enough to survive. Until Lee and Kirby buckled down in early 1964 to see what they could really do with a hero who was also a god, Thor would have to be content with mere survival.

Taking his cue from Thor, who had first appeared in a failing monster comic called *Journey into Mystery,* Lee created two more series in quick succession: *Ant-Man,* to salvage *Tales to Astonish* (TA 35, Sept. 1962) and *The Human Torch,* in solo adventures, for *Strange Tales* (ST 101, Oct. 1962). These titles were the only two to fall below Lee's own standards for originality. The price they paid for this hasty production was a lack of direction and artistic commitment. Ant-Man, a scientist who shrinks himself and uses insects to fight crime, was apparently doubly inspired by an earlier science fiction comic and by DC's Atom; it was an intriguing combination of elements, but Lee put no effort into the project, giving the writing almost immediately to his brother. Kirby stayed for only six issues before Marvel staffer Don Heck began hasty fill-in work. A flirtatious female sidekick called the Wasp didn't help much (TA 44, Jun. 1963), nor did the conversion of the hero into the very different Giant-Man (TA 49, Nov. 1963); at any size, this was the least of Marvel's successes.

The Human Torch (joined by the Thing with ST 125, Oct. 1964) received even less attention from its creator; Leiber wrote it and Dick Ayers, who was most prominent as an inker, drew it from the beginning. The stories consisted of colorless battles with such one-dimensional foes as Plant-Man, the Beetle, and Paste-Pot Pete. The series survived only on the strength of the Fantastic Four's success.

By 1963 Lee had finally found the formula to ensure that all his heroes possessed the originality he sought. The key to the formula lay in the idea of a flawed hero. Two of his earlier co-creations, the Thing and the Hulk, were monstrously disfigured; now Lee and his collaborators moved on to develop heroes who were more subtly impaired, either by common handicaps or spiritual unease.

This served a twofold purpose: first, it set Marvel comics thoroughly apart from those of the competition, populated as they were by flawless heroes; and second, it opened the doors to melodrama, which Marvel's fans valued as highly as adventure. From the latter there also emerged a

A collection of early Marvel heroes: Iron Man, perennial sidekick Rick Jones, the Hulk, Captain America, Giant-Man, the Wasp, and Thor. Pencils by Kirby, inks by Paul Reinman, script by Lee. From *The Avengers 5*, May 1964.

body of ongoing soap operas that led to the growth of a "Marvel universe," an almost organic entity in which the overall unity of the line took precedence over any single series.

This was most pronounced in two heroes Lee created apart from Kirby and Ditko, both featuring physical handicaps. The first of these was Iron Man, who took over the one monster title left vacant by Thor, Ant-Man, and the Human Torch (*Tales of Suspense* 39, Mar. 1963). His alter ego, Tony Stark, is a wealthy inventor and munitions maker, living the life of a blithe playboy until he takes a fateful trip to Vietnam. While accompanying a battalion to see his deadly inventions in action, he steps on a land mine and is captured by the Reds. Even though a piece of shrapnel lodged in his heart gives him only days to live, the fiendish communists demand that he devise weapons for them. Stark fools them, however, constructing a suit of electronic armor—not, as he tells his captors, for their soldiers, but for himself—which both keeps his injured heart beating and gives him tremendous strength and such powers as flight. He escapes the Reds, reborn as a costumed hero, "but," as he tells us, "in order to remain alive, I must spend the rest of my life in this iron prison!"

Like the Thing, the Hulk, and Spider-Man before him, Iron Man was thus another hero both blessed and cursed by his powers. Lee found a new twist on the theme with this new hero, who was actually physically far weaker and more vulnerable than a normal man, and who became a hero only through the use of a device. As happened with Peter Parker, Tony Stark's special status raised a wall between him and human society, for although he found he did not need his full armor to survive, he would always have to wear his massive chestplate under his clothing; if nothing else, this would preclude any intimacy with women for the former playboy.

Lee strove for a tone of hard-bitten realism with Iron Man, having Stark occasionally afflicted by dangerous heart troubles while reacting to his new isolation with anger and snappishness at the people around him—particularly his two loyal employees, Happy Hogan (a sad-faced ex-boxer whom Stark uses as a chauffeur) and Pepper Potts (the cute but unglamorous secretary in love with her boss). He also strove to place Iron Man in the political realities of his day, beginning his tale not in some imaginary war-torn country but in Vietnam, and pitting him against a long series of communist opponents: the Red Barbarian (TS 42, June 1963); the Crimson Dynamo (TS 46, Oct. 1963); the Mandarin, a sort of Red Chinese Fu-Man-chu (TS 50, Feb. 1964); the Scarecrow, who sells stolen Stark weapons to Cuba (TS 51, Mar. 1964); a Russian seductress called the Black Widow (TS 57, Sept. 1964); and still others.

The mere fact that Iron Man had an emotional and political focus made him more interesting than Ant-Man, the Torch, and the early Thor, and the fact that Lee consistently wrote the strip himself suggests that those dramatic and social themes were what really mattered to him. Unfortunately, he had difficulty keeping his emotional scenes from breaking down into predictable melodrama and his communists from being swallowed up by the clichés of propaganda. Furthermore, his artistic partner, Don Heck, was ill-suited to the task of creating costumed-hero adventures. He was a fairly naturalistic, static penciler with a scratchy style of inking who had done good work for Lee on western and war stories during the 1950s. The small size of the Marvel "bullpen," however, pressed him into costumed-hero work in 1963, where his subdued action and messy panels were highly inappropriate. Heck's original conception of Iron Man's armor was a monstrous, bulky affair that seemed to be bolted together from stovepipes; although he streamlined him shortly (TS 48, Dec. 1963), he was never completely able to keep him from looking awkward in action. He also lacked Kirby's background as a writer-artist and Ditko's natural flair for plotting, with the result that Iron Man's adventures never had the compelling quality of Spider-Man's or the punch of the FF's.

Nonetheless, the theme of a hero having to overcome a physical handicap struck a chord with Lee and he promptly repeated the idea with a blind, costumed acrobat named Daredevil (who, due to delays in production, would not appear on the stands until the next year). His remaining senses miraculously heightened by radioactivity, blind lawyer Matt Murdock finds himself able to locate objects and identify people by touch and hearing. Training himself Batman-style in combat and acrobatics, he dons a flamboyant costume and takes to the rooftops to combat crime (*Daredevil* 1, May 1964). In his gymnastic fighting style and freewheeling attitude, Daredevil captured much of the spirit of Spider-Man, and even his foes—the likes of the Owl, Stilt-Man, and the Fellowship of Fear—were reminiscent of such Lee-Ditko gimmick villains as the Vulture, Doctor

Octopus, and the Enforcers. The series was graced by lively art, first by Golden Age master Bill Everett, then free-lancer Joe Orlando, and for nine issues by Wally Wood, the elegant artist who had, as an inker on *Challengers*, given polish and restraint to Kirby's work. With his compact figures posed like graceful statues, his quiet work provided a refreshing balance to the usual rambunctiousness of early Marvels. When Wood left (after DD 11, Dec. 1965) to work for a new comics company called Tower, he was replaced by John Romita, a competent artist whose lack of style took away Daredevil's flair.

The derivative qualities of Daredevil soon began to work against him. A pseudo-vision called "radar sense," dimly reminiscent of Spider-Man's spider-sense, was added to his abilities and threatened to undermine the fascinating innovation of his blindness. In his private life, the similarities to Iron Man—with Foggy Nelson, Murdock's sad-faced partner, and Karen Page, the secretary who loves her employer in silence—were too great. Murdock's blindness, no longer much of a problem for the radar-bearing Daredevil, became mainly a vehicle for agony, self-pity, and star-crossed love. "Farewell, Matt . . . my darling!" Karen thinks during one parting. "If only you could have *seen* me . . . seen the *lovelight* in my eyes!" While Matt thinks, "For a time I almost dared to hope . . . that Karen might feel about me as I felt about her! Yet the emotion I mistook for love was merely pity . . . pity for a man without sight!" (DD 12, Jan. 1966).

Lee did not limit his new crop of innovations to work with minor Marvel artists. His next two offbeat heroes were created with Steve Ditko and Jack Kirby, respectively, and although not physically disabled, each suffered from some kind of alienation from society. (Another creation with Kirby, an entire team of alienated heroes, must be treated later.)

The most impressive new Marvel hero of 1963 was Dr. Strange, for his particular brand of alienation was able to partake of the darkness and eeriness that co-creator Steve Ditko had mastered in his horror and science fiction work. Stephen Strange is introduced in the origin as the world's foremost surgeon, yet also the most arrogant and greedy of men. But Strange is involved in an automobile accident, and when he discovers that, due to nerve damage, he will never be able to operate again, his world falls apart at the seams. He degenerates to a hobo drifter, until one day he overhears two sailors talking about the Ancient One, a sorcerer reputed to possess the power to cure anything. Strange finds his way to the Ancient One's stronghold in the mountains of India. At first the Ancient One refuses to help him because he senses in Strange selfish motives. But later, when Strange discovers that the Ancient One's pupil, Baron Mordo, is secretly planning to overthrow his master, he is filled with concern for the old sage. Sensing this, and pleased to have reached the good side of Stephen Strange, the Ancient One at last makes the former surgeon his disciple in the mystic arts (ST 115, Dec. 1963). Although the new sorcerous hero returns to America and takes up residence in a mysterious old house in Greenwich Village, the eldritch forces with which he tampers and the mystical nature of his studies leave him alienated from his fellow man. Thus, though neither handicapped, monstrous, nor socially antipathetic, he was more completely removed from society than any hero before him.

Realizing that this creation was odd even for Marvel, Lee launched it tentatively as an intermittent backup strip in *Strange Tales* (ST 110, 111, 114; Jul., Aug., Nov. 1963). But the master mage soon drew an esoteric, loyal fandom who won him a regular berth there, behind the Human Torch. They saw immediately that Dr. Strange was different from anything that had come before, but not because of the emotionality or realism that had set Lee's earlier series apart. Strange's powers and fundamental alienation took him, from the start, into weird dimensions far removed from the concerns of men, including the realm of sleep, where he battled the evil personification of Nightmare (ST 111, 116; Aug. 1963, Jan. 1964). In

Dr. Strange confronts Eternity and passes through a Ditko netherworld. Script by Lee. From *Strange Tales* 138, November 1965.

those stories it was Ditko's fantastic landscapes that stole the show—if landscapes they can be called, for his other worlds were vast, open spaces with no up or down, no horizon or vanishing point, only floating pathways linking one aerial island to another, impeded by doorways set in space, disembodied snake-jaws waiting to snap down on the unwary traveler, and legions of mindless, horrid creatures hearkening to the commands of dark lords. Battles were never fought with fists and feet in those worlds, but with incantations ("In the name of the dread Dormammu . . . in the name of the all-seeing Agamotto . . ."), with plasmic blasts of mystic force, with undulating bonds and webs of magic, and often with such tricks of the trade as hypnotism and astral projection. The effect of these brief, tightly plotted stories was an eeriness that bordered on the hallucinatory, one of the very few cases of a comic book that succeeded in being genuinely disturbing.

The repetition of these short mystic voyages might have become tedious, but with *Strange Tales* 126 (Nov. 1964) Lee and Ditko began applying some of the continuity they had mastered with *Spider-Man*. The Ancient One has learned that Dormammu, the most powerful of the mystic lords from whom Strange draws his power, is planning to invade the world of men. Strange enters Dormammu's bizarre universe and confronts his new foe, a manlike creature with a head of fire who surveys all his realm from a throne suspended in space. After fighting him to a stalemate, Strange finds his powers increased and the world of men seemingly safe (ST 127, Dec. 1964). But soon Dormammu enlists Strange's old foe, Baron Mordo, to capture and immobilize their mutual enemy, and Strange must flee Mordo's ectoplasmic servants through all the exotic corners of the earth (ST 130–133, Mar.–June 1965). When Strange again enters Dormammu's dark realm, he is saved from a trap by the rebellious sorceress Clea, who is to become his acolyte and paramour (ST 134, July 1965). Strange's search for the key to containing the ever-more-powerful Dormammu leads him at last on a search for Eternity, the embodiment of all life and matter in the universe; Eternity, however, in classic mythical form, will only say, "You already possess the means to defeat your foes! Power is not the only answer! Events have occurred which require a key . . . and wisdom is that key!" (ST 138, Nov. 1965). In "The End at Last," Strange uses his growing wisdom to play upon Dormammu's arrogance, until the lord of the dark dimension assaults Eternity himself, a fight no one can win (ST 146, July 1966). With this twenty-one-issue story, its scope steadily broadening to include more and more levels of the universe, Marvel began composing the "cosmic picture" that would distinguish it during the rest of the 1960s.

Lee's next experiment with an alienated hero went in a completely opposite direction. The successes of the revived Human Torch and Sub-Mariner made inevitable the return of Timely Comics' third Golden Age star, Captain America, particularly since Jack Kirby, his co-creator, was a driving force at Marvel. But the transference of old powers to a new character, as with the Torch, seemed inappropriate for a war-era hero like Cap, while allowing him to age twenty years would have left him (unlike the non-human Sub-Mariner) decrepit. The problem was avoided when the new costumed-hero team called the Avengers found Cap frozen in an Arctic ice-block, preserved as a young man since a plunge into an icy sea at the end of World War II. Though still filled with fighting spirit, Cap is a man reborn into a strange era; and still more upsetting for him, he awakes to find his beloved sidekick, Bucky Barnes, long dead, having perished in the same incident that left his mentor frozen. "What happens next?" he ponders. "Can't return to my career as Captain America—it would be meaningless without Bucky! I don't belong in this age—in this year—no place for me—if only Bucky were here—if only . . ." Cap, however, briefly finds a surrogate Bucky in the Hulk's young friend, Rick Jones, and, inspired by their heroic example, proudly joins Iron Man, Giant-Man, and Thor in the Avengers (Av. 4, Mar. 1964).

His popularity in that group soon won him a series of his own, backing up Iron Man in *Tales of Suspense,* which would be consistently written by Lee and drawn by Kirby. Although Lee tried to remind us occasionally of the poignancy of Cap's displacement and his almost morbid sorrow over Bucky's death, it was Kirby who dominated the series with his action-filled art. In Cap's first solo adventure we find him attacked by a gang of thugs armed with automatic pistols and an Iron Man–like suit of armor; Kirby treats us to seven pages (of a ten-page story) of flying bullets, hurtling bodies, judo-throws, crunching fists, bulging muscles, and collapsing furniture, free of the encumbrance of plot or captions, executed with the exuberant abandon of a saloon brawl in a big-screen western (TS 59, Nov. 1964). Captain America, an acrobat who fights crime with sinews, muscles, and an indestructible shield that can be thrown like a giant discus, was a perfect vehicle for the wild pugilism that Kirby did better than anyone. During this period Kirby began to leave behind the muddiness that had marred his earlier Marvel work and move into a clean, high-velocity storytelling style that would make him the most popular artist of the 1960s.

The format continued for three more issues, in which Cap fought a gang of acrobatic Nazi assassins, a communist sumo wrestler in Vietnam, and a whole cell block full of convicts. But with the retelling of Cap's Golden Age origin (TS 63, Mar. 1965) all need for characterization, reminders of alienation, and mourning over Bucky's death were abandoned, for it and the next nine issues featured adventures set during World War II, in which Cap and Bucky gaily turned back the tide of fascism. When Cap did return to the present (TS 71, Nov. 1965), it was to enter a later phase of Lee-Kirby work.

Thus, where Dr. Strange's separation from society was obscured by the otherworldly placement of his adventures, Captain America's was circumvented by action-packed nostalgia; evidently, with Ditko and Kirby,

Lee would have little opportunity for the pathos that dominated *Iron Man* and *Daredevil,* series drawn by artists with less forceful visions of their own.

Captain America also illustrates the different approaches to Golden Age revivals employed by Marvel and DC. Where DC put their old heroes on a separate earth, Marvel made them a part of the same historical continuum as its current heroes, thus further unifying their "universe."

The next two series that Lee launched represented a third avenue for his oddball heroes to follow. This was the role of the antihero, a character unaware of his heroic role, not caring much for human society, but none-theless sympathetic to the reader. Lee had introduced his quintessential antiheroes—the Hulk, in his own ill-fated title, and the Sub-Mariner, as a villain in the FF—at the dawn of the self-proclaimed "Marvel Age." At the time, apparently, readers were not prepared to take such characters to their hearts, but as they fell gradually in step with Lee's innovations, their opinions changed. The Hulk made frequent guest appearances in 1963 and 1964, always battling the hero but usually protesting that he only wanted to be left alone; these stories were always followed by surprising outpourings of "bring back the Hulk" letters. When Lee and Kirby launched a comic combining Marvel's heroes into a team (discussed in Chapter 14) the Hulk was pressed into service as a very reluctant hero, and fans seemed to like him in that role (Av. 1, Oct. 1963). At the same time, in the first giant-sized annual of *The Fantastic Four,* the Sub-Mariner at last found his lost race of Atlanteans, relieving him of his main source of rage at the surface world and enabling him to don the noble robe of Prince Namor of Atlantis (FF An. 1, 1963). When he reencountered the FF after the reunion, it was as an arrogant but admirable ally (FF 33, Dec. 1964).

Of the two, the Hulk seemed to provoke a greater response from the fans. Perhaps the lumbering beast who only wanted society to go away and leave him alone said more to the adolescent psyche than did the proud ruler of a wronged people. Thus it was that when Lee decided Giant-Man could no longer carry *Tales to Astonish* alone, he added the Hulk as a second feature (TA 60, Oct. 1964).

The first eight issues came as quite a surprise; the Hulk, the seeming epitome of big-muscle Jack Kirby characters, was to be drawn by Steve Ditko. And it read like a Lee-Ditko series, with a vivid cast of characters interwoven into a complex soap opera and an ongoing plot overshad-owed by the evil of the mysterious Leader, bringing to mind the Green Goblin and Dormammu. Building upon the continuity techniques of other Ditko strips, *The Hulk* broke new ground as the first hero series in which the stories never ended, but rather ran from cliff-hanger to cliff-hanger in a continuous narrative—an effective device for making a long saga out of half-length stories.

With Ditko's departure and Kirby's return to the character (TA 68, June 1965), the series took a dramatic turn. The Hulk's huge fists and mammoth strength were turned to good effect as explosive action squeezed out personal insights and stripped down the soap opera. Where Lee and Ditko had had the Hulk traveling around the world in his tangles with the Leader, Lee and Kirby sent him to the moon, a distant solar system, the far future, and the earth's core. Where Lee and Ditko's Leader plots had revolved around spies and intrigue, Lee and Kirby's resolution involved a quest for an orb of cosmic knowledge (TA 73, Nov. 1965), another sign of the expanding scope that was becoming Marvel's new fascination.

Through it all, the Hulk's personality continued to teeter wildly. At first reminiscent of Mr. Hyde, he was destructive and antisocial but reasonably eloquent. But soon he became a dumb tough guy ("I'll show 'em!" he cries in TA 65, Mar. 1965) and then a subhuman brute, with such dialogue as, "Dead! Saved my life! Died for Hulk! Was friend! Died for Hulk!" (TA 66, Apr. 1965). For a time, with a thin explanation, he regained the mind of Bruce Banner, but gradually it degenerated. It was during this decay that Lee at last began to find the note of angry, injured alienation toward which he had seemingly been groping all along. "Nuts!" says the half-brute when the Leader proposes that they join forces to rule the earth. "I don't want any part of this crummy world! You can have it!" (TA 72, Oct. 1965).

As his thinking became more brutish, the Hulk's failure to understand why mankind persisted in hounding and attacking him became more poignant. This was truest after Rick Jones, believing his monstrous friend dead, finally told the world that Banner and the Hulk were one and the same (TA 77, Mar. 1966); thereafter Banner could have no peace either as human or as monster. When, with the following issue, Bill Everett began penciling and inking over Kirby's basic layouts, the Hulk truly hit his stride (TA 78, Apr. 1966). Everett's exaggerated, cartoonish style emphasized the power and brutality of the character, but the subtleties of his lush inks were able to bring out an undertone of sadness. When the Hulk huddles in misery under a desert sky, moaning, "No place to go! No one to turn to! The world hates the Hulk! ... Why? Why does it never end—?!!" our hearts truly go out to the big brute (TA 80, June 1966). Even though Kirby and Everett left the series after three more issues, this combination of puppy-dog misery with destructive force at last became a consistent characterization that was to last for the next decade and a half.

The Sub-Mariner was a completely different case, an antihero in mankind's eyes who became a real hero by being removed from mankind. In his guest appearances in other Marvel comics, he usually served as an antagonist, but one whose motives could be justified by his loyalty to his own people; but when he squeezed Giant-Man into oblivion to begin his own series alongside the Hulk, his adventures turned solely on his underwater deeds as prince of Atlantis (TA 70, Aug. 1965). Storming about the palace, wooing his blue-skinned but beautiful Lady Dorma, crying out "Imperius Rex!" he was the model of an arrogant but devoted ruler, usually pitted against the Warlord Krang for control of the throne. Only when he occasionally surfaced to battle other Marvel characters did he slip into his old ambivalent role. Although thus remote from Lee's earlier themes of discontent and isolation, the Sub-Mariner gave us plenty of highfalutin gladiator-style adventure, with the added attractions of undersea perils and a hero whose jet-speed swimming approximated flight. Best of all, the series features the art of Gene Colan, newly arrived at Marvel after leaving a line of horror comics published by Warren. His deep shadows and heavy use of blacks, combined with fluid figures and highly naturalistic characterizations, gave his undersea scenes a moodiness, a mystery, and an odd believability that never let the reader forget he was in a strange, exotic land.

By the middle of 1965, Lee had laid the foundations of a unique costumed-hero stable. Although still marred by rough, inconsistent writing, frequently hurried art, and low-quality production, his comics succeeded on the strength of their daring, characterization, running continuity, and emotional power. Revivals and improvements of Golden Age heroes no longer held the day; careful, conservative craftsmanship was no longer enough. "Mighty Marvel," in Lee's own later estimation, had become "a lusty gutsy irreverent mischief-maker in the wondrous world of comix," and despite all his company's flaws, he was succeeding in the marketplace and in the opinions of critical fans. Now he could carry out a further project—the unification of the Marvel universe—a project which pleased the fans so much that it would comprise the next movement in the company's history.

13 The World's Strangest Heroes

With the *Metal Men*, DC proved itself ready at last to create some innovative heroes of its own. Yet Robert Kanigher would produce no more of those heroes, nor would Schwartz or Weisinger, whose comics had attained such a steady level of success that no experimentation seemed called for. Rather, the new characters would emerge from the stable that had suffered worst over the preceding few years, where innovation was most welcome to revitalize its slumping products.

The team system that had been producing the comics of Jack Schiff's stable since the 1940s came to an end in the early 1960s. "On a small scale, the cooperative aspect was good in many ways," Schiff remembers, "but on the large scale that emerged, it became unwieldy." He wanted to return to overseeing a few titles from start to completion of each issue, including plotting the stories himself. Thus, by 1963, Schiff had turned *Challengers of the Unknown, My Greatest Adventure, Tomahawk*, and *House of Secrets* over to his art director, Murray Boltinoff (although the last title was shortly returned to Schiff), and *Aquaman, Blackhawk*, and *Rip Hunter* over to his former story editor, George Kashdan, thereby leaving himself with a manageable load of five comics. Nineteen sixty-four saw a more drastic redistribution of assignments; the three titles featuring Batman were not selling as well as the front office thought they should, and so they were shifted to Schwartz and Weisinger, editors who had recently had more luck with heroes. Weisinger took *World's Finest*, fitting it into his Superman mythos; Schwartz assumed control of *Batman* and *Detective*, causing him to give his science fiction titles, *Mystery in Space* and *Strange Adventures*, to Schiff. (Schiff's involvement with the Caped Crusader would continue, however, in his assisting the makers of the "Batman" TV show in 1966.) This left Schiff with a group of comics devoted entirely, and appropriately, to science fiction and supernatural adventure. It was then that his own style reasserted itself. In his non-series stories, the humanization trend that Marvel had sparked enabled him to shift away from monsters and fantastic happenings, back to characterization. Many were moral tales of the sort in which Lee and Ditko also specialized, in which the protagonist is a scientist, criminal, or plutocrat possessed by greed or fear, whose own weaknesses destroy him as he grabs for control of time, space, or the forces of other worlds. Others, such as "Missing: One Alien," featuring the monstrous but comical buddies L'on and Vaar, were lighthearted romps in which the bizarre aliens became appealing, distinctive characters (TU 84, Sept. 1964). Such supernatural-hero series as *Mark Merlin* and *The Enchantress* meanwhile rose to a prominence denied them by the monster craze. Although a far cry from the beautiful work of the Schwartz stable, Schiff's science fiction and supernatural comics nonetheless showed the stirrings of revitalization.

Adam Strange changed radically in the move from Schwartz to Schiff, with Lee Elias replacing Carmine Infantino and the plots departing from their ingenious scientific bent, but his adventures continued to be fairly sprightly and entertaining until his cancellation in *Mystery in Space* 102 (Sept. 1965). He was backed up in that title by *Space Ranger,* now drawn in a fanciful, small-figured style, reminiscent of Dick Sprang in its detail and charm, by Golden Age veteran Howard Purcell. The Martian Manhunter, meanwhile, continued unperturbed in *House of Mystery* until issue 159 (June 1966), when he abruptly discarded his pet, Zook, and his fantastical nature to become a lone secret agent in an unending battle with the faceless leader of a criminal conspiracy; the stories were refreshing at first, but soon suffered from repetition. The only other old series to continue under Schiff was *Star Hawkins,* which ran intermittently in *Strange Adventures;* its stories were not much more inspired than they had been under Schwartz, but now the art included some of Gil Kane's finest work. Overall, these four survivors ran largely on momentum. The great strength of the Schiff, Kashdan, and Boltinoff stables would be the panoply of new heroes waiting just around the corner.

Kashdan was less successful than Schiff at keeping his comics entertaining and attractive. For one thing, he seemed unable to shake off the effects of the monster craze that had held sway in the first years of the decade. *Blackhawk* continued its decline, while Rip Hunter's adventures were more and more dominated by weird creatures. It became Kashdan's lot to pick up ailing minor series from other editors, with Kanigher's *Sea Devils* in 1964 and Schwartz's *Hawkman* in 1967. Both were damaged in transit. The first lost the technical accuracy with which Kanigher had imbued it and devolved to undersea monster hunts, while in the second, a tired Dick Dillin and Chuck Cuidera replaced Murphy Anderson, and in most issues, battles with aliens and strange creatures replaced interesting earthbound mysteries. From Kanigher and Schwartz, Kashdan also received *The Brave and the Bold,* which he transformed into a showcase for regular costumed-hero team-ups (BB 50, Nov. 1963). The stories brought together such unlikely pairings as Green Arrow and the Martian Manhunter, the Metal Men and the Atom, and Batman and Aquaman. The quality was rarely high, but the idea was fun for kids and the tales were entertainingly written by Bob Haney. And one of the team-ups was to result in a popular new hero group.

Kashdan's greatest success with a series he inherited came with *Aqua-*

man. With the colorful and naturalistic art of Nick Cardy gracefully illustrating the brisk, light scripts, the series was granted a lively, if simple, charm. Aquaman's Atlantis grew during Kashdan's years, beginning with the introduction of Mera, the Sea King's other-dimensional love; their marriage in issue 18 (Oct. 1964) was the first prominent one in the realm of costumed heroes. Soon came their son, Aquababy; Aqualad's girlfriend, Tula (more often "Aquagirl"); and many scientists, leaders, and citizens of Atlantis. The hero's menaces were varied, his adventures usually set in the colorful underwater world but occasionally reaching to the surface, and the series' continuity was greater than most in that extended editorial stable.

Murray Boltinoff meanwhile continued his own inherited series, *Challengers*, at a fairly static level. But it was from his desk that the first of the new breed of heroes came.

They were called "The World's Strangest Heroes" on the cover, and they did their best to live up to the claim. Movie star Rita Farr, test pilot Larry Trainor, and adventurer Cliff Steele were all survivors of horrible accidents; but in surviving, each of them had been weirdly transformed, turned into freaks in the eyes of men. Rita, lost in an African jungle, inhaled vapors that caused her to grow uncontrollably to monstrous size. Strange waves high in the atmosphere created inside Larry Trainor a "strange duplicate," a being of negative energy; when "Negative Man" emerges from its host body, Larry falls to the edge of unconsciousness, and if it does not return in sixty seconds, Larry will die. When Cliff was mangled in a high-speed auto crash, the only way to keep his brain alive was to install it in an experimental metal body, turning him into an expressionless, mechanical "Robot Man."

Outcasts from mankind, embittered by their fates, these three draw deep into self-exile until gathered together by a mysterious, wheelchair-bound genius whom they call the Chief. He trains them to use their freakish natures for the good of mankind, teaching Rita to grow and shrink at will as Elasti-Girl, Larry to make Negative Man a powerful servant, and Robot Man to turn his own body into a powerful, durable weapon. When a mysterious deathless oligarch of crime named General Immortus plots to steal atomic fuel for his own evil aims, the fledgling heroes turn the tables on him through teamwork and self-sacrifice. The press plays up their feat, writing, "Three exiles from the human race battled to save a world that had rejected them," and christening them "The Doom Patrol." "Life isn't over for us!" Rita decides. "It's just beginning!" (*My Greatest Adventure* 80, June 1963).

The Doom Patrol, with its heroes cut off from society and doubting the worth of their own powers, was the first DC comic to incorporate some of the ideas being pioneered by Marvel. It also brought an air of darkness and mystery into the usually sunny world of DC heroes, and continued the swing toward bizarre characters begun by the Metal Men. Boltinoff

Negative Man vs. General Immortus (*left*) and Robot Man and Elasti-Girl (*right*). Art by Bruno Premiani, script by Arnold Drake and Bob Haney. From *My Greatest Adventure* 80, June 1963.

---

displaying an eye for unusual art, assigned Bruno Premiani, an Italian newspaper cartoonist who taught at Argentina's National School of Fine Arts, to draw the strip; using a careful, almost classical approach, Premiani prevented the DP's oddity from turning into comicality of the Metal Men sort. His use of deep shadow and expressive faces accented the mystery and dramatic power of the idea. Writer Arnold Drake kept the torment of his characters always in mind. "When they write about our 'daring exploits,'" says Larry Trainor about the press, "what do they call us? ... [They] never use our human names! We're still just *freaks* to them!" To which Cliff replies, "That's all we'll ever be—misfits—so get used to it!" (MGA 81, Aug. 1963).

The early adventures of the Doom Patrol were among DC's most intriguing creations. The first few stories involved induced hallucinations, the mystery of the Chief's past, and a berserk Negative Man. Robot Man was graphically melted and smashed; in one story he even tore himself apart in order to use his own arms and legs as weapons (DP 87, May 1964).

Apart from General Immortus, their principal villains were the Brotherhood of Evil, a freakish bunch consisting of a disembodied brain, an intelligent, murderous gorilla, and a woman with puttylike flesh who could mold her face into any visage (DP 86, Mar. 1964).

At last the bizarre and outlandish elements that had run through the comics of Schiff and his associates could be put to good effect; where in the past they had only served as hokey menaces for mundane heroes, they now served as the focal point in the creation of the heroes themselves. The new heroes, in fact, were so very outlandish that the nature of their powers required a whole new approach to costumed-hero adventures.

Combining this new bizarre hero style with the Marvel approach to ambivalent characterization, the stable quickly produced its second successful innovation with Eclipso, "Hero and Villain in One Man." Although created by writer Haney and editor Boltinoff, with the vigorous art of Lee Elias (House of Secrets 61, Aug. 1963), *Eclipso* reached its peak when Schiff himself took over soon after, bringing artist Jack Sparling with him.

Eclipso was like a Mr. Hyde to scientist Bruce Gordon's Dr. Jekyll. When Gordon goes to a primitive island to photograph a solar eclipse, a witch doctor slashes him with a mysterious black diamond. Some time later, back in civilization, when the sun is again eclipsed, Gordon is suddenly transformed into a diabolical, half-blue villain. Gradually, as the series unfolds, it emerges that with every eclipse this creature, calling himself Eclipso, will either continue to take over Gordon's body or split from him as a separate evil entity (HS 63, Dec. 1963). After many experiments, Gordon discovers that only intense light can banish his evil side.

Eclipso soon learns that Gordon will probably be able to keep defeating him, but also knows that future eclipses will free him again; so he takes to stealing and hiding weapons that he can use in future incarnations to defeat his alter ego and continue his criminal rampages. His greatest weapon is the black diamond itself, which possesses amazing abilities of transmutation. Once, he goes so far as to use the diamond to create a couple of synthetic, loyal "Moon Creatures" who engineer an artificial eclipse to set their master free of Gordon's virtuous form (HS 77, Apr. 1966).

In keeping with the new breed of Schiff hero, Eclipso's peculiar nature made his adventures different from any others in comics. This was a series in which the only specially powered character was a villain and in which the hero, rather than fighting some new menace every issue, was concerned only with his own alter ego.

The stories were made strong by a mysterious flavor of intrigue and espionage as Gordon and Eclipso matched wits. Eclipso's schemes were often on a vast scale, bringing government forces and Secret Service men into play. They were not confined to one area, which caused the stories to move from one exotic locale to another. Aided in his battle with Eclipso by a fellow scientist and his daughter (who was also Gordon's fiancée), Gordon formed the center of a strong and likable cast of characters.

Rendering the stories was Jack Sparling, the best regular artist in Schiff's stable. Sparling's art was very scratchy and hasty looking, but imbued with a dynamism and an emotional current that electrified the pages. Sparling's figures, as well as his layouts in general, were constructed on a rounded line—fleshy, full-bodied people; lush, sloping backgrounds—along which the action rolled at breakneck speed.

In a burst of inspirations in 1965, Schiff and his writers created five more strange and colorful though short-lived new heroes. The most interesting was Immortal Man, gifted with the ability to die and return to life again and again, always remembering his last life but each time in a different body; with art by Jack Sparling and an odd undercurrent provided by Immortal Man's undying love for a normal woman, the series made sporadic but memorable appearances in *Strange Adventures*. The same title occasionally featured Animal Man, a hero capable of taking on the abilities of any animal that came near him, whose main attraction was some superb art by Carmine Infantino and Gil Kane. *Mystery in Space* starred Ultra, the Multi-Alien, a quadripartite crime-fighter—his right arm had extranormal strength, his left magnetic powers; his left leg could hurl lightning bolts, and his right enabled him to fly—with art by Lee Elias. Less interesting were Prince Ra-Man, a telepath who fought occultish menaces in *House of Secrets*, and Automan, an amiable robot similar to the Doom Patrol's mechanical member, whose tongue-in-cheek adventures popped up in *Tales of the Unexpected*.

More successful was *Dial H for Hero*, which Schiff and writer Dave Wood created as a wide-open forum to experiment with strange heroes. Oriented mainly toward younger readers, it was the most unrestrained of all the new series. Advertised on his first cover as "The Most Original Character in Comic History," Robby Reed is a teenager who stumbles across a strange device from another world, resembling a telephone dial. Whenever he dials the letters H-E-R-O he is transformed into a different hero, but never the same one twice and never with powers that Robby might expect; the constant challenge to Robby is to find a way to use his unexpected powers to cope with whatever crisis is at hand (HOM 156, Jan. 1966).

Nearly every Robby Reed story featured three new heroes in its fifteen pages, which made it a very busy and colorful series indeed. Radar-Sonar Man, Velocity Kid, Baron Buzz-Saw, Quakemaster—the heroes were as numerous as they were outlandish. When Robby did become only two heroes, it was usually because some criminal had swiped his alien device to "Dial V for Villain" (HOM 158, Apr. 1966), or because a nosy female classmate monkeyed with the dial to become a heroine (HOM 169, Sept. 1967). The stories had little to offer but action and color, but they were written with humor and verve, and epitomized the spirit of unrestrained invention that ran rampant in the comics' boom years. They also featured Jim Mooney's best artwork, full of energy, fun, and clever hero designs, displaying a much greater freedom of imagination than his *Supergirl* work.

Dial H proved to be Schiff's last creation for comics. He has said that all the shifting of editorial stables "was preparatory to my decision to retire," which he had been considering since the battles over the monster craze. He tried for some years to persuade DC to establish an educational office, so that the powerful comics medium could be used to inform and enlighten children, but he was denied. And now another new craze was becoming steadily more insistent at DC: the self-parodying, intentional corniness known as "camp." For a variety of reasons, Schiff retired in 1967 to devote himself to political activity and philosophical writings, his titles being divided among Kashdan, Boltinoff, and neophyte editor Jack Miller.

The growing tendency of the weird heroes to turn into self-parody began to show itself in Kashdan's sole entry, *Metamorpho the Element Man*. After Rex Mason is subjected to the rays of a strange meteorite, he finds himself reluctantly able to change not only his form but his very substance, turning any part of his body independently into any element of the periodic table (BB 57, Jan. 1965). Copper legs, bromium body, hands of cobalt and magnesium—he was like a kid's chemistry set come to life. He was also a multicolored, hideous-looking composite creature who shifted to the most bizarre extremes of shape at every opportunity. With such a weird hero, the series could only play upon that weirdness with a rollicking self-mockery that succeeded there as it couldn't have in a more conventional series. Wisecracking like a tough guy in a bad sixties crime movie, the "Fab Freak" breezed effortlessly through tangles with power-mad scientists, goofy-looking aliens, and subatomic universes, but was unable to cope with a pair of rival girlfriends: Urania the E-Girl, who shared the hero's element power, and Sapphire Stagg, armed with her own "curve power" and a great deal of money. Bob Haney wrote the series with purposely cornball humor, and Sal Trapani drew it with tongue-in-cheek grotesqueness.

The new trend picked up momentum in Murray Boltinoff's line, as the adventures of the Doom Patrol began stepping over the fine line between the bizarre and the ludicrous. The seeds were planted with a villain called the Animal-Vegetable-Mineral Menace, whose ability for transformation knew no reasonable bounds (DP 89, Aug. 1964). Soon there followed a new cast member named Mento, a millionaire who possessed a silly-looking purple hat that gave him undefined mental powers (DP 91, Nov. 1964). But the clincher came when the DP were attacked by a giant jukebox (DP 96, June 1965); the freakish quality of the series had turned to self-parody.

Boltinoff had a unique editorial perspective that probably contributed to this change in tone, for in addition to being Schiff's associate, he served as editor of such outright humor comics as *The Adventures of Jerry Lewis*. While this perspective had probably helped him avoid hero clichés in the

DP's early adventures, now it seemed to be preventing him from taking them seriously. A wacky teen hero called Beast-Boy was soon added to the team (DP 99, Nov. 1965), and wooden humor replaced the earlier, character-delineating dialogue.

A comparable change was effected on *Challengers of the Unknown*, where, by 1966, tough Rocky Davis had become a hipster, spouting nothing but lines like, "Drop him, cat—I mean like make with the splitsville!" They began battling characters like Villo, "the world's wickedest villain . . . the master of monumental meanness" (CU 52, Nov. 1966). And the artists on both strips, Bob Brown and Bruno Premiani, unable to draw humorously, simply let their work grow rougher (aggravated in the latter case by worsening eye troubles).

The trend reached its greatest extreme when the "Batman" TV show became a craze in 1966 (to be discussed in Chapter 15) and DC tried to keep up with its self-conscious humor. The greatest victim was *Blackhawk*, which continued its decade-long decline until desperate measures were taken. As Batman himself put it in a guest appearnce in issue 228 (Jan. 1967), "The Blackhawks are washed-up has-beens, out-of-date antiques. . . . To put it bluntly, they just don't swing!" To reverse the steady fall of sales, editor Kashdan's solution was to make costumed crime-fighters of them. No longer would they be Andre, Olaf, Stan, Hendrickson, et al., but Weapons Master, Golden Centurion, the Leaper, and M'sieu Machine (BH 230, Mar. 1967). For the Blackhawks, this overhauling into a way-out camp-strip was the last and worst in a series of unsuccessful measures; they were finally canceled after 243 issues (Nov. 1968).

The year 1966 saw the creation of two humorous hero comics. Jack Miller's *Inferior Five* concerned a bumbling squad of crime-fighters with names like Dumb Bunny and Awkwardman. Boltinoff's *Plastic Man* was a revamping of the zany Golden Age ancestor of both the Elongated Man and Mr. Fantastic; but the concept needed the comic brilliance of its creator, cartoonist Jack Cole, and the lackluster pencils of Win Mortimer and others did not do the trick. Neither series was much of a success.

Closely tied to the camp craze at DC was a loudly touted "teen" orientation that affected humor, romance, and hero comics. The one costumed-hero title conceived mainly in that spirit was *The Teen Titans*, composed entirely of kid sidekicks—Robin, Kid Flash, Aqualad, and Wonder Girl—which grew out of a team-up in *Brave and Bold* (BB 54, July 1964), moved to *Showcase* (Show. 59, Dec. 1965), and started in its own comic with the February 1966 issue. Edited by Kashdan, written by Haney, and drawn most often by Irv Novick and Nick Cardy, it started as a rather standard adventure series but quickly became a vehicle for endless pop-culture references and cute slang that could have seemed convincing only to very young kids. In issue 12 (Dec. 1967), for example, the "Fab Foursome" meet the "frabjous D.J. Deejay . . . the world's first disc jockey in space," whose "dreamy sounds" send "Wonder Chick, Gillhead,

Flasheroo, and Robin-O" off on an implausible battle with an alien that is described by Deejay as "groovy! So gear and ungrotty! Marv and fab!" The Titans won a regular following (many of whom debated in the letters pages whether the Titans were better than the Beatles . . . although without specifying at *what*), but they were left entirely at the mercy of momentary fads.

Kashdan also launched *Bomba the Jungle Boy*, loosely based on Roy Rockwood's old adventure series about a teenaged version of Tarzan (BJB 1, Oct. 1967). Although Jack Sparling contributed some robust, attractive art, the plots and dialogue were weighed down by faddish youth concerns.

It was Murray Boltinoff who, in 1967, began pulling the stable's comics out of their campiness. The Doom Patrol were restored to their darker, more disturbing orientation, and although both art and story suffered in quality, their adventures were again unique and engrossing. But sales had fallen fatally low, and cancellation came in 1968. At the last, Boltinoff, Drake, and Premiani redeemed their series with a final issue as unconventional and disturbing as the strip's beginning. The Brotherhood of Evil lure our heroes to a desert island and try to break their wills by offering them a deal: they will be allowed to live if they will approve the murder of fourteen innocent, ordinary, "useless" people. But the Doom Patrol will not submit, and the Brotherhood torpedoes the island, killing them all (DP 121, Oct. 1968). In the end, it is fitting that the "freaks" who survived to lead a second life, the "world's strangest heroes," should be the first heroes actually to die on the comic book page.

The weird heroes of Schiff, Boltinoff, and Kashdan helped DC learn to innovate and added greatly to the color and variety of the Silver Age, but all essentially remained on a sidetrack of the comics world. Beginning in 1967, however, one of their direct descendants would change the course of comic history.

Marvel's Hero Teams

Marvel's innovations did not cease with their offbeat new heroes. As Lee's co-creations proliferated, he began weaving them together with an internal consistency that no company had ever tried to maintain before. As Mort Weisinger had given Superman a consistent universe that linked seven titles, Lee would now tie together the diverse heroes and subplots of his entire company into a unity that would change the face of comics. He left no doubt that all his heroes really coexisted in the same world, that the Golden Age heroes had existed in that very world a couple of decades before, and that that world included all the real places and social realities that ours does. Within this "Marvel Universe" Lee began redefining the way heroes relate to one another, flying impudently in the face of the DC tradition of camaraderie and chumminess.

Guest appearances of one hero in another's story were old hat, but no one had done them with the frequency or casualness that Marvel began employing in 1963. Heroes, in Marvel comics, would not just get together for periodic teamup issues, as Flash and Green Lantern did twice a year; they would drop in on each other for a brief assist on a case, bump into each other on rooftops, and call each other for help, sometimes to be rebuffed. But most of all they fought. Nearly every time Marvel heroes met, with the exception of numerous cameo appearances, some twist of the plot forced them into combat. In the first two Marvel team-ups, a cocky Spider-Man fights the Fantastic Four to prove his worth (SM 1, Mar. 1963), and the FF are used by the military to wrestle the Hulk into submission (FF 12, Mar. 1963). Sometimes the battles were brought about by the mind-control of some villain, as when the Ringmaster hypnotized Spider-Man into attacking Daredevil (SM 16, Sept. 1964). Other times, Lee had to arrange some misunderstanding, as when the villainous Chameleon fooled Iron Man into believing Captain America was a phony, and Cap obligingly waited until five pages of fight scenes had passed before setting the record straight (TS 58, Nov. 1964).

Whether the heroes were fighting, joining forces, or merely catching one another up on the latest gossip, these crossovers appeared to be among Marvel's most popular features. Soon Lee and Kirby decided to create a regular forum for such team-ups with *The Avengers*, Marvel's answer to DC's Justice League of America (Av. 1, Sept. 1963). In it, Thor, Iron Man, Ant-Man, and the Wasp joiend forces to battle cataclysmic threats that were too much for one hero, particularly villain-teams like Baron Zemo's Masters of Evil, a league of old enemies of the various Avengers (Av. 6, July 1964).

The Avengers were a small team, but an effective mix. The two Lee-Ditko characters, Spider-Man and Dr. Strange, who drew much of their appeal from being loners and oddballs, were wisely left out. The group shifted a little, first when Ant-Man became Giant-Man (Av. 2, Nov. 1963), then when Captain America was thawed out (Av. 4, Mar. 1964), making it more varied and powerful. The Avengers lacked the variety of specialized powers possessed by the Justice League, but with Thor and Iron Man's might, Giant-Man's size, and Cap's gymnastic agility, there was plenty of opportunity for hard-hitting action; where the JLA was perfect for a Gardner Fox plot, the Avengers were ideal for a Jack Kirby slugfest. They did not, however, give Stan Lee much room for his emotional developments. Except for the Hulk, who bounded occasionally onto the scene, these heroes were all a pretty chummy group. The team would only work well as long as Kirby drew it, and he decided not to stay long. With issue 9 (Dec. 1964), Don Heck took over the penciling chores, and although he was a competent renderer of human emotion, he didn't command enough punch to make the high-powered action effective. To keep the Avengers entertaining, a change would have to be made, a change that Lee was soon prepared to make.

Simultaneously with the first issue of *The Avengers* came another team, the X-Men. Another Lee-Kirby project, they were labeled "The Strangest Super-Heroes of All," and all shared a common affliction: they were mutants, young people born with weird powers because of abnormalities in their parents' genes. Scott Summers, known as Cyclops, fired beams of destructive energy uncontrollably from his eyes; Warren Worthington III, the Angel, had huge wings sprouting from his back that enabled him to fly; Hank McCoy, the intellectual Beast, possessed massive legs and feet and an apelike posture that gave him phenomenal agility; Bobby Drake, the Iceman, was able to freeze himself and form icy weapons from his fingers; and pretty Jean Grey, Marvel Girl, was able to move objects telekinetically. All five teenagers were scorned by their peers and feared by society until brought together by a genius in a wheelchair, Professor Charles Xavier, to learn to control their powers and use them constructively.

Xavier, known as Professor X, is himself a mutant with awesome powers of telepathy. He has a deep interest in mutant-kind, calling them *"Homo superior,"* the next step in human evolution. He believes that for the present, however, mutants must learn to live in harmony with *Homo sapiens,* even keeping watch over them, and resist the temptation to take advantage of their powers. Other mutants, unfortunately, do not share his altruism; chief among these is Magneto, master of magnetism, who believes that the destiny of *Homo superior* is to rule. When he attacks American military installations, Xavier sends his young charges, costumed and masked, out to defeat him, and the X-Men ("X" for the "extra" factor in their makeups) become a costumed-hero team (XM 1, Sep. 1963).

Their origin makes clear two paradoxical points: this was, on the one hand, another unprecedented Marvel innovation, and yet, on the other, the idea was strangely similar to that of DC's Doom Patrol. "The World's Strangest Heroes" and "The Strangest Super-Heroes of All" were in both cases a team of freaks and outcasts brought together to be trained and given new lives by a wheelchair-ridden genius. The fact that the X-Men appeared less than three months after the DP makes plagiarism unlikely, given the usual production schedules of comics, and yet the parallels are remarkable. And they continued after the origin story. When Magneto gathered a crew of fellow mutants to attack mankind again, they were christened the Brotherhood of Evil Mutants (XM 4, Mar. 1964), a name oddly similar to the DP's Brotherhood of Evil, who reached the stands that same month.

The mutant theme dominated the X-Men's adventures. Often Professor X would contact a newly discovered mutant, hoping to add him to his group, only to have him yield to selfishness or bitterness and battle the X-Men. Among these were the Blob, an enormous fellow whom no power could move (XM 3, Jan. 1964), Unus the Untouchable, with his all-repelling force field (XM 8, Nov. 1964), and the Mimic, a troubled, arrogant youngster with the ability to copy any other mutant's power (XM 19, Apr. 1966). The enemies of *Homo superior* also figured in the stories, as when scientist Bolivar Trask developed an army of unstoppable robots called the Sentinels to find and destroy all mutants, whom he considered a threat to mankind's future (XM 14–16, Nov. 1965–Jan. 1966).

From the beginning, the greatest appeal of *The X-Men* lay in the large and dynamic cast of characters. The rivalry of the silent, brooding Cyclops and the rich, frivolous Angel for Marvel Girl gave us some of Lee's sloppiest, liveliest soap opera. The Beast, his intellect and baroque vocabulary ("Your powers of deduction," he tells Iceman, "are exceeded only by your affection for the obvious!") contrasting with his brutish appearance and purely muscular special power, was one of comics' most delightful surprises of characterization. Even the villains were fleshed out with unusual flair. Particularly intriguing were Quicksilver and the Scarlet Witch, an extra-fast European mutant and his quasi-magical sister, who were basically good eggs, but had been manipulated into warring against humanity by the scheming Magneto. The master of magnetism himself had a certain dignity in the zealous purity of his mission and his lordly bearing. Perhaps it was because of this colorful cast that the series remained vital even after Kirby left, being replaced by the unattractive art of Werner Roth, at first calling himself Jay Gavin (XM 18, Mar. 1966).

Professor X trains his young X-Men in their Danger Room: the Beast, the Angel, Iceman, Cyclops, and Marvel Girl. Pencils by Kirby, inks by Chic Stone, script by Lee. From *The X-Men* 6, July 1964.

The majestic villain Magneto tyrannizes his Brotherhood of Evil Mutants: Quicksilver, the Scarlet Witch, Mastermind, and the Toad.

On the debit side, the X-Men rarely exploited the element that made them unique, their alienation. That they were feared and often hounded by mankind should have given an utterly unique, fresh cast to the telling of their stories. And yet, with the exception of the Sentinels, this aspect was rarely played up, and the X-Men often behaved like just another band of costumed crime-fighters.

Quicksilver and the Scarlet Witch won the affection of enough fans that Lee decided to make heroes of them. This was accomplished through the revamping of the Avengers, when the old heroes were apparently not helping Lee realize his aims for characterization. All the members but Captain America resigned, and in their place came the two formerly evil mutants, along with an old Iron Man foe who had also proved to have his heart in the right place, a Green Arrow–style archer called Hawkeye (Av. 16, May 1965).

The main thrust of the "New Avengers" was character interaction. Hawkeye was an abrasive showoff with a chip on his shoulder, Quicksilver a proud, humorless outsider, overly distrustful of mankind and protective of his sister. The Scarlet Witch was a naïve, nervous soul, and Captain America the weary, rugged veteran of more battles than the rest of them combined. They were forced to fight as a team to prove their worth to a doubting world, but not for one minute did they get along.

In "The Bitter Taste of Defeat," for example, Captain America orders Hawkeye to refrain from attempting a homemade repair on a piece of specialized machinery. "Knock it off!" Hawkeye says. "Anybody can fix a crummy fuse!" "Look, hot-shot," replies Cap, "you've been riding me ever since you joined us! I chalked it up to your swelled head and big mouth and let it pass! But now . . ." Hawkeye promptly raises his bow and arrow, threatening to "change that parting in your hair," but Quicksilver arrives with a restraining hand. Cap simmers down, but Hawkeye turns his insults on Quicksilver, prompting the Scarlet Witch to blast him off his feet with her "hex power." "I told you to curb those hex bolts of yours!" says Cap, gently but firmly. "You might have injured Hawkeye!" Whereupon Quicksilver barks, "Have a care how you speak to my sister!" And round and round it goes (Av. 21, Oct. 1965).

Although this discord was at first very appropriate for a team of insecure, overambitious misfits, it continued with very little development until it became grating. Something of a new dimension was added when Giant-Man, now called Goliath, joined the team and found himself trapped at a freakish ten-foot height (Av. 28, May 1966), and Don Heck contributed his most active, varied art to the series; but Heck's limitations, an uninspired run of villains, and repetitive characterization prevented *The Avengers* from fulfilling its obvious potential. It would be ripe for change when Roy Thomas took the reins later in 1966.

Although costumed heroes were the source of all Marvel's success in those years, Lee and Kirby made a foray into war comics by creating *Sgt. Fury and His Howling Commandoes*, in which tough, cigar-chomping Nick Fury led an ethnically mixed pack of fanatical soldiers on daring raids into German territory during World War II (SF 1, May 1963). Billed as "The War Mag for People Who Hate War Mags," this Kirbyesque romp through the battlefields read sometimes like an offbeat hero series and sometimes like an unintentional parody of bad war movies. The action scenes were fun, but Kirby soon left that series too, and replacement Dick Ayers was unable to disguise the weakness of the stories.

Lee liked the gruff Nick Fury character, however, and two years later he and Kirby launched *Nick Fury, Agent of S.H.I.E.L.D.* to replace the Human Torch in *Strange Tales* (ST 135, Aug. 1965). Set in the present, this spy series featured a middle-aged Fury as head of an advanced scientific espionage organization reminiscent of TV's UNCLE, battling a mysterious fascist enclave called Hydra. Breaking away from his earlier communist themes, Lee was able to use a great deal of imagination in devising secret oaths, hideouts, and tactics for both his heroes and villains. He and Kirby invented a whole arsenal of such devices as a flying sports car, ESP-amplifying machines, and an airborne "Heli-Carrier" headquarters. But S.H.I.E.L.D., as inventive as it was, was one series that would increase in significance after Kirby departed, in developments to be covered in Chapter 19.

Throughout this proliferation of groups, Marvel's original team, the Fantastic Four, remained at the forefront of innovation and characterization. The foursome proved to be particularly flexible characters, growing together as distinct but devoted members of a family. Sue Storm's ambivalent feelings for the Sub-Mariner finally settled down after his reunion with his people removed her principal reason to pity him, and at last she told him that it was Reed with whom she wanted to spend her life (FF 27, June 1964). Shortly afterward, Reed stepped out of his rigidly cerebral role long enough to ask her to marry him (FF 35, Feb. 1965). Ben Grimm remained the emotional focus of the series, but now a gruff sense of humor was added to balance his misery, with an appealing Brooklynesque speech pattern that included wisecracks about his old haunts on Yancy Street, oaths sworn on a mysterious Aunt Petunia, and William Bendix's old catch-phrase, "Wotta revoltin' development this is!" His running hostility with the Torch evolved into an affectionate needling, and their wild, destructive battles inside FF headquarters provided a humorous counterpoint to the usual fights between Marvel heroes. Reed Richards slowly grew into a harried father-figure as a consequence, loving but losing patience with his impetuous cohorts.

As Lee and Kirby found their footing, the quality of plot and art improved. The most marked improvement was the growth of Dr. Doom, an evil scientist in metal armor who had rivaled the Sub-Mariner as the team's archvillain since issue 5 (July 1962). Gradually he became far more than just another mad scientist, as we discovered his Gypsy origins, found the source of his evil in the wrongs suffered by his family in Europe, and saw him become the autocratic monarch of the Balkan nation of Latveria (FF An. 2, 1964). In the Fantastic Four's finest hour to that time, "A Blind Man Shall Lead Them," they were forced to defeat Doom without their powers in an impressive, two-issue, all-out battle story that helped set the tone for a new phase in Marvel comics (FF 39–40, June–July 1965).

The early days of Marvel were consummated and brought to a close by the Fantastic Four's third giant-sized annual (1965), featuring the wedding of Reed and Sue. This was the guest-star phenomenon taken to its extreme, "the world's most colossal collection of costumed characters, crazily cavorting and capering in continual combat," a riot of twenty-one heroes leaping, flying, and swinging at twenty-one villains and their hordes of acolytes, thugs, and deadly beasts. It wasn't much for plot, but twenty-five cents for forty-two colorful characters was the best buy of the year for hero-hungry kids.

The comic scene had changed completely since that summer nine years before when *Showcase 4* first reached the stands. In the summer of 1965 a trip to the newsstand would reveal Schwartz's stable of revived stalwarts, Weisinger's gigantic supporting cast, and the myraid oddities of Schiff, Kashdan, and Boltinoff, along with the Marvel explosion of innovative heroes. There was also the Mighty Comics Group, an ill-fated effort by the people who published Archie to revive most of their costumed crimefighters of the 1940s in new, hip forms (with a great deal of help from writer Jerry Siegel); and there was Gold Key, who for a few years had been publishing *Doctor Solar: Man of the Atom*, the highly regarded *Magnus, Robot-Fighter*, and other fantastical hero series; and Charlton, briefly reviving an old hero called the Blue Beetle and soon following him with some offbeat new adventurers. By the end of the summer, *T.H.U.N.D.E.R. Agents* would be on the horizon, a series about a squad of extra-normal spies, from Tower Books' new comics line, who counted Wally Wood, Gil Kane, Steve Ditko, Mike Sekowsky, and Reed Crandall among its many superb artists. (Wally Wood would soon even form his own small company, *Witzend*, to publish the offbeat creations of such fellow artists as Ditko and Dan Adkins, which they preferred not to sell to the major firms, a course many others would follow in the years to come.) And there would be more comics in the next year or so, from Dell and Harvey, and a briefly expanding Tower, all reflecting the craze for colorful heroes.

This was a cornucopia of costumed crusaders. By the beginning of 1966, hero comics were heading for the pinnacle of their popularity.

Classic DC

Ironically, in the midst of all the changes in comics, it was the old, steady Julius Schwartz style that would suddenly catapult the field into a popular craze.

As experimentation swept the field, Schwartz went virtually untouched by it. His popularity continued, as did the quality of his output, and he maintained his titles on the same even course. From 1961 to 1964 his roster of comics went unchanged. But by early 1964 it was decided that something had to be done with DC's suffering Batman titles; so it was that *Strange Adventures* and *Mystery in Space*, which were less popular now that the science fiction craze was wearing thin, were shunted to Jack Schiff in order to leave Schwartz free to salvage *Batman* and *Detective Comics.*

All Schwartz had to do was to remold Batman into his own unique style. Gone were the aliens, the bizarre weapons, and the weird transformations. In their place appeared neatly crafted tales of mystery and intrigue centering on costumed thieves and gangs of hoodlums. Fox and Broome, the new Batman writers, reinstated the Caped Crusader's flair for detection and pugilism.

In their first adventure under Schwartz and Broome, for example, Batman and Robin investigate a mysterious crime in Gotham Village, a district of Gotham City torn by controversy (Det. 327, May 1964). One faction wants it razed because the village is a refuge for criminals, while the other wants it preserved as a picturesque landmark. The Dynamic Duo, after some fancy detection, discover that deep under the village is buried a huge hideout for criminals, and that the brains behind the hideout is the chairman for the committee to preserve Gotham Village. As chairman, he had tried to save the village only to prevent his underground lair from discovery.

Bob Kane (along with an increasing number of "ghosts") remained to handle most of the art chores, altering his style in an attempt to reflect Carmine Infantino's, who drew every other issue of *Detective Comics.* The transition, however, proved too severe, for Kane's art lost all of its earlier childlike charm. Joe Giella's inks helped to bring his art closer to the Schwartz look, but it still conflicted with the pristine mold of that stable.

114

Batman's new look: Infantino art and a touch of camp. Inks by Giella, script by Broome. From *Detective Comics* 341, July 1965.

It was one year later that Batman, now cast completely in the Schwartz style, made an unexpected contribution to the fortunes and future of comics. Television producer William Dozier, while on an airplane flight, happened to pick up a copy of *Batman* 171 (May 1965). It featured the return of an old Batman villain, the Riddler. Fox's script abounded in puzzles, for which the Riddler had a peculiar bent, and terrible puns, for which Robin had suddenly become overly fond, all with a light tone of self-parody. Dozier immediately saw in it the possibility for a TV series.

When the "Batman" TV series premiered in January 1966, the show became an instant hit. Dozier had exaggerated the punning and the self-parody, and overnight, comic book "camp" became a national sensation. Comic book heroes became the subjects of magazine articles, the stars of Saturday-morning cartoons, and a fixture on Wednesday- and Thursday-night television. Smaller firms, like the Mighty Comics Group, enjoyed powerful though brief sales boosts, and new series proliferated. Schwartz's *Batman* became the number-one-selling comic book of the year.

Looser DC stables like Boltinoff's, Kashdan's, and Kanigher's hurled themselves wholeheartedly into the waves of camp, but Schwartz, who had inadvertently set things off, managed to get through with very few concessions. In step with the entire DC line, Schwartz's titles now sported more flamboyant and slogan-laden covers, with black-and-white "go-go" checks across the top. In virtually every story, one or another of the characters would drop the word "go-go" (as an adjective, noun, or verb, and with no particular meaning) and occasionally assume a hipper speech pattern, but otherwise Schwartz's style remained the same.

Backing up Batman in *Detective Comics* now appeared the Elongated Man in his own series, written by Gardner Fox and both penciled and inked by Carmine Infantino. Like the new Batman, the Elongated Man stories highlighted plenty of detection and pugilism, but they had a flair all their own. In nearly every episode of this new series, Ralph Dibny and his wife, Sue, drove into a new town just in time to encounter a puzzling new mystery. Ralph and Sue, you see, were inveterate travelers, and the locales they visited, be they rural or urban, desert or tropical, were evocatively rendered by Infantino, and provided a refreshing variety to the series. The stories were light and breezy, and although limited to ten-page backup status, they immediately took their place alongside Schwartz's best titles in consistent quality.

Simultaneously with the new *Batman* and *Detective*, Hawkman was granted his own comic. Written by Fox and drawn by Murphy Anderson, Hawkman and Hawkgirl encountered complex mysteries that reflected both their otherworldly origin and their fascination, as museum curators, for Earth's past civilizations. In their first story, for instance, Hawkman and Hawkgirl have a contest to see whether earthly detection procedures or Thanagarian devices are better suited for catching crooks. In the second, in the ruins of an ancient city in Central America, they battle a Mayan Indian who, with extraterrestial gadgets, has transformed himself into Chac, the ancient god of rain (HM 1, May 1964).

With the waning interest in science fiction and the upsurge of humanization pioneered at Marvel, Schwartz arrived at one of his minor concessions to changing times. Although the basic timbre of his stories remained the same, a large number of them now involved more of the personal sides of his heroes. In *Green Lantern,* for instance, Schwartz launched an intermittent series of backup stories featuring Hal Jordan's two brothers, Jim and Jack, and their stern uncle Jeremiah. Most of these tales revolved around the conviction held by Jim's wife that Jim Jordan was secretly Green Lantern. Some crime or other usually occurred during these family get-togethers, and as Green Lantern was always around to solve it, Jim's wife was further convinced that Jim, not Hal, was in fact the Emerald Gladiator. Another human interest backup series was launched in the pages of *The Atom,* revolving around the invention of a "time pool" by Professor Hyatt, one of Ray Palmer's colleagues (Atom 3, Nov. 1962). In each of them, Ray Palmer, in his secret identity of the Atom, is drawn into the time-pool and thence back in time, where he meets such historical personages as Ben Franklin, Edgar Allan Poe, and Henry Fielding. In each instance he makes a key, albeit unheralded, contribution to history.

Many interesting changes were worked on Batman and his cast of supporting characters, most prominently the death of Bruce Wayne's loyal butler, Alfred (Det. 328, June 1964). Later, however, the producers of the "Batman" TV show decided that Alfred was an indispensable member of the household, so the Schwartz stable contrived to bring him back in a long, continued story line running solely in the Bob Kane–illustrated stories; it emerged that Alfred had miraculously survived, become deranged, and attacked his old friends repeatedly as the mysterious "Outsider," before coming to his senses. The TV show also brought about the introduction of a new cast member, the new Batgirl, who is secretly the daughter of Police Commissioner Gordon (Det. 359, Jan. 1967). Handled much better than the members of the old "Bat-family," she was usually a source of lighthearted fun.

But it was in the pages of *The Flash* that the greatest effort at humanization transpired. Between Barry Allen's marriage (F 165, Nov. 1966) and the subsequent revelation of his secret identity to Iris West, a number of tales revolving around Iris's father, Professor West—an absentminded scientist whose dizziness always landed him in a jam (beginning F 134, Feb. 1963)—and a pair of beautiful stories about movie actress Daphne Dean, a former sweetheart of Barry's, the personal life of the Flash was rounded out to an extent that no other Schwartz character had enjoyed.

Team-ups also became prominent during this period. Flash and Green Lantern guest-starred regularly in each other's titles. Atom and Hawkman shared a few adventures. Batman and the Elongated Man were united in the pages of *Detective Comics* for a few full-length stories. In his own slot, the Elongated Man visited such heroes as the Flash, Green Lantern, and the Atom in their respective cities. Unlike the guest appearances in Marvel comics, however, the DC heroes nearly always met as friends, not as antagonists.

This growing surge of guest stars sparked another new trend in Schwartz's comics. Following on the heels of the revival of Jay Garrick, the Flash of the 1940s, the Justice Society of America—Dr. Fate, Black Canary, Hourman, and the "Earth-2" Atom, Flash, Green Lantern, and Hawkman—returned triumphantly to help the Justice League in a case (JLA 21, Aug. 1963). This crossover became an annual tradition, and from it sprang other Earth-1/Earth-2 team-ups in individual titles. Jay became a regular visitor in *The Flash;* Alan Scott, the Golden Age Green Lantern, dropped in on Hal Jordan (GL 40, Oct. 1965); and the original Atom teamed up with his Silver Age namesake (Atom 29, Mar. 1967). Now, along with modern hero team-ups, visitations from Golden Age heroes became regular events to look forward to.

The next step in the revival of Golden Age heroes occurred in *Showcase* issues 55 and 56 (Apr. and June 1965) when Dr. Fate and Hourman teamed up for a 1940s-style adventure by Fox and Anderson. This triggered a short-lived spotlighting of Earth-2 heroes without participation of their Silver Age counterparts. A Starman/Black Canary team-up came next (BB 61–62, Sept. and Nov. 1965), and shortly thereafter the Spectre, the nearly omnipotent crime-fighting ghost of the 1940s, returned for a three-issue tryout in *Showcase.* The Golden Age team-ups were conventional costumed-hero fare, but the Spectre stood apart with an otherworldly flavor far different from Schwartz's usual scientific slant. In his second adventure, for example, he pursues the mystery of a man with no shadow through "planes of existence that have no counterpart on earth," to "an eldritch world" where he battles the demon Shathan (Show. 61, Apr. 1966). Perhaps because of this difference, the Spectre was the only one of these revivals to receive his own title (*Spectre* 1, Dec. 1967). But ultimately Fox's lighthearted writing and Anderson's restrained art were not adequate for such a mystical concept; the "Discarnate Detective" seemed to be just an old Schwartz hero out of his element.

In such ill-fated ventures as these, it became apparent that a little staleness had crept into the Schwartz stable. Indeed, by the end of 1965, the quality of the entire line was starting to dip. Schwartz and his staff had been toiling on the same titles in the same style for years. The routine was beginning to wear on them, and their inability to innovate with these new ventures showed that they could not longer escape it.

Two specific factors contributed to the downslide. First, John Broome cut back on his scripting, forcing Gardner Fox to take up the slack. But this was not the same Gardner Fox of the early years; Fox's plots, perhaps due to overwork, lost a little of their ingenuity, while his scripting became wordy and bogged down by gratuitous descriptions. Second, artists Infantino, Anderson, and Sekowsky lost much of the clarity that Schwartz had always insisted on. At the same time, the entire DC line had adopted a new style of page layout, shifting to fewer panels per page and far less detail per panel. Schwartz's artists did not adapt well to the change, losing the tight, pristine line that had characterized their work earlier.

Schwartz responded by reshuffling the inking chores in his stable. Sid Greene was assigned to Infantino and Sekowsky in 1966, and succeeded admirably in tightening up their new work. This left Gil Kane, whom Greene had been inking for a few years, to ink his own pencils, a change that was also very much for the better. And DC continued to maintain the superb coloring (by Jerry Serpe and Jack Adler), the lettering (by Gaspar Saladino), and the high printing quality that had distinguished it since the late 1950s. But even this was not enough. A change in the basic fabric of the stories was needed.

A harbinger of what was to come suddenly appeared in the pages of *Green Lantern* 49 (Dec. 1966). Carol Ferris, Green Lantern's longtime sweetheart, suddenly takes up with another man. Crushed, Green Lantern decides he must leave Coast City.

In the very next issue we find Hal Jordan, alias Green Lantern, on the road. We learn that Hal will no longer be surrounded by his old supporting cast or content in Coast City. In fact, we no longer know what to expect from his adventures. Where will Hal go next? Whom will he meet? What odd job will he assume? For the first time, a Schwartz title was not predictable.

Also for the first time, a Schwartz character was now wracked with complex emotions, no longer just the determination to battle evil or wed his girl. Hal was now full of sorrow at having lost Carol, as confused as we were as to what to do next with his life, and desperate to prove his worth to himself as a man, not just a costumed hero.

This desperation led to a vow to rely more on his fists than on his power ring. And what a great vow that turned out to be for the readers, as this was the period in which Gil Kane fully blossomed into the supreme action artist in the field. Kane had long been an admirer of Kirby's, and as Kirby's art improved at Marvel, Kane's followed suit.

Kane now filled every panel with the same fluidity and punch he had long shown in his dynamic covers. When Green Lantern let loose a roundhouse right at an opponent, the reader virtually found himself rolling with the imapct. When Green Lantern hurled his body in a flying tackle, the reader almost expected to find him in his lap. But Green Lantern did not become just a mindless brawler; Kane imbued him with heroic nobility and savage determination through a superb understanding of anatomy and facial expressions. Kane's inking augmented the effect with its rough and masculine, nearly sculptural quality. Through his own work and that of hordes of imitators, Kane would have a profound effect on the comics of the future.

The stories themselves alternated between Hal's footloose adventures on earth and farflung space operas. In the former, Hal moved from city to city, took on new jobs (insurance investigator, toy salesman, etc.), and met new people. In the latter, he traveled to distant worlds to wage furious battle with the likes of Thraxon the Powerful, a fierce warrior bent on conquering the home world of another Green Lantern (GL 50, Jan. 1967), and in a two-part fistic extravaganza (GL 55–56, Sept.–Oct. 1967), with a horde of criminals who had escaped from a prison-planet where they had been sentenced by the Guardians of the Universe for having committed horrible crimes.

Although it happened gradually, the quiet solidity of DC's Silver Age tradition began to unravel in the pages of Green Lantern. It would soon become evident that Green Lantern was only the first, and that innumerable changes were imminent at DC. The seeds of a new era were being planted. The next major change, a far more radical and irrevocable one, will be treated in Chapter 17.

16 The Cosmic Saga

During the early days of Marvel Comics, Jack Kirby's work load had been so great that his artwork appeared rough and hurried, his plots were thin, and his overtaxed imagination was never able to equal the feats it had performed for *Challengers* and earlier series. But as he cut back on his many assignments he was able to bring the full force of his talent and vision to bear on his three favorite titles: *The Fantastic Four, Thor,* and *Captain America.* In the process, he and Lee struck an effective balance in their collaboration, in which Kirby did virtually all the creation and plotting; Lee has related that by the mid-1960s, Kirby would often build a complete story from no more than a few suggestions over the phone. This lightened work load and creative freedom allowed Kirby to stretch his imagination further than he ever had before, in the process blowing open the boundaries of the Marvel universe and creating material almost mythological in scope and strength.

Since Thor's conception in 1962, Lee and Kirby had been flirting with mythological themes, but they nearly always kept to the safe ground of traditional hero fare. The first sign that they wanted to break the bonds of Earth came with the inception of a backup series called *Tales of Asgard* (JIM 97, Oct. 1963). Each of these five-page episodes featured either an actual Norse myth retold or an episode from the early days of the Asgardian gods, in which writer and artist could let their imaginations run wild. The stories, with no link to mankind or the affairs of our planet, were full of the trolls, dwarves, giants, and valiant heroes of European fairy tales. The fact that this series was made not only charming but remarkably convincing by Kirby's bold art and Lee's relatively dignified scripting made it one of Marvel's finest early achievements.

The absence of earthly concerns did not appear to bother Thor's readers, for *Tales of Asgard* was a letter-page success; soon Thor's regular adventures took a turn toward the mythological, beginning with the attack of a pair of Asgardian villains, the seductive Enchantress and her would-be lover, the brutal Executioner (JIM 103, Apr. 1964). The affairs of Asgard and Earth began intertwining, until soon Thor felt torn between the two realms. With the transformation by the evil god Loki of a thug named Crusher Creel into the powerful Absorbing Man (JIM 113, Feb. 1965), those worlds began overlapping into such a complex pattern that the

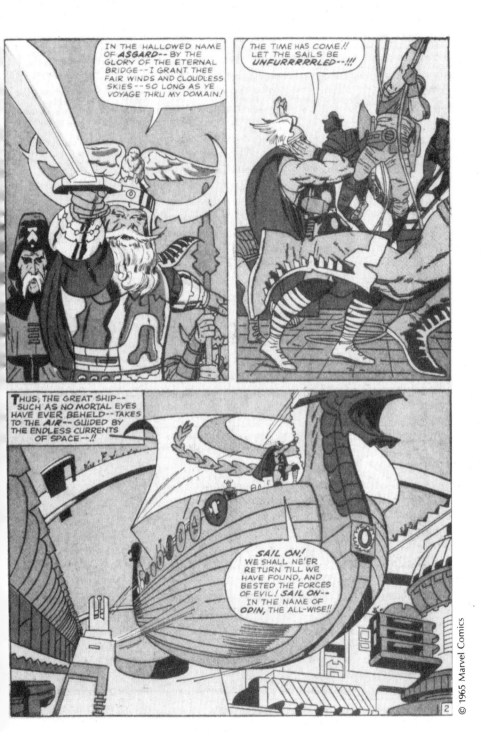

The pageantry and grandeur of the new Kirby. Inks by Vince Colletta, script by Lee. From *Journey into Mystery* 120, September 1965.

story line could no longer be contained in a single issue. Lee and Kirby had already experimented with two-issue stories, a format unusual but not unknown in comics. But before the completion of the three-issue Absorbing Man story, Thor was already engaged in a contest with Loki to procure some magic stones; the tale wended its way through Earth and Asgard for the next five issues. Even before Thor emerged victorious in that contest (JIM 120, Sept. 1965), new menaces had raised their heads on Earth, and events had been set in motion that would take Thor to Olympus for a battle with Hercules (JIM 124, Jan. 1966), and finally to the farthest reaches of space, to meet a godlike experimenter called the High Evolutionary. By the time the sprawling, interweaving plot lines finally converged to a kind of solution (Thor 135, Dec. 1966), twenty-three comics and nearly two years had passed.

Although not a single story by any definition, these twenty-three comics were connected by far more than Marvel's earlier emotional subplots. This was clearly a completely new approach to comic book storytelling. The precedent had been set by Lee and Ditko's use of movie-serial continuity in *The Hulk,* but this free-flowing narrative, bluntly and daringly rejecting the limits of the basic unit of comic book storytelling—the single issue—was forced into existence by Kirby's exploding imagination. With this open field as he was able to create vast, strange worlds and hordes of creatures such as the readers of comics had never seen. The only types of stories that could do justice to these worlds were long quests, epic battles, and grand schemes that set the whole cosmos in motion.

This blossoming of Kirby's creative vision was matched by a great expansion of his artistic range. He wove his mythical realms of equal parts rugged, barbarian majesty and fantastical splendor. Savage landscapes of fire and ice, wild seas, towering palaces, and the boundlessness of space were spread before the fans in large panels, some covering full pages. To his action he added a weight and monumentality that gave his stories a strange feeling of importance, as if they truly were the stuff of legend. His gods really seemed to be something more than human, and the worlds they roamed were distant, endless, and truly mythical. Adding to the "once upon a time" quality of his art were the light, graceful inks of Vince Colletta, who, though usually unimpressive, seemed perfectly suited to the new Kirby.

Lee responded effectively to this change in scope with a serious, sometimes ponderous tone of writing that always reminded the reader that these were the adventures not just of a costumed crime-fighter but a legendary deity. Gradually, he imbued Thor and his fellow gods with a pseudo-Shakespearean speech pattern that set them amusingly apart from the rest of the costumed-hero pantheon. "Evil one!" Thor cries. " 'Tis no ordinary mortal thou hast attacked—but the mighty God of Thunder!" (Thor 135, Dec. 1966).

The most productive union of Kirby and Lee's talents, however, came when this same wave of creativity swept over the Fantastic Four. There Lee was able to flesh out Kirby's mind-boggling creations and plots with memorable personalities and a constant undercurrent of mystery and suspense.

The finest product of this union began (in Lee's retelling) at a lunch conference in which the two set themselves to the creation of the most awe-inspiring menace imaginable in the Marvel universe: Galactus, a giant who roams the cosmos, taking sustenance by devouring the life-forces of entire planets. Kirby made a veritable god of the grandiose being; and a god, logically, required an angel. "When he brought [the art] to me so that I could add the dialogue and captions," Lee recalls, "I was surprised to find . . . a silver-skinned, smooth-domed, sky-riding surfer atop a speedy flying surfboard." This Silver Surfer, Kirby explained, was the herald of Galactus, who warned each world of its impending doom. "I was wild about the new character," Lee says, sensing the mythic power of Kirby's creation. "I found a certain nobility in his demeanor, an almost spiritual quality in his aspect and his bearing . . . something totally selfless and magnificently innocent." As the story develops, the Surfer, moved by the innate nobility he senses buried beneath the fear and hatred in the hearts of mankind, joins with the Fantastic Four to help repel Galactus; for this mutiny his master robs him of his freedom, confining him forever to Earth by an invisible barrier (FF 50, May 1966). Thus cut off from his beloved outer space by a sacrifice he never dreamed he could make, the Surfer became Marvel's most tragic and philosophical figure. "There is still so much I do not know . . . about mankind!" he says. "But now, I shall have the rest of my life to learn—for in finding a conscience, I have lost the stars!" It was ironic, and yet somehow appropriate to the unique collaboration of Lee and Kirby, that the character who would prove to be Lee's—and many fans'—favorite would be one who came to him as a complete surprise.

The exploding Marvel universe: The Silver Surfer confronts Galactus. By Kirby, Sinnott, and Lee. From *The Fantastic Four* 77, August 1968.

The Inhumans: Medusa, Black Bolt, Karnak, Maximus ... Gorgon, Triton, and others. Pencils by Kirby, inks by Joe Sinnott, script by Lee. From *The Fantastic Four* 59, February 1967.

The Silver Surfer first appeared in the midst of an immensely complicated seventeen-issue sequence that, even more than Thor at the same time, told many stories and yet united them into one (FF 44–60, Nov. 1965–Mar. 1967). The stars of this continuing "saga" were the Inhumans, an ancient race of weird creatures from a hidden city in the Himalayas, no two of whom were remotely alike: Gorgon, whose thick legs and cloven hooves gave him a devastating kick; the scaly, amphibious Triton; Lockjaw, resembling a giant, frog-mouthed bulldog, who could teleport throughout the universe; their brooding king, Black Bolt, whose voice could destroy a city; Medusa of the living hair; the karate master Karnak; and, among a horde of others, the beautiful Crystal, mistress of elemental forces (she captured the burning, unreasoning love of the Human Torch, and when she was taken from him, his quest to find her—accompanied by a stoic American Indian friend named Wyatt Wingfoot—became the most powerful unifying element of the series).

Supporting them were the Black Panther, the comics' first black costumed hero and the king of the hidden, scientifically advanced jungle land of Wakanda; the Watcher, a cosmic entity of boundless wisdom, who is preventd by an ancient oath from interfering in the ways of man; and plenty of villains, including Dr. Doom with his grandest scheme to date. And of course the personal melodramas of our four stalwart heroes continued, now complicated by the dilemma of the Silver Surfer.

From a structural viewpoint, Kirby's telling of these tales was undisciplined and often haphazard, and many readers objected with justifiable annoyance and perplexity. The conclusion of the first three-and-a-half-issue Inhumans story, for example, came seven pages into issue 48, where-upon the Galactus plot appeared suddenly out of a clear blue sky (Mar. 1966). Lee himself was troubled enough by the wild hopscotching of Kirby's narrative that one caption read, "Forgive us if our tale seems to ramble . . . but we have so many new elements to introduce . . . so many loose ends to tie up!" (FF 50, May 1966). But to the loyal Marvel fan, who had followed the plot developments from their inception, these two years of *Thor* and *The Fantastic Four* were like a wondrous tapestry of lost worlds, distant galaxies, and uncanny creatures; a trip to the newsstand or the drugstore each month became a new step in a voyage into uncharted realms that seemed to have no bounds.

The boundaries began to show, unfortunately, during 1967, as the stories grew simpler, the new inventions fewer, and straight-ahead fight scenes gradually more prevalent. New ideas continued to appear—a star-spanning race of experimenters named the Kree (FF 64-65, July–Aug. 1967), a scientifically synthesized messiah known only as Him (FF 66-67, Sept.-Oct. 1967), a topsy-turvy world called the Negative Zone, and the hint of strange abilities in Reed and Sue's baby son, Franklin—but the emphasis soon shifted to rapid, lightly entertaining stories. *Thor* contin-ued at a grandiose level for a time, with a long story about Ragnarok, the doom of the gods (Thor 154-157, July–Oct. 1968); much material about the FF's strange worlds moved to that title, helping tie the Marvel universe more tightly together, including an *Origin of the Inhumans* backup series (Thor 146-152, Nov. 1967–May 1968) and revelations of the cosmic impor-tance of both Galactus and Him (Thor 160-169, Jan–Oct. 1969).

For a brief period, Kirby's third title, *Captain America,* had enjoyed a little grandeur of its own. Although restricted by the limited powers of its hero and the established pattern of extensive fight sequences, the series featured an assortment of worldwide conspiracies and secret armies, be-ginning with the return of Cap's wartime archfoe, the Red Skull (TS 72, Dec. 1965). Running subplots included Cap's struggle with his past, his affair with a girl who was an eerily perfect double for his lover of the 1940s, and his involvement with S.H.I.E.L.D. But Kirby's contributions grew sporadic in 1968, and he soon left the series for far different hands to direct (after CA 107, Nov. 1968).

Kirby seemed to be losing interest in Marvel. He left New York for Cali-fornia in the late 1960s, and rumors abounded of disagreements between him and Lee. By the end of 1969, nothing new was springing from the pages of *Thor* or *The Fantastic Four,* and his stories had even lost the ca-pacity to be fun in a purely simplistic, action-packed way. In view of his career record, it was not surprising. The old maverick who had scarcely ever worked as long as two years on one project had been working more than eight years, without missing an issue, on the FF. It was time to seek new pastures.

But he had left a rich legacy behind him. The fans of the gimmick-crazy, pseudo-cosmic, psychedelic 1960s loved his creations, and in the midst of the *Batman* craze he had drawn a great deal of attention, both in and out of fandom, to Marvel. He had laid the foundations of a bigger Marvel universe, one that would give writers of the future a deep well to dip into again and again. His never-ending stories had freed comics from yet another traditional bond, and although the technique was abandoned in the late 1960s, writers and artist-plotters in the next decade would learn to put it to great effect. A new wave of Marvel innovators would spend years juggling, modifying, and synthesizing the ideas and inventions of Jack Kirby.

Deadman

It is odd to note that the same minor DC stables that had just turned out a slew of bizarre heroes, their adventures ranging from the exotic to the outlandish, should, in 1967, produce the grittiest costumed hero yet conceived. Edited by Jack Miller, longtime writer of the *Martian Manhunter* and recent editor of two humor titles, *The Inferior Five* and *Swing With Scooter*, and created by Arnold Drake, the master of freaky heroes, this new character appeared at first glance to be just another in the long series of oddball creations. Upon closer inspection, however, it would prove to be very different—it would prove, in fact, to be the first truly adult comic book in the costumed-hero genre.

The cover of *Strange Adventures* 205 (Oct. 197) pictured a flamboyantly costumed acrobat plummeting from a trapeze. From a corner, the barrel of a rifle protruded into the picture. The caption read: "This man who was just murdered is our hero! His story begins one minute later." Thus were the revolutionary adventures of Deadman launched.

Boston Brand, when still numbered among the living, was an acrobat supreme for a "struggling, fleabag circus." One day, as Brand prepares himself for his "devilishly dangerous and daring" act, a rifle shot strikes him in the chest and sends him hurtling to his death. But when his fellow circus performers crowd around his "corpse," Brand discovers that only his body has died. His spirit has somehow survived, an intangible presence that can neither be seen, heard, nor in any way perceived. This so-called Deadman goes on to discover that Rama Kushna, the "Face of the Universe," as described by Vashnu, the circus seer, has a special fate in store for him. Manifesting himself first as Dora, the baby elephant, then as one of Professor Quigley's trained mice, and finally as a tree, Rama Kushna explains to Deadman that "you shall have the power to walk among men until you have found the one who killed you." To aid Deadman in achieving his quest, Rama Kushna endows him with the capacity to enter anyone's body and gain complete control of it throughout the duration of his possession. Shortly, Deadman learns that witnesses to the shooting claimed that the killer had a hook in place of a hand. Armed with this power and information Deadman is thrust into his unique quest.

Deadman's unusual origin, powers, and quest were not the only ele-

Deadman Agonistes: Neal Adams brings a new realism and drama to comic book art. From *Strange Adventures* 212, June 1968.

ments that made the strip revolutionary. Jack Miller, often writer as well as editor through the first seven issues, summed up Deadman's uniqueness in the letter page of issue 211 (Apr. 1968). Responding to a reader's suggestion that Deadman be teamed up with the Spectre, Miller replied, "Deadman [is] done in a highly realistic manner, while Spectre, although just as effective, [is] done in the more traditionally super-charged and imaginative manner. If you tried to mix [the styles] all you'd have left is hash." The key phrase in Miller's statement is "highly realistic." Where traditional heroes pledged themselves to fighting crime or defending the human race, Deadman existed solely for the purpose of tracking down his killer. Instead of encountering costumed villains, bizarre aliens, evil gods, and the like, Deadman's quest brought him up against such adversaries as dope dealers, motorcycle gangs, villainous circus performers, smugglers of illegal immigrants, and professional assassins; in short, Deadman's adventures featured plausible characters and true-to-life situations. In addition to groundbreaking subject matter, Deadman featured the first mature work of Neal Adams, the man who would prove to be the most influential artist of the decade to come.

Adams was a young artist who had worked his way up through a wide range of advertising art, newspaper strips, and humor comics. With the second issue of *Deadman* (the first issue was hastily cranked out by Carmine Infantino), he was awarded his first regular costumed-hero assignment. Adams promptly combined wildly experimental layouts with a startling naturalism. He showed a flair for action sequences comparable to Kane and Kirby's, but his action was not confined to individual panels; his figures literally burst free of the borders, flying and throwing punches clear into the next page. Yet at the same time, Adams excelled in character nuance. Where most comic book artists would use a stock expression to portray anger, righteous indignation, anguish, or frustration, Adams not only distinguished each vividly, but molded them in accordance with a specific character. His fine, realistic draftsmanship caught every detail: clothes were made from real cloth, hands were built of bone and sinew, and hair either blew in a breeze or became matted with sweat. Adams himself once said that if costumed heroes really existed, they would look the way he drew them.

The writing itself complemented the art by being gritty and realistic. Avoiding both the formal explanatory quality of most DC scripting and the heavyhanded emotionalism of Marvel, Deadman's many writers kept the prose terse but evocative. Captions were merely crisp stage directions that sped the action along, and word balloons contained naturalistic dialogue. Deadman's personal desire for vengeance lent the stories a hardboiled edge that communicated his rage and self-pity as integral elements of the story line, not as extraneous characterization.

The fans quickly recognized and lauded this new development. One letter-writer called *Deadman* the "first adult comic in history." Another described it as the "old-fashioned hit-'em-in-the-guts type that has long been needed in comics." *Deadman*, wrote a third, "is portrayed with the most feeling and realism of any creation in comic books." And Marv Wolfman, a prominent fan soon to become a prominent comic book writer, praised its "adult themes."

The adult themes in *Deadman* were greatly facilitated by the hero's ability to possess bodies; thanks to this power, Deadman was able to infiltrate any situation and experience any predicament firsthand. In the course of his frustrating search for his killer, Deadman clears a young man of a murder charge (SA 206, Nov. 1967), enters the body of a critically wounded old friend and saves his life by instilling in him a ferocious will to live (SA 213, Aug 1968), and is instrumental in bringing a professional assassin to justice (SA 214, Oct. 1968), among many other altruistic deeds.

In one stroke, DC leapfrogged over Marvel. Marvel had broken from DC's childish orientation to pioneer comics for the adolescent, but DC writers now dared to write at their own level rather than condescend to any tried-and-true comic audience. Although *Deadman* was not to prove a great commercial success, it freed writers and artists to press the as-yet-untested limits of the field and to sound the desires of readers.

The first attempts to explore this new ground followed almost immediately.

The DC Experiment

With the Batman craze, DC was riding easily at the top of the comic book world. But crazes have a way of burning out as quickly as they catch fire, and costumed-hero camp proved to be no exception; in its second season the *Batman* show was already losing ratings points, and in 1967 DC first showed signs of a drop in sales. During the same period, the company passed to new ownership, the Kinney Corporation. Added to this was the meteoric rise of Marvel, suddenly threatening DC's long-established primacy. As yet the situation was still in hand, but the company's new publishers realized that if high sales were to be maintained, some post-camp changes would have to be made.

The first step toward such changes was a logical one: hire an editorial director who would control all of DC's stables, and who had a creative background, not just—as with former publishers Jack Liebowitz and Irwin Donenfeld—a financial one. Since the 1950s, Schwartz, Weisinger, and the other editors had run their stables like separate little companies, with their own styles and employees. Now it was felt, not surprisingly, that a more unified approach, coordinated by a single comic book veteran, would be needed. The surprise came when the choice for the job was announced. The new management passed over its established editors and writers, choosing instead an artist, one who had just begun to carve a niche for himself in the new post of DC cover editor: Carmine Infantino. From a purely art-related post, Infantino was thus thrust, with no experience, into a position of great financial and creative responsibility.

Infantino has been both criticized and praised for having little clear idea of a direction for the company but a great openness to new ideas. His first act was to hire a quartet of new editors both to create new titles and to revamp old ones, and—showing an understandable bias in view of his own background—all four of the editors he chose were artists: Dick Giordano, Joe Orlando, Mike Sekowsky, and Joe Kubert.

These new editors not only provided numerous old titles with facelifts, but launched a number of new ones as well. Taking their cue from Deadman, they brought to their comics, whether old or new, an undercurrent of realism and a keen attention to character. Within this framework, however, the operational word was *experimentation*. New kinds of heroes, even new genres, were created and old ones were recast in a completely new light.

The acquisition of Giordano was the finest feather in the new editorial director's cap. After starting at Charlton Comics as both a penciler and inker in the early 1950s, Giordano held on as one of that company's few long-term employees until being made executive editor in the mid-1960s. As an editor he gathered around himself the most creative people available to Charlton, and encouraged them to write and draw comics as they saw fit. Steve Ditko did some of his best work on a revitalized Captain Atom, a revived Golden Age costumed hero called the Blue Beetle, and the Question, a mysterious, morally zealous crime-fighter of his own invention (this was to be the basis for the fanatically moralistic Mr. A, whom Ditko soon created for Wally Wood's new artist-run-and-owned alternative press, Witzend). Giordano also oversaw a martial-arts strip entitled *Judo-Master*, the violence-hating *Peacemaker*, the morally ambivalent *Peter Cannon Thunderbolt*, and finally *The Fightin' 5*, about a squad of adventurers.

When hired away by DC, Giordano brought with him not only Ditko, but a group of rising talents—writers Denny O'Neil ("Sergius O'Shaughnessy"), and Steve Skeates, and artists Jim Aparo and Pat Boyette—and an editorial philosophy radically different from any other at DC. Although he did staunchly advocate an emphasis on realism, characterization, and innovation, he would never forge a Giordano style comparable to the Schwartz or Weisinger styles. "I prefer to work with people whose work I admire and let them do what they do best," he says. "I am not interested in having them do *my* book. . . . I'm interested in creating an atmosphere in which a free-lancer—an artist, writer, letterer, colorist—will feel comfortable doing things the way he feels they should be done. . . . I tried to establish a situation where we were all working together, perhaps having some fun in the process."

Giordano's approach paid its greatest dividends with the three new titles he launched in 1968. Two of these were done by Steve Ditko; each was very different philosophically, and yet each bore the unique Ditko stamp as clearly as his *Spider-Man* work two years before.

The first of these, the Creeper, is the weird, frightening alter ego of hard-boiled journalist Jack Ryder. It is, however, an illusory alter ego. While attempting in vain to rescue a scientist held captive by communists, Ryder has secreted inside his body a device that gives him great strength and speed; at the same time it causes a demonic yellow costume with a green wig and a flamelike red shawl to appear over him, giving him an unholy appearance that unnerves both criminals and police (Show. 73, Apr. 1968). Taking advantage of his horrific appearance, Ryder adopts a haunting laugh and an unearthly pattern of speech: "Ha haaaa!! Stupid mortals! Did you seriously think I am mere flesh?"

Inwardly, however, Ryder laughs at his own histrionics: "I missed my calling! Anybody who can ad-lib lines like that should be writing Dracula movies!" (*Creeper* 1, June 1968). This duality of eerie hero and regular Joe made the Creeper a sort of tough, self-possessed version of Spider-Man. With a complex supporting cast and a regular, many-faced villain called Proteus (whose true face was revealed in the final issue, Cr. 6, Apr. 1969,) this was the closest we would get to a continuation of the themes he had been developing in his last years at Marvel. Spookily drawn by Ditko and written with tough simplicity by Denny O'Neil, it was a brief but exciting series.

Ditko's second contribution, written by Steve Skeates, relied much more heavily on the social issues and youth concerns of the time. Judge Irwin Hall is a tough but reasonable man who believes in our system of checks and balances. His two sons, however, are radical extremes: Hank believes that force is the only effective tool of politics and justice; Don says that "violence only begets more violence," and shuns it in every arena of life. Their disagreement might have remained confined to arguments at college and antiwar rallies, had a group of criminals not seriously injured their father with a bomb; while chasing the criminals they are visited by a supernatural power, "a strange disembodied voice" which grants them great agility, strength, a pair of costumes—an angry red one for Hank, a softly feathered blue one for Don—and highly appropriate new names, the Hawk and the Dove. In rounding up the criminals, their opposing personalities shine through. The Hawk comes on slugging viciously, while the Dove uses his powers to elude, restrain, and baffle his opponents (Show. 75, June 1968).

Arguments about the rightness of violence dominated the interaction of the brothers in *The Hawk and the Dove*. The Hawk chided his brother for cowardice whenever he drew back from a fight, while the Dove called his brother a "sadist," a "witless barbarian," and an "outlaw" for his reflexive attacks on criminals; yet when the Hawk was in danger, brotherly love drew the Dove to his side, fighting in his own cautious manner. In the end, somehow—ineptly, disjointedly, despite a total lack of teamwork—they saw that justice was done (H&D 1, Sept. 1968).

Skeates's scripting, both thoughtful and amusing, dominated the series. For Steve Ditko it was a fairly atypical series, and he left it after issue 2 (Nov. 1968), whereupon Gil Kane contributed some of his most energetic action art for the title's remaining four issues.

Giordano's third new effort was *The Secret Six*, comicdom's answer to the then-popular "Mission Impossible" TV series. In yet another departure from the traditional DC style, here was a team of six intrepid adventurers engaging in international espionage. Rather than wage battle with powerful villains or hostile aliens, the Secret Six recover stolen jewels, thwart power-mad despots, and rescue political prisoners. The tone of the series was realistic, and within this framework the tautly suspenseful stories were set down with bite and vigor.

In the first issue of *The Secret Six* (May 1968), we learn that the team was organized by a mysterious personage calling himself Mockingbird

The Hawk and the Dove: Gil Kane's action art at its peak, with his own inks and script. From *The Hawk and the Dove* 5, May 1969.

The only clue we are given to his identity is that he is one of the six members. Mockingbird, we also discover, has a hold over each of them, and with these trump cards he induces them to take on their dangerous missions. The challenge to guess Mockingbird's identity provided another fascinating element to the stories.

The team consisted of Mike Tempest, a former heavyweight contender who got in trouble with the mob when he refused to take a dive; Dr. August Durant, a nuclear physicist who was inoculated with a rare and fatal disease by enemy agents; Carlo di Rienzi, whose son was crippled when thugs blew up his home; Lili de Neuve, a famous French actress who was framed for a murder and subsequently convicted in court; King Savage, who turned traitor under the interrogation of communists; and Crimson Dawn, a top-flight model hiding a seamy past. In the case of each, Mockingbird either saved their lives, supplied them with miracle cures, or sprung them from disastrous predicaments. Should any of them ever step out of line, Mockingbird will simply revoke the life-saving assistance he has provided them with.

As well as mystery and action, the stories offered in-depth vignettes concerning the personal lives of the members. True to the basic philosophy of the strip, these character sketches were drawn from common life experiences, not from extraterrestrial origins, freak, accidents, or psuedo-scientific fabrications. When Mike Tempest tells his story, for instance, we read of prize matches, crooked managers, fixed fights, a trial at which Tempest testified against a racketeer, and finally of the brutal beating Tempest received at the hands of the racketeer's goons.

The series was created by E. Nelson Bridwell, a former writer for *Mad* magazine who came to comics when he became Mort Weisinger's editorial assistant in the early 1960s, and artist Frank Springer, a former assistant to George Wunder on the *Terry and the Pirates* newspaper strip. Springer's pencils were scratchy and rather stiff, but with the third issue the art chores fell to Jack Sparling, who promptly provided the explosive action sequences so necessary to round out Bridwell's suspense-filled yarns.

Despite the excellent quality of the strip, however, *The Secret Six* lasted only until their seventh issue. To this day, the secret of Mockingbird's identity stands unresolved.

With two exceptions, Giordano was less successful with the titles he inherited from other editors. He was asked, for example, to "play out the string" for three series whose cancellations had already been decided upon: George Kashdan's *Blackhawk* and *Bomba* (following the end of Kashdan's editorial career), and Julius Schwartz's *Spectre*. Having only two issues of each comic to play with, he was unable to work his particular brand of magic to their benefit.

Under Giordano, *The Teen Titans* suffered from a lack of direction, as well as from the absence of a regular creative team. Although the strip was handled by such varied talents as Neal Adams, Gil Kane, Marv Wolf-

Jack Sparling's art barrels along for the Secret Six. Script by E. Nelson Bridwell. From *The Secret Six* 4, November 1968.

135

man, Len Wein, Nick Cardy, Bob Haney, and others, none of them contributed with enough regularity to imbue the series with any consistent approach. The stories consequently ranged from battles with monsters to light mysteries, from invasions of extradimensional fiends to a multi-issue saga (at Infantino's request) in which the Titans renounced their powers and tried to make do as normal teenagers. In the resultant chaos (which Giordano attributes largely to Infantino's "constant interference"), the series, despite a number of excellent yarns, never quite developed an identity of its own and was eventually canceled in 1973, under different editorship.

The innovative editor also inherited *Deadman* from Jack Miller, which he maintained at the same level of excellence, but it was *Aquaman*, another title relinquished by Kashdan, that Giordano improved to the greatest extent. Taking over on issue 40 (Aug. 1968), Giordano's creative team of writer Steve Skeates and artist Jim Aparo immediately launched the Sea King on a richly tapestried, suspenseful nine-part saga. The story begins when Mera, Aquaman's wife, is abducted, and traces Aquaman's frenzied quest to save her; meanwhile, back at his kingdom, Atlantis is threated both by earthquakes and the schemes of an evil deputy leader to overthrow Aquaman's rule.

After this adventure, however, the strip became a little disjointed. The individual stories displayed the same verve that had prevailed under the new creative team, but the strip seemed headed nowhere. Despite this failing, Aquaman was the last holdout of the stable, enduring until Giordano's resignation from editing in 1971.

Another key editor under Infantino, Joe Orlando, first rose to prominence as Wally Wood's artistic collaborator in the early 1950s, then as a very Wood-like horror and science fiction artist for the EC line. After more than a decade of free-lancing—especially work for *Mad* magazine and helping publisher Jim Warren set up his high-quality horror comic, *Creepy*—he came to work for Jack Miller at DC, drawing *Scooter* and *The Inferior Five*, which he would come to edit after Infantino's promotion. His first significant act as editor was to take over *House of Mystery*, dropping *Dial H for Hero* and *Martian Manhunter* and remaking the magazine in the dark, eerie cast of the EC horror comics of his past. With its varied non-series stories, this was one of DC's prime testing grounds for new talent, and many of the major stars of the 1970s entered the field under Orlando.

Orlando avoided straight costumed-hero material, seeking instead to break new ground or revive genres that had fallen into disfavor during the Silver Age. His first new title, *Anthro*, was written and drawn by Howie Post, whose career until then had been spent mainly on newspaper comic strips. The title character was "a lusty young man of prehistory," the impetuous adolescent son of a brutish Stone Age hunter. His low-key adventures revolved aorund the difficulties of living up to his father's demands (Show. 74, May 1968), a romance with a headstrong girl from another tribe of hunters (An. 1, Aug. 1968), and struggles with beasts and the elements (An. 2, Oct. 1968). Later, in an exotic detour, he visited a bloodthirsty early agricultural society of a Mayan type (An. 4, Feb. 1969). The quiet humor of Post's scripting, the rough-hewn naturalism of his drawings, his humane subject matter, and his attention to anthropological detail gave the series a believability and immediacy that justified its first subtitle: "It could be you!" The character of Anthro promised to develop and mature with his adventures, but cancellation made that impossible (An. 6, Aug. 1969).

Perhaps the most delightful of all the new titles during this highly creative period was *Bat Lash*, DC's first Western title since the 1950s (Show. 76, Aug. 1968). Like Giordano's *Secret Six,* Orlando's *Bat Lash* was also comicdom's answer to a TV show, this time the popular western *Maverick.* And like *Maverick, Bat Lash* walked the line between hero and scoundrel.

Bat Lash was a combination of many elements; the strip abounded with humor, action, pathos, and beauty. But in keeping with the spirit of the times, writer Denny O'Neil (assisted often by famed *Mad* cartoonist Sergio Aragones) strove for realism, no matter what slant any particular issue was given. Also highly emphasized was Bat Lash's character, especially his paradoxical nature. In one issue, Bat steals a pocket watch from a priest; in the next, he comes upon a little girl wandering in the wilderness and takes charge of her.

Another strong point of *Bat Lash* was the beautiful artwork by Nick Cardy. Cardy rendered the strip in a highly stylized manner, as if taking a cue from co-scripter Aragones, but balanced this tendency with some of the loveliest nature scenes ever featured in comic books. Whether it be a scorching desert, a snow-covered plain, or a meadow aflame with flowers, Cardy delivered one incomparable vista after another.

The series reached its apex in issue 6 (Sept. 1969), which featured one of the most poignant scenes ever produced in a comic. Bat Lash finds his way to a convent where both his sister and his old girlfriend are cloistered, hoping his "ramblin', gunslingin' days are past," and that he can once again "be the decent fella" he once was. But his sister refuses to go away with him, insisting that although he is as polite and charming as ever, underneath he has become brutal. In the final panel, when a dejected Bat Lash rides away down a lovely wooded lane, his sister, from the convent in which she has chosen to remain, says, "[He's] gone . . . gone forever! Destined always to be a fugitive from the law . . . haunted always by the spectre of death . . . may God have pity on him."

The very next issue was Bat Lash's last. Along with all the other daring and exciting innovations of Giordano and Orlando, it too had failed to catch on. (The last Orlando innovation of 1968 was also the least of his successes; this was writer/artist Joe Simon's *Brother Power, the Geek,* the story of a living bundle of rags that purported to the tell the truth about the underworld of hippies and "flower power.")

Many of the strips discussed in this chapter—*The Creeper, Anthro, The Hawk and the Dove,* and *Bat Lash*—debuted in the pages of *Showcase.* During the same period, *Showcase* featured a number of other titles that did not graduate to their own comics but nonetheless deserve mention. Among them were *Johnny Double* (Show. 78, Nov. 1968), a private detective story; *The Dolphin* (Show. 79, Dec. 1968), the tale of an odd, water-breathing woman; *The Nightmaster* (Show. 82–84, May–Aug. 1969), a sword-and-sorcery saga; and *Firehair* (Show. 85–87, Sept.–Dec. 1969), the story of a half-breed Indian, featuring some of the finest art ever turned in by Joe Kubert (Kubert's great contributions as editor, writer, and artist, which snowballed in the 1970s, will be treated later).

The least successful of the new artist/editors was Mike Sekowsky. His approach to the new realism and characterization leaned toward the faddishly adolescent. *Wonder Woman,* under his tenure as editor, writer, and artist, became an adventurous version of television's "That Girl," as the heroine was deprived of her powers, exiled from Paradise Island, and booted out of the Justice League of America (WW 179, Dec. 1968; JLA 69, Feb. 1969). As Diana Prince, now a mere powerless woman, the former Wonder Woman became the proprietress of a boutique to make ends meet, and hooked up with an elderly oriental gentleman named I Ching, who versed her in the martial arts; their adventures ranged from missions of espionage, to the salvaging of young lives that had run afoul of the law in a big city, to a hard-hitting epic of warfare on Paradise Island. Throughout the series, however, a realistic slant alternated with a fascination for feminine fashion and minor domestic troubles.

Sekowsky's other characters, the New Metal Men, who had already become persecuted outcasts under a brief editorial stint by Jack Miller, were now outfitted with human appearances and provided with such fashionable human roles as model, folksinger, artist, tycoon, and engineer. Where so much of their charm had derived from the contrast of metal form with humanlike personality, now clichéd characterization squeezed out the charm. *Metal Men* was canceled in 1970.

On a minor note, one new title emerged from the older stables. Launched by Weisinger and continued by Schwartz, *Captain Action* was a tie-in with a toy manufacturer, which perished after only five issues (Nov. 1968–July 1969), but featured superb art by Gil Kane and Wally Wood and displayed Kane's growing skills as a writer.

The stable of Murray Boltinoff also responded to the times. Boltinoff turned *Challengers of the Unknown*'s direction back toward its original, slightly supernatural conception. New writers, including Robert Kanigher and rookie Mike Friedrich, added such menaces as the Legion of the Weird, made up of a witch, a Druid, an Egyptian mystic, and the like. But too many writers and artists—ranging from Sparling to George Tuska to Berni Wrightson—left the series uneven, and it was canceled in late 1970.

Boltinoff brought Kanigher and artist Frank Thorne in to revamp *Toma-hawk* as a mature, realistic western comic (shortly succeeded by new editor Joe Kubert). He also revived an old hard-boiled adventure strip with an occult edge called *Johnny Peril,* with Sparling art, in *Unexpected* (U 107, July 1968); but it never found its footing and soon vanished. Boltinoff was more successful in revamping *Unexpected* as a 1950s-style "mystery" comic à la Joe Orlando.

Without exception, the creations of Giordano, Orlando, and their peers failed commercially. The failure of this deluge of wild but effective experimentation was perhaps less a reflection on its popularity than on the overall slump in comic sales which was affecting the industry now that the camp craze had completely passed (a slump speeded by a price increase from 12 to 15 cents for all DC and Marvel comics, which unsettled many young readers). Indeed, even such stalwarts as the Atom and Hawkman had vanished in a general reduction of titles at DC, meanwhile, the Tower comics company had folded, while Gold Key, Charlton, Archie, Dell, and Harvey were cutting back on their titles and once again turning away from costumed heroes and the like, back to their familiar horror, funny animals, humor, and other genres.

But the experiment had been an exciting one, and the field seemed suddenly flushed with the recognition of its newly expanding horizons. Anything, it now appeared, might be tackled in the medium. Attention was being turned toward the new adult "underground comix," and there was increasing interest in maverick efforts like Gil Kane's independently published adventure story, *His Name Is . . . Savage.* Many readers, too, were impressed with DC's new direction and would later, as both fans and young professionals, restore some of its elements to the comics of the future.

First, however, it was becoming increasingly clear that DC would have to channel this new-found creativity in a different direction if the company was to withstand the increasingly serious challenge of Marvel Comics.

The Marvel Expansion

At about the same time that DC unleashed its crop of new titles, its up-and-coming rival was undergoing an expansion of its own; but Marvel was destined to have less trouble with the approaching crisis in sales. Even as the camp rage blew over and DC began to worry, Stan Lee and Martin Goodman were still riding high, watching their line's sales soar until they felt bold enough to expand first their staff, with new and unusual talents, then the line itself, with a number of new comics. This prosperity, like DC's, was not to continue unabated, but it added to Marvel's tremendous momentum and enabled it to make a number of further contributions to the changing look of the field.

Of all Marvel's new staffers, none was to have as great an impact on the company as a whole as the fan-turned-pro Roy Thomas. His first regular assignment was *Sgt. Fury,* but his heart was clearly not in it and he soon turned the chores over to a young discovery of his own, Gary Friedrich. He also did fill-in writing throughout the line, and eventually took over *The Sub-Mariner* (TA 93, July 1967), where, with Adkins, Everett, and Werner Roth, he continued Lee's brand of gladiator battle. His first significant contributions, however, were to be made on the two teams that Lee passed into his hands, the X-Men and the Avengers.

From his first appearance on *The X-Men,* Thomas showed himself to be a very wordy writer of dialogue, intent on adding touches of characterization even to the most insignificant background characters; his opening splash panel, depicting a bank robbery by Unus and the Blob, sports ten different word balloons and a caption, totaling nearly two hundred words, which allow us to understand the incident from the point of view of villains, victims, and bystanders alike. In the course of the issue, the X-Men and the two evil mutants prove very loquacious in revealing details of the story and their personal reactions to it, while along the way a flashback episode gives us the story of how Professor X became a cripple (XM 20, May 1966).

This completism, taking every opportunity to add details and fill in background information, was to be a hallmark of Thomas and, to various degrees, of later writers who came up through fandom. Springing from the careful, almost archival study of comic books, it had the effect of making Marvel stories seem not just like entertainment but like the historical documents of some other world. With this historical perspective came a fascination with comics' past, which Thomas promptly evidenced by resurrecting "a stampede of yesteryear's most sensational super-villains," six old Iron Man and Human Torch villains whom Lee had wisely left forgotten (XM 22, July 1966). Thomas set about linking up scattered pieces of the Marvel universe with knowledge and careful thought, whereas Lee had seemed to be doing so impulsively. He launched a backup feature, for example, detailing the origins and early days of the various X-Men, which Lee had left unexplored (XM 38, Nov. 1967). Also, with his youth and the contact with teenagers that his schoolteaching days had given him, he was able to make the speech patterns, activities, and musical tastes of his adolescent mutants more convincing than Lee had. Thus, because of his background—although he was still learning the basic tools of storytelling—Thomas became an instant favorite of the hard-core fans.

Sales of *The X-Men* nevertheless sagged steadily, perhaps because of poor art by Roth, Heck, and George Tuska, perhaps because Thomas had yet to hit his stride as an entertaining writer. He left the series after two years, and when he returned a year later he was joined by Neal Adams, with the dark, dramatic inking of Tom Palmer (XM 56, May 1969). Together they crafted a hard-hitting, suspenseful series about the mutant-hunting Sentinels, one of the very few X-Men stories to make full use of the original theme of persecution, followed by an exotic adventure in a lost jungle world, featuring a rare glimpse into the mind and personality of Magneto (XM 57–63, June–Dec. 1969). Although these issues combined plot, art, and melodrama into some of Marvel's most acclaimed products, even they were not enough to win back the X-Men's vanished readership and prevent their cancellation in 1970. The complex character interactions and harrowing tone of those stories would, however, set the style for an X-Men revival five years later and thus indirectly help change the direction of comics in the late 1970s.

Thomas made more immediate contributions to comics when he took the helm of *The Avengers* (Av. 35, Dec. 1966). It became apparent quickly that he took comic books seriously not only as historical material but as an artistic medium when he began heightening conflict between the characters and deepening their emotional turmoil. Hawkeye the Marksman received much of his attention, remaining the rebel and misfit of the group but now revealing more complex reasons for his ambivalence, including the torch he carried for the beautiful Russian spy named the Black Widow, who was now turning against her old country and trying to win the trust of S.H.I.E.L.D. Shortly Thomas introduced the Red Guardian, a proud Soviet counterpart of Captain America, who proved to be the Widow's estranged husband. Although the Guardian's goal is to destroy Captain America, in the final story, "The Valiant Also Die," he gives his life to prevent an unconscious Cap from being blown up by a cowardly Russian officer. In the aftermath, the Widow must make peace with her mem-

John Buscema's stately Avengers: the Black Panther, Hawkeye, Thor, Goliath, Captain America, the Wasp, the Vision, and Iron Man. Inks by George Klein, script by Roy Thomas. From *The Avengers* 58, November 1968.

ories and old loyalties, Cap must live with the knowledge that he owes his life to the enemy of his country, and Hawkeye must learn to submerge his pride in his love for the Widow (Av. 43–44, Aug.–Sept. 1967).

By creating these internal dilemmas, raising troubling questions about loyalty and nationalism, and granting heroic proportions to a communist, Thomas deepened Lee's emotional content, adding an air of profundity to Marvel's impetuous character development. He also utilized a flowery, self-important writing style that underlined his serious intentions ("Never, accursed one," cries the Guardian at his death, "not till the heavens crumble, shall Captain America be killed by one so craven as you!"). Literary references and philosophical conversations gave collegiate readers something to chew on, and an increasingly learned tone in the letter pages suggested that such readers were taking notice.

Changes in Avengers membership gave Thomas opportunities to tackle new themes. He used Goliath and the Wasp to try his hand at some heavy marital drama, culminating in a nervous breakdown that caused Goliath to take a new identity, Yellowjacket, and temporarily turn against his teammates (Ave. 59, Dec. 1968). Thor's rival, Hercules, joined, for some mythological content, and the Black Panther enabled Thomas to grapple directly with racial issues. But the most important new Avenger was a sensitive android called the Vision: he was able to turn intangible and fire bolts of force from his head, but his powers were of far less interest than his feelings.

With his plastic body and mechanical voice, the Vision is apparently without emotion, but somehow in his creation he was given human memories and, as a consequence, human feelings. His uncertainty about his true nature fills him with an inexpressible agony (Ave. 57, Oct. 1968). Soon he learns that his brain waves were taken—in a distinctly Thomas twist— from those of a dead hero from 1964 called Wonder Man. Though eased by this knowledge, he is still troubled about his place in human society. His brain, he notes, "is not truly a brain at all, but a maze of printed circuits ... I wonder ... is it possible to be ... 'basically human'?" The Avengers reassure him of his humanity and welcome him to their ranks, drawing a tear from his synthetic eye and thus the title of the story: "Even an Android Can Cry!" (Av. 58, Nov. 1968).

With the mystery-filled origin of the Vision, Thomas showed himself in possession of imagination, emotional force, and plotting talent well able to flesh out his thorough understanding of comics. Although the character's confusion was eventually to break down into self-pity (particularly in an interminably frustrated romance with the Scarlet Witch that would drag on for a decade), and his tragic alienation was to be badly overused, his early appearances brought a new weight and substance to comic book characterization and emotional drama. Thomas, like Lee before him, overstated his themes to get them across, often to the point of mawkishness. But the popularity of *The Avengers* demonstrated undeniably that the comic book medium did have room for thoughts far more ambitious and intelligent than editors had ever assumed.

Thomas was aided on *The Avengers* by the arrival, soon after his own, of penciler John Buscema. Buscema had been one of Lee's favorite young pencilers in the early 1950s, but he had left comics during their shaky years for the more secure field of advertising. Back at the now-prosperous Marvel, he proved to be a steady, prolific worker whose productivity would prove very valuable as the company grew. He had a bold, clear style full of thickly muscled characters in tense, dramatic poses. He used broadly twisted hands and facial features to give impact to Thomas's emotional scenes. He helped Thomas further with his custom of rarely placing more than one or two figures in a panel, leaving out background characters altogether, which prevented the scripter from going overboard on his dialgoue. Soon he incorporated a number of Jack Kirby's action techniques into his art, combining the best of Marvel's melodrama and fight scenes.

Perhaps Marvel's strongest creative force in the late 1960s, although far less prolific than Thomas, was writer/artist Jim Steranko. Steranko was an artist of diverse interests and abilities who would try his hand through the years at book cover illustration, advertising design, writing, and publishing. Comics would never be his sole interest, but he was fascinated with their history and attracted to the notion of telling stories through pictures. He had read a number of Marvel comics and been deeply impressed with Lee's creativity and openness to change. Lee, in turn, was immediately bowled over by Steranko's work; according to the artist, Lee told him, "We don't have anything for you, but you're too good to get away."

Lee started Steranko penciling and inking details inside Kirby's layouts on *Nick Fury, Agent of S.H.I.E.L.D.*, but soon gave him control of all drawing and writing on the series (ST 155, Apr. 1967). Exaggerating the spy-movie elements of the strip into an uninhibited, slightly facetious, James Bond–style romp, he kept the stories sophisticated and ceaselessly fresh. With unrestrained imagination, he armed his agents with devices like the Vortex Beam (which lifted objects through space), the Aphonic Bomb (which exploded without sound), a pocket-sized Electronic Absorber (which saved Fury from a huge jolt of electricity), and a molecular disintegrator called the Q-Ray machine—all in his first, eleven-page story. Steranko also added such behind-the-scenes material as a look inside Spy School and a colorful supporting cast that included the mysterious Countess Valentina Allegro de Fontaine, who was to begin a slyly handled but unabashedly sexual affair with Fury. S.H.I.E.L.D.'s enemies were a legion of ingenious, scheming, advanced scientific fiends, particularly the Yellow Claw, a stock Oriental villain from the 1950s, now revived as a maniac out to conquer the world with gadgetry. The stories were high-speed blasts of technological combat, often jumbled and hard to follow, but

The Steranko page: Design, gadgetry, and special effects swirl around Nick Fury. Inks by Sinnott. From *Strange Tales* 167, April 1968.

written with a subtle campiness that let us know the writer was coming from outside the field, doing this as a lark.

Steranko's greatest impact, however, came not from his writing but his art. Drawing upon the pop-art and psychedelic fashions of his time, he made nearly every page a crazily twisting, tilting design of action-crowded panels, vivid colors, and flashy visual effects (Steranko claims credit, in fact, for getting Marvel to drop the heavy use of gray which weakened its art so much in earlier years). Bodies hurtled and twisted with an abandon that would have given Kirby pause, while spiny, swirling conglomerations of machinery crowded every scene; but most pages nevertheless resolved into cohesive patterns. This attention to the layout of an entire page, rather than merely the separate panels within it, suggested a new dimension of storytelling to the many young artists whose imaginations were seized by his work. And his willingness to innovate visually with nearly every drawing helped loosen up the field for new approaches to comic art. Thus, although he had few significant imitators, Steranko set standards that were to open ground for an explosion of visual innovation during the early 1970s.

He set standards also in his attitude toward his work. With his diverse talents, he had the liberty to approach comics on his own terms, and he did so with a vengeance. "If you're a publisher, and you want my work," he has said, "you get it my way or you don't get it at all." Of Marvel he says, "We had disagreements about the way I told stories. . . . And if I had to sit there and put a lot of Steranko blood, sweat, and tears into it . . . I felt that at least I had the right to say, 'No, you're not going to do this to my work.' "

This independence posed a problem for Lee: "It was simply that Jim, who is something of a perfectionist, would take forever to do a page, and you know what our schedule is. And I used to say, 'For Christ's sake, work faster! So don't put as much work in it! . . .' And he couldn't care less about deadlines. He did it his way."

Because of Steranko's trouble meeting deadlines, Lee—despite a great admiration for his work—felt obliged to bring other artists in, spurring Steranko to seek his living in other fields. Steranko thus became the first of a new breed of artist to rebel against the assembly-line methods of production, a breed who would shortly begin to force a number of changes in the business of publishing comic books

A pair of other new writers drifted through Marvel in those years. Arnold Drake, long a mainstay of Jack Schiff and Murray Boltinoff at DC, used his odd imagination to good effect in the flexible Marvel universe. During a year-long fill-in for Roy Thomas on The X-Men, he crafted an exciting tale (drawn, albeit hastily, by Steranko) involving a mysterious new female mutant named Polaris, the introduction of Cyclops's hot-headed brother, Havok, and a deviously complex scheme by Magneto (XM 50–52, Nov. 1968–Jan. 1969). He also created a futuristic group called the Guardians of the Galaxy for a one-shot story in a new *Showcase*-style title, *Marvel Super-Heroes* (MSH 18, Jan. 1969). Featuring various humans evolved to adapt to different planetary conditions—including a massive Jovian named Charlie-27 and a crystalline Plutonian called Martinex—and stunningly drawn by Gene Colan, it was an impressive enough idea to be remembered for a series of its own seven years later.

Also pinch-hitting frequently was Archie Goodwin, who was making his first forays into the hero genre. Once a prominent EC fan-addict, Goodwin, like many recent comic writers, set out to break into the field as an artist. His scripts, however, shone more brightly than his art, and by the mid-1960s he had become the most respected horror writer in the field, with Jim Warren's *Creepy* and *Eerie* magazines; on another Warren title, *Blazing Combat*, he displayed a tremendous flair for gritty, heartfelt war stories, which was to serve him well in the 1970s. His earliest costumed-hero work for Lee was less impressive, although he did contribute a good set of stories in which Iron Man battled Marvel's regular crime syndicate, the Maggia (TS 99–IM 1, Mar.–May 1968). Goodwin's greatest moments lay still ahead of him.

Stan Lee himself, although holding to a steady course that gave his readers dependable entertainment, would no longer be the great source of innovation he had once been. On *Spider-Man* he continued Peter Parker's collegiate soap opera, but without the complexity or rapid change he and Ditko had given it. Many early villains returned for a few stories, but new manaces, such as a huge, petulant crime czar called the Kingpin, were less satisfying. Despite a certain repetitiveness in the stories (such subplots as Aunt May's periodic bouts with death became almost laughable) and the competent but unimpressive art of John Romita, Spider-Man retained enough personal charm to rise to be Marvel's most popular hero.

Lee approached *Daredevil* with a little more audacity, introducing Matt Murdock's swinging "twin brother" Mike (DD 25, Feb. 1967)—in fact only a role played by Matt, with the aid of his extranormal senses, in order to prevent his friends from deducing his secret identity—and then arranging a moving fake death for him (DD 41, June 1968). But, except for Gene Colan's breathtakingly dramatic art, beautifully inked by Syd Shores, Daredevil never quite outgrew the shadow of Spider-Man.

Colan's art also graced *Iron Man*, enabling Lee to bring a little more dynamism into his stories. Munitions, government, and communism continued to predominate (as in "Here Lies Hidden . . . the Unspeakable Ultimo!" TS 76, Apr. 1966, when the Mandarin attacked the West), but a new drama and intrigue entered the strip.

In *The Hulk*, Lee continued to play with his themes of alienation and persecution, as Bill Everett's art was replaced by the rougher, grimmer renditions of John Buscema and Gil Kane. The series' steadiest artist, however, was Marie Severin, once a respected colorist and staffer at EC comics, where her brother John had been a star penciler and inker; now, with inks by Herb Trimpe, she proved to have a sensitive, naturalistic style of her own (beginning TA 92, June 1967).

Lee was also blessed with good artwork on *Dr. Strange*, where Everett paid tribute to Ditko's earlier work with a beautifully archaic, ornamental style evocative of the mysterious East (ST 147, Aug. 1966). Everett left shortly—when given a chance to draw again the character he had created in 1939, the Sub-Mariner—but in his place came Marie Severin and Dan Adkins, a former assistant to Wally Wood, who used a neat, polished style much like his mentor's. The writing, unfortunately, was only sporadically imaginative, as Lee repeatedly called for hasty pinch-hit jobs from Denny O'Neil, Raymond Marais, Jim Lawrence, and Roy Thomas.

The enlargements of Marvel's staff reflected an overall boom in the company's sales, and new titles inevitably followed. *Fantasy Masterpieces*, which debuted in late 1965, featured reprints of stories from the 1940s and 1950s, relying upon the curiosity or devotion of true Marvelites to keep it afloat. *Not Brand Ecch*, a hero humor comic full of Marvel in-jokes, followed in mid-1967. Shortly afterward, *Fantasy Masterpieces* changed its name to *Marvel Super-Heroes*, showcasing new ideas. The first of those was Captain Marvel (no relation to the Golden Age hero), a noble warrior-scientist of the alien Kree, ostensibly dispatched to Earth to punish mankind for the Fantastic Four's earlier destruction of a Kree robot, but in fact stranded there by a scheming officer who coveted the Captain's beloved (MSH 12, Dec. 1967). Drawn by Colan and leanly written by Lee, the idea was an instant hit, and soon, in Roy Thomas's hands, it graduated to its own title (*Captain Marvel* 1, May 1968), one of a bonanza of new titles to come from Marvel in 1968. Like most of those titles, unfortunately, it was to suffer from changing creative teams and inconsistent work, and like a number of them, it was doomed to failure in two years—even though the final five issues featured some clever science fiction ideas from Thomas, and masterful Gil Kane artwork (CM 17–21, Oct. 1969–Aug. 1970).

Early 1968 looked like a perfect time to expand the line. To begin with, all the two-comic titles—*Tales to Astonish*, *Tales of Suspense*, and *Strange Tales*—were split apart as all six series received their own magazines. The expansion was greeted enthusiastically by the readers, but it would, unfortunately, cause more harm than good. The Hulk did plod steadily along under Lee and Severin (soon followed by Herb Trimpe), and the Sub-Mariner enjoyed some adventures under Thomas and Buscema. But *Iron Man* lost Colan, leaving the art in the less able hands of Johnny Craig and George Tuska, and Goodwin's scripts were unable to keep its quality up. Kirby, perhaps feeling too burdened by the new full-length stories, soon left *Captain America;* Jim Steranko contributed three stylized, disturbing stories (CA 110, 111, 113; Feb.–May 1969) and Gene Colan illustrated a number of issues, but too many changes left the series directionless.

S.H.I.E.L.D. started with promise, as Steranko used the new twenty-page format to experiment with some complicated, offbeat single-issue stories, but the sudden doubling of page production worsened his trouble with deadlines until Lee pulled in a pinch-hitter, which angered Steranko and caused him to leave the strip. Writers like Gary Friedrich and artists like Frank Springer, Herb Trimpe, and a young Kirby imitator named Barry Smith were unable to fill the gap, and the title was canceled after fifteen issues (Nov. 1969).

Dr. Strange was perhaps the best of the newly independent titles, with Thomas taking a literary, cosmic approach to the Doctor's magic, and art first by Dan Adkins and then by Colan, darkly and mysteriously inked by Tom Palmer. But sales flagged, and even an attempt to make Strange a sort of costumed hero, complete with leotard and mask (DS 177, Feb. 1969), could not keep the title from a premature demise (DS 183, Nov. 1969).

One of Marvel's boldest ventures of 1968 was The Spectacular Spider-Man, a magazine-sized, black-and-white, thirty-five cent version of the company's best-selling title. The first issue failed commercially, however, largely because of distribution troubles, and a full-color second issue followed suit; but this would not be Marvel's last attempt to move into the magazine-format market that had done so well for Jim Warren's comics.

The finest of the new titles, in both story and art, was Stan Lee's favorite, The Silver Surfer. Selling for twenty-five cents (when regular comics were still twelve), every issue featured a forty-page story of the Surfer by Lee and Buscema, followed by a ten-page science fiction parable called "Tales of the Watcher" by Lee and Colan. Working on his beloved "Sentinel of the Spaceways," Lee was inspired to his most eloquent, even poetic, writing in scripts that required no hype or pretense to make their quality and profundity clear. In the hero's origin story, all the oddity of a bald, shiny surfer, flying through the sky, bemoaning the contradictions of the human spirit, disappears; it becomes a genuinely moving tale of a man losing both love and home, surrendering his fate into the hands of an awesome stranger, and then renouncing his last possession, his freedom, for a higher principle. The Surfer's meditations upon the contrast between the contented, stagnant world of his origin and the savage striving of Earth produced some well-turned maxims about the purpose of life: "That which is mine for the taking is not worth the taking. Paradise unearned is but a land of shadows" (SS 1, Aug. 1968). This seemed, indeed, like the culmination of Stan Lee's career as a writer. To match this high mark in Lee's writing, Buscema turned in some of his own most sweeping landscapes, evocative expressions, and beautiful figures, superbly complemented by the inking of Joe Sinnott and of John Buscema's brother, Sal.

But even the finest work was not immune to the shaky market of 1969 and 1970. With issue 18 (Sept. 1970), The Silver Surfer joined The X-Men, Dr. Strange, S.H.I.E.L.D., Captain Marvel, Marvel Super-Heroes, and Not Brand Ecch in oblivion (the Surfer was Lee's greatest disappointment among the cancellations, and he claims to have forbidden anyone else at Marvel to revive the series unless he himself was able to write it).

Like DC, Marvel's latest efforts at experimentation failed to forestall declining sales, and like DC, they realized that something fundamental would soon have to change.

The End of the Silver Age

The first signs of dropping sales at DC had prompted a number of new experimental titles as well as a radical overhauling of several minor old ones. But now, as sales failed to improve, it became apparent that even the mainstays would have to change. It would begin slowly, and without a clear direction, but it would ultimately sweep away virtually everything on which the Silver Age had been founded.

One major event that made the changes inevitable was a drastic shift in DC's personnel. According to Gardner Fox, DC's major writers, all veterans of many years who had toiled as free-lancers, were becoming alarmed about the field's shaky stature; concerned over their futures, particularly the financial worries of retirement, they became involved in a dispute with their employers. As Fox remembered it, "Several of the writers . . . myself included, got together to ask for certain fringe benefits from that outfit. Medical insurance, some sort of plan to lay aside some of our income for a retirement pension, that sort of thing. Jack Liebowitz didn't like the idea, so we were soon out on our necks . . . Bill Finger, France Herron, Arnold Drake, Otto Binder. . . ." Hamilton and Siegel had left shortly before for personal reasons, and Jack Miller and Dave Wood soon followed; in 1970, John Broome left Green Lantern and The Flash to spend his autumn years wandering through Asia. In a four-year period, almost the entire old guard of DC writers departed.

To fill this vacuum, DC had to recruit new writers and promote minor ones to major positions. Almost overnight, Denny O'Neil and Weisinger's assistant, E. Nelson Bridwell, were cropping up all over the place, and soon after hiring Jim Shooter, Weisinger added another young fan, Cary Bates, to his staff. One veteran, newspaper comic strip writer/artist Frank Robbins, was soon drafted into the fold. By 1968, three more teenage fans—Len Wein, Marv Wolfman, and Mike Friedrich—were breaking through into professionalism, and within the next few years they would be followed by more youngsters, including Elliot S. Maggin and Marty Pasko. With all these new writers would come, inevitably, a new slant to the old heroes.

Another major factor in these changing times was the breakdown of the editorial monoliths. Now, with Carmine Infantino overseeing the entire line, there was no longer any need for each editor to run his stable as if it

Changing times for the Flash: A new artist and new domestic concerns. Art by Andru and Esposito, script by Broome. From *The Flash* 189, June 1969.

were an independent company. Infantino's own promotion had left personnel gaps on both *The Flash* and *Detective Comics*. Schwartz filled them with Kanigher's principal artist, Ross Andru, and Schiff's Bob Brown, respectively. Giordano's writer, Denny O'Neil, replaced Fox on *The Justice League of America*. Cary Bates worked for both Schwartz and Weisinger, as did Andru. Neal Adams and Gil Kane worked for everybody, including Marvel. Suddenly, the readers no longer knew who would turn up in the pages of *The Flash* or *Superman*.

Despite these new arrivals, the editors maintained the basic elements of their particular styles for a time. Cary Bates, for example, wrote like a Weisinger man when he scripted *Superman* and like a Schwartz man when he scripted *The Flash*. Almost imperceptibly, however, changes manifested themselves. No editor, no matter how strong his personality, could stand for long against the influx of new talents and visions that was beginning to flood the field.

The few changes that took place immediately can be seen by briefly examining one title, *The Justice League of America*, in the hands of Denny O'Neil. Largely, these changes revolved around characterization. Green Arrow, once perhaps the most cardboard comic character of all time, now became a hotheaded champion of the downtrodden. Black Canary moved from Earth-2 to Earth-1 following the death of her husband, and became a modern young woman instead of an aging, nostalgic heroine. Martian Manhunter, who would yield the least to modern ideas of characterization, was sent off to New Mars, a distant planet, and hence out of the DC universe. Wonder Woman, now powerless, and Snapper Carr drifted away. The remaining heroes, although not radically altered, began to interact with a little more depth. Superman was perceived as the awesome hero his powers and heritage would logically make him. Batman became introverted and mysterious, more like the grim avenger his origin had suggested. The Atom told jokes. Flash had a married life to worry about. All in all, the heroes grew from the simple defenders of justice they had been throughout the Silver Age into distinct Marvel-style persons.

This new characterization brought a breath of fresh air, but overall the quality of the comics dropped. This was due primarily to drastic changes in the artistic staffs. In the Weisinger stable, Swan, already forced uncomfortably into DC's new large-panel format, now lost the pristine inking of George Klein and suffered under the heavy, overbearing lines of his replacement, Jack Abel. More and more stories appeared by artists whose styles clashed with Swan's, including Ross Andru and Winslow Mortimer. Schwartz was hit even harder. After Infantino, he lost, in rapid order, Mike Sekowsky, Sid Greene, Murphy Anderson, and Gil Kane—in short, all the giants of his stable. Their replacements, although adequate, did not possess the finesse of the old veterans (Neal Adams, with his atmospheric reworking of the Spectre, being the one exception). Andru, despite his dynamism, lacked the fluidity so necessary to the Flash; Dick Dillin, the new *Justice League* artist, could not solve layout problems as Sekowsky had, resulting in panels cluttered with heroes; Irv Novick and Bob Brown, the successors on *Batman* and *Detective Comics*, were unable to keep the Darknight Detective's nocturnal environment from becoming muddy and lusterless. By early 1970, not a single Schwartz comic displayed the stunning beauty of the Silver Age.

Along with the breakdown of the editorial monoliths came an irregularity of creative teams. Three or four writers, for instance, would alternate erratically on any given strip. At first, while the old editorial styles and classic type of DC storytelling endured, this worked well; the infusion of new ideas from young writers produced fresh, entertaining fare. It was an intimation, however, of trouble to come.

There were also intimations that the visions of the writers and artists would soon eclipse those of the editors. Denny O'Neil would always bring his particular slant to storytelling. Neal Adams had only to apply his unique art style to transform any given strip; in 1969 he took his most significant step, remolding Batman into a frightening night-stalker, and bringing about a totally new conception of his character. Wherever the two went, either individually or as a team, their vision would invariably supersede that of whatever editor they worked for. Other creative personalities of equal strength would soon emerge, parading their own visions, and the entire workings of the comics industry would be forever altered.

In attempting to revitalize the field, it became a virtual necessity to throw out all that had gone before. As the decade drew to a close, and new writers and artists sought to stretch the boundaries of the medium, the Silver Age quietly perished. Gone were the ingeniously plotted short stories, the unified editorial visions, the colorful and decorative art, and most of all, the exuberant sense of fun.

The Silver Age had possibly been the most consistently satisfying period in the history of comics. It was a time when unwaveringly solid craftmanship could exist side by side with the greatest extremes of experimentation. It was a time of the pristine Flash, the wonders of Kandor, the brawling Fantastic Four, the anguished Spider-Man, and the utterly bizarre Doom Patrol. It was a time of few editorial viewpoints, but within the few that there were, a wide spectrum of themes and inventions flourished in an environment of clear, farsighted vision. The readers, however, had withdrawn their support, and a decade would follow in which editors, writers, and artists, new and old alike, would scramble and grapple for a new direction.

Ironically, it was the man who had launched the Silver Age who pronounced its end. In 1970, when *Green Lantern* had seen a drastic drop in sales, Julius Schwartz handed it over to Denny O'Neil and Neal Adams and asked them to see what could be done with it.

PART
TWO

Relevance

The cover of *Green Lantern* 76 looked different. First, the Emerald Gladiator was no longer the sole star of the comic; he had been joined by fellow
Justice Leaguer Green Arrow. Second, the art had changed. The rousing
action scenes of Gil Kane had been replaced by a Neal Adams emotional
study. And third, there was an odd note of discord. Why was Green Arrow
shooting a shaft through his partner's power battery, crying, "Never
again!"?

But the biggest shock came with page one. The first words of the story
were, "For years he has been a proud man! He has worn the power ring of
the Guardians, and used it well, and never doubted the righteousness of
his cause. . . . His name, of course, is Green Lantern, and often he has
vowed that 'No evil shall escape my sight.' . . . He has been fooling himself."

Flying over Star City, Green Arrow's home, Green Lantern sees a "punk"
attacking a fat man in a suit. He intervenes, expecting approval from bystanders, but is greeted instead with a barrage of cans, rocks, and bottles.
Green Lantern is about to retaliate when Green Arrow appears and stops
him angrily. "Green Arrow!" cries Green Lantern. "You're . . . defending
these . . . these *anarchists?!*" Green Arrow explains that the "fat cat"
Green Lantern was defending is in fact a slumlord, and leads him through
a crumbling tenement. When an ancient black ghetto-dweller says to
Green Lantern, "I been readin' about you . . . how you work for the blue
skins . . . and how on a planet someplace you helped out the orange skins
. . . and you done considerable for the purple skins! Only there's skins you
never bothered with . . . the *black* skins! I want to know . . . how come?!"
The self-confidence that had bolstered the Emerald Gladiator since 1959
crumbled all at once—and so a new wave of comics was launched (*Green
Lantern/Green Arrow* 76, May 1970).

Here was a comic that broke with all tradition. *Green Lantern/Green
Arrow* was a comic that sought to educate as well as entertain, a comic
that grappled with pressing social issues. Here was a comic in which the
characters not only acted as adults but were put through stories of adult
concerns. Here was a comic that could not be ignored by the rest of the
field, a comic that must press the medium into a radical self-appraisal, a

Relevance meets space opera: Green Lantern, Green Arrow, Black Canary, and a Guardian of the Universe confront the population explosion. Pencils by Neal Adams, inks by Dick Giordano, script by Denny O'Neil. From *Green Lantern/Green Arrow* 81, December 1970.

reevaluation of its purposes. Taking its example, the comic book community woke up to the serious potential of the medium.

"For me," says Denny O'Neil, "[taking over *Green Lantern*] was unusually interesting and potentially exciting: I had an idea. For a while, I'd been wondering if it might be possible to combine my various professional and personal concerns." O'Neil had been a newspaper reporter and editor, author of a book on presidential elections, a regular contributor to a news magazine, and an admirer of the "new journalists"—Tom Wolfe, Norman Mailer, Jimmy Breslin, Pete Hamill, and Hunter S. Thompson. Revealingly, O'Neil says, "I suppose I considered myself as much journalist as fiction writer. . . . Could a comic book equivalent of the new journalism be possible? What would happen if we put a superhero in a real-life setting dealing with a real-life problem?"

To anchor the space-faring Green Lantern to Earth and human concerns, he was teamed with the new Green Arrow, the former cardboard costumed-archer whom O'Neil had recast as a defender of the poor (in *The Justice League of America*) and Adams, coincidentally, into a hip, bearded rebel (in BB 85, Sept. 1969). "The lusty, hot-tempered anarchist," as O'Neil saw him, not only awoke the "cerebral, sedate model citizen who was Green Lantern" to pressing social ills, but even persuaded one of the remote Guardians of the Universe to join the two of them in a journey of discovery across America. Green Arrow says, "Come off your perch! Touch . . . taste . . . laugh and cry! Learn where we're at . . . and why!" "I feel," replies the Guardian, "there is wisdom in your words." And so the union of the three crusaders for truth and justice was born.

Each issue in the series strove to tackle a pertinent social issue of the time. The trio defended a struggling union in a mining town, unmasked a phony religious prophet, and protected a tribe of downtrodden American Indians. The Guardian soon returned to the planet Oa, and Green Lantern and Green Arrow were joined by the latter's lover, Black Canary. They went on to deal with pollution, overpopulation, feminism, race riots, and destructive industrialism. Running through these stories was the tension between the conservative Green Lantern and the radical Green Arrow, as they butted heads over nearly every issue. As a result, the stories not only dealt with current topics, but attempted to present both sides of each political argument.

Green Lantern/Green Arrow went a long step beyond the likes of *Wonder Woman* and *Metal Men*, strips that, although extensively reworked, stopped at what was essentially just a new plot premise; *Green Lantern/Green Arrow* changed the basic fabric of comic books. Although action and adventure—classic tools of the trade—still abounded, the main thrust of the strip was now social and political relevance. Displaying a growing receptiveness within DC to new creative approaches, the strip marked an emerging predominance of comics controlled by their artists and writers. Backed wholeheartedly by editorial director Carmine Infantino, aided by editor Julius Schwartz, and adored by politically conscious collegiate fans, O'Neil and Adams brought a new ambition to the field. Uniting the realism begun by *Deadman* with the intellectual ambition championed by Roy Thomas, they tried to alter the basic function of comics. With their impact on the field, and their concern being what it was, relevance became DC's watchword for the dawning decade.

Green Lantern/Green Arrow, however, was ultimately unsatisfying. Probably no hero in the DC universe could have been less appropriate to political relevance and gritty realism than Green Lantern. His adventures had always been fanciful, encompassing distant planets, future eras, other dimensions, and a colorful rogues' gallery. With his power ring driven by his own mighty will, he had, of necessity, been the most levelheaded and self-possessed of heroes. The collapse of his confidence and sense of values was too jarring a note; it was hard to believe that the protector of an entire galactic sector would fall apart at the sight of a slum—unless, that is, a writer contrived it so.

O'Neil brought this collapse about by the headstrong influence of Green Arrow. A very powerful personality was needed to exert such an influence on Green Lantern, and in trying to create such power, O'Neil exaggerated Green Arrow into a caricature. Moreover, Green Arrow was a mouthpiece for O'Neil's own 1960s radical orientation, and therefore he always won the political arguments, humbling Green Lantern even further. "Green Lantern was, in effect, a cop," O'Neil has said. "An incorruptible cop, to be sure, with noble intentions, but still a cop, a crypto-fascist." By the end of the series, Green Arrow had become a screaming pontificator, and Green Lantern a whimpering, manic-depressive loser.

The strip might have been more effective if O'Neil, having already wrested the hero from his fanciful orientation, had stayed on course and confined the subject matter to realistic settings. But too many of the stories wove the old fantastical nature of Green Lantern in with the new approach. The overpopulation story, for instance, was set on a distant planet, and the feminist issue focused on harpies from another dimension. This only served to stress further the clash between what Green Lantern had been created to be and the contortions into which relevance had forced him.

Green Lantern/Green Arrow was canceled after only fourteen issues, but in that short time, and despite its drawbacks, it sent waves through the entire field of comics. At DC, O'Neil's most loyal disciple was Mike Friedrich, a young writer recently elevated from fandom. Nearly every story he wrote, whether for *The Justice League of America, The Flash, Superman,* or others, would be laden with overstated political stances, hip references, and obvious contemporary characterizations. Wonder Woman, with O'Neil as editor, was made to endure a brief "women's lib" fling. And, as a last gasp in 1973, veteran writer Joe Simon conceived *Prez,* a comic in which a cute teenager is elected to the presidency and fills his cabinet with minority stereotypes in order to cleanse the corrupt establishment.

Over at Marvel, topical themes had crept in gradually during the late 1960s and never exploded into a full-fledged movement. With a few exceptions, its established heroes were left untouched by current issues, while those chosen to deal with them proved far more appropriate to relevant storylines than DC's.

The first so designated was Captain America. Beginning with the acquisition of a black crime-fighting partner called the Falcon (CA 133, Jan. 1971), Cap ceased to be the symbol of the confident America of World War II, becoming instead the figurehead of the confused America of the early 1970s. In his secret identity he became a motorcycle cop, often intersecting with the Falcon in his secret identity as a Harlem social worker. Reminiscent of *Green Lantern/Green Arrow*, the interaction between the stolid Cap and the fiery Falcon was the focal point of the series. Next *Iron Man* was also recast in the new philosophy, as the hero's true identity, the munitions maker and public figure Tony Stark, was an ideal focus for current political issues.

Spider-Man flirted with relevance when Stan Lee decided to tackle a hefty subject of his own. With characteristic impudence, he chose one that DC had so far shunned, one forbidden by the comics' self-imposed censorship code: drug abuse. In *Spider-Man* 95–97 (Apr.–June 1971), Peter Parker discovers that his nervous friend Harry Osborne has become addicted to tranquilizers, and attempts to save a ghetto kid from a heroin overdose. For the first time in fifteen years, one of the major comics companies had, at the risk of poor distribution, defied the code. Forced into an awareness of changing times, the Comics Code Authority promptly and significantly revised its standards of 1954 and thereby granted more freedom to the industry (almost immediately afterward, *Green Lantern/Green Arrow* took advantage of the new code to have Speedy, Green Arrow's boy sidekick, turn into a junkie).

Beginning in 1972, relevance began quickly to wane. Although a passing trend, it nevertheless helped expand the field of comics, loosening the outdated rules of the Comics Code Authority, broadening characterization, increasing the power of writers and artists, and drawing the aims of Marvel and DC closer together. Those aims, clearly, were away from lighthearted entertainment and toward a more serious, somber brand of comic. The 1970s, from the very beginning, were promising something very different from what had gone before.

 *Marvel: Phase 2*

Despite the cancellations of 1969 and 1970, Marvel pressed on quickly with a pair of new titles. These were *Amazing Adventures* and *Astonishing Tales*, anthology comics showcasing new strips, and they set the pattern that would dominate Marvel at the dawn of the new decade. The company had recently become affiliated with a new distributor, leaving behind the entrenched Independent News (which had specifically limited the number of titles Marvel could publish during the 1960s) in favor of the more flexible Curtis Circulation Company. Strengthened by this new market advantage, Stan Lee and his company were clearly determined to attack a shaky sales situation with new experimentation; and unlike DC, which was looking to relevance and realism as the one key to revamping its line, Marvel would toy with a tremendous variety of genres and styles, launching a spate of titles modeled on DC's *Showcase*, designed to give new series a chance to prove themselves before moving out on their own. During 1972 these would be joined by a number of new series in titles of their own, which led Stan Lee to proclaim what he called "Phase 2" of the Marvel Age of Comics. "Hang loose, heroes," he wrote, "and watch our smoke! Marvel's set to bust loose now, and that means the wondrous world of fantasy won't ever be the same!" For the first time since 1968, it was truly exciting to be a Marvelite.

Ironically, although most of the series featured co-creations of Lee himself, the advent of Phase 2 marked the effective end of his creative control of Marvel Comics. In 1971, when Martin Goodman moved on to other publishing concerns, Lee took over as publisher. Giving up writing at the same time, he poured his attention into creating a line of full-size magazines and, later, into gaining a foothold in the Saturday morning TV market. Roy Thomas, his right-hand man, now became the editor and driving force at Marvel. Under him, a slew of new writers would dominate the company. Following Thomas's style and example, and often working with him, came the prolific young Gerry Conway. Ex-fans Gary Friedrich, Tony Isabella, and Mike Friedrich were assigned to the minor strips. From DC would soon come their compatriots Len Wein and Marv Wolfman. Most significantly, however, the change marked the arrival of a trio of influential young innovators: Steve Englehart, Don McGregor, and Steve Gerber.

Steve Englehart, the first upon the scene, specialized in playing games with established Marvel characters. His first chance to shine came when the Beast, the most articulate and agile member of the defunct X-Men, took over *Amazing Adventures* with issue 11 (Mar. 1972). The first story, written by Gerry Conway and drawn in a spooky, wild style by Tom Sutton, told how the hero, Hank McCoy, inadvertently used a chemical to transform himself into a true beast-man, with savage canines, thick fur, and a pithecanthropine visage. In the process he abandoned his charming old speech-style in favor of a more common angry, agonized one. Englehart took over the writing with the next issue, and began weaving some complex subplots around a varied assortment of characters, including the X-Men, Tony Stark (who is secretly Iron Man), some foreign spies, and—most surprisingly—two stars of Marvel's defunct romance comics line, Patsy Walker and her boyfriend, Buzz Baxter, now slipped unheralded into the world of costumed heroes. The Beast's series ended after seven issues, but by then Englehart had demonstrated a potential that would soon, on *Captain America* and *The Avengers,* become a bright spot in the Marvel firmament (to be discussed in Chapter 31).

The next of the trio was editorial assistant Don McGregor, who was unexpectedly handed the writing chores on the new *Black Panther* series, about the king of a technological wonderland in the African jungle (*Jungle Action* 6, Sept. 1973). He set about the task immediately with remarkable energy and serious intent. He designed a fascinating geography and socioeconomic history for the kingdom of Wakanda, and created a dominant political situation: while the Black Panther lived out his infatuation with the western world by joining the Avengers, his people began to feel he had abandoned them, and a brutal chieftain—Erik Killmonger—laid claim to the throne. McGregor wrote his first thirteen issues as a single story, "Panther's Rage," in which the rightful king battled a long series of Killmonger's bizarre, sadistic lieutenants—with names like Venom, Malice, Baron Macabre, Lord Karnaj, Salamander K'ruel—and took a personal, inward journey to learn his own true values and desires. The Panther became a strong, complex character, forced to choose between the foreign lands that fascinated him—here represented by an urbane Afro-American lover—and the land to which he felt an inherited duty.

To portray the Panther's journey, McGregor dropped all pretense of writing for children and put before the fans the most difficult and ambitious style yet employed in comics. Mixing a style more florid and rococo than Roy Thomas's, with large doses of popular psychology and philosophy, he filled pages with detailed discussions of values and self-perceptions. Contrasting himself with one of his supporters, the Panther ends a long exposition with: "I'm afraid much of Killmonger's revolution has caused me to lose a great deal of my empathy. But Taku, he still listens, senses, evaluates. Inside he is simultaneously outraged by the savagery of men, yet, most often, I think he is merely bemused by their purposes and intrigues" (JA 16, July, 1975). Although some of the writing was eloquent in isolation, it stood in ludicrous contrast to the world of costumed heroes, and rarely felt like natural speech for the characters. The approval that McGregor's writing won from many fans, however, suggested that plotting and smooth-flowing narrative were becoming less important to the readers than exploration of the heroes' lives. Indeed, characterization was quickly becoming the sole concern of some series.

Black Panther was kicked off by the flashy art of Rich Buckler, but it really took flight with the arrival of Billy Graham, whose startling angles, lush, organic backdrops, and lithe, sweaty figures gave the jungle both poisonous menace and erotic allure. His tight, sinewy interpretation of anatomy could convey in a few panels more of the strength and anger of the Panther than could dozens of McGregor's ponderous words.

The third of the innovators made his mark on *The Defenders*, the most successful creation of Marvel's expansion. Premiering in one of the new showcase titles, *Marvel Feature* (Dec. 1971), it concerned a secretive team of heroes composed of assorted loners and oddballs: the Hulk, Dr. Strange, and the Sub-Mariner (who was soon to leave), later joined by an ex-villain named Nighthawk and a human woman with the soul of an Asgardian imposed over her own, the Valkyrie. That such a group could join into a team seemed unlikely even for Marvel, and indeed, writers Thomas, Englehart, and Wein often had to stretch the plots to make them work. But with the arrival of writer Steve Gerber in 1974, the unlikely and implausible became the very fabric of the stories themselves.

Gerber made an art of bending and twisting the established universe into unexpected shapes, and merging different genres. He used dream sequences, strange physical transformations, and tongue-in-cheek plot shenanigans to give the series an air of unreality. His scripting was crisp and effective, his characters distinct and well realized. His version of the Hulk, in particular, was the most delightful ever, blending childlike innocence and dim-witted tenderness with savage strength; eventually the monster adopted a motherless fawn and named it Bambi, thrusting responsibility for its care onto his "smart friend, Magician" (i.e., Dr. Strange; his custom of giving his own descriptive names to everyone he met was one of the great charms of Gerber's Hulk). Gerber's most ambitious work on *The Defenders* came in an eleven-issue sequence centering on the Headmen, a villainous crew of old monster-story characters united by their deformed heads (Def. 31, Jan. 1976). The group's plot involves switching Nighthawk's brain with that of one of their own members, but Dr. Strange retaliates by transferring the villain's mind to Bambi's body, thus starting a carnival of "musical minds." Into the scene come an EST-like cult of self-deprecators who wear clown masks and call themselves Bozos, a band of interplanetary meddlers who want to bring peace to mankind by obliterating all our passion and folly, and a growing cast of visiting heroes and villains. By the conclusion, entitled "World Gone Sane," so many powers are uniting to turn back the rising tide of Bozoism that Gerald Ford finds himself sitting on an asteroid with Dr. Strange (Def. Annual 1, 1976).

Gerber left soon afterward, and although the quality plunged under his various successors, he had given *The Defenders* enough momentum to remain popular. He was aided by the long tenure of penciler Sal Buscema, who, although exhibiting little flair, competently conveyed the stories and concepts.

Most of the other new series of the period began with promise, but all lacked the distinctive flair of an Englehart, a McGregor, or a Gerber, and all were immeasurably harmed by frequent and jarring changes of direction and personnel. The first of them, *The Inhumans*, kicking off *Amazing Adventures* (Aug. 1970), led with four issues of rapid-fire Kirby action, made an about-face to a troubled, humanistic approach under Roy Thomas's writing and Neal Adams's stylized but realistic art, then ended after two issues by Gerry Conway and Mike Sekowsky. The backup strip, about the acrobatic heroine Black Widow, lasted only eight issues under four writers and three pencilers. In *Astonishing Tales* (Aug. 1970), Ka-Zar, a Tarzan-like character from a prehistoric jungle land hidden in the Antarctic, begun under Lee and Kirby, shifted to a fantastical tone under Conway and Barry Smith, then moved to New York City and into a semi-relevant phase under Mike Friedrich and diverse artists. The backup strip, *Dr. Doom*, the first series to star an outright villain, lasted only seven issues but nevertheless featured three writers and two pencilers.

More Silver Age characters were given their own series. The mysterious golden-skinned messiah called Him, who had been scientifically spawned in *The Fantastic Four* and had attained a sort of cosmic stature in *Thor*, now became Adam Warlock, a Christ-figure on the alternate Earth created by the godlike scientist known as the High Evolutionary (*Marvel Premiere* 1, Apr. 1972). Roy Thomas wrote a highly literary and thoughtful origin story, full of biblical parallels; Gil Kane added his dynamic art and Dan Adkins his fine inking, and by the time *Warlock* began its own title (Aug. 1972), it showed tremendous promise. But when Mike Friedrich took over the writing and Bob Brown the art soon afterward, the Christ-figure was recast in a more standard hero-role and rambled to early discontinuation.

Shortly thereafter, *Captain Marvel* returned from cancellation (CM 22, Sept. 1972). This was a series with many ingenious ideas in its favor: Roy Thomas, for example, had paid sly tribute to the Golden Age Captain Marvel by having his Kree warrior share the same space/time with Marvel's ubiquitous teenager, Rick Jones—so that one was always banished to the "Negative Zone" while the other was on Earth—just as young Billy Batson and his powerful alter ego had seemed to. But now weak writing by Conway, Marv Wolfman, and Mike Friedrich, along with sloppy art by Wayne Boring, obscured all the cleverness; the presence, even preeminence, of Rick Jones soaked the stories in excess emotion and hip dialogue: "A warm, loving chick shafted me last night—and that *burns* me—*bad*, man—BAAD!" (CM 25, Mar. 1973).

During the same period of giving minor heroes a chance at the lime-light, Mike Friedrich and Herb Trimpe brought back Ant-Man (*Marvel Feature* 4, July 1972); it was an unsuccessful revival of an unimportant hero, and testified more than anything else to Marvel's unwillingness to let any piece of its past continuity fade away. Next, Dr. Strange was re-vived, but his importance and long duration required that he be treated with the Marvel mainstream titles in Chapter 31.

Not all of the new series featured old Marvel characters. Four titles sprang from the tail end of the "relevance" fad. Foremost among these was *Hero for Hire*. The protagonist is a tough black convict named Lucas, tormented by vicious prison guards. When given an opportunity to un-dergo a medical experiment in exchange for a parole, an assassination at-tempt by one of the "screws" backfires, causing the experiment to grant Lucas tremendous strength and steellike skin. He escapes, but then deter-mines to go straight and work secretly to clear his name; having no job skills, he uses his great strength to become a strongarm for hire, calling himself Luke Cage (HH 1, June 1972). Located in the inner city, his assign-ments revolved around pimps, racketeers, and ghetto parasites. Almost invariably, however, Cage found himself on the side of the angels, and eventually he became a full-fledged hero.

The first four issues of *Hero for Hire* were superbly written by Archie Goodwin, who faithfully preserved the opportunism and moral ambiva-lence of the character. His scripting was hard and terse, with a convincing use of whatever black slang the Code permitted. His artistic partners were George Tuska, with appropriately ugly human portraits, and inker Billy Graham, a young black who evinced a special sensitivity to the subject matter, later assisting with the writing. After Goodwin's departure, the strip's quality dipped under Steve Englehart, then slumped under Tony Isabella and others. To forestall cancellation, Cage was renamed Power Man and made into a more standard hero (*Power Man* 17, Feb. 1974).

Shortly after Cage started, Marvel made a bid for a socially conscious female audience with three comics featuring liberated women as protago-nists. *The Claws of the Cat* starred a tough heroine with athletic ability like Daredevil's and a set of sharp claws for weapons, whose adventures boasted a woman writer, Linda Fite, and artist, Marie Severin (CC 1, Nov. 1972). *Night Nurse* (Nov. 1972) was about the tribulations of a modern working woman in a realistic setting. *Shanna the She-Devil* (Dec. 1972) was a committed veterinarian who, after seeing man's cruelty to animals, ran off to Africa to emulate Tarzan. All three strips were undistinguished and short-lived.

Simultaneously, a low-key effort began on Marvel's part to revive some of their genres of the past. From 1970 to 1972, several comics were created to reprint western, war, and, particularly, monster stories. A new war title, *Combat Kelly and the Dirty Dozen,* and a western, *The Gun-hawks,* were created in 1972; both attempted a cynical, modern look at historical violence, but both failed promptly. Several unsuccessful efforts were also made to revive anthology horror comics. The reprints soon failed as well.

Of the titles in these genres, the most illustrative of the changing times was *Red Wolf,* about a semimystical American Indian hero in the Old West, introduced in *Marvel Spotlight* 1 (Nov. 1971). With a colorful milieu, lush, quiet art by veteran Syd Shores, and an entertaining story by Gardner Fox, Red Wolf was appealing enough to begin his own comic in May 1972. This was Fox's first western comic in over a decade (since he had worked under Julius Schwartz on such series as *Pow-Wow Smith,* about a very different Indian hero), and he was both well and poorly suited to the material. In a field in which more and more writers were young hero-fans with scarcely any diversity to their backgrounds, Fox's experience in pulps, paperbacks, and the varied comics of the past served him well. But at the same time his lighthearted approach blended badly with the more serious treatment now demanded of comics (especially when Red Wolf's adventures moved to New York in the present, after seven issues), and after issue 9 (Sept. 1973) the series, which would prove to be Fox's last, was canceled; it marked the quiet, but not unfitting, departure of a great comic book writer who, sadly, found himself in a time no longer receptive to his talents.

The old-genre comics were not the only ones that stood on shaky ground. Very few of the titles launched in this period enjoyed truly healthy sales, and a number were quickly canceled. But Lee could not have been unhappy with the results of his daring expansion. The fact that several of the new titles survived at all suggested that comics might yet be a vigorous medium and that, despite the troubles of 1969, there was still room for experimentation and boldness. In 1972, DC would begin responding with new creations of its own, but Marvel now had a headstart. Partly because of that headstart, and partly because of DC's difficulty in switching from the Silver Age to the new approach, Marvel had at last equaled—and would soon exceed—its venerable rival in the size of its staff, the number of its titles, and overall sales.

But Phase II was ultimately disappointing and troubling for the readers. Apart from the difficulty of keeping new projects alive, the comic book field seemed to be suffering from sudden confusion and a drastic loss of direction. Series like *The Inhumans, Ka-Zar,* and *Warlock* would begin as one type of comic and veer abruptly into another sort altogether. The new writers behind these and other titles, like rookies hurled from the sandlot into the big leagues, arrived on the scene ill-prepared for the demands of professionalism. Intoxicated by the new ambition of the medium, they fell prey to pretension and self-importance; the basics of storytelling were buried under self-indulgence. Even the best efforts ultimately came to naught. Creators simply would not stay put any longer, and the best ideas seemed destined to be dropped into less capable hands.

During this time of unrest it was the heroes, still the focus of the medium, who inevitably suffered the brunt of the confusion. The attempt to revive old genres was an early inkling that the powers at Marvel thought the long primacy of costumed heroes might be coming to an end. With the heroes struggling for survival, and relevance failing to save them, it became increasingly clear that the future of the field might lie in other types of comics. The rapid growth of "underground" comics during those same years, with their adult content and satirical counterculture orientation, further illustrated the medium's shift away from its traditional subject matter. Many professionals compared the beginning of the 1970s to the beginning of the 1950s, when the costumed heroes had last lost their readership. More and more prophecies of the death of the crime-fighters were heard. Thus, from 1970 to 1973, the doors were thrown open to vigilantes and barbarians, gods and jungle lords, monsters and pulp heroes, every stripe of hero and antihero, both original and adapted, in a mad scramble to find something that would keep comics alive. The next seven chapters treat these various forays into new ground.

The Batman

The changes Neal Adams had instigated for The Batman (as he now became known) in 1969 took full hold in the 1970s. The mysterious Darknight Detective of the 1930s had returned with a vengeance. Driven by an obsessive hatred of all criminals after the coldblooded murder of his parents, he haunted the nocturnal streets of the city, swooping down on terror-stricken evildoers. Such criminals as the Joker, who had been used lightheartedly in the 1960s, now became murderous psychotics. In short, the world of the Batman became a *noir* carnival of fright and insanity.

Shortly after Adams restyled the Batman visually, Julius Schwartz produced a comic that altered the basic story line to match the artist's vision. In *Batman* 217 (Dec. 1969), plotted by Schwartz and written by Frank Robbins, Dick "Robin" Grayson goes away to college, casting the Batman in the more appropriate role of loner. Bruce Wayne modifies his Batman costume, elongating the ears and lengthening the cape, to give it an eerier look, and Bruce and his butler, Alfred, leave Wayne Manor to take up residence in a penthouse apartment atop the Wayne Foundation building so as to live in "the heart of that sprawling urban blight—to dig . . . the new breed of rat . . . out where they live and fatten on the innocent." Thus, although still cast in costumed-hero trappings, the Batman now functioned primarily as a vigilante and detective.

Adams was never to be the strip's regular artist, but appeared only sporadically, and even the story above, pivotal as it was, was drawn by Irv Novick. Although Novick had not gone much beyond the muddy style he had been using, he now strove to emulate Adams; he was aided in this cause by the inks of former editor Dick Giordano, who was Adams's regular inker at DC. Over at *Detective Comics*, Bob Brown was making the same adjustments Novick had, giving the Batman an eerie, diabolical countenance. No matter who the artist was, it quickly became evident, Adams's version of the Batman was here to stay.

The stories kept pace. The guiding spirits, under Schwartz's auspices, were Adams's and writer Denny O'Neil. O'Neil strove to give the Batman the same grittiness he had given to *Green Lantern/Green Arrow*. The Batman no longer punned when he overcame a crook, he now struck wraithlike from out of the shadows. Unfettered by a boy companion, for whom he had had to maintain a fatherly dignity, the Batman was now able to give himself over to his deep-seated rage. The plots themselves shifted appropriately to a macabre cast. The Batman, for instance, now tangled with a coven dedicated to black magic (Bat. 227, Dec. 1970), fought to survive a gauntlet of evil illusions designed by a villain to drive him mad (Det. 408, Feb. 1971), and played Russian roulette with a murdering gambler (Det. 426, Aug. 1972).

O'Neil and Adams's most significant contribution was the creation of the most enduring new villain in the Batman cast of characters, Rā's Al Ghūl. A mysterious, exotic crime lord, Rā's, through a device called the Lazarus Pit, could be restored from the dead repeatedly (Bat. 232, June 1971). He was a brutal adversary, master of all varieties of combat, but he respected the Batman deeply as a "magnificent foe." His exotic daughter, Talia, fell in love with the Batman, and her divided loyalty between her father and the object of her passion provided a focal point for many of the stories. An appearance by Rā's Al Ghūl usually heralded a multi-issue saga, including not only exciting adventures but unfolding revelations of the demonic criminal's nature and further convolutions of the romance of Batman and Talia.

The only other writer who contributed regularly to the Batman during these years was Frank Robbins. An excellent craftsman, Robbins favored tightly woven mysteries over the looser, more action-oriented plots employed by O'Neil. His scripting was terse and restrained, propelling the story along without striving as hard for atmosphere as O'Neil's. Unfortunately, Robbins, who was generally the better of the two plotters, was usually paired with Brown or Novick, whose sketchy illustrations were not adequate to supply the needed atmosphere to his stories; O'Neil's scripts received the lion's share of art by Adams, creating a large body of stories long on atmosphere but short on plot. Robbins occasionally drew his own stories, with an angular, nightmarish effect (the most chilling being the Russian roulette story mentioned above), but these instances, which combined moody art with artful writing, were sadly few and far between.

Most notably, Robbins created Man-Bat, another enduring villain. A hideous man with the face, wings, and fur of a bat, the Man-Bat was really Kirk Langstrom, a zoologist who inadvertently transformed himself by attempting to gain the powers of a bat through a serum of his invention (Det. 400, June 1970). A good but tormented man trapped in the body of a monster, the Man-Bat was an ambivalent foe; his clashes with the Batman combined tense combat with the hero's solicitous attempts to restore him to normalcy. (The Man-Bat, joined by his wife, She-Bat, gained his own title in January 1976, the first issue of which featured superbly atmospheric art by Steve Ditko, but was canceled an issue later. He remains, however, a regular fixture in the Batman's world to the present.)

Another flash of brilliance came, atypically for a decade in which edi-

The increasing sophistication of adventure: Archie Goodwin and Walter Simonson's *Manhunter* meets the Batman. From *Detective Comics* 443, November 1974.

tors had faded into the background, from the brief tenure of a new editor
on *Detective Comics*, Archie Goodwin. As both writer and editor, Goodwin used his training in gritty war and horror stories to good stead on the
new Batman, producing some of the finest work in the field's history. Acclaimed by many fellow professionals as the best writer in comics, Goodwin best demonstrated here his vast talent.

On the Batman's adventures themselves, Goodwin lacked a steady artist, but he seemed capable of coaxing out the very best that Jim Aparo,
Howard Chaykin, Alex Toth, and Sal Amendola had to offer. It was on a
backup feature, however, that his greatest contribution would emerge.

Detective Comics had showcased many backup features through the
years, recently including solo adventures of Robin and Batgirl, but not
until Goodwin's *Manhunter* (Det. 437, Nov. 1973) did any exceed the stature of filler. Written by Goodwin himself and both penciled and inked by
Walter Simonson, the Manhunter was an ambivalent hero shrouded in
mystery. We learn of him slowly through the eyes of an Interpol agent,
Christine St. Claire, who follows him across the globe, recording his exploits. Known to St. Claire as Paul Kirk, a man who supposedly died in
1946, Manhunter functions sometimes as an assassin, sometimes as a
thwarter of assassins and political kidnappers. To further the mystery,
Kirk's adversaries are invariably clones of himself, and as St. Claire's in-
vestigation continues, she is sucked along with him into the midst of a
vast criminal conspiracy. The saga came to an end in *Detective Comics*

443 (Nov. 1974), when Manhunter and the Batman joined forces in an issue-length action extravaganza.

The Manhunter strip was the first truly successful comic to blend the pristine DC craft of the 1960s with the Marvel style of deeper characterization and continuing storyline. The strip was superbly plotted and scripted, featured perhaps the most intriguing and complex mystery ever to emerge from the medium, and showcased the enormous talents of the rising superstar Walt Simonson. In his vivid, impressionistic depiction of the exotic locales visited by Manhunter, and in his brutally realistic fight sequences, which seemed to transcend the merely visual and actually evoke sound— the crunch of bunched fingers driven into a throat, the clank of chains striking armor—Simonson came closer than any artist before him to approximating the cinematic in comic art.

The conclusion of Manhunter's story marked the end of Goodwin's editorial reign, and would also be the beginning of a downturn in the Batman's good fortunes. With the sporadic appearances of Adams, the rare solo efforts of Robbins, and the brief tenure of Goodwin scattered among the reams of stories by Brown and Novick, the Batman had always, even at his best, been inconsistent; but now, with the departure of these men, inconsistency would characterize the state of the Batman to an even greater degree for the rest of the decade. Superb contributions by such veterans and rising stars as Toth, Aparo, Chaykin, and Simonson would flash in and out of view over the next few years, but for the most part *Batman* and *Detective Comics* were never as good as the fascinating new interpretation of the character promised.

This inconsistency of creative teams was something new to comics. In the past, when a reader bought a comic he was not just buying the adventures of his favorite hero, but the product of the same group of men who for years had fashioned those adventures. But now, with titles like *Batman, The Inhumans,* and *Warlock,* readers never knew what to expect from month to month. Readers who had been accustomed to the reliability of old were perenially frustrated when their favorite artists began dropping out of sight after tantalizingly short stints on these and other titles. Some consistency did exist—as with Sal Buscema's long stay on *The Defenders* and George Tuska's stint on *Hero for Hire*—but it usually came from the nondescript workhorses of the field.

The most prominent artist of the period, Neal Adams, instigated a move toward sporadic contributions when he rebelled against working conditions at DC and Marvel; he felt that artists should receive residuals for their work, or retain outright ownership of it, and he formed a guild that strove to protect the rights of artists. (Among its first efforts was an attempt to secure compensation for the creators of Superman, Jerry Siegel and Joe Shuster.) The struggle was slow and uphill, causing strife between free-lancers and management. Like Jim Steranko before him, Adams would turn to other fields for income, eventually founding an independent art studio, paving the way for much talent to seek employement elsewhere.

One comics professional, writer Mike Friedrich, took the move a step further by forming his own publication, *Star*Reach*, in 1974. In the tradition of the underground comics and of Wally Wood's *Witzend*, *Star*Reach* provided an alternative to the big publishers which allowed creators to retain complete ownership of their material; among Friedrich's first clients were Neal Adams and his partner in the new studio, former editor Dick Giordano.

The Batman's world did provide one rare instance of consistency at DC, *The Brave and the Bold*. For most of the decade that title, which paired the Batman with various other DC heroes, was manned by the creative team of editor Murray Boltinoff, writer Bob Haney, and artist Jim Aparo. Although none of these men were giants in the field, they were all competent craftsmen, and *The Brave and the Bold*, despite the lack of continuity brought on by its ever-changing cast, boasted a solid Silver Age approach in which tightly plotted entertainment held sway (albeit woven into the persona and milieu of the new Batman).

But *The Brave and the Bold* was the exception. The Batman's solo adventures fell further into disarray. Both the bright young stars and the old workhorses departed the titles, leaving them in the hands of a multitude of writers who never stayed long enough to give them any direction, and such artists as John Calnan and Ernie Chua, who lacked both the atmosphere of Adams and his peers and the solid storytelling ability of Brown and Novick.

There would continue to be moments of excellence, particularly writer Steve Englehart and artist Marshall Rogers's six-issue sequence of political corruption in Gotham City and poignant romance with the ethereal Silver St. Cloud, which came to a stunning climax when the Batman was pitted against the most ingenious and maniacal Joker ever portrayed (Det. 471–476, Aug. 1977–Apr. 1978). But these moments were even fewer and farther between than they had been in the first half of the decade and, generally, the slump continued. *Batman* and *Detective Comics* would remain worth glancing at on the newsstand, in the hope that another solitary masterpiece might lurk within, but the hope was far more often than not crushed, and the exciting new edge that Schwartz and Adams had given the Batman a decade before had become a tired cliché.

24 Conan and Kin

At the same time the new Batman was emerging, Marvel produced a far more dramatic departure from standard hero fare. Surprisingly, it was Roy Thomas, heretofore almost exclusively dedicated to costumed heroes, who pressed into existence a title that introduced to comics a new genre, a whole new set of story elements, and the first real challenge to the primacy of hero characters since the end of the Golden Age.

Although science fiction, war, western, and other popular genres had long held places in comics, the field of heroic fantasy, with a few such exceptions as *Viking Prince,* had generally been ignored. But Thomas had a long-standing affection for the barbaric sword-and-sorcery stories of the old pulp magazines, and was determined to see them brought into the comics, despite fantasy's poor track record. In Robert E. Howard's *Conan* he found a barbarian hero who won over fans and casual readers alike, took hold even in those shaky years, and endured to produce offspring.

Adaptations, such as Dell and Gold Key's *Tarzan* series, were not new to comics, but they had never been tackled by either of the two major companies, or by a major comic book writer. Thomas, evincing both his love of Howard's stories and his English teacher's instincts, worked carefully to duplicate the style and elements of the originals. Since the pulp stories abounded in bloodshed, sorcery, and sexuality far beyond the usual boundaries of comics, this resulted in a gradual expansion of those boundaries, including further challenges to the Comics Code. Although Thomas would never be able to capture Howard's content completely, he was nevertheless able to bring a refreshing new boldness to comics.

Howard's hero, Conan the Barbarian, was a wandering thief and mercenary in a fantasied time before the dawn of history, the Hyborian Age. Beginning as an impetuous youth in the Scandinavia-like land of Cimmeria, he battled his way through turbulent kingdoms and decadent empires loosely based on ancient Rome, Egypt, and medieval Europe; through the roles of buccaneer, warrior, and general, he rose at last to be king of powerful Aquilonia. Thomas retold the tales in careful order, trying not to miss any significant Howard stories. Conan began battling the Cimmerians' enemies in the far north (*Conan the Barbarian* 1, Oct. 1970), went on to confront a "grim gray god" modeled on the Norse Odin (C 3,

Barry Smith's eerie, beautiful Conan. From *Savage Tales* 3, February 1974.

Feb. 1971), then journeyed south to the corrupt city of Zamora, where he freed a pathetic, otherworldly creature from imprisonment in a tower, in a truly poetic tale of contact between savage and civilization, innocent wildness and wise decrepitude (C 4, Apr. 1971). In issues to come, the barbarian would grapple with many an evil seductress, decadent sorcerer, and scheming plutocrat; such horrors as a minotaur (C 10, Oct. 1971), a huge spider-god (C 13, Jan. 1972), and a serpent made of living gold (C 24, Mar. 1973) would leap from all the hidden corners of his exotic world.

In fleshing out these tales, Thomas produced without question the finest scripting of his career. Not bound to emulate Lee's quasi-realism, he wrote vivid descriptions and stylized dialogue with elegance and distinction. He also paid homage to Howard with minute attention to the places and customs of the Hyborian Age, including maps and text features that provided a wealth of background information. In the stories we follow

Conan's wanderings closely, always aware of where he has been and where he is going, both geographically and spiritually; we not only follow him from exotic land to exotic land and from adventure to adventure, but from brash youth to maturity.

Transcending even the excellence of the writing, the real magic of *Conan* lay in the artwork of Barry Smith. Smith had begun as a Marvel pinch-hitter with a distinctly Kirbyesque look, but with this regular assignment his art evolved from issue to issue with remarkable speed. As early as issue 4 he displayed an utterly unique approach, and by the time he left the series after issue 24 (Mar. 1973), his style, best described as baroque, was the rage of the field.

Smith's pages were a delicate embroidery of stylized figures parading against beautifully ornate backgrounds—glass towers, bone-filled dungeons, lanternlit bazaars—composed of small, dense panels in defiance of the current passion for sweeping layouts of the Kirby and Adams types. In keeping with the Adams school, however, Smith proved quite able to capture human character both in facial expression and physical posture. Conan himself exuded icy savagery; his women were dreamy, mystical, and almond-eyed; the greedy merchants and officials he encountered were corpulent and gross in every feature. Smith's art was a startling blend of the naturalistic and the fanciful.

During Smith's stay on *Conan*, unfortunately, a disturbing trend in comic art came forcefully to light. In issue 4, featuring the best Conan art to that time, Smith was effectively inked by Sal Buscema, but in the very next issue the art looked rough and choppy, seeming to have regressed to that of a less developed Smith. The reason was the inappropriate, heavy inking of Frank Giacoia, probably necessitated by Smith's lateness in completing his pencils and the necessity to use whatever inker was available. Inkers would play musical chairs during Smith's entire stay, some appropriate (Buscema, Dan Adkins, Smith himself), some not. This tendency would plague Marvel and, to a lesser extent, DC, all during the 1970s. Again and again the reader would be disappointed to find his favorite penciler disfigured by the wrong inker, his style neutralized by an incompatible finisher. This had often been a problem for Marvel in the 1960s, when a small staff had necessitated some ill-conceived artistic unions, but in the 1970s the problem seemed to spring from the disorder caused by sudden growth, and from the less compliant, less obedient attitude of many artists toward employers and deadlines.

With or without appropriate inking, Smith remained the source of most of Conan's magic. Unfortunately, he soon followed Steranko and Adams out of the comic book field. In just four short years, three artistic superstars had entered comics, only to vanish in a wink; with such precedents, it seemed unlikely that emerging stars would be willing to remain in the business, and comics appeared to be in for a difficult and frustrating time.

Smith's successor, John Buscema, inked by Ernie Chan, also known as

Ernie Chua (who would later pencil the strip), recast the wandering bar-barian in a brawnier, simpler mold and lost most of Smith's beauty and richness. Although Thomas's writing did not noticeably change, *Conan* somehow read like a completely different, inferior series. This drop in quality, coming solely from a change in artists, revealed a trend that had been growing over the last few years: with the Marvel method of artist participation in the plotting, the rise of many young visionary artists like Adams and Smith, and a sudden surge of fan interest in the finer points of art, it became clear that comics were increasingly being looked upon as a graphic, much more than a verbal, medium.

A second Robert E. Howard hero, living in a pre-Hyborian age, entered comics in *Kull the Conqueror* (June 1971). Kull was like an older version of Conan, taking the throne of "ancient, decadent Valusia" by the sword, aided by an American Indian-like sidekick named Brule. Written by Thomas, drawn by Marie Severin, and inked by her brother John, *Kull* was a dignified, restrained fantasy that pleased Conan's fans but failed to seize a large audience. Through discontinuation and recontinuation, under such neophyte writers as Gerry Conway, Steve Englehart, and Doug Moench, and with a conversion to a more violent and horrific tone under horror-artist Mike Ploog, when the series became *Kull the Destroyer*, (KD 11, Nov. 1973), the barbarian king squeaked through the decade, off and on, to the present day.

Two other sword-and-sorcery series enjoyed even less success, running for short periods in a comic that had been reprinting early Marvel monster stories, *Creatures on the Loose*. The first, *Gullivar Jones, Warrior of Mars*, was based on a book written in 1905 by an obscure adventure writer named Edwin Arnold, one of the forerunners of Edgar Rice Burroughs. Adapted by Roy Thomas, with later writing by science fiction author George Alec Effinger, it told of an Earthman who became a master swordsman and adventurer on the brawling world of Mars, much like Burroughs's John Carter series (CL 16, Mar. 1972). Gil Kane contributed two issues of dynamic art before giving way to the attractive but static Gray Morrow, among others; the series ended after six tantalizing stories. Its successor, *Thongor of Lost Lemuria* (CL 22, Jan. 1973), was adapted by Effinger from the books of Lin Carter (a Robert E. Howard scholar who wrote some sword-and-sorcery of his own), but with poor conception and rough Val Mayerik art, it passed quickly. Marvel tried, through guest ap-pearances and one-shots, to introduce some other barbarians, including Michael Moorcock's mysterious Elric (C 14–15, Mar.–May 1972), John Jakes's Brak (*Chamber of Chills* 2, Jan. 1973), and Howard's female war-rior, Red Sonja (C 24, Mar. 1973); but although Sonja would reappear later, Conan would remain its only real success in the new genre.

Conan had taken comic book fandom by storm under Smith, and even under Buscema it continued to be one of Marvel's more successful titles. In addition to sparking these other comics in the sword-and-sorcery genre, it led to a large black-and-white magazine-sized comic entitled *Savage Tales,* published outside the Comics Code. This was dominated by a Conan story and included a variety of risque science fiction and adventure stories (ST 1, May 1971). The first issue was not a success, but after a two-year hiatus the magazine returned, soon joined by *Savage Sword of Conan,* which focused entirely on sword-and-sorcery (Aug. 1974); between them, they would help secure Marvel's footing at last in the magazine market dominated by Warren. (And, a few years later, a parody of Barry Smith's Conan, the adventures of a heroic aardvark named Cerebus, would add new impetus to the young independent comics movement.)

But despite these successes, and despite the durability of the sword-and-sorcery genre, *Conan* would not prove the key to saving the medium.

Kirby Was There

For months the ads read, "Kirby is coming!" The word spread like wildfire through fandom in 1970: Jack Kirby, after eleven years at Marvel, had signed a five-year contract at DC which promised him unlimited creative freedom. Speculation ran rampant about what new worlds he would create without Stan Lee's influence. At last the long-awaited blurb appeared—"Kirby is here!"—but in an unexpected corner: *Superman's Pal, Jimmy Olsen.*

Kirby relates that Carmine Infantino originally approached him to revamp the entire Superman line, from which Mort Weisinger had just retired. Kirby responded with a counteroffer: He would take on *Olsen,* and if he could reverse that title's dismal sales, he would be given complete creative control—editing, writing, and drawing—of three titles he would create himself. Infantino consented, and Kirby was granted an unprecedented opportunity to prove his creative prowess, thus opening the door for future writer/artists to parade and develop their visions.

If any readers doubted that he could spring back from his late, stale days at Marvel, his first Jimmy Olsen story put those doubts to rest. A revived Newsboy Legion, Simon and Kirby's version of the Dead End Kids from 1941, roared up in a high-tech car called the Whiz Wagon and drove Jimmy off to the forested Wild Area. There they found a hairy cycle gang called the Outsiders engaged in highly scientific warfare with the Raiders, a brutally reactionary band of vigilantes. Into this already mixed bag of elements flew Superman, while overshadowing the story loomed a semi-mystical Mountain of Judgment, turning the once-trite world of Olsen into one of the oddest melanges a comic book fan was ever likely to read (JO 133, Oct. 1970). In it Kirby united the four seemingly irreconcilable elements that would dominate his work for DC: cosmic scope, gritty violence, topicality, and nostalgia.

He began grappling with themes even more overtly mythical and symbolic than he had at Marvel, forging a writing style oddly combining beat-talk with blunt, savage philosophizing. "Go! Go! Go!" cries an ecstatic biker. "Death is *fast!* Death is *loud!* Death is *final!*" He also began drawing on the classics, which he called "the most powerful literature there is," as when one Outsider describes the Mountain of Judgment as

Science and savagery: The monumental villainy of Jack Kirby's Darkseid, with a retainer named Steppenwolf. Inks by Mike Royer. From *New Gods 7*, March 1972.

"like Moby Dick! You go there to meet it—and die!"

But Kirby's wonders were just beginning. At the beginning of 1971 he pulled the veil from his grandest and most unified creation, a realm of existence he called the Fourth World. The greatest expanse of this realm unfolded in a title called *New Gods,* telling of no less than "the titanic struggle for the fate of mankind." "There came a time when the old gods died," says the opening narrative, and from the ruins of their domain arose two worlds: New Genesis, "a golden island of gleaming spires that orbits a sunlit, unspoiled world," and Apokolips, "a dismal, unclean place . . . an armed camp where those who live with weapons rule the wretches who build them . . . [where] life is the evil . . . and death the great goal!" (NG 1, Mar. 1971). The master of Apokolips is the great, stone-faced Darkseid, a monumental, self-possessed embodiment of destruction. Arrayed against him are the glorious young gods of New Genesis, spearheaded by Darkseid's own son (as we discover later), the grim Orion, who wields the powerful Astro-Force against his father. The New Gods and their foes resembled Kirby's earlier Inhumans in distinctness and variety—including the impetuous Lightray, the knowledge-seeking Metron with his universe-spanning Moebius Chair, the cruel scientist Desaad, and a group of undersea demons called the Deep Six—but the scope of their adventures was much greater. Orion's mission, which he must accomplish through subterfuge on Earth as well as combat in the Fourth World, was to prevent Darkseid's conquest of mankind and his acquisition of the dreaded Anti-Life Equation.

Congruently, a series called *The Forever People* followed the efforts of a colorful group of extranormal flower children from New Genesis to frustrate Darkseid's agents on Earth (FP 1, Mar. 1971). As their most interesting member, a naïve, mystical woman called Beautiful Dreamer, commented, "We have fun names!": Big Bear, Vykin the Black, Mark Moonrider, and the cowboy-suited Serifan. They also had amusing hippie speech patterns, a giant tricycle that teleported them through space and different dimensions, and adventures set against such mind-boggling backdrops as Desaad's jolly but sinister amusement park, Happyland.

Next came *Mr. Miracle*, the adventures of a fantastic-escape artist and his gnomish assistant, Oberon, who travel America performing Houdini-style stunts, but are secretly agents of New Genesis (Mr. M 1, Apr. 1971); soon their lives were complicated by a partnership with a musclebound, hotheaded Amazon named Big Barda (Mr. M 4, Oct. 1971). Mr. Miracle's greatest foe was Granny Goodness, whose matronly veneer hid the soul of a sadistic dominatrix, and who tenderly coddled a computer called Overlord while devising exquisitely horrible death-traps for Mr. Miracle. Behind the façade of an orphanage she trained brutal but infantile warriors for the service of Darkseid.

Within these three titles (with *Jimmy Olsen* and the non-Kirby *Lois Lane* often tying in as a fourth and fifth), the vision that had begun growing in Kirby's work at Marvel six years before came to full flower. Some of his Marvel ideas resurfaced, now distilled to pure Kirby terms, including a version of the Silver Surfer—a skier who was transfigured by Darkseid into a cosmic herald of death called the Black Racer—bereft of Lee's inclinations to humanization and internal agony. The Marvel ideas of charcterization played no part in these new creations; the Fourth World was a theater for elemental drama, for the clash of absolutes, for grand symbolizing about the nature of life and death, good and evil. Beside the powerfully symbolic and multi-faceted Darkseid, even the awesome Galactus began to seem like just another comic book villain.

Kirby determined to use his unprecedented creative freedom to make his message unmistakably clear. "I felt there was a time," he says, "that a man had to tell a story in which he felt . . . there was no bullshit. There was absolute truth." Even Darkseid told the truth for Kirby, as when he observed a funeral for a fallen New God, saying, "Oh, how heroes love to flaunt their nobility on the face of death! Yet they know better than most that war is but the cold game of the butcher!" (NG 4, Sept. 1971). "And he's right," says Kirby, remembering the day he "was handed a helmet, an M-1 rifle, and two chocolate bars and told to polish off Adolf Hitler." That Darkseid, and not any of the many heroes who opposed him, was ultimately the focus and the most fascinating personality of the Fourth World stories was a departure for comics but a logical result of Kirby's thought. "People like villains because they know that in us the villain lives," he says. "The villain is as valid as the hero."

Although Kirby unquestionably took the moral sense of his stories very seriously, he approached the adventures themselves in a spirit of fun. His art was rapid and lively, his plots—the most compelling and best crafted of his career—abounding in fight scenes, extravagant costumes, and fantastic machinery. A deluge of ideas poured from every issue, always with surprising and slightly tongue-in-cheek names: the Boom Tube, which transported characters between the Fourth World and our world; the Mother Box, which kept the New Gods in touch with their homeland; and many such threats as Doctor Vermin Vundabar's Murder Machine, which the cover said was "like a diabolical car wash!! It traps you on the way in—and kills you on the way out!" (Mr. M 5, Dec. 1971). In all, he showed that he could effectively tackle the very big and very serious with scarcely a trace of pretension.

Sometimes, perhaps, Kirby's imagination went a little too far out (especially in *Jimmy Olsen*, where vampires, Scottish sea serpents, and even comedian Don Rickles traipsed through the pages); but even then, all of his work blazed with the unmistakable Kirby verve. The Fourth World provided one of those rarest and most meaningful of moments in comic book history: a truly individual vision, free of trends and fads, of editorial policy and the demands of mainstream fandom. In those pages full of archetypal power, explosive action, and bizarre invention, Jack Kirby—the man who had been both workhorse and maverick, street-fighter and mythic poet, salesman and creative genius during all of comics' most critical junctures—brought his tumultuous career to a dazzling consummation, and in the process created three of the finest series of their time.

For a while there seemed nowhere to go but up. The titles were apparently selling well, Kirby was committed to them, and their promise seemed boundless. Thus it came as a stunning blow both to Kirby and his fans when DC inexplicably canceled *New Gods* and *The Forever People* after eleven issues (Nov. 1972), and *Mr. Miracle* after eighteen (Mar. 1974), having already turned *Jimmy Olsen* over to editor Murray Boltinoff (Apr. 1972). The "titanic struggle" of New Genesis and Apokolips was left unresolved. (With these cancellations, Kirby felt a growing discontent with the standard business of comic book production, in which all his great ideas remained the property of DC, and he gained only a free-lancer's fees; he thus began, like Neal Adams, and *Star*Reach's* Mike Friedrich, to be a force for legal and financial, as well as creative, change in the field.)

With each creation after the Fourth World, Kirby's talents seemed to flag. First he turned out a pair of one-shots for DC's sole experiment in black-and-white magazines, *In the Days of the Mob* and *Spirit World*. His next actual series, *The Demon*, was the moody and entertaining story of occultist Jason Blood, who was transformed by the ancient spirit of Merlin into a nearly uncontrollable demon named Etrigan, in order to battle the magical forces of darkness (Sept. 1972). Although a rare and potent blend of horror and heroics, *The Demon* failed to build as other Kirby creations had, and perished after sixteen issues.

Next came *Kamandi*, a twist on *Planet of the Apes*, about a human boy in a post-nuclear-war future in which other animals have gained intelligence and reduced mankind to bestiality (K 1, Nov. 1972). Another clever idea, it was allowed to become repetitious when Kirby settled for a long series of different talking animals (including even talking snails) instead of more complex plot variations. The longest-lived of Kirby's DC creations, *Kamandi* ran to 59 issues (Nov. 1978), but the last nineteen were drawn by various artists under the editing and writing of DC newcomer Gerry Conway.

Much more ingenuity entered the pages of *OMAC*, about a "One Man Army Corps" in a future of robotics gone mad, which introduced such ideas as a female "Build-a-Friend" with which the hero falls in love, and a sentient orbital satellite shaped like a giant eye, but it ran only eight issues (Oct. 1974–Dec. 1975). Along the way, Kirby contributed a few nostalgic war stories to *The Losers*, briefly revived a Golden Age hero called the Sandman, and helped launch a pair of new series, *Kobra* and *Richard Dragon, Kung Fu Fighter*. But only his Fourth World would be truly remembered.

Kirby's art took a slow but steady turn for the worse during the same period. The large pencils that had once been so effective now became too big, and the details sketchy, with the result that his compositions became disjointed and unclear, while his stories began to speed by too quickly to be satisfying. He was also not much helped by the rather rough inking of Mike Royer, who replaced Vince Colletta early in Kirby's stay at DC. At the same time, his scripting, always unusual, began to swing toward the oblique and confusing.

When he'd first arrived at DC, Kirby had been the favorite of fandom, the star of the field, living up to the nickname Stan Lee had hung on him: "the King." His arrival promised to champion the cause of the artist-creator, to further the shift of comics into a graphics-dominated medium, "to keep the medium," in his own words, "ever flexible and sustaining." But within a few years the great body of fandom had pulled away from him, dealers in old comics were cutting the prices of his back issues, and sales of his comics were beginning to dip.

Kirby had carried to a wondrous conclusion the explosive innovation of Marvel in the 1960s, but the fans of the 1970s seemed no longer interested. In the slick, serious days of O'Neil and Adams, Thomas and Smith, perhaps Kirby's rambunctious creations, so uniquely combining awe and delight, could be too easily dismissed as "comic-bookish." When his contract came up for renewal, he and DC were unable to come to terms, and in 1975 he left them.

"Dear Joe"

All during the 1970s, only one editorial stable at DC maintained a distinct personality. This was the stable of Joe Kubert, one of the artists whom Carmine Infantino had promoted to the position of editor in 1968. Unlike his predecessors at DC, Kubert functioned as editor, writer, and artist, but because of his excellent craftmanship and the support of a carefully gleaned roster of co-creators, he was able to overcome the pitfalls that had faced Lee and Kanigher.

Kubert exuded a robust love for comics which transfused his entire stable. He threw himself wholeheartedly into his creations, and his writers and artists responded with the same zeal; the appearance of Kubert's name on any comic promised that his staff would invariably produce their very best work.

This sense of delight spread to his readers. His letter pages were probably the most intimate in comics. Under the salutation "Dear Joe" appeared innumerable war missives with the buddy-buddy tone of a GI writing to a stateside friend. The letters were neither critical dissertations of the sort inspired by Schwartz, nor the fanatical pledges of loyalty sent to Lee, but glowing accolades of respect and admiration. His responses were equally warm, and the result was a close bond between editor and reader.

Kubert's first assignment in 1968 had been to take over the war titles from Kanigher: *Our Army at War*, featuring Sgt. Rock; *GI Combat*, featuring the Haunted Tank; *Star Spangled War Stories*, featuring first Enemy Ace, then the Unknown Soldier; and *Our Fighting Forces*, featuring the Losers. Without making any obvious changes in the strips themselves, Kubert subtly raised their level of quality. The stories now seemed a little more human, the art more vivid and polished.

The surrendering of his editorial reins freed Robert Kanigher to concentrate solely on his writing. Kubert had the utmost respect for Kanigher's talent, and so made him his principal writer for the entire stable. Kanigher evinced a true understanding of warfare and captured the souls of men on the battlefield. He never glorified war, portraying instead the pathos of civilians and soldiers alike. His poetic yet natural dialogue, his historical accuracy, and his sharp eye for the little tragedies underlining the horrors of war, made these perhaps the greatest of all war comics.

The cornerstone of DC's war stable was Sgt. Rock, the tough leader of a platoon called Easy Company, which had been running since the late 1950s. Kanigher employed an intimate first-person voice here as Sgt. Rock addressed each story directly to the reader. A perennial foot soldier, Rock detests war but slogs wearily on, determined to see his buddies through to the war's end. Although an accomplished warrior, Rock, under Kubert, was first and foremost a man, his heart always sensitive to the sad episodes around him. Classic stories include "Medic" (OAAW 218, Apr. 1970), in which a medic is ridiculed by his fellow soldiers for showing up when "the shooting's all over." The story is a highly sensitive depiction of a medic's duties on the battlefield, and ends when he gives his life shielding his comrades from enemy fire. In "It's a Dirty War" (OAAW 228, Feb. 1971), Rock, having killed a German boy who had ambushed him, undertakes a trek across dangerous terrain to inform the boy's family of his death; haunted by the tragedy, Rock feels the dead boy's eyes following him from the night sky.

Perhaps the most acclaimed war comic in the stable was *Enemy Ace*, the exploits of Hans von Hammer, a German fighter pilot of World War I. Kanigher had introduced him in the mid-1960s, showing some daring in picking the enemy as a protagonist. Enemy Ace, however, was the most human warrior to emerge from comics. Like Rock, he detests war, but his sense of horror goes so deep that he is alienated from his men. His men see in him only a coldly proficient death machine of the "killer skies," and fail to see the anguish that eats him away; at night, lying in his bed, the words "killer, killer, killer" seem to echo from the walls. His only companion is a wolf, a killer like himself, whom he joins on his hunts in the woods. A strange bond grows between man and beast, and on one occasion the wolf even saves von Hammer's life (SSWS 145, July 1969). Kanigher's lyrical prose and Kubert's elegant art captured not only the austere torment of von Hammer, but the romance of the times as well.

Of lesser note were *The Haunted Tank*, in which the ghost of Civil War general J. E. B. Stuart watched over one of the U.S. tanks named after him and its crew; *The Losers*, in which four old DC war characters whose titles had been canceled banded together and squeaked through disastrous adventures; and *The Unknown Soldier*, about a master of disguise who undertook dangerous espionage missions (a great many *Unknown Soldier* stories were written by Bob Haney). Although not as consistent as *Sgt. Rock* and *Enemy Ace*, they all nevertheless featured much fine art and writing.

All the strips were graced with superb art. Along with substantial contributions by Kubert himself, the lead series featured many stories by veteran free-lancers Russ Heath and John Severin. Both were meticulously neat, and thoroughly knew the paraphernalia of war. Heath's layouts were hard-driving and swift, and his characters' expressions starkly echoed the agony of their lot. Severin's art was grittier and grimmer, reflecting the dark tone of the EC comics where he had made his name. With these three masters at the helm, DC's war comics were the most consistently handsome of their time.

Kubert's titles also included a regular run of excellent backup features. Many were one-shot stories, finely drawn by the likes of Mort Drucker, Ed Davis, Walt Simonson, Ken Barr, Alex Toth, Frank Thorne, Neal Adams, and George Evans. But most notable were two regular strips, *U.S.S. Stevens* and *Gallery of War*. The first was written and drawn by Sam Glanzman, and concerned a naval destroyer in the Pacific Theater. The focus shifted among many protagonists, from the various crew members to the ship herself to the enemies who attempted to sink it, but in each case a poignant human touch prevailed. The second strip was an anthology of famous historical battles, including "The Fall of Constantinople" (OFF 126, Aug. 1970), the slaughter of Roland at "Roncesvalles" (OAAW 224, Oct. 1970), and a Civil War story entitled "The Brave Soldiers" (OAAW 228, Feb. 1971), in which children were recruited to bolster the depleted Confederate Army. They were drawn with expressionistic vigor by Ric Estrada and written with historical veracity by Kanigher.

In 1973, Archie Goodwin took over the editorial reins on *GI Combat* and *Star Spangled War Stories*. Influenced by the EC comics of which he had been a prominent fan, and having foreshadowed Kubert's approach in his own work at Warren, Goodwin was an ideal choice to take up some of the slack when Kubert took on some new projects. Except for a few changes in personnel—most notably Frank Robbins, whom he recruited to help him out with the writing chores—Goodwin maintained the titles on the same even keel of excellence established by his predecessor.

Kubert not only lavished loving attention on the stories themselves, but on the overall packaging of the comics as well. They included such extra bonuses as two-page "Battle Albums," detailed illustrations of weapons and military vehicles augmented by informative texts, and "Table Top Dioramas," three-dimensional, do-it-yourself models of battle scenes. Such extras delighted the children, soldiers, and history buffs who comprised Kubert's broad following.

In 1972, Kubert branched out into a new genre with three titles: *Tarzan*, *Korak*, and *Weird Worlds*. DC had just taken over the rights from Gold Key comics to adapt Edgar Rice Burroughs's novels, and had determined to do them up in style. From the start, they would turn six of Burroughs's creations into comic books—Tarzan and his son Korak, John Carter of Mars, Carson of Venus, Pellucidar, and Beyond the Farthest Star—all under Kubert's direction.

The most prominent and longest-lived, *Tarzan*, was written, penciled, and inked by Kubert himself. Beginning with a remarkably faithful four-part adaptation of Burroughs's first Tarzan book, and setting with it a precedent for fidelity to both the plots and spirit of the originals to which the stable would adhere, Kubert made the Lord of the Apes a quietly

Joe Kubert's elegant Ape-Man. From *Tarzan* 228, February 1974.

noble scholar and warrior, at home both in the jungle and in civilization (*Tarzan* 207–210, Apr.–July 1972). Mixing multipart adaptations with single-issue original stories for the next three years, Kubert not only gave us classic jungle adventure, but a fully developed world with a well-rounded character at its center. In addition to being acclaimed by Burroughs's fans as the most faithful adaptation in the medium, Kubert's Tarzan was such a self-contained and universal hero that he also reached the pure comic fan.

Kubert's writing was extraordinarily simple, but still lyrical and moving. His artistic style, always marked by finesse, here loosened and broadened to capture the panoramic sweep of the tropics. Stripped of clothing and hardware, the lean, attenuated figures danced gracefully in battle, flight, and tribal ritual. The trees of the jungle became characters in their own right, sometimes sheltering, sometimes menacing. His animals, particularly the semi-intelligent great apes, were not only zoologically accurate, but infused with character and nobility. On those occasions when Tarzan visited civilization, the backdrops of the early twentieth century in which the series was set were transformed into another jungle, this one of brick and wood and human malevolence.

Korak, the son of Tarzan, enjoyed little of his father's excellence. Written less successfully by Kanigher and roughly drawn in imitation of Kubert by Frank Thorne, the stories remained stuck on a single, rather unimaginative note: Korak searching for his lost beloved. Murphy Anderson later drew the strip briefly, but although the look improved, the stories unfortunately did not. Korak's brief day in the sun came after his own title was canceled and he assumed a position as a backup in *Tarzan;* drawn by Alex Niño for four issues (T 231–234, July 1974–Jan. 1975) and severely reduced in length, the stories were little gems of tropical mood and atmosphere. (Niño was one of a number of Filipino artists imported by DC when Carmine Infantino became attracted to their dark, moody styles— and perhaps to the lower rates charged by artists in their country. Among them were Nestor Redondo, Franc Reyes, Pablo Marcos, Alfredo Alcala, and E. R. Cruz. This would prove to be an important step in a growing American awareness of the international comic scene.)

Kubert's third title, *Weird Worlds,* featured two series in the manner of Marvel's *Astonishing Tales* and *Amazing Adventures.* These were *John Carter of Mars,* Burroughs's epic of swordplay on the Red Planet, gorgeously drawn by Murphy Anderson, and *Pellucidar,* featuring adventures in a savage, inverted world at Earth's core, with attractive artwork by an associate and emulator of Neal Adams, Alan Weiss (WW. 1, Sept. 1972). Other short strips, appearing respectively in the pages of *Tarzan* and *Korak,* were *Beyond the Farthest Star,* farflung interplanetary tales pristinely rendered by Dan Green, and *Carson of Venus,* which told of an earthman's perilous odyssey through an arboreal world; with art by rising star Mike Kaluta, it featured the most unique and decorative illustrations of the four series. Showcasing scripts by Len Wein, Marv Wolfman, and Denny O'Neil, all four were faithful and entertaining adaptations, but all were abruptly discontinued before their story lines could come to full flower.

Under Kubert, the stable also included a number of carefully selected reprints, particularly during a company-wide increase in 1974 to longer, varying formats. Beautifully wrought stories by newspaper comic artists Hal Foster, Burne Hogarth, and Russ Manning provided the fans with retrospective Tarzan adaptations of former decades.

The last product of the Kubert stable was *Rima the Jungle Girl,* a female answer to Tarzan's success, based on W. H. Hudson's *Green Mansions* (R 1, May 1974). Although well written by both Kubert and Kanigher, with attractive art by Nestor Redondo, the series failed after seven issues. Kanigher also wrote a fantastical backup strip for the title, *The Space Voyagers,* which showcased more of the art of Alex Niño.

Kubert would not see DC's *Tarzan* to its end. He left as artist after issue 235 (Mar. 1975), turning the work over to Franc Reyes, then departed as editor and writer after issue 250 (May 1976). *Tarzan* became one of Joe Orlando's numerous non-crime-fighter series, written by Denny O'Neil and Gerry Conway, and drawn by promising newcomer Jose Garcia Lopez and others. After eight substandard issues, the title was canceled. Kubert meanwhile withdrew from drawing and writing in his war titles as well, devoting his energies to a new School for Cartoon and Graphic Art, and to making a contribution to the growing independent press movement with *Sojourn: New Vistas in Narrative Art,* which brought a number of battle-scarred artistic veterans—Dick Giordano, John Severin, Doug Wildey, Lee Elias, and others—into the arena of alternative publishing. Although he remained as editor of *Our Army at War* (later retitled *Sgt. Rock*), his unique touch seemed no longer present, and the genre of war comics began to slide into obscurity. Neither they nor jungle lords, it seemed, were fated to take the place of the costumed heroes.

27 Horror from the Swamps

Another editor who promoted what had been a minor genre at DC into a major contribution was Joe Orlando. Like Kubert, Orlando not only forged new ground outside the costumed-hero field, but gave many young talents the opportunity to break into the business. Unlike Kubert, however, Orlando's stable was largely lacking in creative unity; the major exceptions were the handful of "mystery," or horror titles on which he lavished most of his attention.

Although Orlando's various new titles of 1968 (*Anthro, Bat Lash,* and *Geek*) quickly folded, the titles he and Murray Boltinoff had converted into horror comics—*House of Mystery, House of Secrets,* and *Unexpected*—survived. Modeled on the EC comics of the 1950s, these were anthologies of short tales of supernatural menace (somewhat watered down for the Code), which were of consequence mainly in that they showcased such young artists as Mike Kaluta, Alex Niño, Berni Wrightson, Gray Morrow, Alfredo Alcala, and Don Newton—all practitioners of the dark, stylized, pre–Silver Age look then in prominence.

Horror, both pure and in combination with other genres, would be Orlando's trademark during the early 1970s. It was a trademark for which he was well suited, with his early experience at EC and important later role at Warren. In addition to purely supernatural material, he would edit Gothic romances, such as *Secret House of Forbidden Love,* titles that mixed genres, such as *Weird War* and *Weird Western* (the latter starring a physically deformed, alienated gunslinger named Jonah Hex), and a gruesome humor comic called *Plop* (which, with Infantino's backing, became an unsuccessful try at producing a high-quality, advertisement-free comic book).

The most enduring Orlando title to be built around a regular character, *Phantom Stranger* was at first another vehicle for miscellaneous horror stories (Show. 80, May 1969; PS 1, June 1969). A revival of a mystical, ghostlike DC character from 1952, the Phantom Stranger would flit in and out of tales of human greed and the supernatural, warning each central character of the danger of his evil ways, always to be ignored and see the character consigned to a horrible fate. Later, under Len Wein and Jim Aparo, the Stranger became an ambiguous hero in his own right, battling a criminal cult called the Dark Circle (PS 20–24, Sept. 1972–May 1973), but soon the original concept returned, with many writers and artists. Before the title's cancellation in 1976 it featured a pair of interesting backup strips: *The Spawn of Frankenstein,* based on Mary Shelley's creations and graced by some beautifully ornate Kaluta art; and *Black Orchid,* about a mysterious costumed heroine whose origin and true nature (like the Stranger's) was hidden even from the readers as she grappled with both urban crime and the outre. The Orchid had begun in *Adventure Comics* under Michael Fleisher and Tony DeZuniga, and now continued with art by Nestor Redondo and Fred Carillo.

Scripter Michael Fleisher was not a full-time comic writer, but a researcher working on a projected seven-volume *Encyclopedia of Comic Book Heroes* in the DC archives; during the course of his research he sold a number of odd, unique scripts to Orlando. His major project was a once-again-revived Spectre, appearing in *Adventure,* for which Orlando edited a baffling variety of titles in the early 1970s. The Spectre's return (Adv. 431, Jan. 1974), now infused with the macabre, came about through an incident in Orlando's life. "I had just been mugged in broad daylight on upper Broadway. . . . The feeling of helplessness and anger and loss of manhood (my wife was with me at the time) as I watched the two muggers strutting away with my wallet gave me the Walter Mitty idea of fantasy revenge." Fleisher threw himself with disturbing relish into the idea of a hatefully vindictive Spectre, writing of "the leeches of the underworld [who] crawl forth from their slimy crevasses to rob the helpless and slaughter the innocent," and having his ghostly hero punish them horribly with magic, as when he turns one gangster into a wooden statue and then cuts him into little pieces with a buzz-saw (Adv. 435, Oct. 1974). Jim Aparo's eerie art made the series fairly effective, but Fleisher's writing made it too disturbing for many fans to read. Fleisher would shine more brightly when he replaced writer John Albano on Orlando's hard-hitting western series, *Jonah Hex.*

The most memorable product of the Orlando titles proved to be neither a revival or an adaptation, but an original creation of a young writer, working with the editor himself, for a one-shot horror story in *House of Secrets* (HS 92, Sept. 1971). Since he was buying scripts from Otto Binder in 1969 and 1970, Orlando wanted to pay homage to that writer's classic pulp creation from the 1930s, a sensitive, sympathetic, alienated robot named Adam Link; when fan-turned-writer Len Wein came up with a horror story idea about a man turned into a plant-creature, Orlando saw it as the perfect vehicle for his notion of a sensitive soul trapped in an inhuman body.

It was a moving and well-realized idea, but probably would have remained buried in the pages of the horror comics if not for the chillingly evocative art of Berni Wrightson. Wrightson, a young artist whose style seemed to spring from the pages of twenty years before (showing the strong influence of horror artist Graham "Ghastly" Ingels and fantasy art-

Berni Wrightson's Swamp Thing: Fear, violence . . . and an odd humanity. Script by Len Wein. From *Swamp Thing* 5, July 1973.

ist Al Williamson), was already carving a great name for himself as a horror artist at Warren. One of his collaborators there, writer/artist Bruce Jones, says, "Berni Wrightson knows a lot about maggoty grave dirt. And he didn't learn about it by collecting Spider-Boy and Captain Jock-Strap. . . . He learned it in darkened rooms, sitting mesmerized by Karloff's performance in *Bride* . . . and by taking long, solitary walks through the neighborhood cemetery and wondering what your dead Uncle Chester looks like *now*. . . ." Using deep shadows, lines twisted like jungle creepers, and faces contorted in desperation, greed, and terror, Wrightson was able to tear the deepest fears from the hearts of his readers and send them flowing over the page. In "Swamp Thing," he made of the bayous a single malevolent organism, rich with the smells of rot and fecundity, from which the protagonist oozed like a wayward, sentient clump of moss.

The story became the one fan sensation of the DC horror comics. Carmine Infantino requested a series about the character almost immediately, and after a year of development, Orlando, Wein, and Wrightson launched the Swamp Thing in his own title (Nov. 1972). They developed the tale of Alec Holland, a scientist secluded in the bayous while developing a fertility formula for plants; when foreign agents bomb his laboratory, he, the formula, and the marshes around him merge into a creation of mucky vegetation that could only be called the Swamp Thing. Hideous in appearance and unable to speak, Holland nonetheless retains his intelligent, all-too-human soul, condemning him to shamble through the bogs in lonely misery.

The three creators worked very closely together, plotting the first nine issues page by page in the editor's office, thus bringing the artist into the process of creation at a much more intimate level than was yet common for DC (Wrightson even plotted the tenth issue mainly on his own when Wein fell ill). The threesome proved to be clever and compelling plotters, able to keep a rather limited character fresh and unpredictable. Intrigue and drama were contributed to the stories by a regular supporting cast: government agent Matt Cable, trying to puzzle out the connection between the Swamp Thing and the (so he thinks) deceased Dr. Alec Holland; a lunatic, physically withered scientist named Arcane, who wants to transpose his mind into the Swamp Thing's body; Arcane's daughter Abigail, who becomes involved with Cable; the members of a mysterious 'Conclave" out to capture the Swamp Thing; and an affectionate little mutt who befriends the Swamp Thing but has had his skull wired by the Conclave to turn him into a tool of espionage.

The monster reached the height of his poignancy and effectiveness when he left his marshy roots, donning a trench coat and hat in an attempt to move among men again. Among the varied, spine-tingling adventures through which he wandered were a clash with a village of witch-hunters, an encounter with an eccentric maker of clockwork people who has created "living" replicas of Alec Holland and his deceased wife, and a guest appearance by the Batman, in which Wrightson's spooky portrait of the Darknight Detective ranked among the decade's best (*Swamp Thing* 7, Dec. 1973).

To all the stories Wein contributed florid descriptions in the horror-genre tradition (with an added dose of would-be poesy à la Roy Thomas, as when a cry of fright "echoes through the ancient battlements like the death-knell of a dream") and moving interior monologues for the alienated monster. Thus the Swamp Thing, though drawing much from the horror-comic tradition, transcended his genre to become a unique blend of monster, antihero, and hero.

The series' best days, unfortunately, ended after ten issues. Wrightson followed the pattern of all the fans' favorites of the day in leaving the strip, and Orlando replaced him with one of the Filipino artists then so much in favor, Nestor Redondo. Although a dark, atmospheric artist, Redondo lacked all the drama and evil of Wrightson, costing the character much of his emotional impact. Wein left three issues later, leaving the writing in the inexperienced hands of David Michelinie; the series lasted to issue 24 (Sept. 1976), but with little of its original impact.

No other horror creation at DC created such waves, and even *Swamp Thing* saw only limited success. But a horde of creatures at Marvel, including one oddly similar monster from the swamps, were soon to set off some of the strangest developments of the decade.

Marvel's Monstrous Heroes

Soon after Joe Orlando and Murray Boltinoff brought 1950s-style horror back to DC, Marvel tried a pair of anthology titles of its own, *Tower of Shadows* and *Chamber of Darkness*, but both had been turned into reprint comics within ten issues. A number of such reprint titles in the early 1970s—*Creatures on the Loose, Monsters on the Prowl, Where Creatures Roam, Where Monsters Dwell, Fear, Beware,* and others—kept the horror genre dimly alive there, but their emphasis was heavily on Kirby and Ditko monster stories from the early 1960s. In 1972 and 1973, Marvel tried again with *Worlds Unknown, Journey Into Mystery, Chamber of Chills,* and *Supernatural Thrillers,* ambitiously adapting well-known works of horror and creepy science fiction by the likes of H. G. Wells, Theodore Sturgeon, Fredric Brown, and Robert E. Howard; but despite fine writing and art, those too failed.

Even more than at DC, Marvel's only real successes in the horror genre were to come with series that starred continuing, sympathetic, special-powered characters. Evidently, although the costumed crime-fighters themselves might be generally out of favor, they had made an indelible imprint on the field during the Silver Age, and no series could now catch on without at least boasting a regular superhuman protagonist (usually complete with girlfriends, running subplots, and regular foes). And, as at DC, the story that first launched Marvel on the road to successful horror was an apparent one-shot about a swamp creature, this one in the magazine *Savage Tales* (SavT 1, May 1971).

Written by Gerry Conway, drawn by book cover illustrator Gray Morrow, and reportedly created by Stan Lee, that creature, the Man-Thing, reached the newsstands only a couple of months before DC's Swamp Thing. Although the publication dates were too close together for there to have been any possibility of post-publication plagiarism, the similarities between the two "things" were remarkable: both were scientists transformed into creatures of living moss by their own experiments, both were cut off from mankind and hounded as monsters, but both tried to do the right thing and come to the aid of the defenseless. (Both, ultimately, were modeled on a creature from late in the Golden Age called the Heap, which may help explain why no legal action ever grew out of the similarities of the two swamp creatures.) The Man-Thing differed from the Swamp Thing in only one important respect: incapable of his counterpart's lucid, tortured thoughts, he shambled along mutely, revealing his emotions and dim glimmers of humanity only through his actions. This set the monster apart not only from fictional society but from the reader, threatening to make him a badly limited, one-dimensional character.

The Man-Thing began his own series in the former monster-reprint comic *Fear*, with issue 10 (Oct. 1972). Although not as well developed a concept as the Swamp Thing, he was lucky enough to fall quickly into the hands of writer Steve Gerber. Seeking a key to make the Man-Thing interesting, Gerber took flight into the realms of magic, alternate reality, and hallucination. First the slime creature establishes a sort of mental link with a young psychic named Jennifer Kale, whose grandfather, Joshua, is a student of the occult. She in turn meets Dakimh the Enchanter, a 20,000-year-old wizard who flits among the dimensions, keeping track of the "cosmic forces" that "prevent alternate realities from converging—and possibly destroying one another." The "nexus point" of those forces, as it turns out, is the very swamp in which the Man-Thing dwells, and the presence of a construction crew there, draining the swamp in order to build an airport, has disturbed the "cosmic balance." And if that balance "is not set aright, the very structure of reality will collapse," warns the Enchanter: "A plague of insanity would sweep across the cosmos. . . . Your world will be inundated by a tide of blade-wielding barbarians . . . or beasts who walk and talk like men. . . !"

But such predictions prove mild compared to the unrealities Gerber treats us to. A butter knife left on a table becomes a sword, and then the peanut butter in the jar beside it swells up and becomes a barbarian swordsman determined to kill Jennifer Kale. Jennifer, in a dream-reality, becomes a beautiful witch-girl in a realm where barbarians, World War II dogfaces, old biplanes, and rocket ships all wage war on a "blood-red plain—'neath this verdant sky—among these stones surely sculpted by a somnambulant lunatic." And who should be shambling across that plain? Only the Man-Thing, who has somehow become the key to restoring order throughout all the alternate realities of the cosmos (*Fear* 18–19, Oct.-Dec. 1973).

Soon Man-Thing, in his quiet way, finds a pair of friends: first Korrek, the great warrior made of peanut butter, and next one of the "beasts who walk and talk like men," a smart-mouthed, cigar-chomping duck named Howard, wearing coat, tie, fedora, and spats without shoes. Howard, of course, comes from a reality in which he is the norm, and he is as surprised by the cosmic disorder as anyone—"Finding yourself in a world of talking hairless apes," he says to Korrek, "now *that's* absurdity!"—but he is inclined to express his surprise more through smartass remarks than cries of amazement. Howard appears to die before order is finally restored, but neither the fans nor Gerber would let him stay dead long.

Gerber invented a writing style all his own, uniting the flowery Marvel style, a tongue-in-cheek sense of humor, and truly audacious pretension. No one else would have begun a story with the declaration, "Reality: Plato found it in the shadowy confines of a cave—Descartes, in a syllogism ...'Cogito ergo sum' ... 'I think, therefore I am.' They blew it—both of them." No one else would have had a character say, "Allow me but a moment, sir, and I'll explain everything—literally, *everything*. The universe!" But it was Gerber's very audacity that made him charming. He was at his best with the small absurd touches. When he tried to throw everything back into order, in a vast "Congress of Realities," the plot was a little too jumbled and arbitrary; and for his big shock ending he came up with the anticlimactic revelation that the gods who control the cosmos are a couple of dogs—in the last panel he even tries to suggest that the reader spell G-O-D backwards (*Man-Thing* 1, Jan. 1974).

Perhaps Gerber's best writing job of all came five issues into the Man-Thing's own title (May 1974). In a sensitive, haunting tale, a pathetic little

Mike Ploog's humorous approach to horror: Ghost Rider. Inks by Frank Chiaramonte, script by Gary Friedrich. From *Marvel Spotlight* 7, December 1972.

carnival clown commits suicide, then, as a ghost, gathers four people and the Man-Thing in a lonely corner of the swamp. In the next issue the ghost compels the five to act out the story of his wretched life—physically becoming the characters they represent, even as children—while three cloaked figures sit as "critics," judges of the clown's soul (MT 6, June 1974). As a moral fable, a supernatural story, and the very sad, stylized portrait of a man, it is a work of true feeling and originality. The story was also marked by the evocative art of newcomer Mike Ploog, who replaced the stiffer penciling of regular artist Val Mayerik to great effect.

Gerber fell short on a number of stories, but his high points were so imaginative and radical that he still stands as one of the few truly distinct writers in the field. Unfortunately, his esoteric and intellectual challenges were not much use in selling comic books to kids, and *Man-Thing* vanished after issue 22 (Oct. 1975).

Although the first and most unusual of Marvel's monster-heroes, the Man-Thing was not the most successful. A wave of continuing-character horror comics began in late 1971 as a result, surprisingly, of the drug-abuse *Spider-Man* stories Stan Lee had written months earlier. When the Comics Code authority rewrote its regulations in response to those stories, among the old rules withdrawn was the injunction against "walking dead, . . . vampires and vampirism, ghouls, . . . and werewolfism." Marvel promptly turned out a werewolf, a few vampires, and a rejuvenated corpse in series of their own.

The first of these was *Werewolf by Night,* appearing in the second issue of *Marvel Spotlight* (Feb. 1972), and beginning in its own title seven months later. It starred Jack Russell, a rather hip and alienated young man who is cursed to turn into a werewolf at every full moon, and his sister Lissa, who loves him and wants to understand him, but is always sundered from him by his curse. With writing by Conway, Wein, and Wolfman ("At last!" read the credits. "A werewolf written by a Wolfman!"), the words were poetic—with a vivid first-person voice—but the stories tended to be directionless. The series' main appeal was the art of Mike Ploog, who, for all too brief a time, was the mainstay and style-setter for Marvel's horror titles.

Combining a lively, cartoonish line with a rich inking style reminiscent of the old EC artists, Ploog was able to unite exciting, action-filled stories of the type favored at Marvel with the atmosphere demanded of horror. An odd humor ran through his drawings, preventing any writer from making his material too self-important or ponderous, but he would often surprise the reader with scenes and characterizations of touching poignancy.

Ploog left the series after issue 7, then returned for five more before departing for good (WBN 16, Apr. 1974). Although tremendously prolific at times, he would, like so many others, stay for only short periods on any one strip. After his departure the stories improved somewhat, as newcomer Doug Moench tried to develop some complex supernatural sub-plots, but by then the art chores had fallen to Don Perlin, whose work lacked all of Ploog's atmospheric beauty. The title survived until its forty-third issue (Mar. 1977).

Soon after the Werewolf's debut, another movie-influenced monster began in his own title, *Tomb of Dracula* (TD 1, Apr. 1972), which would prove to be Marvel's steadiest and most acclaimed horror title. The art was by Gene Colan, who would stick with it to the end; he turned in some of his eeriest and most dramatic art, often inked by Tom Palmer, who gave clarity and solidity to his often oblique images. The stories began on a sound note, with Conway and Archie Goodwin centering on a troubled, weak-spirited foe of Dracula's named Frank Drake, and adhering to the tone of Bram Stoker's original novel. But it was with Marv Wolfman's arrival soon afterward that the series hit the stride it was to keep for the rest of the decade.

Wolfman avoided centering his plots too much on Dracula himself, as that would have taxed a character who was, ultimately, rather limited. Instead he focused on people whose lives had somehow fallen under Dracula's shadow, either by losing a loved one to the vampire's bite or by getting involved with those out to destroy vampirism. He developed a large cast of characters—the old vampire authority Quincy Harker, descendant of a character in Stoker's novel; Frank Drake, in search of his past and himself; the jive-talking black vampire-slayer named Blade; Harold H. Harold, the humorously nervous, opportunistic writer who sees Dracula as a potential best-seller; the naïve, silly Aurora, who thinks Dracula loves her; Rachel Van Helsing, the tough, levelheaded descendant of the man who killed Dracula in Stoker's book—whose paths would cross, separate, and recross again in unexpected patterns over the years. Perhaps Wolfman's most interesting creation was Hannibal King, a hard-boiled private eye who also happens to be a vampire, and uses his investigative talents to destroy the minions of Dracula. King's stories—told in a tough, wise-cracking, albeit fairly clichéd, first-person voice—generally involved everyday clients in urban settings whose troubles were linked to both crime and vampirism. They provided some of Wolfman's best character studies.

Gradually the personality of Dracula himself became multifaceted and capable of growth. We learned of his ambivalent feelings about his own bloody past, his proud adherence to the peculiar ethical code by which the vampires live, his love for a human woman, his beloved son Janus and hated daughter Lilith, and the odd mixture of distaste and respect that he accords the people who are determined to slay him. His ability to die and be reborn was used to good effect, particularly when Harker and his other foes felt compelled to bring him back to life themselves in order to combat a greater evil (TD 40–41, Jan.–Feb. 1976). Wolfman was able, through all these elements, to unite horror, mystery, humor, tragedy, and warmth

The horror of Dracula brought to life by the atmospheric Gene Colan. Inks by Tom Palmer, script by Marv Wolfman. From *Tomb of Dracula* 41, February 1976.

in—of all unexpected places—a vampire comic.

Unfortunately, it was the very number and variety of elements that left the title ultimately troublesome. With so many subplots running, some would be abandoned for a year or more at a time, then pop up unexpectedly with too much having been resolved "off camera." Many issues ran mainly on subplot continuity, without much really happening. And Wolfman wrote too much for Dracula's loyal body of fans; after a couple of years it became virtually impossible for a new reader to pick up a single issue and understand who all those characters were and what they were trying to accomplish—an easy pitfall of the continuity-minded Marvel style. Wolfman proved, however, that he could write superbly in spots and keep a team of characters fascinating to regular readers for over seven years; the comic ran seventy issues, then ran six more in a large black-and-white format, ending in 1980.

The next entry in the parade of monsters would prove to be the longest-lived of all. This was *Ghost Rider*, first appearing in *Marvel Spotlight* (MS 5, Aug. 1972), written by Gary Friedrich and drawn by Mike Ploog (who, although unfortunately unable to ink his own pencils, was usually fairly well finished by Frank Chiaramonte). The hero, Johnny Blaze, was an egocentric stunt-motorcyclist who fell halfway under the power of Satan and every night became a "biker" with a blazing skull for a head. Attempting to use his powers for good, Blaze found himself always being manipulated and occasionally controlled by Satan and his various cults; fortunately, good always triumphed, often through the intervention of Johnny's cycle-riding girlfriend, Roxanne. The most interesting aspect of the series was the fact that Satan appeared in person, a startling move for a mainstream comic book company, which will usually go far out of its way to avoid offending anyone's religious beliefs.

Although the strip was never particularly compelling or artful, a small but steady readership—presumably drawing from lovers of both motorcycles and the supernatural—kept Johnny Blaze glowing through various writers and artists after every other horror hero had passed from the scene. The final issue of his own title, number 80, came in 1983.

While Wolfman was doing his best writing for Dracula, Gary Friedrich was turning in his own for another classic character, *Monster of Frankenstein*. The series began with a careful, heartfelt adaptation of Mary Shelley's original story, capturing not only its horror but the sadness of the monster's persecution and longing for love (MF 1–4, Jan.–July 1973). Friedrich clearly had a feeling for the story, adapting it with fidelity and poetry; his scripts were accompanied by Ploog's most moving and evocative art, emphasizing tragedy over horror and vividly picturing the early-nineteenth-century setting. The stories turned toward silliness, however, as soon as the adaptation ended and the monster found himself in the present. When Val Mayerik replaced Ploog three issues later, there was little of interest left, and cancellation came the next year.

Another Gary Friedrich series, *Son of Satan*, sprang from the milieu of *Ghost Rider:* exorcist Daimon Hellstrom discovers that he is, literally, the son of the Prince of Darkness and uses his own diabolical powers and "psycho-sensitive trident" to battle his father (MS 12, Oct. 1973). But in this case the writing was unimpressive, the Herb Trimpe art lacked mood, and although it did run in its own title for eight issues, the series quickly faltered.

Other horror heroes fared even less well. Steve Gerber and Gil Kane produced *Morbius, the Living Vampire*, an intriguing series about a tragic fellow artificially transformed into a vampire, which combined horror and science fiction (Fear 20, Feb. 1974), but it never gained its own title. A Haitian magician named Brother Voodoo had a series in a revived *Strange Tales* (ST 169, Sept. 1973), but only for a few uninspired issues. In a weird twist on Marvel continuity, the son of newspaper publisher J. Jonah Jameson, Spider-Man's nemesis, found himself transformed into Man-Wolf, and as such ran in a few titles through the 1970s (beginning in Creatures on the Loose 30, July 1974); his later adventures were entertaining escapades into science fiction and sword-and-sorcery. Perhaps the worst idea of the horror boom was the resurrection of an old Lee-Kirby monster as the central character in *It, the Living Colossus*, running briefly in *Astonishing Tales*. A few other creations were given tryouts—including a *Living Mummy* series, a *Son of Satan* spinoff called *Satana, the Devil's Daughter*, a Jewish monster-hero called the Golem, and a team-up of Dracula, Werewolf, and others as the Legion of Monsters—but, not too surprisingly, none of them caught on.

One advantage of the horror trend was that it enabled Marvel at last to gain a firm foothold in the magazine-format, non-Code market. Lee had been trying to break into that market, controlled by Jim Warren with *Creepy* and *Eerie,* since 1968. With *Vampire Tales, Dracula Lives, Tales of the Zombie,* and *Monsters Unleashed* in 1973 he finally succeeded. In those titles, big-name writers and artists applied their talents both to continuing characters and self-contained stories, all with a more purely horror and less hero-influenced slant. With their success, many more would follow: *Deadly Hands of Kung-Fu,* the return of *Savage Tales, Savage Sword of Conan, Planet of the Apes, Marvel Preview* (showcasing various features, including much science fiction), a *Mad*-style humor comic called *Crazy, The Rampaging Hulk, Howard the Duck,* and others, all by 1976; among Lee's most forward-looking experiments in the format was *The Comix Book,* an attempt to bring underground comics to the attention of the mainstream. Although most of these black-and-white magazines were short-lived, they were to set the stage for a valuable Marvel contribution to nontraditional comic publishing in the 1980s.

By the mid-1970s the horror trend had run its course. Although some series survived, scarcely anything new was being added to the genre. Like relevance and sword-and-sorcery before it, it had not been the key to saving comics from the insecurities of the 1970s. In some respects it had been a backward-looking trend, with its emulation of old EC work and, at the same time, incorporation of some Silver Age elements, suggesting that some fans and creators might already be looking to the past for quality in comics. And it was, in fact, almost at the same time that the field was swept by a fascination with its own ancestry and history.

29 The Golden Age Revival

The interest in comic book history which had been growing since the days of Jerry Bails and Roy Thomas's *Alter-Ego* led to a number of books about the early days of comics, beginning with Jules Feiffer's *The Great Comic Book Heroes* in 1965, followed by Dick Lupoff and Don Thompson's *All in Color for a Dime* and *The Comic Book Book,* and culminating in 1970 in the most influential of them, artist Jim Steranko's *History of Comics.* With one of fandom's hottest young favorites touting the glories of the Golden Age, suddenly every fan was curious to see the original comics of the 1930s and 1940s.

DC met the demand in 1972 with a comic called *Wanted: The World's Most Dangerous Villains* (Aug. 1972), devoted solely to reprints of Golden Age and a few Silver Age hero-stories. This was followed by the similar *Secret Origins* (Mar. 1973), and then two titles reprinting old Simon and Kirby material, *Boy Commandos* (Oct. 1973) and *Black Magic* (Nov. 1973). Soon they added tabloid-sized "limited collector's editions" for special reprints (later featuring special-occasion new material, and shortly afterward imitated by Marvel). When DC increased its comics to a forty-eight-page, twenty-five-cent format in 1972, filling the extra pages with Golden Age reprints, it was able to satiate the demands of the hard-core fans (That same year, two other companies, Warren and the alternative publisher Dennis Kitchen, joined the trend with reprints of Will Eisner's classic *Spirit* series.)

But the appearance of the reprints was merely a prelude to one of the biggest bombshells in the memory of comic fandom: In 1972, DC bought the rights both to reprint and revive the comics of their two great competitors of the 1940s, Quality and Fawcett, and in short order they brought about the return of one of the premier heroes of the Golden Age, Captain Marvel.

Because Marvel Comics had trademarked the title Captain Marvel during his absence, the old hero had to return in a comic called *Shazam,* named after the magic word that transforms young Billy Batson into "The World's Mightiest Mortal." The title became the most anticipated new comic since Kirby's Fourth World, particularly when it was announced that original artist C. C. Beck would return to draw it. When issue 1 (Mar

1973) appeared in print, it was so frantically hoarded by dealers and collectors that very few copies reached the stands.

The editor chosen for the new title was Julius Schwartz, a natural selection in view of his successes with Golden Age revivals at the beginning of the Silver Age. Unfortunately, the series did not develop as well as the combination of artist and editor seemed to indicate. In the 1940s, Captain Marvel had been handled with a humorous, almost self-parodying tone that contrasted fundamentally with the ambitious, dark, self-important style of the 1970s, a style that Schwartz had helped to launch with the new Batman and Green Lantern. Perhaps because his own perspective on comics had changed too greatly, Schwartz was unable to set a consistent tone for the strip. Since Otto Binder had retired from comics in 1970, his experience with Captain Marvel could not be drawn upon; the writing chores were divided among Denny O'Neil, E. Nelson Bridwell, and others, who seemed unable to decide whether old-fashioned fun, cute hipness, or self-satire was the right approach to the character.

Beck, disturbed by what he saw as campiness and confusion, withdrew as artist after a few issues. Kurt Schaffenberger, himself an old Fawcett veteran, filled in for him effectively but not regularly. Other artists, most frequently the rough Bob Oksner and the too-realistic Don Newton, were not appropriate to the old-fashioned material.

At its best, Shazam provided colorful costumed-hero adventure of a type all too rare in the 1970s. Beck's art, and Schaffenberger's after it, was very simple and cartoonish but told stories remarkably clearly and entertainingly. The Captain's entire wonderful Golden Age cast was revived, including Captain Marvel Jr. and Mary Marvel, the talking tiger named Mr. Tawny, and the Sivana family of bickering evil scientists. With its emphasis on lighthearted fun, Shazam found its audience mainly among young children, and a television version soon appeared on Saturday morning.

A new character tied in with Captain Marvel, the heroine Isis, later gained her own TV show and comic book (Nov. 1976). The comic, however, was scarcely more than a TV tie-in, with weak stories by Steve Skeates and Jack C. Harris and bland art by diverse hands. It perished after eight issues.

Although Shazam was successful enough in sales to survive five years, mainly on the strength of the young readers who followed the Saturday-morning show, it quickly lost the support of the older fans. While the Golden Age seemed intensely interesting when written about glowingly by Jim Steranko, the return of Captain Marvel brought home the fact that most of the old comics were light costumed-hero fare of the type that fandom had wanted to leave behind at the end of the Silver Age. Eventually the support of juvenile readers faded as well, after the cancellation of the TV show, and Shazam was discontinued after issue 35 (June 1978), to be preserved only as a backup feature in World's Finest.

The old heroes appeared in other quarters as well. The Justice League of

America, which had been hosting annual guest appearances by the Justice Society of Earth-2, now introduced other old teams. The year 1972 saw the return of the Seven Soldiers of Victory, a team of minor DC heroes from the 1940s (JLA 100–102); in 1973 came the return of the Freedom Fighters, a group of such Quality heroes as Doll Man and Uncle Sam (JLA 107–108); and 1976 brought a team-up with Captain Marvel, Bulletman, Spy Smasher, and other old Fawcett heroes. The Freedom Fighters, along with the Justice Society, were later to gain their own series, but in a time when DC was less concerned with reviving the Golden Age than with merely grinding out new titles, a time to be discussed in Chapter 36.

One of the most intriguing chapters in Steranko's history was "The Bloody Pulps," about the pulp-magazine predecessors of the comic book crime-fighters. Both major companies responded to the curiosity of comic fans by purchasing the rights to adapt old pulp heroes, Marvel first with *Doc Savage*, but DC far more effectively with Maxwell Grant's original darknight detective, *The Shadow* (Shad. 1, Oct. 1973). Assigned to the adaptation were writer Denny O'Neil, who would also serve as editor, and artist Mike Kaluta.

The stories were workmanlike mysteries of the Batman sort, set in the nocturnal city streets of the 1930s, involving bootleggers, crime syndicates, a "freak show killer," and a masked Oriental assassin. But the high point of the series was the atmospheric, stylized art of Mike Kaluta. Each of his panels was like a painting in its own right, evoking the eerie, thrilling covers of the pulps. The superficial details of his art were historically accurate, but he transcended mere accuracy with ornamental renderings that captured the romance of the times. His oblique angles and dramatic shadows recalled the *film noir* masterpieces of the era.

The beauty and drama of the pulps: Mike Kaluta and Berni Wrightson team up on the Shadow. Script by O'Neil. From *The Shadow* 3, March 1974.

Kaluta, unfortunately, like so many of his artistically sensational peers, did not remain long on the series, drawing only five issues. His successor, Frank Robbins, drew it through issue 9; his angular art, though dark and eerie as his Batman work, was so different from Kaluta's that *The Shadow* began to lose its fan support. With issue 10, Filipino artist E. R. Cruz took over, turning in a respectable job in the moody Kaluta tradition, but the title was canceled after its twelfth issue (Sept. 1975).

DC also tried an adaptation of the pulps' Avenger, as *Justice Inc.*, by O'Neil and Kirby, but nothing came of it (JI 1-4, June–Dec. 1975). By late 1975 *Shazam* had lost its early momentum, *The Shadow* was gone, and old reprints had been squeezed out by Silver Age material and new backup stories. DC's fling with the 1930s and 1940s had ended.

Marvel had entered the Golden Age revival as early as DC, but with far less fervor. A year before *The Shadow*, they had revived the pulp hero Doc Savage (D. Sav. 1, Oct. 1972). The bronze-skinned strongman and his squad of handymen enjoyed fast-paced adventures of an old-fashioned cast, battling such colorful criminals as the Silver Death's-Head in straightforward Steve Englehart stories. Ross Andru supplied good action art, with fine inking by Tom Palmer, but the series soon fell into other hands and was canceled after eight issues; in 1975, though, it did enjoy a brief return in a magazine format.

Marvel issued one reprint comic with a fair emphasis on Golden Age material, *The Human Torch*, but even it favored early 1960s stories (HT 1, Sept. 1974); Lee's stable had been doing well with reprints of its own early products since the mid-1960s. The only significant effect of the Golden Age revival on Marvel's mainstream titles was the brief appointment of Bill Everett as writer and artist on *Sub-Mariner* (Sub. 50, June 1972). Abandoning the highfalutin approach that Stan Lee had brought to the character since his revival in 1962, Everett returned to his corny, semi-humorous style of the 1940s. He brought a troublemaking young cousin of the hero's, named Namorita, into the picture, and shifted the Prince of Atlantis's vocabulary from such exclamations as "Imperius Rex!" to the likes of "Great Gar!" and "Sufferin' Shad!" His art gave a beautiful, nostalgic look to the series, but the character had been changed too radically for contemporary readers, and soon Steve Gerber was brought in to restore the writing to the Marvel norm. Everett's death soon afterward deprived the field of his lush, decorative art as well. The strip rambled after that, to be canceled with issue 72 (Sept. 1974).

The man responsible for Everett's return to that character was his young admirer and onetime roommate, Roy Thomas. Thomas's background as a prominent student of Golden Age comics later put him in a position to launch the last entry in the revival, *The Invaders* (beginning in Giant-Size Invaders 1, June 1975), which would prove to be Marvel's most successful. Featuring the combined adventures of Captain America, the Sub-Mariner, and the Golden Age Human Torch in the early days of World War II, *The*

Invaders gave Thomas a chance not only to play with the historical material that fascinated him, but to add some retroactive twists to the early continuity of the Marvel universe, including the creation of such new "old" heroes as Union Jack and Spitfire. Frank Robbins drew the stories with an angular, choppy vigor that recalled such Golden Age action artists as Mort Meskin; he was assisted by Frank Springer in later issues, who would eventually handle much of the art himself, in a good emulation of Robbins. The adventures centered on the three heroes' struggle against Axis aggression, mixing up fights against such villains as the Red Skull, Master Man, and Warrior Woman with participation in actual historical battles. The stories were fun in the beginning but grew increasingly uninspired, and the series never won over the fans who had been so history-minded a couple of years before; and yet, perhaps because it starred three such prominent and colorful heroes,it garnered a broad enough readership to outlive most of the titles released by Marvel in the mid-1970s, and ran to issue 41 (Sept. 1979). It sparked a spinoff in two issues of *Marvel Premiere* (MP 29–30, Apr.–Jan. 1976), *The Liberty Legion,* composed of a number of Timely Comics heroes from the 1940s, but that failed to earn its own title.

The Golden Age revival was the first clear case of a comic book trend sparked by the interest of dyed-in-the-wool fans. Comics were beginning to show an inclination to aim themselves more at the esoteric market of their loyal followers than at a more general readership of children, and the rapidly increasing number of comic conventions, fan journals, and comic book specialty shops suggested that that market might soon be a force to be reckoned with. But the time had not yet come for such new aims. Although the best revivals generated devoted fan followings, those fans were apparently not yet numerous enough to support them. Perhaps the creators of the comics were not yet ready for their fans, either, for the irregularity of the titles persisted in frustrating their most dedicated followers. In the continuing quest for successful alternatives to traditional heroes, for comics that could reach the older and more discriminating readers, still more avenues would have to be explored. Science fiction was about to emerge as the most exciting of those avenues; but in the meantime, the only comics that seemed solidly entrenched were those telling the adventures of the old costumed heroes.

The DC Mainstream

With all the attention being lavished on new genres by both companies, the titles that had formed the backbone of the 1960s were left to run solely on momentum. Some changes were attempted in many of the titles, but they were neither significant enough nor executed with sufficient aplomb to snap them out of a deepening malaise that had taken root at the end of the Silver Age. Having abandoned those things that had once made it great, DC seemed at a loss as to how to revitalize its principal titles.

In most cases, the quality of art decreased as the old titles fell into the hands of less talented artists, or good pencilers were paired with inappropriate inkers. The writing suffered apace as young writers struggled to learn their craft and the few remaining veteran writers trudged along sluggishly; writing assignments, moreover, changed hands again and again, as did editorial posts, and most strips lacked any direction. The physical packaging of the comics worsened as well. Scrambling to find a look that would sell, comics adopted innumerable formats and cover designs, most of which proved to be cluttered and tasteless. The coloring suffered, the printing suffered, even the quantity suffered as the number of pages gradually decreased from twenty-four to seventeen. In the midst of this, a new mind-set pervaded the field, and the old heroes, particularly at DC, were painfully contorted to fit the mold.

In general, a great insularity set in among the creators of comics at both companies. The fans-turned-pros seemed to draw all their style and subject matter from other comics (particularly Stan Lee's), and very little from the world at large; from this grew comics that were not only repetitive and lacking in distinction, but which eschewed the traditional broad readership of children in general, in favor of an audience of fellow fans.

By the early 1970s the Marvel style had become the norm. Its once-radical approach to characterization had, with its rise to preeminence and the hiring of fans as writers, inundated DC. Suddenly every DC hero had to find his own niche in an emerging stereotypical range of stock comic book personalities. All heroes had to be either hotheaded, alienated, bitter, frivolous, hard as nails (if female), or slow and genial. Between any two given heroes, a conflict had to be contrived where there had formerly been no reason for any to exist. Although these character traits and conflicts had started with the idea of making heroes believable, they were now exaggerated to the point that they became as fantastical as the powers of flight and X-ray vision. Character nuances, moreover, were stuck in wherever a thought balloon could be squeezed, and expressed in language that was forced, falsely hip, and sadly predictable. (Wordy captions were utilized to cram in more of the same; where they had formerly been used simply to propel the plot, they now became devices for the writer to make his presence felt.) What had begun as an exciting innovation in the 1960s had become an embarrassment a decade later.

DC had been flat on characterization in the 1960s, and the company's desire to borrow from Marvel in that area was understandable, but the decision to adopt the Marvel style of plotting as well seemed unnecessary and unfortunate. The two-story-per-issue format that had cultivated so many tightly plotted tales was scrapped in favor of full-issue stories. Many series turned toward continued story lines, but they were generally executed haphazardly and without craft, and lacked the epic quality of the Marvel sagas they strove to emulate. Bits of contrived foreshadowing and insincere melodrama were injected into the series in an effort to create Stan Lee–style continuity, but they were unable to provide the suspense that the lackluster stories generally needed. Still more often, Marvel-style slugfests squeezed out genuine plot devices altogether, despite the fact that only Jack Kirby could have made such sequences truly entertaining. With the breakdown of the editorial monoliths, no one appeared to demand the clarity and unity that had marked DC's stories during the Silver Age, and the new plotting style seemed to become an excuse for lazy, uninspired, or untutored storytelling. Some good stories did appear, of course, but they were swallowed up in an ocean of creative confusion and shopworn devices.

The Justice League of America, the meeting place of DC's primary heroes, most clearly evinced these points. Julius Schwartz edited the series for most of the decade, but no writer remained on it for more than a few years, and so no sense of cohesive development was possible. Denny O'Neil, Mike Friedrich, Len Wein, Cary Bates, Elliot S! Maggin, Marty Pasko, Steve Englehart, Gerry Conway, and others marched in quick succession through the pages, and none of them, despite Schwartz's presence, seemed able to break from the affectations and repetitions of the times. The art team, Dick Dillin and Frank McLaughlin, were dependable, but their work tended toward the stiff and cluttered, and suffered further from washed-out colors and poor production. Each character was saddled with a caricatured personality, and internal bickering ran amok: the radical Green Arrow and the Thanagarian policeman Hawkman feuded for years, happy-go-lucky Snapper Carr became an embittered youth and turned against his old JLA pals, and it was not uncommon for any two heroes to come to blows over a minor disagreement. The Justice League's adventures remained varied, several isolated stories were quite good, and

Troubles for the Justice League: Green Arrow snaps at Hawkman, while the Batman and Aquaman step out. Pencils by Dick Dillin, inks by Frank McLaughlin, script by Cary Bates. From *The Justice League of America* 121, August 1975.

a number of big developments in the DC universe—most notably the marriages of Ray "Atom" Palmer to Jean Loring and of Adam Strange to Alanna of Ranagar—occurred in its pages. The overall product, however, was a far cry from what it had been in the previous decade.

Of the DC mainstream titles that survived into the 1970s, few fared better than the Justice League. The Batman has been discussed already. *The Flash*, running steadily under Schwartz, Cary Bates, and Irv Novick, attempted to preserve the light, playful tone of the Silver Age, but was uninspired and weakly drawn. *Green Lantern/Green Arrow* fell to backup stature in *The Flash* under O'Neil and various artists, where, after the relevance phase, the stories amounted to little; they returned to their own title in 1976 under O'Neil and artist Mike Grell, resuming a swashbuckling, science fiction slant, but the stories were of little merit. Wonder Woman continued her pattern of ceaseless change: Robert Kanigher returned as editor and writer in 1973, joined by various undistinguished artists, and gave her back her Amazonian role; in 1975, Schwartz, Marty Pasko, and Kurt Schaffenberger gave her a lighthearted air and had various DC heroes guest-star in each issue; finally, in 1977, O'Neil, Pasko, and artist Jose Delbo set her adventures in the 1940s to tie in with the "Wonder Woman" TV show. No approach proved very successful. Aquaman returned for a brief stint in Joe Orlando's *Adventure Comics* under Steve Skeates, Paul Levitz, and Grell in 1974, and then, in 1977, for a briefer stint in his own magazine under Levitz, David Michelinie, Jim Aparo, and Don Newton.

The only hero who at first rose above the DC doldrums of the 1970s, although still falling short of the heights he'd reached in the 1960s, was Superman. Mort Weisinger's retirement in 1970 had made change inevitable for the Man of Steel; without his iron-handed control, no other editor could have sustained his peculiar but consistent vision. The more vocal fans, in any case, had begun complaining about the endless variations he had played for a decade on his conservative world, and although the sales of his titles were still among DC's best, the temper of the times favored the fans. So it was that when Julius Schwartz took the helm of *Superman* with issue 233 (Jan. 1971) he introduced a spate of changes to the life of Clark Kent and the adventures of Superman.

The new era began on a strong note. The art, first of all, uniting Weisinger's star penciler, Curt Swan, with Schwartz's best inker, Murphy Anderson, was the best of Superman's long career; with Anderson's precise finishing, Swan was able to display his new facility for bold, dynamic, "modern" layouts. And Denny O'Neil, to whom Schwartz entrusted the revamping job, brought about three major changes in an intriguing six-part story line.

Perhaps fandom's greatest complaint about Weisinger's Superman was the abundance of kryptonite, that convenient weakness of the hero; O'Neil arranged to have all kryptonite on earth turned to iron in an explosive chain reaction, but had that same explosion create a weird evil Superman with a body of sand and the mind of an alien. The creature was able to rob Superman's powers, and although it eventually left Earth, it thus accomplished a second major change: the Man of Steel was thereafter only half as powerful as he had been under Weisinger. Third, in the same storyline, Clark Kent abandoned his long career as a mild-mannered reporter for the *Daily Planet* to become a news anchorman for the Galaxy Broadcasting System (which had bought the *Planet* in a Jack Kirby story a few months before). In the years to come, a new set of relationships would form around Clark: the vaguely sinister Morgan Edge would replace the blustering Perry White, Jimmy Olsen would become an independent adult, and eventually Superman would openly vow his love for Lois Lane.

The reduction of Superman's powers enabled Schwartz and his writers—most often Cary Bates and Ellios S! Maggin—to handle his adventures in more standard costumed-hero form, pitting him against a variety of gimmick-foes like the space-faring cowboy called Terra-Man, and even such old Schwartz villains as Star Sapphire. The lore developed by Weisinger, in keeping with DC's tendency during the 1970s to repudiate most of its Silver Age contributions, was either scrapped or downplayed. The Imaginary Stories, which had grown so common in the late 1960s, were eliminated entirely, for they did not fit the new Marvel-influenced attention to continuity. Kandor was rarely mentioned. The only new contribution to Kryptoniana was an admirable backup series, *The Fabulous World of Krypton* (beginning in Sup. 233, Jan. 1971), in which various writers (most notably Cary Bates) and artists told the entire history of that planet.

Although the new direction at first promised much excitement, a great sameness soon afflicted the stories. Even at half his powers, Superman was still an unwieldy hero, and it was too easy for the young creators of comics to dismiss him as corny and neglect him. Then, in 1974, Murphy Anderson left comics; his successors, Frank Chiaramonte and Bob Oksner, had none of his elegance and polish. Stripped of his lore and his finely finished art, Superman became nearly as dull as he had been in the 1950s.

While Schwartz's staff made these changes in *Superman*, Murray Boltinoff followed along during short tenures on *Action* and *World's Finest*. With stories by Bates and veteran Leo Dorfman, Boltinoff (as he did on *Brave and Bold* and *Superboy*) produced light, old-fashioned stories that incorporated the new elements without trying to add any of their own; although usually entertaining, they were rarely exciting.

The members of Superman's family fared less well. Superboy was the most fortunate, thanks again to the inking of Murphy Anderson, this time over the pencils of Bob Brown. Jimmy Olsen, after Kirby's departure, returned to his Silver Age look under Boltinoff, Dorfman, and Schaffenberger, but only for thirteen issues. Lois Lane took on a hint of feminism under various hands, none too enduring or inspired (although a backup strip, *Rose and Thorn*, featured the adventures of an interesting schizoid heroine by Kanigher, Andru, and Esposito). Supergirl, having inherited *Adventure Comics* from the Legion of Super-Heroes, fell first into Mike Sekowsky's hands in 1970, following the faddish orientation of that artist/writer/editor's Wonder Woman, then into Joe Orlando's, under whom she coasted unimpressively until 1973; she then ran in her own title for ten lackluster issues (the first five of which featured the female magician Zatanna as a backup strip). In 1974, Olsen, Lane, and Supergirl were combined in a comic entitled *Superman Family*, which also featured stories starring Krypto, Superboy, Nightwing, and Flamebird. *World's Finest Comics* dropped *Batman* in 1970 and became a companion to *The Brave and the Bold*, featuring Superman in team-ups with other DC heroes. The title reverted to its old format in 1973, teaming Superman and Batman again under various creative hands.

For DC's mainstream heroes, the 1970s were a decade of innumerable superficial changes and perpetual shifts in creative teams. Yet even in the face of such flux, their adventures were mired in a bland, all-pervasive sameness. To a reader glancing over the newsstands at mid-decade, the shift to other genres seemed a blessing. Not since the 1950s had heroes been so bland, and if something was not done soon, they seemed fated for creative oblivion, if not extinction. Only one old DC hero-title shone brightly: *The Legion of Super-Heroes*, to be discussed in Chapter 32.

31 The Marvel Mainstream

Marvel's established heroes fared better, on the whole, than DC's in the early 1970s. While DC seemed to orient its series either toward the elite of fandom or toward the youngest and least discriminating of readers, Marvel continued to cultivate the loyalty of its body of adolescent "true believers." The success of a new company-run fan club called Friends of Ol' Marvel (FOOM) in 1973 was so much greater than that of the old M.M.M.S., in fact, that the size and loyalty of Marveldom Assembled was apparently greater than ever before. Supported by such loyalty, Marvel's mainstream titles continued to sell well, eclipsing DC's, and less importance was placed on exploring new genres.

New ways were found to market the old heroes. *Marvel Team-Up* (premiering in March 1972), based on DC's *The Brave and the Bold*, featured Spider-Man in pairings with other Marvel characters; *Marvel Two-in-One* followed (Jan. 1974), with the Thing cast in the role of host. Both were uneven series, but succeeded on the strength of their stars' popularity. Next came *Giant-Size Super-Stars* (May 1974), an oversized comic offering adventures of the Fantastic Four outside their usual continuity; in short order followed giant-sized versions of nearly every popular Marvel title, particularly hero series, including a revived X-Men. Spider-Man gained more exposure in *Spidey Super-Stories*, tied in with television's educational "Electric Company" and geared to young children (Oct. 1974). Yet another Spider-Man title, *Spectacular Spider-Man,* would join the ranks in 1976 as a part of a new explosion of Marvel titles; it continues to the present as a regular companion to *Amazing Spider-Man*. For Marvel, at least, the shaky years of the early 1970s seemed to have passed, and a new boom seemed on its way. (The company's optimism was enough to embolden Chip Goodman, son of Marvel's original publisher, to launch a comics company of his own, called Seaboard, which would bear the pre-Marvel house name Atlas; edited by Stan Lee's brother, Larry Lieber, and releasing new creations by such popular artists as Steve Ditko and Howard Chaykin, it was an ambitious project that was fated to end in failure.)

The cost of success, however, proved to complacency. A "house style" of story and art spread through the company, creating a unified line of comics that could be depended upon to be at least passably entertaining, if often bland and occasionally tedious. The approved storytelling style was a synthesis of the approaches of Lee-Kirby and Lee-Ditko. Each story seemed composed of formulaic proportions of action and emotional subplots; never as much combat as an old *Fantastic Four,* never as much melodrama as an old *Spider-Man.* The scripting itself was generally derived from Roy Thomas's style, marked by florid description and high emotionalism, steeped in the Marvel mythology. Great emphasis was placed on having each strip interact with every other part of an unbroken company continuity. Guest appearances were demanded of every character, creating such spectacles as a battle between the Man-Thing and the thoroughly urban Daredevil. Overall, the Marvel heroes maintained an even if unexciting course.

The art was equally even, but also equally bland and unimpressive. The great workhorses were John Buscema, whose style became steadily sketchier and less imaginative as he turned out more work, and his brother Sal, who had a strong sense of plotting and forward motion but little originality or finesse; together with a legion of imitators, they forged a Marvel look that seemed to combine the least impressive work of John Romita (now company art director) and an earlier John Buscema. The pages were laid out in straight comic-strip manner, usually containing the standard six panels per page; the backgrounds were sparse, the figures chunky and devoid of emotional nuance. The inking was laid on by innumerable hands in styles usually derived from the heavy, cumbersome lines of Frank Giacoia and John Tartaglione.

Marvel's overall packaging fared even worse than DC's. Rather than have the artist of a title do his own cover, one of a few cover artists was usually pulled in to impose the company's new uniform "cover look." Those covers were busy and heavy on action, usually so crowded with motion and written blurbs that they ended up painfully cramped and messy; this reached its worst in 1971, when huge logos and colorful frames squeezed the illustrations into the bottom half of each cover. Perhaps the clearest sign of Marvel's artistic troubles in those years lies in the innumerable covers drawn for them by Gil Kane; his talent for action had always lent itself to solid, dynamic cover art, but at Marvel his work looked so hastily executed, and was so badly inked and so restricted by the new format, that it only exemplified the general ugliness of the line.

Much of this uniformity of art and story was due to the fact that Marvel, even as it expanded exponentially, continued under a single editor until late in the 1970s. Roy Thomas had inherited the job from Stan Lee, but found it too stressful and unrewarding and returned to full-time writing in 1974, turning the position of editor over to former DC writer Len Wein. Wein also stayed only a short time, being followed by his friend and colleague Marv Wolfman and recent DC editor Archie Goodwin before a more durable editor-in-chief was found in 1978. Except for an occasional title controlled by a writer/editor, the lone editor generally ran the creative end of the whole company; by the time a multiple-editor system similar to that at DC was finally adopted in 1978, the Marvel style was solidly entrenched.

The dominant movement during the first years of the new decade was an elaboration and unification of the Marvel mythos created by Lee and Kirby during the mid-1960s. Lee himself departed in good style by contributing a quartet of epics in the old-fashioned Marvel mode. First, Thor set off on a quest to find the omnipotent and all-destroying Infinity, confronting the ominous Silent One, the death-goddess Hela, and Karnilla, beautiful queen of the Norns who guide the fates of men and gods alike (Thor 184–188, Jan.–May 1971). His confrontation with Hela continued, leading gradually to a war with the Trolls and a journey to the Well at the World's End (Thor 194, Dec. 1971); this set the stage for the second epic, in which Asgard fell before the powerful Mangog, Odin apparently died, Pluto battled Hela for control of the land of the dead, and Loki's machinations promised to bring on Ragnarok, the doom of the gods (Thor 200, June 1972).

The Fantastic Four meanwhile battled a mentally powerful invader from beyond the stars called the Overmind, who possessed Reed Richards's mind and thus forced our heroes to turn to their archfoe, Dr. Doom, for aid and leadership (FF 113–116, Aug.–Nov. 1971). Then, in what was virtually Lee's parting shot as a writer of comic books, an interplanetary herald called Gabriel the Airwalker announced the return of Galactus, setting up a battle that would involve the Silver Surfer, a witch named Agatha Harkness, and all the nations of Earth (FF 120–123, Mar.–June 1972). With competent art by John Buscema and Joe Sinnott, all of these were entertaining stories and a fitting farewell to the old days of Marvel.

At the same time, Roy Thomas was attempting, true to form, a far more ambitious handling of the Marvel universe. Beginning with a seemingly minor guest appearance by Captain Marvel and one of the robotic Sentries of the alien Kree (Av. 89, July 1971), Thomas used his *Avengers* to weave what he intended to be the largest-scale, most profound cosmic saga ever to appear in comics. Over the next few issues emerged a Kree plot to reduce *Homo sapiens* to the primitivity of our ancient ancestors; at the same time, several venerable Avengers began acting suspiciously, and the crime-fighting group was abruptly disbanded (Av. 92, Oct. 1971). In an ingenious twist, Thomas revealed that the suspect Avengers were in fact impostors sent by the shape-shifting alien Skrulls, and that the plots of both alien races were only minor fronts for a galactic Kree-Skrull war in which Earth, like some Pacific island in World War II, would be devastated just because it happened to be in the way. With issue 93 (Nov. 1971), regular artist Sal Buscema was replaced by Neal Adams, who, with the aid of Tom Palmer's inks, brought tremendous force, beauty, and believability to Thomas's far-ranging story line. His first job was to make a microcosmos of the inside of the android Vision, as Ant-Man made a fantastic voyage through his colleague at tiny size in search of a key to the mysterious events surrounding them. Next the plot led to the Great Refuge in the Himalayas, where the Kree-Skrull War had involved the Inhumans; Adams brought the same blend of humanity and oddity to them as he had in their own series only a few months before (Av. 95, Jan. 1972).

The climax of the war must stand as the consummate unification of Roy Thomas's unique vision. The Avengers journey to the Kree home world to encounter the Supreme Intelligence: the disembodied, combined minds of all the Kree's greatest thinkers. Seeing that the war must end, the Supreme Intelligence grants temporary mental powers to Rick Jones, who shares the time/space continuum with Captain Marvel of the Kree. From Jones's mind then springs an army of the heroes of Timely Comics' Golden Age: the Fin, the Blazing Skull, the original Vision, the Patriot, the old Angel, and others. Thus, in an odd and rather arbitrary finale, all of Thomas's most evident concerns—cosmic scope, the Marvel universe, the Golden Age of comics, and a hip teenager—are fused into a single plot twist (Av. 97, Mar. 1972).

The Kree-Skrull War, combining the greatest mythopoeic aspirations of fandom's favorite writer with some of the most atypical and ambitious work of its favorite artist, was immediately hailed as a masterpiece. Unfortunately, as inventively plotted and beautifully drawn as it was, the saga suffered from Thomas's determination to make the prose as profound as the story line.

Too often, he crammed deep meditations into the mouth of whatever character Adams had penciled into the panel, many of which were at once pretentious and silly. When, during one action sequence, for example, Ant-Man sees one of his ants killed, he reflects, "Human beings are funny—they think no living things but themselves capable of feeling pain. That's because—they've never heard an ant scream. Well, I have— and it's a sound to haunt a lifetime worth of dreams! A sound like lost souls in torment or the wailing of a forsaken child—and I don't ever want to hear that sound again—not EVER!" The writing also abounded in contemporary references; the ant who was killed was named Crosby, to go with its partners Stills and Nash, while Iron Man comments on the story by saying, "I've seen a lot more than fire and rain in my time . . . but this . . ." (Av. 93, Jan. 1972).

The stories thus exemplified the curse of serious comics in the 1970s: in striving to tackle grandiose subject matter, the young writers of the time, trying to rise to the occasion, erroneously utilized a style that was distractingly ponderous, badly written, and unsuited to the medium. (A great exception to the rule was on the horizon, but his contribution was so far from the mainstream that it must wait until Chapter 33.)

A more symbolic approach to cosmic adventures came with the return of Dr. Strange in *Marvel Premiere* (MP 3, July 1972). After a period of many writers and artists, Steve Englehart and Frank Brunner joined forces to recast the sorcerous hero as a brooding, eloquent explorer of dark, dank, Lovecraftian nether-realms (MP 9, July 1973). Their most notable work came when Strange gained his own title again, with a twisting, unsettling journey into a topsy-turvy world within a crystal ball, where Strange encountered and withstood Death himself (DS 1–5, June–Dec. 1974). Englehart's writing kept the story vivid and surprising, while Brunner's art—bold and atmospheric, reminiscent of that of Neal Adams—was well suited to the material. Brunner shortly departed comics, however, and although Gene Colan replaced him fairly effectively, the stories grew increasingly less interesting. Although always good enough to maintain its esoteric fan following, *Dr. Strange* had lost most of its original pizzazz by the late 1970s.

The series that most successfully and playfully enriched the Marvel cosmos was another title dominated by Englehart—*Captain America.* Just prior to Englehart's arrival, Gary Friedrich had written a long story, set against the relevance-inspired backdrop of ghetto unrest, that pulled off a fascinating unification of Marvel's secret armies and criminal organizations of the 1960s: the Supreme Hydra proved to be the son of the crime czar called the Kingpin, while Hydra and affiliated cabals turned out to be controlled by that master Nazi schemer, the Red Skull (CA 147, Mar. 1972).

Englehart brought such revelations to the characters of Captain America and the Falcon themselves. First, skillfully blending the "relevant" orientation already described in Chapter 21 with an interest in Marvel minutiae, he solved a particularly annoying riddle of continuity: How could Cap have gone into deep freeze for twenty years in 1944 as told in *The Avengers,* when, as veteran comic collectors loved to point out, there had been a run of Captain America stories in the early 1950s? To explain the paradox, he introduced a rabid commie-hater of the McCarthy era who had declared himself a second Captain America and gone on a binge of jingoistic violence until the government had to put him in suspended animation. But come November 1972 (CA 155), this overly patriotic Cap escapes, mistaking the original hero for a comsymp imitation of the 1970s, and runs off to mop up the Reds in his own style. The real Captain America must battle him, coming to some distinctly Vietnam-flavored realizations about the dangers of patriotism and his own heroic role.

Soon, the revelation that the head of an evil Secret Empire is really (in a Watergate-inspired twist) the President of the United States leads to the collapse of Cap's belief in the nation he symbolizes and thence to his resignation as a hero (CA 176, Aug. 1974). For the next year Englehart's stories not only brought some surprising twists to the hero's life but caught much of the political confusion and bitterness of the time. The former Cap first lets the Falcon fight alone for a few issues, then assumes the irresponsible new identity of Nomad, "a man without a country," who lives the adventurous life of a costumed hero but essentially stands for nothing. But when an overenthusiastic teenager declares himself the new Captain

America and is killed by the Red Skull, the true Cap reaffirms his destiny (CA 183, Mar. 1975). The ensuing battle with the Red Skull brings one more gut-wrenching revelation for the oft-tested hero: his partner, the Falcon, is himself a pawn, in part even a creation, of that supreme Nazi (CA 186, June 1975).

Such revelations and hidden connections would soon become an almost obsessive motif of the Marvel house style. But Englehart's stories were fresh and well written enough to interest even readers not born and bred in the Marvel universe.

Cap's developing continuity was broken off abruptly in late 1975, when Jack Kirby returned to Marvel. For the most part, Kirby would pour his energies into new titles, but he also wanted to tackle the character he had co-created in 1941 and revived in 1964; unfortunately, his current bent for interdimensional adventure and action without restraint was inappropriate for the hero. After he left in 1977, various writers—Thomas, Gerber, Don Glut, Roger MacKenzie, Chris Claremont, and others—tried to reestablish the complexity of Englehart's tenure, but there were too many cooks for the broth to be consistently palatable.

Englehart also enjoyed a fan-acclaimed, subplot-filled stay on *The Avengers* from issue 105 (Nov. 1972) to 152 (Oct. 1976). He shook up the membership roster frequently, cutting Hawkeye and adding a mysterious Vietnamese heroine named Mantis (whose slowly-unraveling origin would be a dominant subplot for a year and a half), with her friend the Swordsman, an arrogant ex-villain; next cutting Captain America, the Black Panther, and others in order to add the Beast and another mysterious woman, this one from outer space, named Moondragon; later adding the once-relevant Cat and a formerly dead hero named Wonder Man. He

The Avengers of 1974: The Black Panther, Mantis, the Swordsman, the Scarlet Witch, Captain America, the Vision, and Thor. Art by John Buscema and Dave Cockrum, script by Steve Englehart. From *The Avengers* 125, July 1974.

also gave a new, surprising origin for the Vision (Av. 134–135, Apr.–May 1975) and got him married to the Scarlet Witch (which did not, unfortunately, end the long agony of their melodramatic relationship). Rapid turnover has since been standard for the Avengers' roster.

A persistent problem with Englehart, however, as with most continuity-minded writers of the 1970s, was that in focusing on subplots and personal development he seemed to bring far less care and imagination to bear on the actual adventures. While his work with characters was probably the most ingenious the field had yet produced, his villains and plots had neither the slam-bang fun of early Marvel nor the inventiveness and finesse of Silver Age DC; too many of his stories led the reader merely to skim them, looking for subplots.

Englehart was also plagued by irregular and substandard art. Sal Buscema did steady work with him on *Captain America* (with the Nomad sequence being done mainly by Frank Robbins), but *The Avengers* was handled by Rich Buckler, George Tuska, Jim Starlin, Don Heck, Dave Cockrum, Sal Buscema, George Perez, Keith Pollard, and Bob Brown—almost all badly inked—during a four-year period. As usual, the rule seemed to be that the least inspired artist had the longest run. After Englehart, the series fell into the hands not only of many more artists but of no fewer than nine writers before the decade finally stumbled to a close.

The rest of the Marvel mainstream was far less interesting. Apart from expanding and complicating the company's universe, attempts to change and mature the line centered on more ambitious emotional developments. The prime movers in that approach were Roy Thomas and his frequent colleague Gerry Conway, who were presumably trying to remain true to Stan Lee's original philosophy but whose products were generally contrived and unsatisfying.

Thomas's principal target was *The Fantastic Four,* where he forced Reed and Sue to become bitter enemies and had Sue file for divorce, where the Torch lost his beloved Crystal to Quicksilver of the Avengers, and where the Thing's manhood was threatened by the obnoxious Thundra, a product of comics' fling with women's lib. After much excessive soap opera, Thomas's successor, Conway (with artist Rich Buckler doing an amusing imitation of early Kirby) wrapped up the loose ends and tried to get back to straightforward entertainment, but the inspiration had somehow dissipated. For the rest of the 1970s the Fantastic Four enjoyed competent stories and attractive house-style art, but no more.

On *Spider-Man,* Conway tried to keep the subplots lively and surprising, but he and his successors ultimately took them to the point of absurdity, as when Peter Parker's girlfriend Gwen is killed by the Green Goblin, then returns as a clone, and finally leaves Parker in order to go "find herself." The series was further marred by hasty-looking Ross Andru art, inked by all the wrong people. Even worse, Parker's writers in the 1970s seemed unable to distinguish between pathos and bathos; instead of the troubled but always strong and determined Parker of early days, he became a whiner who was unable to tackle or even accept any of the challenges of life. A number of Marvel heroes would undergo this weakening of their characters during the deluge of emotionalism in those years. It was as if the young writers, having just made the jump up from fandom, lost sight of the concept of heroism and used their beloved characters to battle internal emotional wars of their own.

Conway was more effective with Daredevil, whom he moved to San Francisco—thus making him the first Marvel hero to live in any city other than New York (DD 87, May 1972)—and put him through a jet-set love affair with the dashing Black Widow. Aided by the sensitive, sophisticated art of Gene Colan, he was able to create a generally convincing adult relationship between the two heroes; his successor, Steve Gerber, brought even finer nuances into the scripting by highlighting the lovers' different attitudes toward crime-fighting, partnership, and love. Colan departed, however, followed soon by Gerber, and the series would be shuffled among unconcerned writers and artists until it could safely be listed among Marvel's worst.

Other Marvel titles fared similarly. *Iron Man* was handled by a variety of second-string writers, with art dominated by George Tuska, who turned in some vigorous layouts but grew weaker and rougher as the decade wore on. *The Incredible Hulk* enjoyed more stability, with long writing stints by Thomas, Wein, and Roger Stern and solid art by Herb Trimpe, until 1975; then Sal Buscema took over until the 1980s; but the character's limitations became steadily more apparent, particularly after the success of the Hulk's television show in 1978 discouraged experimentation. *Thor* also continued at a steady but unexciting pace as first Conway, then Wein, then Thomas strove vainly to maintain the epic flavor of the late 1960s, with John Buscema slugging along as artist for nine years.

Gradually, what had looked like an exciting decade of new frontiers became an endurance test for creators and readers alike. As flawed as they were in various ways, the developments of the early 1970s had kept Marvel's heroes alive and interesting. But by 1974 the company seemed content to let its major titles ride on their earlier successes, downplaying experimentation in favor of formulas that had been proven in the marketplace. The bulk of their comics seemed suited only for the already committed Marvelite. The fan looking for vitality and innovation would have to look away from the established heroes and turn, if not all the way to the growing independent press, at least to a few minor but promising titles of the big companies. From the surprisingly diverse fields of science fiction, martial arts, and sword-and-sorcery would come four islands of excellence in the late 1970s.

The Legion of Super-Heroes

After being dropped from its backup status in *Action Comics* in 1970, the Legion of Super-Heroes went into limbo. Six months later, however, it resurfaced in *Superboy* 172 (Mar. 1971) for a one-shot backup story. Written by E. Nelson Bridwell and drawn by George Tuska, it was an unremarkable work, but it excited the body of diehard Legion fans. One of those fans, Mike Flynn, wrote a letter to *Superboy* proposing a Legion Fan Club. Such proposals had been made for every comic book, but Flynn's sparked an unexpected reaction. Hundreds of fans rallied to his cause, and DC soon saw its way to giving the Legion another shot as headliners.

The editor on *Superboy* since 1970 had been Murray Boltinoff, and it was he who brought back the Legion as a sometime filler. With their fifth appearance (Supb. 184, Apr. 1972), Boltinoff settled on the creative team of writer Cary Bates and artist Dave Cockrum to handle the strip. Much to the delight of many Legion fans, they cast the stories firmly in the Silver Age tradition. The team was perfectly suited for such an approach. Bates had been trained under Weisinger in the late 1960s; Cockrum had been a big fan of Boltinoff's *Doom Patrol,* and his art displayed a clean, unencumbered sense of fun. Combined with Boltinoff's old-fashioned orientation, they produced classic DC fare that still kept in step with more modern trends.

With *Superboy* 197 (Sept. 1973) the Legion, including Superboy, was promoted to regular lead status in the magazine. Now having more room to work in, Bates and Cockrum produced such excellent stories as "The Fatal Five Who Twisted Time" (Supb. 198, Oct. 1973), featuring the spectacular return of the Legion's mightiest foes, and "The Legionnaire Bride of Starfinger" (Supb. 200, Feb. 1974), featuring the wedding of Bouncing Boy and Duo Damsel. Enhancing these stories was the visual diversity that Cockrum lent the Legionnaires themselves. Providing them with new, more varied costumes and creating greater individuation among the characters—Timber Wolf looked more ferocious, Brainiac 5 grimmer—Cockrum took what was essentially Silver Age material and made it palatable to the 1970s mentality.

Despite a couple of key changes in the creative team over the next two years, the Legion maintained its successful blend of old and new. When

Cockrum left the strip in 1974, Mike Grell took over the art chores (Supb. 203, Aug. 1974). Even more than Cockrum, Grell's art was wholly contemporary, echoing Neal Adams in its flamboyant action and photorealistic faces. The next change came soon afterward, when Jim Shooter returned to comics to split the writing chores with Cary Bates. Shooter had quit Weisinger's stable upon finishing high school five years before, putting his interest in comics behind him. But fan intervention changed that. In 1974, two members of the Legion Fan Club, Harry Broertjes and Jay Zilber, persuaded him, during an interview, to return to DC.

With two former Weisinger boys at the helm, the Legion held firmly to its tradition, but now an odd new quality began to manifest itself. In the guise of classic Weisinger fare, Shooter and Bates imbued the stories with daring undertones. In "Braniac 5's Secret Weakness" (Supb. 204, Oct. 1974), for example, Braniac 5 builds a robot of Supergirl in his sleep and later convinces himself that the machine is his real, flesh-and-blood lover; in "Who Can Save the Princess?" (Supb. 209, June 1975) Princess Projectra contracts a "pain plague," a disease that causes such great anguish that no one has ever survived it; to save her, four Legionnaires must take turns diverting the unbearable pain into their own bodies; in "The Trillion-Dollar Trophies" (Supb. 221, Nov. 1976), the Legion is attacked by Grimbor, the "greatest master of bondage, restraint, and security in the universe," and his woman Charma, a mutant whose powers evoke abject devotion from men but violent hatred from women. Brought vividly to life by Grell's art, the stories proved that adult concerns need not exclude the tight, pol-

Brainiac 5 keeps track of the burgeoning Legion of the 1970s. Pencils by James Sherman, inks by Bob McLeod, script by Paul Levitz. From *Superboy and the Legion of Super-Heroes* 241, July 1978.

ished craftmanship of traditional DC comics. These concerns could be woven finely into the plots themselves, not tacked on as disconnected subplots.

Perhaps more than any other comic in the 1970s, the Legion of this period foreshadowed the developments of the decade to come. During the Silver Age, Marvel had specialized in innovation and humanization, often at the expense of polish, while DC had contented itself with superbly crafted juvenile material. In the 1970s, Marvel had rested on its laurels, while DC struggled—abortively, more often than not—to ape Marvel. If comics were to grow again, it became evident that a successful synthesis was in order; the urge to enrich and expand the medium would have to be coupled with mature, professional storytelling by creators who truly cared about their product. *The Legion of Super-Heroes* was the first to demonstrate this synthesis. Written by Bates and Shooter, who had been trained by the toughest story editor in the field, and drawn by Cockrum and Grell the Legion was the child of a quartet of young minds who strove to expand the medium while still prizing its tradition.

As with most of the great ventures in the 1970s, however, the Legion's time had not yet come. In 1977, Boltinoff surrendered the editorial chair to the revisionist Denny O'Neil, Shooter left for an editorial position at Marvel, and Bates and Grell went on to other DC titles. O'Neil brought in a Legion fan named Paul Levitz—who, at twenty-one, had already served as Joe Orlando's editorial assistant and was beginning to do quite a bit of writing and editing of his own—to write the strip, and newcomer James Sherman to draw it, and under this new regime the Legion went the way of the rest of the DC mainstream. Tradition went out the window, and in regularity and artificiality reigned. In an effort to further differentiate the members, each Legionnaire was issued a stock, exaggerated personality while plots ambled from event to event without any complexity, and the strip was suddenly rudderless. The personnel behind the comic now seemed powerless to affect it. Editors came and went—Al Milgrom replaced O'Neil in 1977, and Jack C. Harris replaced him in 1979—and pinch-hits by artists and writers abounded. Between issues 225 (Mar 1977), when Levitz and Sherman took over, and 248 (Feb. 1979), when they were replaced by Gerry Conway and Joe Staton, the team required help from writers Conway, Jim Starlin, Paul Kupperberg, and Len Wein and artists Staton, Ric Estrada, Grell, Walt Simonson, Starlin, and Howard Chaykin. In an attempt to compensate for the irregularity of artists, inker Jack Abel was utilized on a steady basis. With a heavy, domineering pen Abel succeeded in making all these artists look similar but, in the process obliterated their strong, individual styles.

Despite it all, Levitz on occasion displayed the promise of a budding talent. In a tabloid-sized edition of *The Legion of Super-Heroes*, Levitz wove a complex, century-spanning mystery around the wedding of charter members Lightning Lad and Saturn Girl (All New Collectors Edition

C-55, 1978), and in a five-part extravaganza called "Earth War" (Supb. 241, July 1978—Supb. 245, Nov. 1978), teamed first with the fluid, inventive James Sherman, then with the cartoonish but dynamic Joe Staton, he engineered an all-out battle that reshaped the Legion's thirtieth-century milieu. But Levitz's talent would have to wait to reach its full flowering, for he was replaced in 1979 by Gerry Conway.

The waning decade saw a total decline in the fortunes of the Legion. Conway would soon be replaced by Roy Thomas, Staton by Jimmy Janes, but neither team was able to right the strip again. By now, however, the Legion had amassed twenty years of rich lore and tradition, and it could not be kept down for long. Another resurgence, perhaps the strongest of all, occurred in 1981, and will be discussed in the final chapter of this book.

Cosmic Zap

The great cosmic outer-space adventure had been an integral part of the Marvel universe since 1965, but not until the coming of Jim Starlin did it assume the stature of a new genre. In the past, science fiction comics had almost always been either anthology titles or hero series with fantastical backdrops, but Starlin created tales that were continuing sagas, unlike the anthologies, and yet were true science fiction.

Starlin emerged as an artist doing pinch-hit work at Marvel in the early 1970s. His style developed slowly, but at full force it combined the ornate decorative beauty and small panels of Barry Smith with the powerful action and twisting figures of Gil Kane in a groundbreaking synthesis. When he took over both the art and the plotting of the aimless, failing *Captain Marvel* with issue 25 (Mar. 1973), he was just beginning to hit his stride. Before his stay on the title ended, he would emerge as one of the prime creative forces of the decade.

In his nine-issue *Captain Marvel* saga, Starlin was still essentially working within the established Marvel universe. The plot line was a complex space-war involving such prominent characters as the Thing, the Avengers, and the Skrulls, along with such newcomers as a bald, mystical, extraterrestrial woman named Moondragon, and Thanos, a tyrant from Saturn's moon Titan, out to enslave the universe by obtaining an old Lee-Kirby creation, the Cosmic Cube; along the way, Captain Marvel, in an encounter with a personified metaphysical force called Eon, is granted an extrasensory "cosmic awareness" (CM 29, Nov. 1973). The stories were slightly marred by poor scripting by various hands, an abundance of inkers—some bad, some good, but their very abundance depriving the strip of a consistent look—and a plethora of guest stars and supporting characters who obscured the originality of Starlin's thought. But from underneath it all emerged the rich complexity that was his to weave, and the preoccupation with the ultimate, implacable evil that would make his next effort, *Warlock,* a comic to be reckoned with.

Warlock was another Marvel title that had tottered and floundered since its inception. Bringing it back in *Strange Tales* 178 (Feb. 1975), Starlin took firm hold of it and immediately molded it to his own vision. Hardling all the scripting chores himself, blessed by good and steady inking—by himself and Steve Leialoha—and unhampered by the necessity to tailor his ideas to the set Marvel universe and include needless guest stars, Starlin was finally able to hew a vision of his own.

In a far-reaching eight-issue story, Starlin told of the ultimate confrontation between good and evil. The combatants were Adam Warlock, part costumed hero and part messiah, and the Magus, godhead of the Universal Church, an insidious organization bent on enslaving the cosmos. "I am the Ultimate Force!" announced the evil god. "Depending upon my mood, worlds live or galaxies die! The very fabric of time, space, the mind, or the soul are mine to command! I am *power* absolute!" Soon Warlock was shaken to learn that the Magus was not merely some external villain, but the dark side of his own soul.

The saga, until the final issue's confrontation (W 11, Feb. 1976), was enlivened by the fact that neither Warlock nor the Magus dared destroy the other lest they both die, and by the wildly imaginative scenes and adventures that Warlock encountered on his quest to find his evil self. There was the Death Ship, populated by aliens of many defeated races, pressed into slave labor by the Universal Church; a cosmic kangaroo court composed of bizarre creatures—one all eye, one all mouth, one nothing but a six-tentacled head—who put Warlock on trial and killed all the witnesses who defended him; and the Land of the Way It Was, a realm of clowns, scarecrows, and the Madness Monster, a creator of nonsense who claimed to be everything Warlock sought. All were created in Warlock's mind by a strange helmet.

The world of Adam Warlock was populated by a diverse and colorful supporting cast, including Pip, a hedonistic troll; the Matriarch, calculating temporal head of the Church, who desired to dethrone the Magus; the Magus himself, a demonic, inverted messiah; Thanos, with his scheme for total stellar genocide; and Gamora, his beautiful, hapless servant, who befriended Warlock. The most intriguing of all was Warlock himself, grim and complex, whom the fates decreed, in his own words, "savior, god-layer, demon, and the avenging hand of light!" Possessed of a vampiric soul-gem that could, when unleashed, suck the soul of any being into Warlock's own, he fought to contain the ultimate evil while at the same time struggling to keep his own lusty fury under control.

Here Starlin's art attained its full, awe-inspiring power. His page layouts were masterpieces of design, his worlds were wonderlands of hallucinatory weirdness, and his synthesis of Smith and Kane equaled the finest work of either of his influences. He developed a repertoire of personal storytelling gimmicks—Ditkoesque symbolism, shifting visual/narrative viewpoints, quick panel progressions suggesting stop-action camera work—that told his stories in terms uniquely suited to the comic book medium. His scripting was verbose, for his complex plots required many words to make them comprehensible; but it was never overladen with the ponderous philosophizing so often associated with "cosmic" comic writ-

Warlock, Thanos, and Gamora, in Jim Starlin's exploding cosmos. From *Warlock* 15, November 1976.

ing. His ideas were genuinely profound, and his writing was mature and unassuming enough to serve the profundity well.

After the end of the Magus epic, *Warlock* endured for four more issues before its cancellation (W 15, Nov. 1976). Those four were desultory and unsatisfying, for Starlin needed a huge canvas to put his talents to full effect, but the fans had seen neither the last of Adam Warlock nor of those immense abilities of Jim Starlin. In *Avengers* Annual 7 (1977), Thanos reveals the reason for his plan of stellar genocide: it is a love offering to Death, his beautiful and beloved mistress. Joining with the Avengers to stop him, Warlock sees both Pip and Gamora die, then is fatally wounded himself. "My mistress awaits you," says Thanos. "Tell her I follow shortly behind you, bringing an offering of undreamed-of magnitude ... the stars!" But even in death, Warlock's story is fascinating, as he meets his own former self, prevents the Magus, through a time paradox, from ever having existed, and finds himself in a strange afterlife. Starlin concluded the story of Thanos in *Marvel Two-in-One* Annual 2 (1977), where Captain Marvel reenters the picture to help the Avengers and the Thing destroy Thanos's plot.

Aside from four issues of *Dr. Strange* in late 1977, the conclusion of the Thanos story also marked the end of Starlin's work in the Marvel cosmos. As a major contributor to Mike Friedrich's independent *Star*Reach*, he had already shown his desire to work unfettered by company policies and mythologies. His most important work in the years to come would be on creations all his own, with which he and Marvel together would help pave the way for a new approach to producing comics in the 1980s.

If the Marvel universe had seemed grand before Jim Starlin's arrival, now it had expanded until it bordered on the infinite. And in Starlin, comics had found not only a great imagination but an artisan who could communicate the true profundity and symbolic power of his ideas with force, awe, and beautiful craftsmanship. Uniting the populous Marvel pantheon with the absolutism of Kirby's Fourth World, the broad view of true science fiction, and the psychedelic quality of some underground and independent comics, Starlin's brief tenure at Marvel was like a blinding flash of revelation. On the heels of Thomas's Kree-Skrull war, Englehart's Dr. Strange stories, and the many strange worlds of Steve Gerber, *Warlock* was the crowning touch of the huge Marvel world-view, a view that fellow writer Don McGregor once called the "cosmic zap." In a beaker of psychedelia, audacity, and playfulness, that "zap" transmuted past creations into new visions, took the comic book ideas that had once struck awe into the hearts of children and rekindled them so that they could do the same for the hearts of adults.

Warlock sired no direct offspring, but Starlin's art, at least, had a prompt impact. Most of the major artists to rise to prominence in the next few years—George Perez, John Byrne, Keith Giffen, Craig Russell—shared his decorative dynamism.

Russell was the first of them to put his talents to good effect, working with Don McGregor on another Marvel science fiction strip, *War of the Worlds*, later called *Killraven* after its hero. Launched by Gerry Conway, with art by Neal Adams and Howard Chaykin, the series revolved around the premise of what might happen if H. G. Wells's Martians were to invade Earth again in the near future, as in his novel *War of the Worlds*, but this time emerge victorious (*Amazing Adventures* 18, May 1973). The stories were set in a hideously altered future in which humanity has become a race of abject slaves to the tentacled Martians, and centered on a band of guerrillas fighting for emancipation, particularly the brash and violent Killraven. McGregor took over the writing soon afterward (joined in issue 17 by Russell), giving his readers a brilliantly envisioned future landscape—human breeding pens where the offspring of the enslaved provide the Martians with food; all manner of mutated beasts lurking in the ruined cities and poisoned seas; a host of horrible Martian overseers who relish torturing mankind—strangely but chillingly wrought by the delicately lovely pencils of Russell. Unfortunately the stories were marred by McGregor's tendency to overwrite at every turn (with characteristic ambition, he tried to make each story a unique, significant work of a different type, describing them variously as "social satire," "fantasy head trip," "realistic and relentless drama," "a bizarre love story," "a moralistic comic book of rather epic proportions") and by the abrupt discontinuation of the series before the story line could be satisfactorily concluded (AA 39, Nov. 1976).

A number of Marvel's bright young talents got to try their hands at science fiction in the next few years. Most prominent among them was Steve Gerber, who revived the Guardians of the Galaxy, the team of futuristic heroes created by Arnold Drake in 1968, as guest stars in the *Defenders* then started them in their own series in a new tryout title, *Marvel Presents* (MPr. 3, Feb. 1976). Although not one of Gerber's most inspired jobs, the series was an enjoyable, high-energy space opera about a crew of argumentative quasi-human adventurers saving the universe from such threats as the Planet of the Absurd and the antilife Topographical Man; its resolution came with the surprisingly graphic depiction of physical union between the latter threat and the astral projection of a female character in what Gerber called the "Cosmic Consummation" (Although "Copulation" might have been more apt). Gerber called the plot "the supreme affirmation of life," but it also shows a good dose of his usual satire and audacity (MP 7, Nov. 1976). The series was taken over the next issue by Roger Stern, a solid storyteller with a more standard Marvel approach, but was canceled after twelve issues (Aug. 1977). The art was consistently handled by Allen Milgrom, who drew essentially in the "house style," but usually brought in a little extra dimension of imagination.

During the same period, writer Doug Moench and the versatile, energetic artist Rich Buckler (with newcomer George Perez) created Deathlok the Demolisher, a futuristic combination of human and computer, for *Astonishing Tales* (AT 25, Aug. 1974). The series was short-lived, never allowing the seeds of the fascinating future world that Moench planted flourish, but it did introduce a remarkable character in Deathlok himself: rather than a simple internal monologue, his thoughts came to us in the form of internal conversations between the tough human portion, Luther Manning, and the cold, overattentive, almost nagging data readouts of the computer.

To Steve Englehart and Al Milgrom fell the considerable task of continuing *Captain Marvel* after Jim Starlin's departure. They used much of Starlin's cosmic material, some of it well, but seemed too overwhelmed by their predecessor's scope to get a firm grip on the stories. They were followed by uneven work from writer Scott Edelman and various artists, but with issue 56 (May 1978) Doug Moench took over the writing and Pat Broderick the art. With a tighlty controlled but dramatically powerful line, aided by the clean inks of Bob McLeod and Bruce Patterson, Broderick was able to remind readers of both Starlin and Gil Kane, and with Moench contributing imaginative stories, the Captain was able to meet cancellation (CM 62, May 1979) with dignity (an attempt to continue him in the new *Marvel Spotlight*, July 1979, failed; in 1982 it would fall to Jim Starlin to write the final chapter in the hero's life).

Marvel's black-and-white magazines, at first devoted solely to horror and sword-and-sorcery (whose grisly subject matter was made possible in this format by the lack of Code supervision), made a foray into science fiction with *Planet of the Apes* in 1974, adapting the book, movies, and TV series of that title, with writing by Conway and Moench and art by Mike Ploog, Tom Sutton, and others; it was to lead the way into an explosion of adaptations of popular science fiction programs, movies, and even toys in the second half of the 1970s, an explosion described in Chapter 36. Next came *Unknown Worlds of Science Fiction,* an anthology of adaptations of highly regarded stories by some of the best-known and most sophisticated artists in the field, including Al Williamson, Neal Adams, Wally Wood, Howard Chaykin, Richard Corben, and others (some only in reprint). In 1975 *Marvel Preview* appeared, which intermittently featured a space-spanning antihero, Star Lord, conceived by Steve Englehart (whose interest in the supernatural gave the character an astrological bent). The series was actually written by an emerging writer named Chris Claremont, who fleshed out the character and had fun writing what he called "classic Bob Heinlein/Ed Hamilton ... space opera, complete with heroes, villains, a couple of ingenues, neat visuals [mainly by John Byrne, with Terry Austin inks], and a wild technology." As such, it was one of Marvel's more entertaining contributions to the usually sombre magazine-format market.

Despite the brevity and unevenness to which their titles were subject, Jim Starlin and his colleagues contributed, from 1973 until about 1977, one of the few wholly original bright spots in the comics of that decade. Their work helped to keep comics experimenting and reaching, and their best creations left memories that would enliven the resurgence of heroic comics in the 1980s.

Masters of Kung Fu

It is ironic that the most enduringly superb new series of the 1970s should spring not from the demands of discriminating fans but from a popular craze that the fans scorned. But due to the vision of a single writer and a talented quartet of artists, the series overcame the onus of its origin and went on to reach new heights in the field.

Master of Kung Fu began as an effort to cash in on the martial-arts craze kicked off by the "Kung Fu" television program and the Bruce Lee martial-arts action films. Created by writer Steve Englehart and artist Jim Starlin for the pages of *Special Marvel Edition* 15 (Dec. 1973), the strip's protagonist was Shang-Chi, offspring of Sax Rohmer's creation, the diabolical Fu-Manchu. Shang, we learn in the origin story, has been duped by Fu-Manchu into thinking his father represents the forces of good, while Sir Dennis Neyland Smith and Dr. Petrie, also creations of Rohmer, represent evil. Thus the hapless Shang is sent by his father to assassinate his enemies; he fails, however, and the result is that Shang is thereafter caught between the eternal war waged by Fu-Manchu, who condemns his son for having failed him, and Smith, who thinks Shang an agent of the evildoer he has sworn to destroy.

The series caught on, and with issue 17 (Apr. 1974), *Special Marvel Edition* became *Master of Kung Fu*. Unfortunately, the creative team departed, and so began a scramble to find permanent replacements. In the interim, the series evinced a predictable lack of direction; Shang-Chi either battled with his father, whom he had openly declared an enemy by now, or tangled with Smith and his loyal agent, Black Jack Tarr. The stories were bland and unimaginative, and *Master of Kung Fu* seemed ticketed for certain artistic oblivion.

But then, with issue 29 (June 1975), a dramatic change occurred. One would never have suspected anything of consequence was afoot by looking at the cover; in a scratchy illustration grievously cramped by the enormous logo, Shang is flying through the air at a hideously deformed opponent. Two obtrusive captions read, respectively, "Action as you've never seen it before!" and "Fists of fury versus slashing swords of death!"

The splash page promised even less. The writing was credited to Doug Moench, who had turned out several inconsequential tales for the strip,

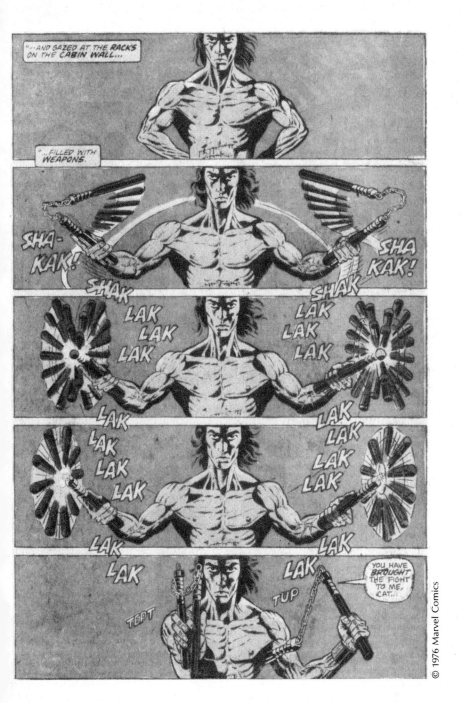

Paul Gulacy and Doug Moench make movies on the comic book page. Inks by
Dan Adkins. From *Master of Kung-Fu* 39, April 1976.

and the art to Paul Gulacy, a penciler who, although he had initially displayed strong promise, had seemed for months to be going nowhere. But for the reader who took heed of the caption reading, "Exploding: a blisteringly volatile new direction for mighty Marvel's dynamic master of kung fu," and turned one more page, a startling transformation lay in store.

Gulacy's art had suddenly improved a hundredfold. His action sequences now vibrated with motion, his layouts were innovative and moved the story along with cinematic clarity, his anatomy and facial expressions were strong and vivid, and the overall appearance of the strip was tight and meticulously neat. Although occasionally maligned for the striking resemblance of his work to Jim Steranko's, a point that cannot be argued, Gulacy nevertheless excelled in portraying mood and atmosphere where Steranko had fallen short.

The story line now promised an exciting new direction as well. Shang-Chi has come to be in the employ of MI-6, a British Secret Service agency. Shang, we discover, will now be operating alongside a close-knit circle of special agents including Smith, the gruff Black Jack Tarr, and one Clive Reston, who, through a series of veiled allusions, we can assume to be the great-nephew of Sherlock Holmes and the illegitimate son of James Bond. Smith, as team leader, will be aided by his old friend Dr. Petrie.

In their first mission, the team is to infiltrate the island of Carlton Velcro, a notorious drug dealer.They succeed, but much to their dismay discover that Velcro has turned the island into a nuclear arsenal for the purpose of conquering the world. In the course of defeating Velcro, Shang must fight his minion Razor Fist, a mountain of a man whose arms, from the elbows down, have been replaced by wicked steel blades. The story is reminiscent of the best of *S.H.I.E.L.D.* and *The Secret Six*, but goes far beyond them in its vivid cinematic depiction of realistic violence.

But *Master of Kung Fu* did not stop there; it was far more than an action-packed romp. It featured a tight, intricate plot, a number of terse but expertly wrought character sketches of a sort that would dominate the series, and, most importantly, an in-depth examination of the fascinating personality of Shang-Chi himself through the use of first-person narration. As Shang fights Velcro's guards and later Razor Fist, we are privy to his abhorrence of violence and yet, at the same time, his determination to overcome the man whose drug trafficking has ruined the lives of countless addicts. In this three-part saga, Moench established himself overnight as the most lyrical and elegant scripter in the field of comics; Shang's probing meditations and sensitive awareness of the world about him were expressed in keen, melodic language such as no writer had ever before attained in the pages of a comic book.

The Moench/Gulacy team promptly turned out two more superb stories. The first was the three-part Mordillo saga (MOKF 33–35, Oct.–Dec 1975). Mordillo's island, on which the story was set, was a huge playground populated by all manner of animate and deadly toys. Everything, from the choo-choo trains to the mechanical animals to the tin soldiers, either spoke or wielded lethal weaponry. Most delightful and innovative, however, was Mordillo's lieutenant, Brynocki, a three-foot-tall robot modeled on the mascot of Bob's Big Boy restaurants. Brynocki, fiercely loyal to his creator, assumed various roles, from cowboy to train conductor to chef, and for each he donned the appropriate garb and spoke the appropriate lingo.

The other story revolved around one Shen Kuei, otherwise known simply as Cat, an agent of the Chinese. The second installment of this two-part masterpiece included one of the most vivid and suspenseful fights in the history of comics (MOKF 39, Apr. 1976), as Shang and Cat, also a martial-arts master, engaged in combat. The fight, which neither contestant seemed able to win, was finally decided when Juliette, a double agent in the employ of MI-6, who had fallen in love with Cat in the course of her mission, drove a knife into her own shoulder to demonstrate the futility of their battle.

Moench and Gulacy reached their peak with issues 40 through 50 of *Master of Kung Fu,* an eleven-part opus that featured the return of Fu-Manchu. Issues 40 through 43 (May–Aug. 1976) served as a prelude to the story, planting clues that something sinister was afoot and introducing a dynamic new character, Larner, a former agent of MI-6 who was pressed back into duty to help battle Fu. Larner, a demolitions expert, had been booted out of the Secret Service following a mission on which his lover, another agent, had died. Embittered by her death, Larner took to drink and idleness, but during the course of the story he overcame his bitterness and regained his dignity as both a heroic agent and a human being.

Another character, who had been introduced during the Mordillo sequence, rose to prominence during this epic. She was Leiko Wu, another agent of Smith's, who was to become Shang's lover. She too was a martial-arts expert and, along with Smith, Shang, Tarr, and Reston, became a regular member of the closely knit team.

The story revolves around Fu-Manchu's scheme to revivify his long-dead ancestor Shaka Khan, the greatest of all warlords in ancient China's legends, and with him to depopulate most of the earth in order to remold it into the "glory which was old China." Manchu intends to do this by destroying the moon and thus hurtling the earth into an ecological apocalypse. The individual issues are told from varying viewpoints, including Shang's, Reston's, Leiko's, Black Jack's, Smith's, and Fu-Manchu's. All afford fascinating insights into the characters' personae. The epic also includes Larner's heroic death, one of the very few truly poignant tragedies in comics, the introduction of another recurring character, Fah Lo Suee, Shang's sister and a ruthless villainess in her own right, and an action-packed climax aboard Fu's satellite. Throughout the entire epic, moreover, Moench mastered the integration of words with art with unprecedented effectiveness, a mastery that would serve him well for the strip's duration.

Gulacy left *Master of Kung Fu* after issue 50 (Mar. 1977), and although the art on the strip would suffer by comparison to his for several years, he and Moench had established such a strong momentum that his departure, although lamented by the fans, did not seriously wound the quality of the series. Two precedents in particular set by Moench and Gulacy insured the continuing excellence: the first was a method by which *Master of Kung Fu* was able to circumvent to a large degree the disturbing irregularity of creative personal so prevalent in the 1970s; whenever Gulacy, or any future *Master of Kung Fu* artist, missed a deadline and a pinch-hit art job was required, Moench was careful to write a story that was both self-contained and divorced from the strip's continuity. Therefore a reader, if he chose, could afford to skip inferior issues without missing anything of consequence. Secondly, the characterizations of Shang, Smith, Tarr, Reston, Wu, and even the major villains were not only rich and well rounded, but the varied interactions between them were the first to achieve that adult authenticity toward which comic books had been striving since the late 1960s. With this solid foundation, Moench was able to maintain the extraordinarily high level of quality through partnerships with artists Jim Craig, Mike Zeck, and Gene Day.

Gulacy's successor, Jim Craig, did an admirable job of approximating Gulacy's style, but his work was marred by the overwhelmingly heavy inks of John Tartaglione. With him, Moench, following the dissolution of Smith's team after the grueling battle with Fu-Manchu, crafted first a four-part story introducing War-Yore, a villain who assumed the guise of various historical warriors, then the eight-part "China Seas" (Moench's tribute to Milton Caniff's classic *Terry and the Pirates*), which followed the various paths of the primary characters as they gradually converged again to battle and defeat Kogar, a murderous smuggler.

With the arrival of Mike Zeck, who brought a lighter but still energetic look to the comic, a new avenue was opened in Shang-Chi's development. In "Nightimes" (MOKF 71, Dec. 1978), a story reportedly suggested by new Marvel editor Jim Shooter, Moench spotlighted a quiet day in the lives of Shang and Leiko. On the surface, the story told of an evening of exercise, dining, moviegoing, and lovemaking, but underneath ran a current of serene, profound introspection that would come to permeate and further strengthen the series. Zeck enjoyed the longest stint of any artist on *Master of Kung Fu,* an uninterrupted run from issues 71 through 101 (June 1981), collaborating most significantly with Moench on the return of Brynocki, in which the robot takes over Mordillo's island (MOKF 73–75, Feb.–Apr. 1979), and on another multi-issue Fu-Manchu saga, in which the diabolical villain is again bent on destroying the "vile present mired in its foul western decadence (MOKF 81–89, Dec. 1979–June 1980). The story, in addition to a multilayered plot and plenty of rousing action, included the most in-depth examination of a villain's mind ever afforded by the genre.

Although Craig and Zeck performed admirably, the series did not fully return to the heights achieved under Gulacy until the arrival of Gene Day in 1981. Day, utilizing a baroque style and experimenting freely and most successfully with layouts that were masterpieces of design, would help to make *Master of Kung Fu* one of a body of superb series to blossom in the 1980s, part of a renaissance to be discussed in the final chapter.

Master of Kung Fu, although originally born of a fad, stood alone in the last half of the 1970s, a solitary masterwork untouched by other trends and genres in the field. Its relatively realistic subject matter and its solid, believable cast of characters made it the consummation of what *Deadman, Manhunter*, and every comic that tried to be adult had striven for. While never attracting the ranks of "Marveldom Assembled," it nevertheless earned a loyal following whose letters showed them to be the most intelligent and critically astute to follow any single title in comics. Unified by the strong, clear vision of Doug Moench, it was a work of rare artistic integrity.

Master of Kung Fu was not the sole creation to spring from the martial-arts fad. Marvel also brought out *Deadly Hands of Kung Fu*, a magazine-format anthology comic, and *Iron Fist*, a strip concerning a wandering half-breed martial-arts expert named Danny Rand. Rand's mother was an American, his father a scion of the mythical Chinese land of Kunlun, which periodically phases in and out of our dimension. Although born on our world, Danny is orphaned and raised by the masters of Kunlun in a training sequence reminiscent of TV's "Kung Fu." Upon attaining adulthood, he comes to America to avenge his parents' deaths, but is himself unjustly accused of murder (MP 15, May 1974). The series tells of his struggle to clear his name, with lots of flying hands and feet thrown in.

Launched by Roy Thomas and Gil Kane, *Iron Fist* was quickly delivered into a number of different hands. Its best moments came with the team of writer Chris Claremont and artist John Byrne, especially after it began in its own title (Nov. 1975). They built up a supporting cast, including a tough black female detective named Misty Knight, and added some variety to the story line. But after fifteen issues the title was canceled, and Iron Fist teamed up with another combative hero trying to clear his name, Luke Cage (PM 48, Dec. 1977). Although at first it offered an interesting interplay of personalities, *Power Man/Iron Fist* has as yet failed to find a real identity or rhythm of its own.

On a minor note, DC responded with *Richard Dragon, Kung Fu Fighter* (May 1975), a short-lived martial-arts series based on a book by novelist Jim Dennis, and *Karate Kid* (Apr. 1976), which was notable only in that it starred a member of the Legion of Super-Heroes and featured occasional Legion crossovers.

The kung-fu craze blew over as quickly as its predecessors and, with one important exception, contributed little to comics. The search for a winning genre or formula was growing increasingly frustrating, and was soon to lead to some disastrous publishing decisions.

The DC Barbarians

DC entered the sword-and-sorcery genre much later than Marvel. There were a couple of noble but abortive attempts in 1973: *Sword of Sorcery*, an adaptation of Fritz Leiber's witty Fafhrd and the Grey Mouser, with effective Denny O'Neil scripting and sweeping art by the dramatic and ingenious but seldom seen Howard Chaykin (along with work by two of his equally maverick friends, Walt Simonson and Jim Starlin); and *Ironwolf*, an exciting Chaykin creation that ran only in the last three issues of *Weird Worlds* before its cancellation. It was two more years before the company launched a full line of barbarian comics, the beginning of a wave of new publications that would sweep DC for the next few years.

The first three titles were *Beowulf*, beginning as an adaptation of the epic poem but quickly degenerating into pseudo-science fiction, *Claw*, which writer David Michelinie based fairly effectively on the fantastical worlds of Michael Moorcock, and *Stalker*, about a lonely swordsman, beautifully rendered by Steve Ditko and Wally Wood. None were ultimately satisfying, and all were short-lived; the most enduring of them, *Claw*, ran only nine issues (it returned in 1978, but was again canceled after only three more). A fourth title, however, was to become a permanent fixture in the DC line.

Warlord, after a one-issue tryout in DC's *First Issue Special* (Dec. 1975), was given his own title two months later. It was the brainchild of Mike Grell, one of the first of a new breed of creators who, functioning at once as originators, writers, and artists, would guide their comics according to their own personal visions. Grell's vision was clear and strong, and *Warlord* would prove to be not only a fresh and daring series, but one of the very few creations of the mid-1970s to last until the present day.

Warlord tells of the exploits of one Travis Morgan, an Air Force lieutenant colonel who is shot down over the North Pole by the Russians. He bails out of his plane at the last moment and inexplicably finds himself "in a world of eternal sunlight—a timeless world where prehistoric beasts still roam a towering tropical forest" (WL 1, Feb. 1976). The horizons curve upward here, and Morgan soon deduces that this world, called Skartaris, is at the center of the earth. He soon meets and befriends a female warrior named Tara, who teaches him the credo by which the people of Skartaris live: Life is a constant struggle for survival in this savage world, and you must always expect the unexpected; let your guard down but for an instant, and that instant will cost you your life. Morgan and Tara are then separated, and Morgan quickly discovers what Tara meant, when he is captured and made first a galley slave, then a gladiator. In the gladiatorial pens of the savage kingdom to which he has been condemned, he realizes where his personal destiny in Skartaris lies: to lead men to freedom. After organizing and executing an escape from the pens, he scours the land, emancipating men everywhere from their oppressors. Soon he is followed by a tremendous army of liberators, and men everywhere come to sing the praises of the mighty Warlord.

Simultaneously with Morgan's personal development, Grell gradually unfolded the mysterious origins of Skartaris itself. In "The Secret of Skartaris" (WL 5, Mar. 1977), Morgan and Tara stumble upon a cave housing a vast computer center. Morgan accidentally triggers a switch, and from the computer issues a history of the mysterious world at the earth's core. Skartaris, we learn, was discovered by survivors of Atlantis when that fabled continent sank beneath the Atlantic Ocean. Finding themselves in a primeval forest of unspoiled beauty and limitless fertility, the Atlanteans built a mighty civilization that quickly surpassed even that of their ancestors. In time, however, the new civilization split into numerous city-states that ultimately engaged in a cataclysmic war that destroyed it. Countless generations later, in Morgan's time, "Skartarans have evolved to various states of barbarism and medieval civilization dwelling among the ruins of once-great cities . . ."

Grell also established a solid supporting cast for *Warlord*. Most prominent among them were Tara, Queen of Shamballah, the greatest of Atlantean city-states, and the mother of Morgan's son; Machiste, a fellow gladiator from Morgan's days of bondage and later a lieutenant in Morgan's liberation army; Mariah, a Russian archaeologist who starts a new life in Skartaris; and Deimos, the power-mad high priest who becomes Morgan's archenemy. But far and away the most interesting character of all is Morgan himself. An adventurer and warrior born, Morgan believes that "you have never lived until you've almost died! For those who fight for it, life has a flavor the protected will never know!" (WL 3, Nov. 1976). In the savage world of Skartaris, he has found the stage upon which his bold, lusty spirit can truly soar.

As a writer, Grell proved himself a very capable plotter. His stories, although rarely intricate, moved along briskly and clearly. Unlike so many of his contemporaries, he did not feel compelled to fill his pages with excessive verbiage and highfalutin prose; primarily an artist, he was content to let the pictures tell the stories. Grell's art was expressive and dynamic, often capable of sweeping action sequences along without any words at all, and the end result was a breezy, visually stunning series.

Grell's vision unfortunately began to waver after the fifteenth issue. That story ended with a cliff-hanger in which Warlord's newborn son was kidnapped by Deimos. Morgan and Tara took off after the villain, but the urgency of their mission was displaced during three issues of unrelated, desultory adventures. From that point on, Grell would alternate brilliant stories—as when Morgan and Tara catch up with Deimos, and Morgan is forced to kill his full-grown son who, unbeknownst to him, is actually a clone (WL 21, May 1979)—with severe lapses of direction.This tendency got totally out of hand when issue 30 (Feb. 1980) told of an imminent war with Morgan at its center, only to be interrupted for eleven issues when Morgan was snatched away by a giant bird and plunged into a long, rambling interlude during which the war was all but forgotten.

As the series wore on, Grell got carried away by his own inventiveness. Skartaris became too vast, and Grell stopped building upon established realms in favor of charting new ones. Thus the fascination of the gradually accumulating history and geography was diluted; Skartaris was stretched too thin, and the series' continuity lost focus. In a world where anything can and does happen, and the novel becomes commonplace, all sense of familiarity and intimacy is lost; it is difficult to care for places and people when they are left behind as quickly as they are discovered.

Fortunately, Grell did not toss all of his inventions aside. A number of other characters and lands took root in his mythology. Among them were Ashir, a charming rogue prince; Wizard World, a sorcerous realm in Skartaris's past, in which Machiste and Mariah, now lovers, make their home; Joshua, Morgan's young son, who the Warlord believes is dead; Shakira, a mysterious cat-girl who becomes Morgan's traveling companion; Jennifer, Morgan's daughter from the surface world who tracks him to Skartaris and, in time, becomes a sorceress; and Mikola Rostov, a Russian werewolf who flees to Skartaris hoping that under the eternal sun at the earth's core he can escape his lycanthropic curse.

Grell held to his personal vision of *Warlord* for his entire tenure, resisting crossovers with other DC characters and incorporation into the company mainstream. He finally left the strip as penciler in 1981, although he would be credited as writer until 1983. According to Grell, however, much of the writing in those later years was handled by his wife, Sharon. She brought a depth and quality of characterization to the Warlord which Grell felt exceeded his own, and her work would inspire some of his most important future creations.

But those creations would not appear through DC Comics. Grell's independence and desire to control his own material made him a natural candidate to turn to the independent press. Many other artists of his generation—Neal Adams, Jim Starlin, Walt Simonson, Howard Chaykin, Frank Brunner, Gene Day, Craig Russell, Steve Leialoha, and others—had already dabbled in that field, especially in *Star*Reach* and its sister publication, *Imagine*, but without any significant commercial success. By 1981 some crucial changes had occurred in the comic book market, however, and Mike Grell would be among the first creators both to take advantage of them and to help them along.

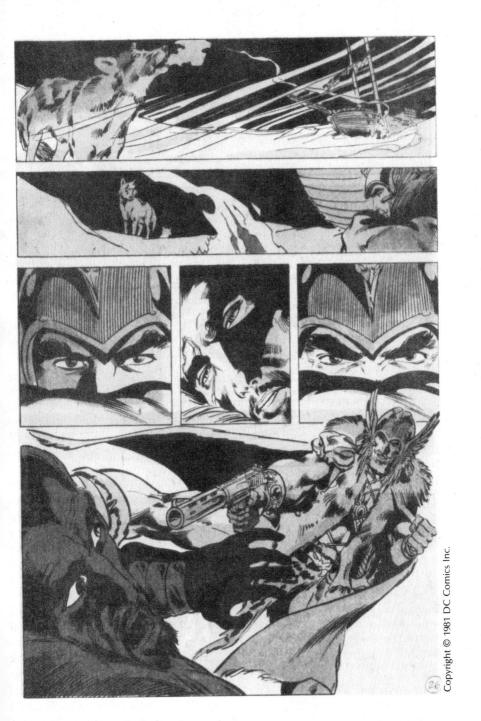

Sparse wording and strong action narrative from one of the new writer/artists:
Mike Grell's Warlord. Inks by Bob Smith. From *Warlord* 50, October 1981.

36 Explosions and Implosions

If the 1970s can be characterized as a mad scramble for new ideas that would sell, then that scramble reached a lunatic peak in the middle of the decade. Over a three-year period from 1975 to early 1978, DC and Marvel turned out at least eighty-five new comic book titles, along with reprints and magazine-format titles that raised the total of new periodicals to more than a hundred. A wide spectrum of genres was attempted: costumed hero, science fiction, sword-and-sorcery, war, horror, movie and TV tie-ins, humor, and more. Many old titles were revived. A small army of new talents was showcased. Superficially, it looked like a boomtime for the field. Yet of all the new comic books, more than half perished within their first ten issues, well over two-thirds within their first fifteen, and all but seven by the time of this writing.

This ill-fated deluge was unleashed by DC, at first under the auspices of publisher/editorial director Carmine Infantino and a few young editors whom he had recently hired, in desperate reaction against the ebbing tide of sales. The corporate hand may have been forced in part by the doomed attempt of Chip Goodman's Atlas/Seaboard to storm the market in early 1975 with more than twenty titles, in nearly as many genres; with work by Steve Ditko, Wally Wood, Neal Adams, Howard Chaykin, Mike Ploog, and others, it must have seemed like a potential threat for the few months before the company folded. After years of frustrating experiments, it seemed as if an attempt was being made to see if quantity alone could force the market back to health. DC may not have been surprised that nearly all of its new titles failed; it was apparently hoped that sheer volume would increase the company's profits. Marvel soon followed its example, nearly matching DC's output. The result, from both companies, was a plethora of hastily conceived and sloppily executed comics in which good writers were rarely paired with good artists, and creators rarely remained on their own creations, which also drained talent from established titles and left them even worse off than they had been before. It was no surprise to anybody that nearly all of the titles failed.

The deluges came at the worst possible time for comics. Increasing distribution and sales problems made the success of any new comic extremely difficult. Inflation continued to drive comics out of the range of kids' allowances: a twenty-five-page DC that would have sold for twelve cents in the 1960s cost fifty cents in 1978; a seventeen-page Marvel sold for forty. Magazine dealers and retailers meanwhile found it harder to justify giving display space to such a low-yield item, and comics disappeared from drugstores, newsstands, and supermarkets. Shops specializing in comic books and related items were beginning to pop up all over the country, promising an eventual alternative to the traditional marketing network, but they were not yet numerous enough or prosperous enough to counteract the downward spiral of distribution and sales.

On the creative end, talent was left at an all-time low ebb, for most of the bright lights of the early 1970s had followed Steranko and Adams to other fields, or to independent publishers like Mike Friedrich's *Star*Reach*. (Further competition would soon come from *Heavy Metal*, a slick magazine modeled on the French *Metal Hurlant*, publishing "adult" comic strips of science fiction and fantasy orientation.) Mainstream comics no longer attracted creative people from other fields, as they had in the 1940s and 1950s, and so young fans were almost the sole source of new talent; with the profusion of titles, inferior and undeveloped artists and writers were thrust to the fore. The booming quantity only served to stress the plummeting quality. And, in typical form for the decade, the few exciting talents who emerged generally vanished after teasingly short stints, and even the shortest-lived series were subject to jarring changes of direction.

In such a troubled period, perhaps it was inevitable that both companies would experience significant management shake-ups. DC's owners, the Kinney Corporation, had recently merged into giant Warner Communications, and in early 1976 the management chose to replace Carmine Infantino with a publisher from outside the comics field, Jenette Kahn. Kahn had founded an innovative children's magazine called *Kids* in 1969, which was written and drawn by children for each other; she had followed it after a few years with a pair of lucrative juvenile magazines, *Dynamite* and *Smash*. Her hiring suggests that DC's corporate owners may have been leery of letting comic book insiders continue to run the show, and that they wanted someone with the qualifications to go after the shrinking readership of children.

At first, under Kahn, the new titles kept coming, although she also increased cancellations until the line began to shrink. In early 1978 she christened the final wave of the deluge the "DC Explosion," in which not only were more titles created, but new pages were added to the existing titles in order to make room for numerous backup strips; it is a label that might well be attached to the entire expansion, beginning in 1975. Only a few months after the "Explosion" was declared, Warner ordered an unprecedented cutback of comics, along with the release of two editors and a reduction in format to make DC's products match Marvel's in size and price. By the end of 1978, after this "DC Implosion," only a half-dozen of the more than fifty new titles and reprints DC had launched in those years were left alive. Since then, Kahn has overseen a significant reorganization of the company, working with a pair of editors from DC's more successfully experimental days: Joe Orlando, now creative director, and, more recently, Dick Giordano, the current executive editor. She has won a reputation over the past eight years of working well with creative people and being very open to writers' and artists' demands for new rights, spearheading some contractual changes that have helped alter the relationship of creators to publishers.

Marvel's reorganization began during the same period. In January of 1978, associate editor Jim Shooter, after less than four years back in comics and only two years of editorial work, was boosted to the top of the ladder as editor-in-chief. He has since provided the kind of tough, steady control that Marvel lacked during the 1970s, winning the deep allegiance of some creators, the great enmity of others, and generally making himself the most strongly felt editorial presence in comics in many years. Under him, many of the company's assistant editors were raised to full editorial status (and such new editors as Warren's accomplished Louise Jones were hired), creating a more efficient multi-editor system resembling DC's.

Shooter combines an editorial approach that seems to have been learned from his original mentor, Mort Weisinger, with commonsense business acumen. On the creative front, he set about training new writers, artists, and editors in the basics of comic book storytelling, in a manner that Weisinger might have done. On the business front, he quickly proved to be attuned to the growing fan market, specifically the "direct sales" market of comic book specialty shops, as opposed to the usual newsstand distribution; this would soon enable him to lead his company into some bold, much more intelligently conceived new publishing projects that would contribute to the comic book renaissance of the 1980s. He also oversaw a major trimming of the inflated Marvel line; in his first year-and-a-half as editor-in-chief, nearly twenty titles from the explosion years were cut.

Although little of longevity or long-term significance emerged from this watershed period, a survey of the comics released during the explosion does reveal a few isolated moments of quality and several glimmers of things to come. The first wave of the expansion, beginning at DC, was dominated by the sword-and-sorcery comics discussed in the last chapter (one of which, *Warlord*, is among the few titles from the period still surviving). Hard on their heels came some more DC series featuring big, brawny heroes: a realistic caveman strip called *Kong the Untamed*, which lasted only five issues; *Hercules Unbound*, in which the Greek demigod battled aliens on a post-holocaust future Earth, with beautiful although short-lived artistic contributions by Jose Garcia Lopez, Wally Wood, and Walt Simonson; and *Starfire*, in which a beautiful swordswoman fought for freedom on a distant planet and frequently lost her blouse. Marvel followed in the same vein with a female barbarian named Red Sonja (a spinoff of the *Conan* series); *Skull the Slayer,* about an adventurer who gets stranded back in time and fights fantastical menaces; *Tarzan,* the rights to which Marvel inherited from DC, but which it executed with far less flair, and the companion title, *John Carter,* featuring some fine art by veterans Gil Kane and Carmine Infantino (the latter going to Marvel when he returned to the pencil after his deposition at DC).

The next type of comic to begin pouring out with the deluge was the revival of past series. Most of them seemed ill-considered, for *Blackhawk, Challengers of the Unknown, Aquaman,* and the New Doom Patrol (featured for three entertaining issues of *Showcase*) quickly returned to oblivion. *Plastic Man* and *Teen Titans* lasted a little longer, each for ten issues, but their quality was dismal. Two teams from the 1940s were given adventures in the present day: the Freedom Fighters, a team of old Quality Comics heroes who now struggled under innumerable creative hands; and the Justice Society of America in *All-Star Comics,* which got off to a good start under Gerry Conway and Wally Wood (inking himself and other pencilers), but meandered its way first to a slot in *Adventure* and then to cancellation. (At the same time, *The Invaders* and *Justice Inc.* were closing out the earlier Golden Age revival.) The best of the revivals were DC's *Metal Men,* drawn with great verve first by Simonson, then by Joe Staton; and *The Inhumans,* Marvel's lone entry, featuring solid adventure stories by Doug Moench and artists George Perez, Gil Kane, and Keith Pollard.

Jack Kirby's presence lingered on, both through his own efforts and through earlier ideas that fell into other hands. His last act at DC was the co-creation (with Steve Sherman) of *Kobra,* one of the few good ideas of the Explosion, which told of a pair of telepathically linked brothers, one good and one evil; but Kirby worked only on the first issue, and the series, although continued with integrity by writer Marty Pasko and artists Keith Giffin, Rich Buckler, and Mike Nasser, was canceled after six more. DC also revived Kirby's *New Gods* and *Mr. Miracle,* the latter featuring lovely art by up-and-coming stars Marshall Rogers and Michael Golden; neither, however, lasted longer than eight issues. Returning to Marvel in 1976, Kirby unleashed a wide spectrum of titles which, unfortunately, all shortly rambled to oblivion: *The Eternals,* featuring astronaut-gods à la Erich von Däniken; *Devil Dinosaur,* about a Tyrannosaur and his ape-boy companion; an adaptation and extension of the movie *2001;* a lighthearted spinoff of that called *Machine Man* (later taken over by Steve Ditko); and the hastily executed return of *Black Panther.*

Costumed heroes abounded. DC found various ways to increase the exposure of its old heroes: *The Joker, Man-Bat,* and *Secret Society of Super-Villains* were offbeat sources of guest appearances by assorted heroes; a second Justice League title, *Super Friends,* was created as a tie-in with a Saturday-morning cartoon; Green Lantern got his own title back; *DC Super-Stars, DC Special, Batman Family,* and *Super-Team Family* mixed reprints with new adventures; and *DC Comics Presents* took on an old function of *World's Finest*, costarring Superman with a different hero each month. Jenette Kahn devised "Dollar Comics" in 1977, in which each contained a number of different series, as in the comics of the 1940s; in addition to converting some old titles to that format, she also launched the dollar-size *DC Special Series*, centering various characters on a different theme each issue.

Marvel lumped some of its old heroes together—Hercules, Angel, Iceman, Ghost Rider, and Black Widow—into a bush-league version of the Defenders called *The Champions*. They also created their own bad-guy showcase, *Super-Villain Team-Up*, and gave Spider-Man a second title, *Spectacular Spider-Man*. But most of Marvel's attention went into the creation of new crime-fighters. Marv Wolfman created *Nova*, a light series about a teenage hero, which featured some of Infantino's boldest new artwork. Two series reached for a feminist readership, *Ms. Marvel* and *Spider-Woman* (who, despite her name, was a fresh character with original powers, not a simple attempt to cash in on Marvel's most popular hero); both titles were written at times by Chris Claremont, who has made a strong mark with his heartfelt characterizations of women, and the latter title displayed fine art by Infantino and Steve Leialoha. All three of these titles enjoyed unusually long runs for the period: *Nova* lasted twenty-five issues, *Ms. Marvel* twenty-three, and *Spider-Woman*, surviving to 1983, fifty. Lasting for nineteen issues was *The Human Fly*, a slapdash rendering of the unlikely adventures of a real-life daredevil. Less successful was *Black Goliath*, a black ghetto hero created by Tony Isabella, which was dropped after five issues. Finally, *Omega the Unknown* was about a mysterious interdimensional hero, displaying Steve Gerber's usual predilection for the cosmic and peculiar; it was canceled after ten issues, however, and Gerber was never able to bring the hero's mystery to an adequate resolution.

DC's new heroes were all characterized by extremely short runs. *Ragman*, an interesting Kanigher-Kubert creation, lasted only five issues. *Black Lightning*, another ghetto hero by Tony Isabella, staggered through eleven. *Isis* ended after eight. *Steel the Indestructible Man*, a steel-skeletoned World War II hero, lasted five, as did *Firestorm*, Gerry Conway's atomic-powered teenager.

Other genres were tackled with little success. Both companies tried horror, martial arts, and TV tie-ins (Marvel winning that category with a slew of Hanna-Barbera cartoon comics). DC added lone new titles to its war and western lines: the latter was *Jonah Hex*, moving out of *Weird Western* and into his own series; under the lean, hard-boiled writing of Michael Fleisher and the evocative art of Dick Ayers and Tony DeZuniga, the violent adventures of that alientated gunslinger have been able to endure poor sales and hang on well into the 1980s. Marvel, meanwhile, had begun taking on Hugo, Stevenson, Melville, Homer, Verne, and

Absurd fantasy and sharp satire: Frank Brunner and Steve Gerber's Howard the Duck goes "barbarian." Inks by Steve Leialoha. From *Howard the Duck* 1, January 1976.

others in its unsuccessful *Marvel Classics Comics.* Science fiction, which has grown increasingly dominant in the field since the release of *Star Wars* in 1977, was briefly represented at DC that year by *Shade the Changing Man*—a typical Ditko soap opera about a persecuted other-dimensional hero who seeks refuge on Earth—and *Star-Hunters,* about corrupt corporations and an interstellar odyssey in the future.

Off in its own little corner was Marvel's *Howard the Duck.* Highlighting Steve Gerber's impish writing, the adventures of the cigar-chomping duck effectively parodied the Marvel trends and genres of the time. The art of Frank Brunner and Gene Colan made it a graceful and amusing package. Running for thirty-one issues, plus nine in a magazine format, Howard retained a loyal and steady following. (His success, however, precipitated a crisis in comic book production when Gerber, arguing in favor of creators' rights, sued Marvel for ownership of the character. This led to Gerber's departure from mainstream comics and bad fortunes for his creations; but it has helped force a change in the formerly more rigid relations between creators and publishers which has made possible some of the great strides of the medium in the last few years.)

As if this deluge of titles wasn't enough, myriad new ideas were paraded through showcase-style comics in a desperate scramble to find an idea that would click. The first was DC's *First Issue Special,* followed in time by *Marvel Presents, Marvel Chillers, Marvel Feature,* and the revived *Showcase* itself. Of the twenty-three ideas premiered in the five, only three went on to gain their own titles. Marvel also presented old heroes in new lights with *What If...?*, which tackled speculations ranging from "What if the Avengers Had Never Been?" to "What If Sgt. Fury Had Fought World War II in Outer Space?"

New formats were also tackled, with Marvel expanding its line of black-and-white magazines and both companies their lines of tabloids. DC and Marvel attempted a few joint ventures in the tabloid format, beginning with an adaptation of *The Wizard of Oz*, then, more appropriately, a meeting between Superman and Spider-Man, opening the way for other such crossovers. Marvel also made ventures into the bookstore market, with paperback prose novels about their heroes and an oversized "graphic novel" about the Silver Surfer by Lee and Kirby.

Perhaps the only financially lucrative development of the explosion was Marvel's discovery of the movie and TV tie-in. *Logan's Run, Godzilla,* and *Man from Atlantis* enjoyed only limited success, but *Star Wars* proved to be a solid seller and continues to the present. Later, after the explosions and implosions had passed, *Star Wars'* success prompted Marvel to launch *Battlestar Galactica, Star Trek,* and still more in the 1980s; 1979 also saw the debut of three comics based on toys—*Shogun Warriors, Rom,* and *The Micronauts*—of which the latter two are still running.

A decade earlier, DC and Marvel had gone through a similar experiment with numerous new titles. Then, as in the 1970s, most of those—*Deadman, The Creeper, The Silver Surfer,* and others—had perished after short runs. But in the 1960s, even in failure those comics had seemed to leave the field emboldened, creative, and hopeful. The implosion of a decade later, by contrast, left the field in a shambles. It seemed to readers that a sense of hopelessness permeated even those strips that survived. Jim Shooter recalls that when he first took the helm of Marvel, increasing numbers of creative personnel were despairing of comics' future, looking to television, advertising, slick magazines like *Heavy Metal,* and other fields for income. Even with a drastic reduction in titles, the talent was still too thin to go around. The best writers and artists who remained appeared unable to do their best. To compound the malaise, new printing processes were introduced that replaced metal printing plates with plastic, producing blurry lines and muddy, often indecipherable lettering; degenerating apace, the colors grew steadily more garish and inharmonious. And adding insult to injury, prices continued to soar while story lengths diminished. By 1979, while mainstream comics reached their nadir, even the independent-press movement seemed in danger, for that year the acclaimed *Star*Reach* and *Imagine* ceased publication; and although some new companies—Aardvark-Vanaheim, WaRP Graphics, and Eclipse—had entered the fray, they had yet to prove themselves able to survive.

But despite all the obstacles, one series emerged from the explosion that would, once again, change the face of comic books.

The New X-Men

It started on a note of nostalgia. *The X-Men*, a fan favorite that had perished from lack of sales five years before, was resurrected in a one-shot, giant-sized issue (GSXM 1, Summer 1975). In a story written by Len Wein and drawn by Dave Cockrum, Professor X, the leader of the group, recruited an international team of mutants—Nightcrawler, Storm, Wolverine, Colossus, Sunfire, Banshee, and Thunderbird—to rescue his X-Men from deadly peril. The new team succeeded, and the issue ended with the greatest assembly of extra-powered mutants that Marvel had ever presented. Would these be the new X-Men? The one-shot left the question unanswered.

The issue was resolved a few months later when *The X-Men*, which for five years had contained only reprints, became the home of the New X-Men with issue 94 (Aug. 1975). Most of the old members, we discovered, preferred to leave the team. Angel, Iceman, and Marvel Girl departed (the Beast had switched to the Avengers months ago), while Cyclops remained to lead the new team. Of the newcomers, Sunfire elected to return to his native Japan, and Thunderbird died in the following issue. Thus, with issue 96 (Dec. 1975), the new team was set, and the most successful and influential series of the 1970s was underway.

The New X-Men were far more varied than any other team had ever been. This distinction, however, had little to do with their powers: Storm's mastery of weather, Nightcrawler's teleportation, Colossus's "organic steel" body, Wolverine's animallike agility and self-healing metabolism, Banshee's sonic scream, and Cyclops's devastating optic blasts. In that respect, they were no more varied than the Justice League of America or the Avengers; the true source of their uniqueness and diversity lay in their strong personalities and the complex relationships among them.

For too long, comic book writers had grafted stock, two-dimensional personalities onto heroes to create an illusion of characterization. The tough woman, the hothead, the anguished introvert, etc., had popped up in many different costumes but without variance in attitudes or speech patterns. The X-Men, however, were far more complex. Their very backgrounds, multilayered personalities, and changing interactions would open the way for a revolution in the field.

Kurt Wagner, a.k.a. Nightcrawler, suffered as a deformed circus acrobat in Germany, persecuted for his demonic appearance. Regardless, he is intelligent and charming; unlike other physically misshapen heroes, he is not bitter and lost in self-pity, but naïve and affectionate. Ororo, known as Storm, has the most traumatic background of the team. Orphaned as a young girl, she became a pickpocket and master thief in the backstreets of Cairo to survive. When her elemental powers manifested themselves, however, she was able to enjoy years of make-believe as a self-styled goddess in East Africa. As an X-Man, she is torn between her motherly devotion to all things and her lust for the power she commands. Peter Rasputin, a.k.a. Colossus, is a big, simple Russian farmboy. Boundlessly loyal to his comrades, he is often befuddled by his role as an American hero. The strongest of the X-Men, he is also the most gentle. In sharp contrast is Logan, the ferocious Canadian Wolverine. Barbaric and ruthless, he nevertheless lives by a rigid code of honor. He is the most self-sufficient and confident of comic book heroes, and so makes no excuses for his philosophy of violence. At first hotheaded and selfish, he has evolved into the cool, dependable backbone of the team. Rounding out the group are Banshee, a sentimental Irishman; Cyclops, the obsessive, high-strung field leader; and Professor X, the uncompromising mentor and father figure.

The man who breathed life into these characters was Len Wein's successor, Chris Claremont, who began as scripter with issue 94 and almost immediately after took over as sole writer. Claremont took his time with the characters, leading them along slowly and carefully, bringing about change and growth in an utterly believable and fully developed manner. It became quickly evident that he cared very deeply about the characters. Exploring them ceaselessly through mature introspection and dramatic scenes, he not only fleshed them out thoroughly, but wove them into a close-knit, tumultuous, but loving family.

The relationships were many and varied. Wolverine often challenged Cyclops's authority, but gradually a feeling of great mutual respect grew between them. Storm, frightened of her own powers, felt an almost perverse fascination for Wolverine's ferocity. For Colossus and Nightcrawler, on the other hand, she felt a deep, sisterly affection. Colossus and Nightcrawler became warm comrades, Nightcrawler's urbanity contrasting amusingly with Colossus's simplicity. Later, Nightcrawler and Wolverine became fast friends, staging impromptu physical contests, the loser springing for beer; Wolverine always won. When Colossus's self-confidence wavered, it was Wolverine who harshly restored it. Their relationships were ever-changing, every-richening.

Their adventures were also set apart from the rest of comicdom. Claremont, harking back to the original premise of the series—that mutants should band together to survive mankind's unthinking hatred of their extraordinary powers—made the X-Men a focus of hostility rather than crusaders against crime. His first big epic, in fact, pitted the X-Men against the Sentinels, those giant robots programmed to hunt down and eradicate all mutant-kind (XM 98–100, Apr.–Aug. 1976). From that point on, nearly every one of their adventures began not with them answering some call for help, but with them being attacked.

Claremont takes the theme of persecution very seriously. "The X-Men are hated, feared, and despised collectively by humanity for no other reason than they are mutants," he says. "So what we have here, intended or not, is a book that is about racism, bigotry, and prejudice. . . . It's a book about outsiders, which is something that any teenager can identify with. It's a story about downtrodden, repressed people fighting to change their situation, which I think anybody can empathize with."

The artist and co-plotter of these adventures was *Legion of Super-Heroes* veteran Dave Cockrum. As on that DC title, he displayed a love of colorful heroes in abundance and lively action. His fun, almost childlike quality was a perfect complement to Claremont's concern for adult emotions and soap opera. Although sometimes cluttered and erratically inked, his work was rambunctiously vital.

Claremont and Cockrum, in these early years of the strip, teamed up for two very significant creations. The first was the creation of Phoenix, or more properly, the transformation of Jean Grey, formerly known as Marvel Girl, into a being of immeasurable power. This happened when Jean, after the defeat of the Sentinels, piloted a spacecraft into a solar storm. In the midst of this storm she died, yet found herself endowed with the power to resurrect herself. Emerging from the craft, she proclaimed, "Hear me, X-Men! No longer am I the woman you knew! I am Fire! And life incarnate now and forever . . . I am Phoenix!" (XM 101, Oct. 1976). Jean's new-found power, however, was undefined, and so began a three-year subplot in which her powers expanded and eventually overwhelmed her.

In the new Jean Grey, Claremont displayed his fascination with transcendent and near-perfect women. His women were not merely mortal, but embryonic goddesses. Claremont himself says, "It always seemed to me there was never any reason why a character should be any less heroic, courageous, intelligent, aggressive, simply because that character was a woman. It always seemed to me that a character—the characterization should evolve from the character itself and should not be bound by the fact that it is a male or a female." But in following this precept he took an extra step; his women are not only as strong as men, but even stronger. In Jean's love affair with Cyclops, he dramatized his determination that women should not only usurp male dominance but still remain "compassionate, warm, humorous, witty, intelligent, attractive"; in short, that they should be impossibly perfect creatures. Largely because of this, his X-Men succeeded at winning a sizable female following where all the more overt attempts to do so had failed.

The other creation of Claremont and Cockrum was to have profound implications for comics in the years to come. This was the introduction of a galactic empire, the Shi'ar (XM 107, Oct. 1977). Among its many contributions were Lilandra, the empress who would become Charles Xavier's interplanetary sweetheart; the Imperial Guard, a delightful takeoff on DC's Legion of Super-Heroes; and the Starjammers, a small squad of interstellar troubleshooters commanded by Corsair, who, in a dramatic twist, turned out to be Cyclops's father. This galactic empire would not only figure prominently in the expanding X-Men cosmos, but would (along with the extraordinary impact that the movie *Star Wars* had on the comic book community) kick off a craze for star-spanning empires in the 1980s.

The last issue of the Shi'ar story introduced a new artist to the pages of *The X-Men* (XM 108, Dec. 1977). This was John Byrne, who had worked with Claremont on *Iron Fist* and *Marvel Team-Up.* Whereas Cockrum had been light and fast and action-packed, Byrne now brought a new sophistication to the strip. He excelled in characterization, possessing a great subtlety and quiet drama that lent further nuances to the cast. Paired with Terry Austin, one of the most attractive and stylized inkers in the field, Byrne created a look that was at once dynamic and lovely. His drawings teamed with detail and ornamentation, yet the stories surged along with power and clarity. He quickly became the fan sensation of his day, and re-

Phoenix using her power to help the New X-Men in flight: Storm, Wolverine, Nightcrawler, Cyclops, Colossus, Banshee, Polaris, and Havok. Pencils by John Byrne, inks by Terry Austin, script by Chris Claremont. From *The X-Men* 127, November 1979.

versing a decade-long trend, he stayed on the strip for over three years.

Byrne was very creative, and with Claremont he expanded the X-Men universe exponentially. To old characters such as Cyclops's brother, Havok, Havok's wife, Polaris (both mutants), Moira McTaggert (Professor X's former girlfriend), and the old X-Men, who made occasional guest appearances, were added new wrinkles. A parade of new characters debuted: Wolverine's Japanese girlfriend, Mariko Yashida, an ethereal noblewoman; the Canadian hero team Alpha Flight; Kitty Pryde, a bright, perky thirteen-year-old mutant who began as the first truly convincing youngster in hero comics and went on to become one of the key members of the team; and an extended family of others.

Villains took on new dimensions. Magneto, who had formerly represented the stock archvillain, now took on an intriguing ambiguity. Where before he merely sought to enslave mankind, now, through conquest, he strove merely to insure the survival of persecuted mutant-kind. Although still posing a great threat, he was no longer simply evil. Claremont developed a fascinating kinship between Magneto and Professor X. Magneto believes that mankind is intractably bigoted and that mutants can survive only by taking command; Professor X believes that man can be taught not to hate, if mutants prove that their differences can be beneficial. To achieve their desired ends, however, both can be equally ruthless, arrogant, and coldly Machiavellian. And yet both can display unexpected moments of warmth and nobility.

Of the new villains, the most complex were the members of the Hellfire Club, an organization determined to dominate the world through political manipulation and the accumulation of wealth. The organization was vast, but the true source of power lay in the Inner Circle; most prominent among them were Sebastian Shaw, who, although secretly a mutant, owned a corporation that built Sentinels, and Emma Frost, a mutant who ran a private academy dedicated to bringing both young mutants and the offspring of the rich under the Club's influence. Unlike the usual villains of comics who would pop up for a confrontation and quickly disappear again, the Hellfire Club would lurk in the background for years, casting an all-pervasive, threatening pall over the series even when they were not spotlighted.

The culmination of the Byrne years came with the Dark Phoenix saga, the most dramatic and talked-about comics event of the time (XM 134–137, June–Sept. 1980). Jean Grey's powers, which have been growing increasingly awesome, finally explode as she becomes the all-destructive Dark Phoenix. Intoxicated and blinded by her power, she devours a sun, bringing about the death of an alien race and incurring the wrath of the Shi'ar empire. The empire clamors for her blood and it falls to the X-Men to procure her for the trial. Awesome battle scenes follow, made poignant by the fact that Jean Grey's persona flits in and out of Dark Phoenix's power-warped mind. Claremont and Byrne originally intended her to subdue her power and be forgiven, allowed to go off with her lover Cyclops. But, according to Claremont, editor-in-chief Jim Shooter was disturbed by the fact that a Marvel heroine had murdered billions of innocents without seeming to pay for her deeds. "Shooter wanted Jean punished," Claremont says. "He wanted her to suffer. . . . [He] feels that it is his responsibility . . . to see that nothing goes out of the office that reflects a moral position that he does not think Marvel should take. . . ." In the end, Claremont and Byrne opted to have Phoenix kill herself when, in a lucid moment, she realizes that she cannot control her power and that the universe will be happier and safer without her. This death of a major and beloved character would overshadow the series for months to come and definitely clinch *The X-Men's* place as the most sensational comic of its time.

This very sensationalism, however, was one of the problems of the series. Claremont sometimes heaped on too much anguish, too much sensitivity, too much introversion. His characters were not only made to endure great hardship, but were made too self-conscious about it. "The pain is too great!" they were made to think again and again. Cloying also was his lack of restraint in reminding us repeatedly of how perfect, albeit tortured, his women were. The realism he brought to his characters, although very refreshing and welcome, was often at odds with their flamboyant powers and fantastic adventures (this has continued to be one of the great difficulties facing comic book heroes in these days of aspiration to maturity and sophistication in the field). It became almost ludicrous when, in the midst of fleeing the giant Sentinel robots or saving the universe, the characters fretted about such mundane problems as romance, insecurity, or troubled friends—all with a kind of pop psychology that would have been more at home on a "sensitive" television show about "real contemporary people." This tendency reached its extreme when Kitty, in her early teens, was supposed to have become, almost instantly, as wise and mature, as sagacious and poised as any other X-Man because she had ventured into sorcerous domains and fought epic battles in space.

Despite its faults, the new *X-Men* has been one of the most engrossing of all comic series, so multilayered and compelling that the reader can easily overlook the false notes in his eagerness to learn more about these endearing characters. The runaway fan favorite of its time, and Marvel's biggest commercial triumph of the late 1970s, it revitalized the waning fortunes of hero adventures and restored that genre to the limelight of comics. It started a trend toward closely knit hero teams with an emphasis on family-like interaction that has swept the lines of both Marvel and DC. And it helped, through the Shi'ar, to kick off a craze for galaxy-spanning space opera that has become a very lively sub-genre in the 1980s.

The X-Men also showed that good quality and serious intent could sell comics, and may have inspired numerous writers and artists to take a har-

look at their handling of other established heroes and consider how they might be done better. With *The X-Men* it became clear that the old heroes could recover their popularity, despite hard times, if handled correctly; and it became clear that the weighty emotional concerns of the 1970s could be incorporated into comics in a mature manner, without sacrificing entertainment value. The series was also fortified by a steady creative vision. When John Byrne left in 1981 he was replaced by Dave Cockrum, who picked up seamlessly where he had left off four years before; with only one writer and two artists for its first seven years, the strip broke a decade-long trend and showed the value of consistency.

More than any other comic, the new *X-Men* made possible the revitalization of the Marvel and DC mainstreams in the 1980s.

PART
THREE

A Look Ahead

Early 1980 did not bode well for comics. *The X-Men* and *Master of Kung-Fu* were going well, but the rest of the field ranged from the uneven to the dismal. The medium, at a glance, looked more hopeless than it had in 1956.

What happened next was an unprecedented turning point for comics. By the summer of 1980, the first glimmers could be seen of an upheaval that would send wave after wave of creativity breaking upon the field. The Silver Age, by contrast, had come into being rather slowly. Although Flash had premiered in 1956, DC did not reach its full stride until 1959; even then Marvel was still two years down the line, and it would take another few years to discover its identity. But beginning in 1980, change, positive change, occurred with such rapidity that a veritable renaissance can be said to have started overnight.

It must remain for future historians to pick out all the patterns, all the causes and effects that are even now molding comics into unforeseen new forms. The lightninglike changeability and instability of the field, moreover, make it nearly impossible to project where comics will be in only a few years' time. Nonetheless, there are some general tendencies clearly visible, and new developments that carry a clear importance for the future of the medium. This chapter cannot attempt as comprehensive a survey of its subject as have the preceding chapters, but it will try to seek out and put in some perspective whichever recent developments are fresh, innovative, and exciting, and whichever seem to promise the potential to change and improve the world of comics.

Synthesis

In the 1970s it was easy to imagine that a band of bellyaching impostors had supplanted the great heroes of the Silver Age. That new breed of costumed hero might not have been so objectionable if its malaise had been incorporated with well-crafted writing and not shoved obtrusively into the story lines, or portrayed with clear and attractive narrative art. But the young creators of the time seemed so desperate to forge ahead, turning their backs on the Silver Age and regarding all that had gone before as trivial and outdated, that they threw out the baby with the bathwater. Years of lore and tradition were forgotten. The comic book heroes of the 1970s were left to exist in a vacuum, their adventures colorless, the art dull, and the scripting self-conscious and undeveloped.

But the 1980s have brought a maturation of that generation of young writers and artists, and with it an awareness that the past was not all dross. Such modern elements as continuing subplots, character development, and mature tone remain dominant, but to them in many cases have been welded the basics of craftsmanship: plots are better structured and the stories more fun; scripting has greatly matured; the lore and heritage of many strips has been brought back into play. The art has also recently regained its sense of fun, through clarity, dynamism, and much-improved inking, coloring, and printing. DC artists no longer seem to feel bound to churn out quasi-realistic imitations of Neal Adams; some key Marvel hero-artists have broken from the mold of Sal Buscema and John Romita. This synthesis of old craftsmanship with new concerns, the most refreshing recent development to affect the comic book mainstream, might prove to be the key to saving the troubled costumed heroes.

The first signs of this synthesis appeared at DC, most forcefully with *DC Comics Presents* 26 (October 1980), where the New Teen Titans made their debut. Edited by the creator of the New X-Men, Len Wein, and written by his old colleague Marv Wolfman, the New X-Men's original editor the new team echoed that recent Marvel sensation in many respects. Like Claremont on the X-Men, Wein and Wolfman attempted to weave distinct personalities, a sense of family, and adult concerns with the farflung adventures of a hero team; they strove for the same combination of weighty personal drama and grand-scale exuberance that had enabled Claremont, Cockrum, and Byrne to push costumed heroes back to the forefront of comics. And as the first new comic to follow in the New X Men's weighty footsteps, the Titans' own title (Nov. 1980) rose meteorically to the top of DC's sales charts, signaling that company's first major commercial success in many years.

The team consisted of Robin, the levelheaded leader, Kid Flash, the reluctant speedster, and Wonder Girl, all from the old Titans; joining them were a mystic "empath" named Raven, a naïve but powerful alien woman named Starfire, a half-man/half-machine called Cyborg, and Beast Boy of the old Doom Patrol, now called Changeling. Although their adventures have been comprised largely of standard heroic fare, they have been unified by a tight company of regular villains and enriched by the complex, fascinating backgrounds of Raven and Starfire, which Wolfman has woven into the series to great effect.

Ironically, *The New Teen Titans*, while succeeding largely because of its similarity to a current sensation, also planted the seeds that have grown into the new synthesis. Although Wolfman often fell short of Claremont's ability to breathe life into comic book characters, his great strength lay in

260

his new penchant for tightly woven plots, clear scripting, and boisterous action—all of which reflected his background as a DC fan during the Silver Age. He was teamed with penciler George Perez—who has perfected an ornate, small-paneled, tightly composed approach to drawing that suggests the best work of Barry Smith—and the meticulous inker Romeo Tanghal; such a clear, pristine style had not been seen at DC since the likes of Carmine Infantino and Murphy Anderson. Working together, their stories carried echoes of the better DC comics of the 1960s.

The tremendous success of *The New Teen Titans* awoke DC to an important realization: for a comic to succeed, good creative people had to be obtained, and they had to be encouraged to remain on their strips. Publisher Jenette Kahn instituted such benefits as royalties, incentives for new creations, and bonuses designed to increase staying power, measures that Marvel was soon to adopt as well. (The success of those measures is evident: Wolfman and Perez remain the team on the Titans until this writing, late in 1984, and whatever the magazine's faults, it is unified by their unwavering attention.) Consistency, at long last, was on the way back.

Whereas the Titans echoed the 1960s only incidentally, a new step had to be taken before the synthesis could be fully accomplished. That step would be a virtual reaction, an attempt to return almost completely in some stories to the manner of the Silver Age. Its greatest proponent was writer Cary Bates, on *Superman, The New Adventures of Superboy,* and *The Flash.* After a decade of generally uninspired storytelling in a somewhat old-fashioned manner, Bates knuckled down in 1980 and 1981 to revive the light, intricate, gimmicky style of the old Schwartz and Weisinger writers. He produced such nostalgic fare as a four-part Superman Revenge Squad story (Sup. 365–368, Nov. 1981–Feb. 1982), a riddle about a pair of evil Kryptonians who claimed to be Superboy's true parents (NAS 27–28, Mar.–Apr. 1982), and many Rogues' Gallery appearances for the Flash; his masterpiece came with a special three-hundredth issue of *The Flash,* in which a harrowing internal journey both recaps the hero's career and raises the chilling suspicion that that entire career might have been no more than a delusion of a demented Barry Allen (Aug. 1981). Bates's unfailingly entertaining and ingenious scripts were greatly aided by his artistic collaborators: Curt Swan, now blessed with better inkers than in the 1970s, continued to be the backbone of Superman (occasionally joined by a returning DC giant, the powerful Gil Kane); Kurt Schaffenberger, his pristine and charming art nearly unchanged since the Weisinger years, drew Superboy; and a third Silver Age veteran, Carmine Infantino, returned to the DC fold to resume the art on the Flash, whom he had helped revive twenty-five years before, now employing a loose, wild, but still dynamic style.

Bates has since greatly reduced his work on the Superman family, but a significant step back to a Silver Age approach in those comics has recently been taken, appropriately by editor Julius Schwartz. Recognizing that the Man of Steel still appeals mainly to children and that the kids' market (ironically one of the most neglected of recent years) may be a crucial one if new generations of readers are to be introduced to the medium, Schwartz has converted *Action Comics* into a two-story-per-issue format featuring self-contained tales of Superman lore in the strongly plotted, childlike DC tradition. Mixing old-fashioned stories with wildly comical guest-appearances by Keith Giffen's lunatic villain, the Ambush Bug, *Action* holds the promise of a return to earlier glory for the greatest of comic book heroes.

In early 1982, DC reached the quintessential synthesis of old and new with *The Legion of Super-Heroes* under writer Paul Levitz and artist Keith Giffen. Levitz, a longtime Legion fan, has pulled extensively and imaginatively from Legion lore, combining it with a vastly improved understanding of storytelling. His scripting is as unencumbered as early Legion stories, and he has added to it a mastery of the art of writing cinematic scenes; his stories, whether epic battles, reinterpretations of Legion lore, or explorations of the characters, are told through vignettes of great economy and sophistication. He is perfectly complemented by Giffen, whose depiction of the future is the most truly futuristic in comics. Giffen, the series' co-plotter, is also among the most creative storytellers in the business, ingeniously employing unusual color-printing techniques, pseudo-computer graphics, sight gags, and highly dramatic transitions to great effect. He has recently left the series, but his successors appear interested in following his example, and the Legion remains a superb blend of old and new, neither rooted completely in the 1960s nor bogged down by the legacy of the 1970s.

The Legion, long supported by a loyal body of fans, is an excellent example of the new emphasis placed upon the fan market by publishers With significant portions of sales now coming through largely fan-supported comic book shops, the creators of comics like the Legion feel they need not be compromised by a necessity to reach a mass readership. The Legion is so steeped in the details of its own lore that it can be difficult for a new reader to enter the series in midstream (which might prove commercially limiting in the long run, although it is one of DC's best-selling titles at present), but for the veteran fan it is a long-awaited delight.

With such successes as the Titans and the Legion, DC has drifted increasingly toward old-fashioned fun throughout its costumed-hero line while high-powered teams with extensive character interaction and an X-Men-like feeling of family have become the dominant trend in hero comics of the 1980s. Roy Thomas, recently ending his long stay at Marvel to move to DC, has launched *All-Star Squadron*, which brings together innumerable heroes of the Golden Age in adventures set in the 1940s, and *Infinity Inc.*, which teams up several children and students of those heroes in the present. Although crammed with verbiage and historical minutiae in the Thomas manner, the abundance of colorful heroes and th pristine art of Jerry Ordway and others have made them attractive additions to the DC line. (Thomas's longtime colleague, Gerry Conway, has been less effective, sadly, in his painful attempt to transform the Justice League of America into a gang of hip-talking, faddish young folks à la Wolfman's Titans.) The Batman, meanwhile, has formed a team of outcasts and oddballs in *Batman and the Outsiders*, under the auspices of writer Mike Barr and artist Jim Aparo, which also displays the improved characterization and brisk spirit of the self-proclaimed "New DC."

A collaborative team of two new writers has recently appeared, capturing the same spirit that veterans like Wolfman and Bates have been rediscovering: Dan Mishkin and Gary Cohn. Their series about a weirdly costumed, multipowered Hollywood stuntman who takes gleefully to the heroic life, *Blue Devil* (co-created with young artist Paris Cullins) was advertised with the slogan, "We're bringing fun back to comics!"—and indeed it partakes of much of the breezy, tongue-in-cheek adventure of the Silver Age Schwartz comics.

Although much of DC's mainstream continues to be muddled or stagnant, this synthesis of old entertainment value with new sophistication has clearly brought tremendous improvements to the line, making its venerable heroes once again vibrant and strong enough to tackle the future.

Meanwhile, Marvel has only returned to its past in this manner on a few isolated occasions, and with a basically different approach—Marvel's writers and artists have, of necessity, looked to the past for a sense of excitement and unbounded imagination more than for lessons in craftsmanship—but the results have been equally entertaining. The longest-running example is *The Fantastic Four*, which John Byrne has been writing and drawing since he left *The X-Men* in 1981. In casting out the mawkish emotional developments of the 1970s, weaving his best stories around Lee-Kirby creations of the mid-1960s, tackling the Marvel cosmic saga in a spirit of fun rather than would-be profundity, and simplifying his art to recall Kirby's dramatic storytelling, he has recovered much of the vigor of early Marvel. But Byrne is often able to unite these elements with masterful plots full of mystery, suspense, and a cohesion that their inspirations lacked. He has also shown a refreshing flair for adding new dimensions to such long-overworked creations as Galactus, Dr. Doom, and the alien Skrulls.

But the most impressive synthesis of old and new at Marvel has come, surprisingly, from an avant-garde star of the 1970s, Walt Simonson. As writer and artist of *Thor*, he has recovered the strip's early inventiveness and mythic power without sacrificing a bit of his utterly unique dramatic style. He has also woven a knowledge of genuine Scandinavian customs, legends, art, and architecture into the stories to give his lengthy epic of Ragnarok and "The Cask of Ancient Winters" a rich texture that even Jack Kirby's *Thor* lacked.

The major contribution of Marvel Comics to the world of heroes has, however, not been in such recoveries of past glories but in its openness to some unique creative visions and their dramatic new approaches to comic book content and storytelling.

New Visions

The keenest vision at the start of the decade was that of writer Doug Moench, who, along with artist Bill Sienkewicz, launched a new series called *Moon Knight* in November 1980. Centering on a mysterious dark-night crime-fighter who holds three secret identities simultaneously—ruthless mercenary, rich playboy, and cab driver—the series was a complex, occasionally unsettling character study. Sienkewicz, who at first appeared to be just another in a legion of Neal Adams imitators, matured on the strip into a master of design and atmosphere, exceptionally able to capture the eerie, pulp-inspired quality of the series. During the same period, Moench, along with artist Gene Day, raised *Master of Kung-Fu* to new heights of lyricism and beauty. Unfortunately, a purported disagreement with editor-in-chief Jim Shooter about the future of the series led Moench to leave Marvel and join a number of ex-Marvel writers and artists at DC (where, among other assignments, he now handles the adventures of the Batman). The fortunes of both of his series fell soon after his exit.

Another enormously facile writer appeared in an unexpected corner with the revival of Ka-Zar, who was now joined by the chic, feminist jungle-woman Shanna (Mar. 1981). The writer was Bruce Jones, a veteran of Warren and Marvel's black-and-white magazines; his clever scripting brought a bright, urbane, suggestive humor to the jungle lord that rescued him from the stock pomposity that is usually the lot of "savage" heroes in comics. The fantastic elements of the series—hidden lands bird-people, a friendly saber-toothed tiger—meshed well with the humor and were attractively drawn by Brent Anderson. After seventeen issues however, *Ka-Zar* was pressed into a more standard mold, and Jones soon left Marvel.

But by far the most explosive of the visionaries was a young artist/writer named Frank Miller. In 1979 he began as regular penciler in a forgotten corner of the Marvel line, *Daredevil* (DD 158). His art—sketchy, even abstract, but amazingly fluid, displaying a highly cinematic flair for crisp brutal action—was radical enough. But it was when he took over the writing of the title from Roger MacKenzie with issue 168 (Jan. 1981) that he took a hard look at the nature of costumed crime-fighters and found a startling new approach to them.

With his very first story Miller introduced Elektra, the most fascinating character to hit comicdom in many a year. The daughter of a Greek ambassador, Elektra became a merciless bounty-hunter after her father's assassination. The story spans the years from Matt Murdock's ill-fated love

Frank Miller's brutal action and sensuality: Elektra traps Daredevil. Inks by Klaus Janson. From *Daredevil* 179, February 1982..

affair with her in his college years to their violent, ambivalent meeting in the present, in their roles of crime-fighter and hired killer. A poignant love story and a tense thriller, Miller's first story hit the medium like a bombshell.

Coming in at the end of a decade of wordy, introspective, unimaginative fare, Miller distinguished himself not only as a good plotter but as a dazzlingly effective storyteller. Like *Warlord's* Mike Grell before him, Miller, as both writer and artist, relied heavily on his pictures to move the story along. Captions, which for years had been used as vehicles for overbearing and superfluous exposition, were stripped by him to clipped mood-setters and quick transitions. His dialogue was hard-boiled, pointed, and refreshingly mature; he had apparently learned much of his craft from his editor on *Daredevil,* Denny O'Neil (whose writing for the Batman a decade before had pointed toward Miller's style), but promptly outshone his mentor. His pictures (aided by Klaus Janson's impressionistic inks) complemented his terse writing with their taut dramatic flair.

Issue by issue, Miller unfolded a criminal underworld of frightening believability, a dark urban realm of stoolies, enforcers, junkies, and pushers. After creating Elektra, Miller transformed three established characters into fully rounded citizens of Daredevil's world: Ben Urich, a cynical, down-at-the-heels reporter who deduces the hero's secret identity; Bullseye, a psychotic hitman obsessed by a need to kill Daredevil; and the Kingpin, once a dull, standard villain, now remade into the brooding, implacable crime lord of New York City, a villain made all the more threatening by the fact that his terrible power derived not from any superhuman abilities but from his iron grip on the world of crime. Blended into this believable world were startling elements of the exotic and the supernatural: Elektra became associated with a band of mysterious Japanese assassins, while Daredevil enlisted the aid of a tough old codger named Stick, who dealt with paranormal powers. This juxtaposition proved that "hard-boiled" comics need not lock themselves into realism and social relevance in order to be effective.

The tradition of realistic violence that had led from Deadman to the new Batman to Manhunter to Wolverine found its culmination in Frank Miller's world. Remorselessly, Miller evoked the truly dark, ugly side of crime, combat, and vigilantism. Daredevil's battles with opponents were not noble fisticuffs but bone-crunching street brawls; Elektra was truly ruthless in her assaults, with an arsenal of Oriental death-devices. In issue 181 (Apr. 1982) this violence reached its culmination in the grittiest scene ever presented in a mainstream comic book. In a vicious fight between Bullseye and Elektra, Bullseye not only kills his opponent but, relishing every blow, breaks her jaw, slits her throat, and thrusts a knife through her body. Costumed heroes were clearly no longer just entertainment for children.

From this episode arose a disturbing ambiguity in the character of Daredevil himself, echoing but exceeding the obsessive element that O'Neil had once given the Batman. During Miller's remaining tenure, the hero became horrifically obsessed with Elektra's corpse—even digging it up in the cemetery—more ruthless in his fight against crime, shaken in his moral convictions, and oddly linked to the Kingpin. In Miller's last issue (191, Feb. 1983), Daredevil sits at the bedside of Bullseye, whom he has beaten to within an inch of his life, and subjects him to a game of Russian roulette.

Miller, like others before him, then migrated from Marvel to DC; and although *Daredevil* has since returned to mediocrity, his style has gradually altered the face of the field. Dialogue has grown crisper, captions smaller, and subject matter often more frankly treated. This has given the costumed heroes an alternative to the synthesis style, presenting an avenue for them to remain alive and powerful for older readers.

Since the departures of Moench, Jones, and Miller, Marvel's mainstream comics have produced less in the way of startling innovation. Jim Shooter has committed himself to an across-the-board improvement in his company's product, but with less emphasis on diversity or new visions than on mastering the basic craft of storytelling. "We want to make sure that everything is at least good," he says. "Our people have been encouraged to be the cutting edge of the medium, but I think they can do more with the fundamentals of their craft than in a scattershot way." Distressed by the creative and editorial chaos afflicting Marvel in the 1970s, he began to train his writers, artists, and assistant editors in layout, pacing, and narrative techniques. The departures not only of Moench, Jones, and Miller, but of Roy Thomas, Gene Colan, Marv Wolfman, Len Wein, George Perez, and others in recent years have left openings for a flood of new Marvel talent: Tom DeFalco, J. M. DeMatteis, Jim Owsley, Peter Gillis, Jo Duffy, and others among the writers, and many such artists as Bob Hall, Ron Wilson, Alan Kupperberg, and Ron Frenz. Thanks to the training of Jim Shooter (or of young editors trained by him), their work is indeed clearer and more readable than most of the craftless comics of the 1970s.

So far, unfortunately, only a few of the new writers and artists (such as Roger Stern, Alan Zelenetz, Bill Sienkewicz, and Butch Guice) have yet gone beyond the training to develop truly creative styles of their own. Most Marvel titles still chug along in an uninspired manner all too reminiscent of the "house style" of the 1970s. The uniformity of the series is increased by the fact that Marvel's biggest selling point continues to be the unity of its "universe," which seems to discourage most writers and artists from breaking with the established look of the company; to an increasing extent the entire line functions like a single title, with plotlines begun in one series, picked up in another, and sometimes continued to till a third. This can have the effect of pulling all the titles down to the same level.

Nonetheless, there continue to be bright spots, and signs can be found of growing vitality in some areas. Chris Claremont and Dave Cockrum started the decade off well in *The X-Men,* and their work was topped when Claremont was teamed with the exciting young artist Paul Smith soon afterward; although the series has been rambling recently (since John Romita, Jr., took over the artistic half of the collaboration), it remains a great commercial success and trendsetter. It has also spawned some interesting spinoffs: *The Dazzler,* about the amorous adventures of a singing and dancing mutant in Hollywood; *Alpha Flight,* John Byrne's lively tales of a loosely connected group of Canadian heroes; and most impressively *The New Mutants,* telling of the education and rites of passage of a group of mutants in their early teens, wherein Claremont (working with the widely varied artistic contributions of the neat Bob McLeod, the solid Sal Buscema, and the startling Bill Sienkewicz) explores the youth and naïveté of the characters in some of his most insightful writing.

A new contribution has recently come from the long-term editor of the New X-Men (who also worked with Bruce Jones on the new *Ka-Zar*), Louise Jones Simonson. This is *Power Pack,* in which four siblings from five to twelve years of age are granted unearthly powers and given a dangerous mission, thus combining the current interests in hero groups, science fiction, and the kids' market. With solid characterizations by its novice writer and elegant art by June Brigman, it may also be a foreshadowing of what the increasing numbers of women in the creative roles of comics have to contribute to the medium.

The success of such ventures as *Power Pack,* along with the continued improvement of the time-tested old heroes, might help bring about a return of Marvel and DC to their full creative capacity. But it has become increasingly clear as the 1980s have progressed that mainstream comics are no longer the likeliest breeding ground of creations that are both artful and truly original. Of the three visionaries discussed at the beginning of this section, only one has continued to work in the mainstream, and that one, Moench, has done better work elsewhere. A sudden wave of experimentation in formats and distribution techniques, combined with a boom in small independent publishers, has thrown the field open to new approaches. After Miller's departure from *Daredevil* in late 1982, a survey of the comics available at a newsstand or 7–11 store might have left an impression that the cutting edge of the medium had become badly dulled. But a trip to a more specialized retailer would have revealed a rapidly expanding world of superb and unique new creations.

The Independents

"I think that if people are actually involved from the top to the bottom in a common endeavor," Mike Friedrich said of his *Star*Reach* experiment, "really involved, everyone is going to be more productive. . . . If the writers and artists have a piece of it, they're going to be more involved and ar going to do a little bit more than if they don't."

From its beginning with Wally Wood's *witzend* in 1967, through the boom in "undergrounds," through such projects as veteran artist Jack Katz's series of "graphic novels" (*The First Kingdom*) beginning in 1974, to *Star*Reach* and *Sojourn*, the independent comic book publishing movement held to one policy: the full rights to each work would be retained by the creators, not by the publishers. The work in them was thus marked by unusual integrity and individual creative visions, but publication was limited to mail order and a small number of specialty shops, and the money was never adequate to lure the better writers and artists away from the major companies to any significant extent. Most such publishing ventures folded, including Friedrich's (which nonetheless survives as a literary/artistic agency and packager for other publishers).

But a proliferation of comic book shops in the late 1970s, along with the efforts of pioneering distributors like Phil Seuling and Bud Plant, eventually created a market capable of sustaining independent ventures. In late 1977 a young Canadian cartoonist named Dave Sim created a *Conan* parody starring a barbarian aardvark named Cerebus; with no more than one five-hundred-copy advance order, he and Deni Loubert formed Aardvark-Vanaheim, Inc., to publish it. At first no more than a remarkably skillful parody of Barry Smith's sword-and-sorcery art, with the "earth-pig born" ludicrously injected into it, *Cerebus* began to build an audience during 1978 with such funny supporting characters as the airheaded female barbarian Red Sophia and the blustering sorcerer Elrod the Albino, with his Foghorn Leghorn speech pattern ("Mind your manners, son! I've got a tall pointy hat! Status, boy! You can argue with me, but you *can't* argue with status!"). By issue 20 (Sept. 1980), Sim had broken fully from his Smith imitation, emerging as a unique and witty stylist in both art and story, building a complex political and religious world-picture around his aardvark and seeing *Cerebus* earn a large and devoted cult following. Aardvark-Vanaheim prospered, and by late 1984 published six regular series.

In 1978, Wendy Pini launched her large-format heroic-fantasy series *Elfquest*, with her husband, Richard, as co-publisher in WaRP Graphics. It quickly built its own very loyal following and has gone on to great success not only in the comic market, but in the broader world of the regular book trade.

At about the same time a company called Eclipse, run by the brothers Jan and Dean Mullaney, began publishing one-shot graphic novels, including *Sabre* by Don McGregor and Paul Gulacy (the first graphic novel ever published exclusively for the direct market), and *The Price* by Jim Starlin. In the summer of 1981 they followed with their first regular publication, the black-and-white *Eclipse* magazine, which serialized creations as diverse as Steve Englehart and Marshall Rogers's mythological *Coyote*, Don McGregor and Gene Colan's *Ragamuffins*, about real kids in 1950s America, and a hard-boiled detective series called *Ms. Tree*. A year later the company took a chance on the regular color comics format with

Sabre, printed on high-quality paper and distributed, at an above-normal price, only through the "direct sales" market of comic shops and their kin. It is a complex series about a black adventurer and his lover fighting for right and dignity in a chaotic future world; and although deeply flawed, both in McGregor's writing and the art of Billy Graham and Jose Ortiz, by self-conscious daring and experimentalism, it remains a showcase of the artistic liberty allowed by the independent press. And by succeeding well enough through its limited market to embolden Eclipse to go on expanding, it proved that independent comics could make the jump from marginal experimentation and cult status to become viable alternatives, perhaps even rivals, of Marvel and DC.

Eclipse has expanded impressively in the last three years, lately under the excellent editorship of Cat Yronwode. *Eclipse* magazine was replaced by a regular-format color comic, *Eclipse Monthly*, showcasing projects ranging from Marshall Rogers's absurdist fantasy *Cap'n Quick and a Foozle* to B. C. Boyer's Eisner-influenced *The Masked Man* (both continuing in their own comics) to Doug Wildey's elegant western, *Rio*. Rogers teamed up again with Englehart briefly to explore some mystico-sexual themes in *Scorpio Rose*. The young company offered some explicit support of artistic independence with the publication of Steve Gerber's *Destroyer Duck*, the income from which went to help finance Gerber's lawsuit with Marvel over the ownership of Howard the Duck; joined by a pair of unlikely artistic partners—Jack Kirby and the atmospheric Filipino inker Alfredo Alcala, contributing their efforts in support of creators' rights—Gerber produced five issues of biting and entertaining satire of the corporate mentality in the entertainment business. Although these three comics have since been replaced by other titles, each made a distinct contribution to advancing the cause of the independents.

But Eclipse's greatest gifts to the comic book world have come with a quintet of titles that not only hold historical significance but offer consistent high-quality entertainment with great potential for long lives and steady improvement. The first was *Ms. Tree* (Jan. 1983), created for *Eclipse* magazine by the prolific mystery novelist Max Collins and a beginning artist named Terry Beatty. Michael Tree herself is a hard-boiled female private eye, but completely free of the "tough woman" stereotypes that run rampant through comics and television; her hard-hitting adventures, in which violence is treated quite frankly and un-comic-bookishly, center on her fierce grudge against the mobsters who murdered her detective husband. The plots are intricate mysteries worthy of Collins's numerous novels, and his prose is effectively sparse and finely honed. Terry Beatty whose training was in humorous cartooning, has made an impressive adjustment to a stylized, dreamlike, but extremely coherent and attractive art style. Collins, Beatty, and Eclipse also put together a fine package for the comic, with a "Mike Mist Minute Mist-eries" filler, "Famous Detective Pin-Ups" by Frank Miller and Mike Grell, and Collins's personable, dialogue-like letter pages. After nine issues, Eclipse let *Ms. Tree* go, but Col lins and Beatty have been able to keep it in publication through Aard-vark-Vanaheim, a good example of one of the biggest advantages of crea-tor-owned comics: even if the original publisher decides that a series doesn't fit its line, the series can go on, as it could not have in years past. (Greater flexibility is afforded creators and characters as well, as demon-strated by *The P.I.s*, a "miniseries" from a younger independent, First Comics, in which Ms. Tree guest-stars with one of First's characters, a pri-vate eye named Michael Mauser, created by writer/artist Joe Staton; Col-lins writes the series, which is drawn by Staton and Beatty.) *Ms. Tree's* continued success is also proof that the direct-sales comic market can support restrained, intelligent, adult material, and that straightforward development of genres other than science fiction, fantasy, and costumed crime-fighting can find a place in the medium. The series may have a very liberating effect on the whole field.

Two Eclipse titles are the brainchildren of Mark Evanier, a writer with some experience at Marvel or DC and seemingly limitless credentials as a television scripter and a writer of comics for the Gold Key group. With art-ist Will Meugniot he created *DNAgents* (Mar. 1983), about a team of five genetically created special agents for a huge, merciless corporation. Al-though the stories revolve around standard comic book heroics, they gain a delightful emotional quality from the fresh characterizations—reminis-cent of the old Metal Men, of whom Evanier is obviously fond—as the naïve heroes (with the bodies of adults and the maturity of five-year-olds) seek identity and independence from the corporation that created them. Meugniot's offbeat, uninhibitedly sensual art, graced by the lush inks of Al Gordon, gives life to the diverse characters. (The series has also sparked Eclipse's first "miniseries," starring the DNAgent named Surge, with the attractive art of Rick Hoberg.)

From one of the adventures of the DNAgents sprang Evanier's second series, *Crossfire* (June 1984), drawn by a comics veteran of thirty-five years, Dan Spiegle (with whom Evanier had recently worked on an ill-fated but very distinctive revival of *Blackhawk* for DC). Although ne-glected by most fans and many critics, Spiegle's art is some of the raciest and most fluid in the business, with a storytelling ability perfectly suited to the adventures of bail bondsman Jay Endicott, who has inherited the costumed identity of a dead industrial spy named Crossfire, and uses it to fight crime. Evanier combines three distinct elements in the series: heroic adventure of the lively sort that the original Spider-Man exemplified, tough crime drama, and his inside knowledge of the current Hollywood scene. In his scripting he shows a uniquely relaxed, conversational style full of sarcasm, satire, and an obvious love of his subject matter. His lengthy text pages and answers to letters display a man who knows and loves Hollywood and comics, and wishes to share that knowledge and love with his readers.

The year 1984 has seen the release of two other very promising series. Doug Moench's *Aztec Ace* (Apr. 1984) is a strange excursion into the paradoxes of time travel, relating the efforts of one man from the far future to prevent the dissolution of the time-stream as we know it by halting the evil machinations of a time-manipulator named Nine-Crocodile. Into numerous historical epochs, jumping from Aztec Mexico to Dashiell Hammett's San Francisco, Moench's wordy, complex scripts introduce such temporal oddities as "doxie-glitches," "scrambacks," "Quetzalcoatl reanimate," "Montezuma conterminous," the Ebonati Shadow-Knights, and a jukebox filled with the hit songs of every age; the art is handsomely designed by Dan Day, brother of Moench's late artistic partner on *Master of Kung Fu*, Gene Day.

For sheer delight and entertainment, perhaps no other current comic can top Eclipse's *Zot!*, written and drawn by an inspired young cartoonist named Scott McCloud. Zot is an exuberant teenager in a colorful costume, living a wild hero's life in the fabulous "farflung future of . . . 1965!" McCloud's world is a distillation of all the beautiful, sanitary, adventurous futures Americans were promised up until the early 1960s, the futures of

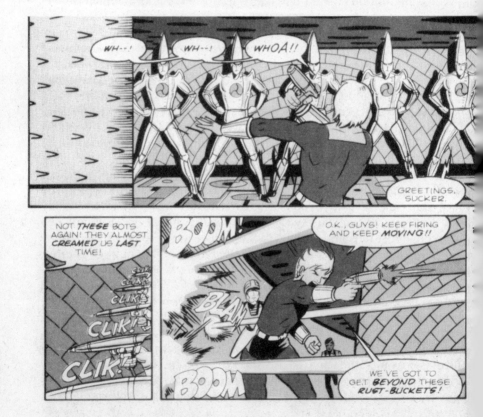

Caricature, Art Deco design, and high-velocity narrative: Scott McCloud's Zot confronts Dekko's robot minions. From *Zot!* 4, July 1984, Eclipse Enterprises.

Schwartz science fiction comics and Disney's Tomorrowland, with their multicolored skyscrapers, protective robot servants, flying cars, and congresses of bizarre but convivial aliens. Into this world is thrust a sad thirteen-year-old girl named Jenny and her belligerent older brother Butch (who is promptly turned into an articulate ape). They join Zot in his mad pursuit of the key to the Doorway at the Edge of the Universe—which, in typical McCloud fashion, is visualized as an ordinary wooden door with a skeleton-key lock, sitting amidst the vastness of outer space. McCloud deals in themes and inventions completely his own; there is, for example, the mad artist Arthur Dekker, who, developing a hatred of life after a bout with cancer and a tragic love affair, becomes obsessed with the inorganic decorativeness of Art Deco, transforms himself into an image of the Chrysler Building, and assaults the world with Deco robots and weapons. McCloud expresses a great debt to Japanese comic art and animation, especially the work of the seminal Osama Tezuka, and it shows in his unfailingly original sense of design and his flamboyant cartooning. A deceptively simple series, Zot! weaves intelligent themes and artistic techniques into a fabric of pure playfulness, and suggests hero adventures of the classic type without ever treading old ground.

Along with Eclipse have come a number of new, farsighted independent publishers. The first company actually to bring out a regular-format comic book among the independents was Pacific Comics, published by Steve and Bill Schanes and edited by David Scroggy in San Diego, California, which launched a new Jack Kirby space opera, Captain Victory and His Galactic Rangers, in late 1981; but the strip, typical late-Kirby fare, aroused little interest. Pacific's second title, however, attracted a little more attention. This was Starslayer, the creation of writer/artist Mike Grell, which told of a Celtic barbarian whisked to the far future; like Grell's Warlord, it featured plenty of the swashbuckling action that Grell had made his forte. In issue 2 (Apr. 1982), a backup feature entitled The Rocketeer premiered; written and drawn with great wit and charm by newcomer Dave Stevens, this tale of a 1930s stunt aviator who comes into possession of an experimental rocket-pack was effectively reminiscent of the old pulp tradition, and became an instant hit. When, after another backup appearance, it was announced that The Rocketeer would graduate to a lead status in a new publication entitled Pacific Presents, and that a new title by comic book titan Neal Adams was soon to debut, it seemed that Pacific was truly on its way.

Almost immediately, however, innumerable snags afflicted the company. Dave Stevens, due to prior commitments, was unable to work on The Rocketeer with any regularity; Pacific Presents #2 was delayed for several months, and the final installment would not see print until late 1984 (when it was published by Eclipse). Mike Grell signed a contract with another independent and after six issues took Starslayer with him; and Ms. Mystic, the Neal Adams title released in October 1982, saw a delay of over a year before the second issue hit the stands, squelching most of the interest the first one had generated. Things would have looked very grim indeed for Pacific, and the company might very well have sunk into obscurity, if not for the timely arrival of a new writer to the fold.

Bruce Jones was just winding down his two-year stint on Marvel's *Ka-Zar*, looking for new opportunities now that both Marvel and Warren had cut back on their black-and-white magazines. Coming to Pacific, he launched two anthology titles, *Twisted Tales* (Nov. 1982) and *Alien Worlds* (Dec. 1982), serving as both co-editor (with April Campbell) and sole writer. The debut issues of both titles were so impressive that Pacific, rather than being a foundering company, was suddenly the publisher of two of the finest comics in the field. With these new comics, moreover, Pacific switched most of its line to heavy, glossy magazine paper, printed in rich colors both subtle and brilliant (with a cover price of $1.50, now a commonplace), and in addition to serving up excellent quality, they sported the most elegant and handsome packaging in the stands.

Twisted Tales and *Alien Worlds,* like those titles at Marvel and DC which strive to synthesize the old and the new, derive much of their strength from the past. Pacific, of course, had no tradition to speak of, so for his inspiration Jones looked back to the heyday of EC comics. In the 1950s, EC had set the standards for comic book storytelling, particularly in the fields of horror and science fiction, and now Jones sought to follow in their footsteps. Teamed with many of the finest, most atmospheric artists in the field—Al Williamson, Richard Corben, Mike Ploog, Tom Yeates, Tim Conrad, Scott and Bo Hampton, John Bolton, Ken Steacy, Bill Wray, Rand Holmes, and many others—Jones has not only revived the greatness that was EC, but very possibly exceeded it. Demonstrating a mastery of the short story that has not been seen since the days of Gardner Fox and John Broome, an amazingly fertile imagination, and a grasp of the truly horrific for the one title and the mind-boggling for the other, Jones has emerged as one of the finest writers in comics.

Jones and co-writer/editor Campbell followed with another comic, *Somerset Holmes,* a thriller about a mysterious woman suffering from amnesia and hunted by unknown assailants, drawn by Brent Anderson, Jones's collaborator on *Ka-Zar.* They also began a new science fiction series, and Pacific meanwhile launched a number of non-Jones titles, including work by Roy Thomas and Craig Russell, Sergio Aragones, Roger MacKenzie and Pat Broderick, Paul Smith, Will Meugniot, Jack Kirby, and others (along with some superb reprint albums, including fine color printings of Berni Wrightson's classic horror stories for Warren). But in 1984 it became suddenly doubtful that any of these promising creations will have the chance to blossom as they should: Publication snags and delays became more frequent until, late in the summer, Pacific announced that it had suspended operations. Other publishers, particularly Eclipse, have arranged to continue some Pacific titles, but most (including the Bruce Jones comics) only long enough to clear out inventory and wrap them up. The demise of this most prolific and ambitious of the independents has forcefully reminded the business that the direct-sales market remains an untested and insecure business.

Another unfortunate casualty of 1984 was John Davis and Richard Bruning's Capital Comics of Madison, Wisconsin. Beginning quietly in 1981 with a black-and-white, low-distribution magazine called *Nexus,* its great achievements were in introducing newcomers to the field rather than in granting creative freedom to frustrated veterans, in the manner of most Eclipse and Pacific titles. The newcomers in the case of *Nexus* were writer Mike Baron and artist Steve Rude, who quickly became two of the brightest lights in the comic book firmament.

Their creation, set in the twenty-fifth century, tells of a planet-hopping "independent adjudicator" named Horatio Hellpop, who is transformed into the powerful Great Nexus by mysterious forces and is thereafter driven by strange dreams to hunt down and kill such heinous criminals as mass murderers and slavers. Joined by a bizarre supporting cast of humorous aliens and animate disembodied heads that fly through the air, Nexus roams an ever-unfolding universe of vast invention and mystery.

Upon the breakthrough of his series into the regular color format in 1983, Nexus gained a new partner—an apelike alien sporting a Mohawk haircut—and the comics gained one of their most original characters. Judah Maccabee—hero, professional wrestler, gourmet cook, and self-proclaimed adjudicator—is an explosive bundle of humor, rage, appetite, and braggadocio. He struts and hams his way across the pages with a histrionic speech style that jumbles eloquence, slang, and wit all together: "Not now, my little potato-bug," he tells his amorous girlfriend. "Papa's wrestling with an existential dilemma. . . . Yes! Yes! I shall inculcate Great Nexus in the art of tavern-hopping! The lad hath ne'er tasted aught but table wine!" (Nex. 5, Jan. 1984).

Writer Baron, apparently an outsider to both the professional end of the field and to the ranks of hard-core fandom, has created a breathtakingly fresh, lively style that holds humor and cosmic mystery in perfect equilibrium. His partner, Rude, has himself perfected a dynamic synthesis of polished richness and bold vitality. *Nexus* is not to be outdone either in raw vigor or careful execution; it points the way to new frontiers in the union of serious experimentation with exciting storytelling.

Capital launched a pair of other titles in 1983 which both showed great potential during their short runs: *Badger,* a creation by Mike Baron without Steve Rude, about a psychotic costumed hero in partnership with a fifth-century Druid; and *Whisper,* by sometime Marvel writer Steven Grant and the budding action artist Rich Larson, featuring a young American woman reluctantly pressed into the role of a Japanese *ninja.* In all its ventures, Capital explored new approaches to coloring, printing, and packaging (including an issue of *Nexus* with a "Flexi-Disc" soundtrack record built in) that seemed destined to push it to the forefront of the independent movement. But in early 1984 that most delightful and conscientious of new publishers suddenly suspended publication, and al-

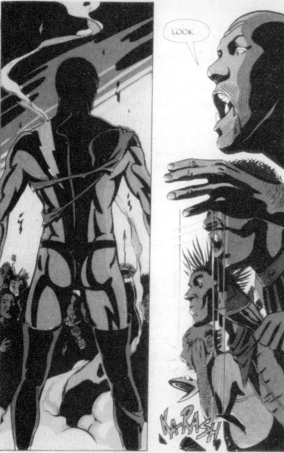

Steve "The Dude" Rude displays flashy effects and rich characterizations as Judah Maccabee and Great Nexus defend Clonezone the Hilariator from an angry nightclub crowd. Script by Mike Baron. From *Nexus* 5, January 1984, Capital Publications.

though *Nexus* and *Badger* are continuing with another publisher, its collapse is still a significant blow to the field. Should the dimming of such bright lights as Pacific and Capital be an omen of trouble ahead for the independents in general, the exuberant spirit that is sweeping comics might wane, and another devastating slump might well befall the medium.

The steadiest of the independents is also one of the youngest. Rick Obadiah and Mike Gold's First Comics of Evanston, Illinois, began, like Pacific before it, on a rather inauspicious note. Its first release was *Warp* (Mar. 1983), an adaptation by diverse hands of a cycle of heroic fantasy plays by Stuart Gordon and Bury St. Edmund, which has had trouble transcending the boundaries of its overworked genre. Next came *E-Man* (Apr. 1983), a revival of a tongue-in-cheek hero of the Charlton company from about ten years before; with bold, caricaturish drawings by Joe Staton and writing first by DC alumnus Marty Pasko, then by Staton himself, it has been a refreshing venture into comic book self-parody, but never a great success. Soon Mike Grell contracted with First to publish *Starslayer*, but he would no longer be writing or drawing it himself (and his absence has been felt in the finished product).

But with the first issue of Grell's new creation, *Jon Sable, Freelance* (June 1983), First's fortunes began looking up considerably. Leaving behind his fantastic settings in favor of a completely contemporary milieu, and incorporating whatever he may have learned about characterization from his wife's contributions to *Warlord*, Grell has here truly found his niche. His protagonist leads a strange, complex, often very funny double life: Sable is an ex-mercenary who works as a bodyguard, detective, and adventurer on jobs too dangerous or specialized for other men, yet he also has a knack for writing children's stories, and so masquerades as a bland kiddie novelist named B. B. Flemm. With a light, unobtrusive mastery of emotional nuance, drama, and expression in both writing and art, Grell has made Sable/Flemm one of the very few wholly individual, real characters in comics. Grell's art has evolved into a unique, sketchy style that is stiff at times but is admirably suited to his realistic subject matter. His breezy storytelling manner is superbly applied to the heady exploits of his hero, and he seems equally comfortable with scenes of every imaginable emotional tone and intensity—ranging from Sable's grief, rage, and horror at the murder of his wife and children to his amusing embarrassment at the discovery that one of his new male friends is gay. In all, the series promises not only light adventure that is refreshingly free of comic book heroics and space travel, but a full exploration of a fascinating character.

Quick upon Sable's heels came another creation of a writer/artist who never quite seemed able to find his groove in the 1970s, a creation utterly different yet equally sophisticated and fully developed: Howard Chaykin's *American Flagg!* (Oct. 1983). The setting of this complex, ingenious strip is twentiety-first-century America, a future world like nothing ever seen before in comics, a world whose intelligent conception is worthy of the best in satirical science fiction. It is a world following "the year of the domino . . . 1996 . . . when *everything* went to hell," a year that left the world's political structure in a shambles, most of the United States decimated, and the remainder under the control of an octopuslike corporate entertainment complex called Plex-USA™. What is left of our culture is a gross, hedonistic caricature of modern consumer society. It is a world haunted by the random violence of "gogangs" like the Genetic Warlords and Ethical Mutants, by insane political groups like the Arab Nazis, Animal Mutilators, and Gotterdammercrats; a world whose favorite video show is "Bob Violence," packed with such subliminal messages as "Kill, rape, death, sex, mutilate"; a world where drugs are in constant use, and the brutal police force, the Plexus Rangers, use the wonder drug Somnambutol™ ("The Tender Riot Ender: It's like a wet dream . . . without the hot parts!") for crowd control. Official corruption is endemic, morals are nonexistent, and the entire society runs on a ceaseless barrage of crass hormonal stimulation.

Into this mess comes Reuben Flagg, a video star who once played a Plexus Ranger and is now—through a very modern confusion of image with substance—pressed into actual service with the force. Flagg himself is a fascinating set of contradictions: he deeply resents the betrayal of the true American dream ("The American spirit—the honest, openhanded driving force of solidarity—has been castrated . . . by slimy fat cats who use patriotism like a tart uses cheap perfume."), yet he indulges unquestioningly in all the bizarre sexual treats his world proffers. Amid a bafflingly large supporting cast—dominated by the corrupt mayor of Chicago, a coterie of sexually demanding women in garter belts and spike heels, a cartoonish robot called Luther Ironheart, and a talking cat named Raul—he fights an exasperating battle to clean up the smelliest pockets of a worldwide venality.

The central character of Chaykin's stories is the society itself, and through his crowded panels, clever wordplay, and sly background details he makes it far more hilarious, repulsive, engrossing, and disturbing than any world yet attempted in the medium. His stories can be overcomplicated and hard to follow, but his cleverness often keeps them delightful even when the plots are lost. His dramatic, inventive, design-conscious art expertly interweaves the sleek technology and heated, perverse eroticism of his future. *American Flagg!* quickly became the most critically acclaimed and, by most reckonings, the best-selling product of the independents, outselling some Marvel and DC titles. It has strengthened the standing of the entire movement and opened the door to sophisticated subject matter that adds a new dimension to the phrase "adult comics."

First has produced two more fresh twists on science fiction with *Mars* and *Grimjack*. The former (now cancelled), by newcomer Marc Hempel and Mark Wheatley, told of a young earthwoman on a hallucinatory journey through Mars, which human science had turned into a weird, living

278

Howard Chaykin's ingenious blend of satire and action from *American Flagg!* 4, January 1984, First Comics.

Ld+3

world where many of the features and residents seemed almost to be creations of her own unconscious mind; through dreamlike, ambiguous stories and a flagrantly dramatic, cartoonish art style suggesting Japanese models, Hempel and Wheatley made *Mars* one of the most intriguing creations of recent years. *Grimjack* is a spinoff from *Warp* by writer John Ostrander and artist Timothy Truman, which tells of a hard-boiled maverick who functions like a private eye on the fantastic, multidimensional world of Cynosure. Perhaps the best feature of *Grimjack* is the backup strip, *Munden's Bar,* clever stories of the rowdy saloon owned by Grimjack himself in the sleaziest quarter of Cynosure, displaying work by many talented guest artists.

First has been a more conservative entrant in the independent boom than Eclipse and Pacific, bringing out new titles slowly and eschewing the fashionable slick paper in favor of a lower price than its competition; it has also been the steadiest of the new companies, bringing each of its seven titles out monthly without fail. The company's future appears very bright: In addition to the *Ms. Tree* crossover in *The P.I.s,* it has contracted with DC to publish team-ups between heroes of the two companies, in the first joint venture of a major firm and an independent; it is also continuing *Nexus* and *Badger* from where Capital left off, and has picked up *Elric* from Pacific. First may provide valuable lessons for survival in the difficult business of direct sale comics.

Some smaller companies are also making their way in the business. The most impressive is Fantagraphics, which, since the mid-1970s, has been publishing the most intellectually ambitious and critically demanding news-and-review magazine about the medium, *The Comics Journal.* Under editor Gary Groth it expanded into the publication of comics of its own in late 1981 with the black-and-white magazine *Love and Rockets.*

Of all the recent comics emphasizing adult, genuine characterizations, none can exceed *Love and Rockets* for authenticity and emotional depth. Produced by two Mexican-American brothers, Jaime and Gilbert Hernandez (with a third brother, Mario, contributing some material), it features two running series: Jaime's amusing and touching tales of an odd near-future world in which costumed heroes and scientific gadgetry flit through the background while our protagonists, young Maggie Chascurrillo and her gang of friends, a blend of pachucos and punk-rockers, go about the business of their transient lives and volatile loves; and Gilbert's incisive, naturalistic look at life in the Mexican village of Palomar (beginning with issue 3, Fall 1983). Jaime's art is subtly composed and simply rendered but very lively and compelling, with an emotional strength that beautifully evokes the very full characterizations of his street-smart, fun-loving girls. His stories are remarkable in their juxtaposition of Latin, punk, mainstream American, and science fiction elements; his dialogue is often startlingly naturalistic. Gilbert, on the other hand, uses a simplified, expressionistic style suggestive of Mexican popular art. Through love and murder, dissipation and redemption, he follows his common people with an unflinching but always affectionate and humorous eye. In telling his soap opera of life in the streets and behind the closed doors of Palomar, he seems more akin in spirit to the likes of John Steinbeck and Sherwood Anderson than to any of his predecessors in comics; his first Palomar serial, "Heartbreak Soup," is like a Mexican *Winesburg, Ohio* in its portrait of the sad yearnings and small tragedies of its townsfolk. *Love and Rockets*, with its affection for the joys and travails of believable people, is the most radical departure to date from mainstream comics. (The work of the brothers Hernandez has also appeared in *Mister X*, from a small Canadian company called Vortex, in which they have developed a disturbing image of a model city gone wrong, from an idea by Dean Motter and Paul Rivoche.)

Fantagraphics has lately added a couple of color comics to its line: *Dalgoda*, by writer/critic Jan Strnad and artist Dennis Fujitake, about an appealing, doglike alien who comes to Earth for military aid when his planet is threatened by a warlike race; and *Hugo*, a wild and slightly bawdy funny-animal series by Milton Knight, Jr.

One small company with promise is Comico, which publishes *Mage*, *Evangeline*, and *The Elementals*. The first is the story of an ordinary man who discovers he has sorcerous powers and must protect the Earth from doom, by a unique and somber storyteller named Matt Wagner. The second, by Charles Dixon and Judith Hunt, concerns the adventures of a very tough nun in a hostile future. And the third, by the dynamic Bill Willingham, stars a costumed-hero team whose members draw their powers respectively from the four elements.

One venerable independent, Aardvark-Vanaheim, has been enjoying new growth in recent years. Under publisher Deni Loubert it has added Bill Loebs's caustic tale of pioneer days, *Journey*, the utterly charming *Neil the Horse* by Arn Saba ("Making the world safe for musical comedy!"—a rare goal for a funny-animal comic), Valentino's sharp parody of mainstream comics, *Normalman*, Bob Burden's bizarre *Flaming Carrot*, and Collins and Beatty's *Ms. Tree*. Along with *Cerebus*, this stable of unassuming black-and-white comics serves as a sort of bridge between the independents and the iconoclastic undergrounds.

In addition to these, a number of other small companies—Spectrum, Americomics, Just Imagine, a revived Archie Adventure Series, The Guild, Southstar, Chance Enterprises, and others—have tried to find their footing in the business. More appear to be on the way: Neal Adams and his associates have, at this writing, just begun releasing Continuity Comics, which promises work from some highly unusual and seldom seen artistic visionaries. Some companies have failed, others are as yet unproven, but their mere existence opens up new possibilities. There is also an increasing visibility of foreign comics on the American scene. The general discovery of Japanese comics and animation has hit creators and critics like a bombshell (especially since the publication of Frederik L. Schodt's study of the subject, *Manga! Manga!*). The British companies Eagle and Quality are finding wider and wider export markets for series like *Judge Dredd* and *Warrior.* Eclipse Comics has announced publication of two British series, *Marvel Man* and *Axel Pressrod.* And Continental publishers like Dargaud, who originally inspired the production of graphic novels and similar formats in America, continue to meet with great success. Out of this confluence of independent publishers and foreign imports must come as yet unpredictable new directions for comic books.

And, in the last few years, Marvel and DC have been taking steps to make sure that they too participate in finding those new directions.

The New Market

Just as important as the mushrooming of the independents have been the marketing and packaging innovations of the major companies, particularly Marvel. After the shake-ups of the "explosion" years, Jim Shooter (working with the company's new vice-president of publishing, Mike Hobson, and its publisher in absentia, Stan Lee) quickly began orienting new projects toward the growing fan market and its dependent direct-sales outlets. Marvel's great success in new ventures has offered significant proof to distributors, dealers, and new publishers that alternatives to the uniform comics of the newsstands can be profitable.

The company launched its new wave of publishing innovations in early 1980 with *Epic,* a high-quality color magazine modeled on the French *Metal Hurlant* (and its Yankee cousin, *Heavy Metal*), which showcases unconventional fantasy and science fiction strips of an adult orientation Under the editorship of former writer Archie Goodwin, *Epic* has remained a varied and experimental magazine; perhaps more importantly, it provided the first regular market for creator-owned material among the established companies. Among the creators attracted to it was Jim Starlin whose long serial, *Metamorphosis Odyssey,* an exploration of the same universe to be featured in Eclipse's *The Price,* would soon prove to be the starting point for Marvel's most liberating new venture.

By early 1981, Marvel began moving seriously into the direct-sales market (even briefly hiring *Star*Reach's* Mike Friedrich as direct-sales manager). First, three titles with strong fan support but low overall sales—*The Micronauts, Moon Knight,* and *Ka-Zar*—were converted into longer higher-quality comics available only through direct sales. Next came the creation of a comic exclusively for the fan market, which was also the firs series to be published on the slick, expensive paper that is so popular now: *Marvel Fanfare,* which, with its stories of such popular heroes as Spider-Man and the X-Men executed by fandom's favorite writers and artists is clearly aimed at the more discriminating hard-core Marvelite. In the years since, the greater dependability and profitability of the direct-sales market have made it a significant portion of Marvel's, and now DC's, over-all income.

Nineteen-eighty-two saw Jim Starlin once again involved in a bold new project for Marvel, this time by writing and drawing *The Death of Captain Marvel*, the first Marvel Graphic Novel. Since this first surprising twist on the Marvel universe, the book-sized, higher-priced Graphic Novels have gone on to spotlight such established characters as the X-Men and Killraven, as well as showcasing new creations of Walt Simonson, Dave Cockrum, Steve Gerber (now patching up his differences with the established companies), and many others. Their success has shown that comics need not be bound to continued series or their usual magazine format; Marvel has since been joined in the venture by DC, First, and Fantagraphics.

Marvel's third Graphic Novel, Jim Starlin's *Dreadstar*, both capped off his *Metamorphosis Odyssey* and laid the foundation for Marvel's most effective use to date of the new market: the Epic Comics Group. Shooter, Starlin, and Archie Goodwin developed *Dreadstar* into a continuing title, on high-quality paper but in standard format, in late 1982. As in *Warlock*, Starlin created a vast, interstellar setting for his latest cosmic saga; *Dreadstar* concerns a two-hundred-year-old war between two galactic empires, the Monarchy and the religious Instrumentality. Unlike *Warlock*, *Dreadstar* is set in a far distant future in which the entire Milky Way has been obliterated. The stories (as with so many series in the wake of *Star Wars*) revolve around a band of space-faring guerrillas fighting for peace and freedom. Led by Vanth Dreadstar, a mystical, sword-wielding human who spent over a million years in suspended animation, the band consists of Syzygy Darklock, a half-human, half-mechanical sorcerer; Willow, a blind telepath who sees through the eyes of an alien simian with whom she shares a mental rapport; Oedi, the sole survivor of a race of genetically molded cat-men; and Skeevo Phlatus, a blue-furred galactic smuggler.

Starlin has continued to improve as both writer and artist. Although not as imaginative as *Warlock*, *Dreadstar* moves at a much brisker pace and displays more mature characterizations. In place of his earlier flights of fancy, Starlin has woven a complex future history that should provide a solid springboard for innumerable adventures. Whereas the premise for *Warlock* produced but one strong story line, *Dreadstar* should prosper for years to come and set new standards in comic book entertainment value.

The success of *Dreadstar* has led to a very promising expansion for Goodwin's Epic Comics. Epic's second title, *Coyote*, was an Englehart-Rogers creation combining mysticism, science fiction, American Indian lore, heroics, and sexuality; Englehart's determination to broaden the perimeters of the field (along with the artistic contributions of Steve Leialoha and Dave True) made it a liberating, if short-lived, venture. The third, *Alien Legion*, is another series in the *Star Wars* mold, but reverses the usual anti-imperial emphasis by centering on the adventures of mercenary troops with questionable backgrounds who are charged with maintaining peace on the fringes of a galactic empire. Imaginatively created by Carl Potts, strongly scripted by one of the better new writers in comics, Alan Zelenetz, and solidly illustrated by Frank Cirocco and Terry Austin, *Alien Legion* is among the most promising entrants in its mushrooming genre. More recent projects, especially the Doug Moench–Paul Gulacy *Six from Sirius*, speak well for Epic's prospects.

Marvel has recently taken some criticism for allegedly trying to flood the shaky direct-sales market with hastily packaged reprints of old comics, but such ventures as Graphic Novels and Epic Comics clearly show the company's importance in developing the new markets that may prove to be the medium's salvation.

Marvel has also used its regular line to explore the limits and desires of the fan market. For its hordes of dedicated followers it has produced some works of broad self-satire—*The Fantastic Four Roast, The No-Prize Book, The Fumetti Book*—as well as one of its most ingenious and helpful creations, *The Official Handbook of the Marvel Universe,* a fifteen-issue compendium of drawings, statistics, and biographies of all of its major characters. Marvel has also picked up a DC innovation, the miniseries, to feature supporting characters; the best have been Claremont and Miller's lean, hard-hitting *Wolverine* and writer/artist Bob Layton's rollicking, hilarious *Hercules.*

The company's biggest recent hope for using the fan market to revitalize its line has, however, proven artistically disappointing. This is *Marvel Super Heroes Secret Wars*, a twelve-issue series written by Shooter and drawn by Mike Zeck and others, which ties into the continuity of nearly every Marvel hero and at first promised to revise the entire line. But it has proven to be only a very standard, though large-scale, battle between popular heroes and villains, thus showing Marvel's continuing ability to be very daring on one hand and surprisingly complacent on the other. *Secret Wars* has proved, nonetheless, to be the most popular comic book series of (in Shooter's estimation) the last twenty-five years, and Marvel's sales continue to be far and away the best in the business (generally between fifty and sixty percent of the total market). It is unlikely that that company will ever engage in an overhaul as thorough or rapid as that going on at DC, which has recently begun battling to get itself back into contention in the comic book sales wars.

DC followed Marvel quickly into direct sales, first with a one-shot called *Madame Xanadu*, then with *Camelot 3000*, the first series of its "adult line," telling of the resurrection of King Arthur and his knights, a thousand years hence, to combat an alien invasion (Dec. 1982). Designed as a twelve-issue "maxi-series"—the first of its kind—it spun some intriguing and innovative variations on Arthurian themes and, in very good taste, presented some of the most erotic and kinkiest sexual situations in comics (especially in the character of Tristan, still in love with the maiden Isolde, but now himself resurrected in the body of a woman). It was evocatively and beautifully drawn by a British artist, Brian Bolland, and written with rapid-fire action by Mike Barr. Unfortunately, it suffered from repeated and worsening publication delays, a problem that has tripped DC up a few times in its efforts to move into the new market.

Another slick-paper DC science fiction series, *Omega Men*, sprung from the DC mainstream, where Marv Wolfman and Joe Staton created them for *Green Lantern*. This series tells of another galactic war and another band of freedom fighters, but has generally been a refreshing and unusual entrant, focusing more on an interstellar cold war and the fascinatingly varied lives of the different Omega Men than on *Star Wars*-like adventure. Unfortunately, the shifting of writing chores among Roger Slifer, Tod Klein, Doug Moench, and others, along with comparable changes in the art crew, have left *Omega Men* somewhat directionless. A more consistent "adult line" product is the *Sun Devils* maxi-series, wherein writer Gerry Conway and the maturing artist Dan Jurgens tell of the efforts of a band of renegades to set back the Hitler-like machinations of a galactic warlord. With Conway's surprisingly fresh and lively writing, his complex and intriguing plot, and Jurgens's exotically designed other-worlds, it is a good realization of the potential of its genre.

DC has had very good luck, artistically as well as commercially, with the heavily worked "galactic empires" genre. Springing not only from *Star Wars* but from Claremont and Cockrum's Shi'ar Empire in *The X-Men* and from Marvel's *Micronauts* (in which writer Bill Mantlo developed a complex geography and history for his subatomic universe, complete with numerous distinct alien races), that genre has opened up a brave new world to adventure comics, not tied to any restrictive old continuity or the formulaic fisticuffs of the costumed heroes, which provides a rich source of original plots, milieus, and characters. Perhaps the best of the lot began as a video game tie-in but has been transformed by its writer into an exploration of some of the most delightful and well-rounded characterizations in comics: *Atari Force*. Set in another dimension, it is the story of a band of human refugees from a war-torn Earth who join with a group of colorful aliens to repel a despot called the Dark Destroyer, who is intent upon conquering the "multi-verse." Writer Conway, showing a spirit of invention and a skill that have been missing from his mainstream work, spins his plots around his characters, revealing their natures artfully through their actions and interactions. Among them are Morphea, a dinosaurlike empath with a strong maternal instinct, Babe, an enormous, hulking alien baby cared for by Morphea, and Pakrat, an incorrigible thief. But most notable is Dart, a young female mercenary who is the most fully realized and charming of the new breed of tough comic book women. *Atari Force* is published in regular newsstand format and is not part of the Adult Line, but it is fully divorced from DC's mainstream continuity. Strengthened by the lush, sweeping art of Jose Garcia Lopez and Ricardo Villagran, it has been an impressive success for the company. (To add to its lustre, Conway was recently replaced by Mike Baron, writer of *Nexus*, who has made the characters even sharper and the stories even fresher than ever.)

On a more experimental front, DC has used its Adult Line to launch two wildly avant-garde titles affording bizarre glimpses into Earth's near future. One, *Thriller* (Nov. 1983), was a perfect case of self-conscious experimentation carried away by its own zeal. Written by Robert Loren Fleming and drawn by Trevor von Eeden, the strip concerned the crime-fighting exploits of a team of strangely powered operatives led by the mysterious Thriller, an ethereal female entity of undefined power. Although Fleming and von Eeden drew heavily from the action-filled pulp tradition, they shrouded their tales in a dense cloud of obscurity; over the chaotic layouts and expressionistic renderings of von Eeden, Fleming wrote in a sparse, riddle-laden prose that was designed to challenge the reader but only served to confuse him. *Thriller* quickly perished, giving DC a warning of the pitfalls of treading new ground.

Far more successful was *Ronin* (July 1983), the first creation of the field's new superstar, Frank Miller, after leaving Marvel. This six-issue miniseries told of a young masterless samurai from feudal Japan who, as the result of a demonic spell, is resurrected in a hideous post-holocaust Earth. Centering on the Ronin's duel with the demon who cursed him to live in this world he never made, the story leads us through the savage remains of a war-ravaged New York City and the inner workings of the Aquarius Complex, a corporation devoted to the creation of organic cybernetics and coordinated by a sentient, sinister computer named Virgo. Miller's developing art style (now heavily influenced by the French artist Moebius), his frightening vision of the future, and his innovative storytelling have here combined into one of the few truly significant steps taken in the recent history of comics. A stunning juxtaposition of words and art, *Ronin* is told in cinematic terms, relying on the integration of dialogue and dynamic imagery to whisk it along; the oblique, sometimes fragmentary images infuse the story with a breathless sense of motion and agitation. It is also a stunning piece of production for DC, with innovative coloring by Lynn Varley and a very sophisticated, costly package. Heralded as a masterpiece by most of Miller's contemporaries in the field, as well as a solid financial success, *Ronin* sets standards for which all comics may have to strive if they are to move beyond their subcultural status. It might well be history in the making.

DC has been uneven, apparently somewhat uncertain, in its use of direct sales so far. (Its Graphic Novel line, for example, has been slow-starting but ambitious, including the long-delayed conclusion to Jack Kirby's Apokolips saga, as well as some impressive new creations.) In addition to experimentation like *Ronin* and light entertainment like *Sun Devils*, it has also published Marv Wolfman's *Vigilante*—an unsuccessful merger of stock costumed-hero fare with would-be gritty violence—and special slick-paper versions of *The New Teen Titans* and *The Legion of Super-*

Heroes (an experiment likened to hardcover editions in the book industry, with the regular newsstand edition being reduced to reprint status, as with paperbacks), which have not differed much from the mainstream product. But the fact that the company continues to gamble on these projects shows an important willingness to tackle the changing times with changes of its own.

DC has made some contributions to publishing through its regular line as well. The most liberating for the field in general has been the mini series, which began in 1979 with *World of Krypton* and has since been used to make additions to company lore through *Tales of the New Teen Titans, Sword of the Atom,* and others. These three-, four-, or six-issue series have made it possible for concepts to be published that do not necessarily have long-term series potential, for stories to have true beginnings, middles, and ends, without the obligation of a series to keep its main characters predictably alive and unchanged; it is an idea that has been taken up energetically by Marvel, Eclipse, Pacific, and First. Maxi-series of twelve issues, allowing for much more development, began with *Camelot 3000* and entered DC's mainstream with *Amethyst, Princess of Gemworld* (May 1983), the charming story of a thirteen-year-old suburban girl who discovers that she is secretly the rightful ruler of a fairy-tale land of magical jewels; intricately plotted and entertainingly written by Dan Mishkin and Gary Cohn (who have since created *Blue Devil*), and rendered with delightful flourish by the highly individual artist Ernie Colon, it recently earned its own title and has become one of DC's brightest prospects.

Now a maxi-series promises to alter forever the nature of the DC mainstream: This is *Crisis on Infinite Earths,* written by Marv Wolfman and drawn by George Perez, scheduled to run through 1985. In twelve issues, Wolfman plans to strip down and overhaul the entire cumbersome DC continuity that has been building since 1938, refashioning some heroes drastically, eliminating others entirely. It is confirmed, for example, that the Flash and Supergirl, two characters who have been running since the 1950s, will be killed. It will be a bold attempt to throw off the weight of the past, make possible a sense of unity and simplicity comparable to the Marvel universe, and start from scratch with the heart of the DC line; and it is only one of the many events planned in conjunction with the company's fiftieth birthday in 1985.

The man behind DC's progress since 1981 has been executive editor Dick Giordano, one of the most creative editors of the 1960s and a participant in some of the important publishing movements of the 1970s. "I have a vision," he has written. "A vision of comics being all that they can be. ... [I] want to publish a line of DC Comics ... that will have people working together who care about their material, each other, their reader, and comics in general. Creators who work toward a common goal for love of the work and a desire to entertain and please an audience ... as well as themselves." DC still has a good distance to go before it meets Giordano's vision, but the line has improved immensely since the last decade. Now Giordano is looking to 1985 as "a critical year" for the company, a year of significant revamps, new series, and whole new publishing ventures. "The key word to DC's direction," Giordano says, "is diversity. Diversity of format, of genre, and of style."

Toward this end, DC has expanded its editorial staff with many people new to the comic business, and gone in pursuit of beginning artists and writers through talent coordinator Sal Amendola and his "New Talent Search"; many of the fruits of that search are seeing print in a unique comic called New Talent Showcase, which provides a source of income and a training ground for promising newcomers. DC is also showing an increased interest in the comics creators of other countries, especially Britain, from which pencilers Brian Bolland and Dave Gibbons and writer Alan Moore have been imported.

Although costumed crime-fighters and space opera will no doubt continue to be the DC mainstays for some time yet, an important area of expansion for 1985 will be into other genres. At both Marvel and DC sword-and-sorcery remains the only reasonably successful minor genre and it is no longer nearly as vital as it was. DC's once-thriving war line has shrunk to two neglected titles, its humor comics have vanished, and its sole surviving western is Jonah Hex, which (though generally still excellent under Michael Fleisher and Tony DeZuniga) has been cut back to bimonthly publication. But Giordano now hopes to pursue the female market through new, sophisticated romances and humor with a woman's slant; he plans a humor line, beginning with the return of Sheldon Mayer's Sugar and Spike; and he has talked of a line of quality mystery, police, and detective comics. Such ventures, if executed with energy and integrity, should prove to be a critical part of the company's renewed growth, and may prove the key to the breakthrough of comics into the entertainment mainstream.

A glimpse into the tremendous potential of the less fashionable genre is afforded by DC's last remaining horror title, Saga of the Swamp Thing. Revived in 1982, the muck-monster passed with his twenty-first issue (Feb. 1984) into the hands of artists Stephen Bissette and John Totleben and British writer Alan Moore. Moore, from his first issue, began turning out the finest scripting seen in American comics since the best of Moench's work on Master of Kung Fu. First reinterpreting the origin of the Swamp Thing in startling terms, then converting an old Schwartz villain named Jason Woodrue from an ordinary crook into what may be the most sinister and demented lunatic ever portrayed in the medium, next turning Jack Kirby's old Demon into a poetic, elemental, true child of hell, Moore has been redefining the perimeters of comic book horror. His fluid, lyrical stunningly poetic prose can seemingly translate anything into an image of chilling beauty ("At night you can almost imagine what it might look like if the Swamp were boiled down to its essence, and distilled into corporeal form; if all the muck, all the forgotten muskrat bones, and all the luscious decay would rise up and wade on two legs through the shallows; if the swamp had a spirit and that spirit walked like a man. . . . At night, you can almost imagine."). Along with the mysterious, fantastical art of Bissette and Totleben, he has raised *Swamp Thing* to the top rank of current comics. DC has here set a standard, not only for its own future ventures into various genres, but for the whole comic book business as it faces the critical years ahead.

If the new surge of energy in comic books is any indication, there is cause for optimism that improvement will continue as the decade unfolds. If writers, artists, and publishers, in stretching the boundaries of their medium, can reach out to a wider audience, moving beyond the dependable but limited market of the hard-core fan, comics might prosper to an unprecedented degree and finally break into the main body of American entertainment. Already, with comics such as *Swamp Thing, Ronin, Dreadstar, Love and Rockets, Jon Sable, Nexus, Twisted Tales,* and *Ms. Tree,* the field offers work fully as imaginative and well wrought as that of any other entertainment medium. The best of them need make no apologies for the limitations of their medium, and many of the rest offer fun, escapist entertainment of a type that no other field provides.

But the future remains in doubt. The direct-sales market is still limited mainly to tried-and-true fans, the independent publishers have yet to prove themselves over the long haul, and the world at large remains generally unaware of the field. Although the fans seem rabid for more and more, it is questionable whether growth can continue if a wider audience is not attracted. As happened with Atlas, *Star*Reach,* and the DC and Marvel explosions of the mid-1970s, a continued expansion could yet result in another implosion. Such a collapse at this critical juncture would be an unprecedented disaster for the medium.

Comic books now stand at the moment of their greatest potential. If the new companies can survive to provide a place for increasing innovation and individual creativity, if writers and artists will dare to tackle new genres and subject matter, and if Marvel and DC can continue to expand the new market while committing themselves to accessible quality entertainment, the medium's growth should be boundless. As this decade nears its halfway point, the prevalent mood of the business, for the first time in many years, is one of soaring optimism. The true Golden Age of Comics might lie just over horizon.

Index of Titles

292